Internet Babylon:
Secrets, Scandals,
and Shocks on the
Information Superhighway

GREG HOLDEN

APress Media, LLC

Internet Babylon: Secrets, Scandals, and Shocks on the Information Superhighway
Copyright © 2004 by Greg Holden
Originally published by Apress in 2004

ISBN 978-1-59059-299-1   ISBN 978-1-4302-0684-2 (eBook)
DOI 10.1007/978-1-4302-0684-2

Trademarked names may appear in this book. Rather than use a trademark symbol with every occurrence of a trademarked name, we use the names only in an editorial fashion and to the benefit of the trademark owner, with no intention of infringement of the trademark.

*This book is dedicated to my virtual community,
otherwise known as the Internet. Be it ever so scintillating,
there's no place like home.*

Contents at a Glance

Contents

About the Author

Greg Holden, a formidable opponent in Trivial Pursuit, collects odd facts in his mind the way some folks collect pens, watches, or vintage clothing. Oh, wait, he collects those, too, along with other assorted objects that follow him home from garage sales and antique malls. A computer geek back in the days when most of his fellow newspaper reporters were still pounding away on typewriters, Holden was excited by the World Wide Web in its early days and has been devoted to it ever since. For one thing, it allowed him to leave the confining cubicle of his nine-to-five editorial job at the University of Chicago and form his own company called Stylus Media, which specializes in technical writing, publications management, and desktop publishing. Okay, so most of his books are pretty straightforward computer how-to manuals. But when he gets the chance, he loves to branch out to write books such as *Literary Chicago: A Book Lover's Tour of the Windy City* (Lake Claremont Press, 2001) and *Karma Mama, Dharma Dad: Answering Everyday Parenting Questions with Buddhist Wisdom* (June, 2004). But whether it's driving past half a dozen Holiday Inns to get to a bed and breakfast known for its unusual architecture or clicking his mouse just one more time to find the funniest Web site ever, Holden keeps his eye out for the unusual, the offbeat, and the exceptional.

Acknowledgments

THIS BOOK EXISTED as a gleam in its author's eye long before it found a home at Apress. First and foremost, I want to extend thanks to my agent Neil Salkind of Studio B, who shows great faith in me and the ideas I always have ripening on the vine. Jim Sumser at Apress had the vision to realize that the time was right to harvest this book, and he made significant contributions to the content. Tracy Brown Collins and Laura Cheu have my thanks for pruning it into a coherent form.

It was really exciting while writing this book to make connections with people I don't know personally. In some cases I'm glad to have never met them, but all inspired the events I was able to document. They include, in order of appearance, Colette Howard; Gary Cohn; Saddam Hussein; Osama Bin Laden; Todd Matthews; Jacqueline Gay; Mary Lockhart; O. J. Simpson; Sterling Silver Rose; Sean Pinkerton; Reata Strickland; Monica Lewinsky; Linda Tripp; Al Gore, who was instrumental in taking the initiative toward the support of ultimately inventing the Internet; Jeffrey Dahmer; Trent Lott; Richard Nixon; Pierre Salinger; the space aliens who secretly work in Area 51; Barney the dinosaur; Bert the Muppet (last name unknown); Justin Dagen; Clare Swire (yum); Stanley Kubrick; Nostradamus, who predicted this book would appear; the Doctress Neutopia; Mahir "I Kiss You!" Cagri; the person who stole Microsoft's software; Scott Fahlman, for inventing the :-) symbol; J.R. "Bob" Dobbs; Jay Williams of the South West News Service; the Pets.com sock puppet; Pierre Omidyar, who invented eBay; Marilyn Manson; Uri Geller; and the Butter Cow Lady.

More wonderful than any in this cast of characters is my intrepid assistant, Ann Lindner, who can be credited (or blamed) for many of the puns in the text and headlines ("Elvis is their rock and their roll").

Part One
The Rich and (In)Famous

Family Values
in Babylon

*Don't forget about the importance of the family. It begins with the family.
We're not going to redefine the family. Everybody knows the definition of
the family. [Meaningful pause] A child. [Meaningful pause] A mother.
[Meaningful pause] A father. There are other arrangements of the family,
but that is a family and family values.*

—Former Vice President Dan Quayle, quoted on
the Official Internet Quayle Quote List[1]

MEMO TO MR. QUAYLE: The Internet begs to differ with you. In the world of the
Internet that I will call *Internet Babylon*, families come in many more flavors than
just the nuclear variety. If you are unhappy with your family of origin, or if you are
looking for all or part of your family, you can find a solution online. Join a newsgroup, type messages in a chat room, surf over to a support group's Web site, or
subscribe to a mailing list. These are all ways to become part of an online community that can function much like a family. For many, online groups become
families of choice, enabling the dissatisfied to redefine themselves, aligning with
like-minded groups that fit their circumstances and needs.

And, of course, being wired to the global network means that we are all part
of one big family—a family in which the well-behaved kids as well as the "black
sheep" get a voice. On the "black sheep" side, you'll find America's first family of
killers, the Mansons, still spewing their peculiar mixture of love for the environment
and hatred for police and much of the rest of humanity. The children of such heads
of household as Saddam Hussein are online. And one of the largest, richest, and
most notorious families around, the Bin Ladens, has left its traces on the Net.

Internet Babylon is also a place where people come together and where family
members who have been separated by time and circumstance can discover connections. Whether it's the offspring of a rock star who played Johnny Appleseed
with women around the country or harried e-commerce executives who commute
and work 80-hour weeks, the Internet is all about different modes of connection.

---

1. http://www.xmission.com/~mwalker/DQ/quayle/qq/quayle.quotes.html

Then there's the question of whether to have a family in the first place. Never mind marriage, church, or the proverbial stork. With a click of a mouse and a few clicks of the keyboard, the Internet brings the promise of children to those who might never be able to conceive on their own. Sometimes the family comes in the form of frozen sperm delivered by FedEx, sometimes by surrogate parents who connect through the Internet. And if you're confronted with the proverbial leaky condom and don't want to have a child, the Internet promises that "morning-after" remedies will be brought to your door within the critical 72-hour time period.

In regard to the quality of one's family life, it isn't enough to be occupying the same space. To be functional and happy, family members need to communicate, to share memories, to celebrate their personalities, and to cope with illnesses. Going online has given families access to a wider range of medical help than was ever possible before. It's even helped some amnesiacs regain their memories, and some 60-something Alzheimer's patients hold on to their memories and their ability to communicate by typing daily *blogs* (Web logs).

On the Net, it's all in the family—making, remaking, and taking charge of your family and making it work for you. The following are some stories of people whose families really "click" (mouse click, that is).

Family Togetherness, Internet-Style

Time was when finding long-lost relatives and meeting domestic partners was a matter of physically getting up and going somewhere—to the local pub, to the National Archives, to a relative's house. No more. The Internet is a perfect medium for family connections. It is increasingly common for an Internet address called a *uniform resource locator* (URL) to be printed on a formal invitation to a wedding or reunion to direct guests to a Web page that was specially created for the event. Countless far-flung relatives exchange e-mail messages to keep in touch. Millions of individuals strive to reunite with ancestors and long-lost relatives using genealogy databases. And *kazillions* of others hope to meet a mate or start a family with a little help from the matchmaker Internet.

Screamin' Jay Hawkins Put a Spell on 'Em

The phrase "Who's your daddy?" has been used as trash talk on inner-city basketball courts. But it's a serious matter both to those who knew from birth that they were the child of Screamin' Jay Hawkins, a rhythm-and-blues singer, as well as those who only later in life began to suspect that he was their father.

Hawkins was able to reunite many of his children after his own death by way of the Internet. This form of immortality was a tall order, even for Hawkins, who had a booming voice and incorporated elements of voodoo and tribal rituals into his act. But after opening many shows by emerging from a coffin placed onstage, Hawkins was able to gain a sort of life after death as a result of his own interpretation of the phrase "family values." Hawkins himself claimed to have fathered as many as 75 offspring, and many of them were able to verify their identity and locate their siblings through the ultimate "family reunion" Web site (see Figure 1-1).

Figure 1-1. The Jayskids.com Web site attracted lots of attention when it went online in 1999.[2]

_____

2. http://www.jayskids.com/

The story about Hawkins having so many children—like so many other legends, rumors, and tales—has taken on a life of its own on the Internet. A search for the phrase "Screamin' Jay Hawkins" on any of the major search services will turn up as many media stories about how many children the singer supposedly sired as links to fan Web sites. The story overshadows his music and the powerful stage persona he created. Newspapers and magazines big and small reported on the search for the children and the planned reunion at the House of Blues in Cleveland, Ohio, in 2000. But virtually nothing can be found online about what eventually happened to the far-flung siblings.

It turns out that only a handful of Hawkins's children ever assembled at the House of Blues in Cleveland for the planned reunion. Perhaps half a dozen of his daughters stay in touch and meet regularly. The children's attitude toward being identified varies. The eldest children, who actually knew Hawkins before he left their home in Cleveland to launch his career, have expressed resentment toward the "newcomers." Some children are interested in whatever chunk of Hawkins's estate might be coming to them. Some of his sons don't want to have anything to do with meeting the other children. But for a few of the daughters, it's been an enriching and positive experience just to know something about their father and to get to know their new sisters.

One of those sisters, Colette Howard, remembers the day she first learned about—and saw—her illustrious father. She was ten years old and had just returned home from school. Her mother insistently motioned her toward the TV to watch an afternoon talk show. She saw a man emerge from a coffin, a bone protruding from his nose. He began singing wildly, howling and screaming. "This is your dad," her mother told her. She looked on in wonder.

"I think we never did talk much about him again though once in a while when I would ask her a question, she did tell me about him."

Howard, now 50, a technician for the Occupational Safety and Health Administration in Cincinnati, Ohio, has a story that is typical of Hawkins's offspring. Her mother, Mildred Walker, was a dancer who performed in the same show with Hawkins in Cleveland. Later, they had an affair in Canada. By the time she learned she was pregnant, the singer was on the road again, and she could not contact him. On a later visit to Cleveland, Hawkins saw Walker again and held his baby, Colette. He asked Walker to come away with him, but by that time she was engaged to another man and turned him down. Colette never actually met her father. She tried to visit him on the set of the movie *A Rage in Harlem*, in which her father had a small part, but he had left the previous day.

Although both she and her mother harbored some bitterness toward Hawkins, today she is glad to know her heritage and to have connections with her siblings.

"Since my father passed away, I have gained five sisters," says Howard. "We really keep in touch with another by phone and e-mail. We exchange Christmas cards." A sixth sister in Hawaii (Melissa Ahuna, a hula dancer) also kept in touch with the group until she moved recently.

The Jayskids.com Web site and the responses it attracted were "pretty interesting," Howard says. Creating and maintaining the Web site became a crusade for Maral Nigolian, an investment banker who first became interested in Hawkins after hearing his hit song, "I Put a Spell on You." Nigolian befriended the singer in his final years and visited him in Paris shortly before he died in 2000 at age 70. He was still performing even in 1996 (see Figure 1-2). Hawkins told her that he had 75 children and that he hoped they would meet one day. When Nigolian realized at the singer's funeral that none of these children was actually present, she decided to get them together and throw a party. Where better to find them than on the Internet?

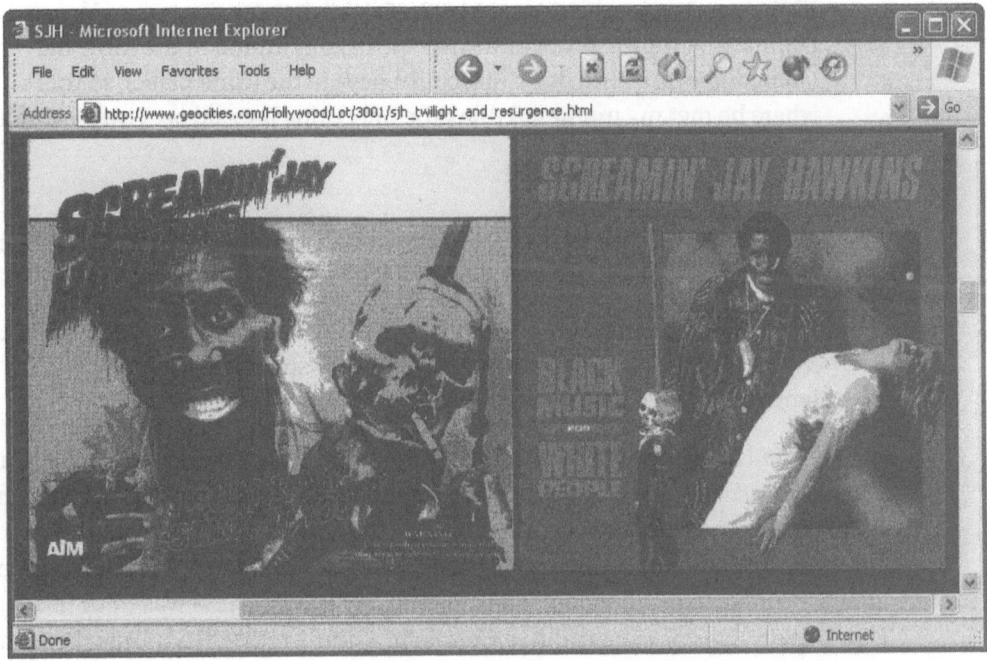

Figure 1-2. Hawkins had a wild persona as well as a wild sex life.[3]

Nigolian hired a designer to create the Web site, which asked on its home page: "Are you one of Jay's kids?" The site included video clips of Hawkins revealing just how many children he had fathered and an audio clip of the singer's quirky telephone answering machine message. Visitors to the site were greeted with the message, "If you believe you may have had a child by Screamin' Jay Hawkins, or if you believe you are a child of Screamin' Jay Hawkins, please click here." Visitors could then leave messages stating why they thought Screamin' Jay Hawkins might

3. http://www.geocities.com/Hollywood/Lot/3001/sjh_twilight_and_resurgence.html

be their father. When the site first went online in 1999, the designer warned Nigolian that she should expect only a few visits. But immediately the site attracted hundreds of visitors, and the number soon climbed to thousands. Eventually more than 2,500 submissions flooded in from Hawkins wannabe-offspring. Examples from the original Jayskids.com site include the following:

- **HD, Barberton, Ohio; birth date 6/12/81**: Well, I look exactly like all of the pictures that I have seen of him, and my mother once said that she went to one of his concerts and went backstage....

- **RJ, New Orleans; birth date 12/24/64**: He's my father. My mother had a brief relationship with Mr. Hawkins in early '64. She said he "put a spell" on her.

- **JD, Juarez, Mexico; birth date 11/22/77**: Well, it was a time when Jay used to come to the south border and party. He usually attend to the same bar (sometimes he spend five consecutive days in the same place), so that's where he met my mother...I think the only thing Jay said is "Viva el tequila."

- **SP**: F#ck, I just want the cash.

- **JJ, Orange, CA; birth date 7/03/75**: Well, I'm fully white, and I know who my real father and mother are...but if there is money involved, I'll be anyone's kid!

- **MP, Korea; birth date 11/11/67**: Screamin' Jay had a tour of duty in Korea. My mother didn't speak any English, but they spoke the international language of rhythm and blues and love.

Nigolian recognized that most of the comments were jokes. Because Hawkins had a good sense of humor, she was not offended. She was more interested in the claims that turned out to be legitimate.

To understand the attraction of the Web site, it is helpful to know something about the man who called himself Screamin' Jay Hawkins. He was born Jalacy J. Hawkins on a bus passing through Cleveland, Ohio, in 1929. His mother brought him to an orphanage, and he was raised by a group of Blackfoot Indians. He soon showed boxing skills and was once middleweight champion of Alaska. After spending time in the army, he arrived in New York City in 1952 and became a nightclub singer.

In May 1953, he snagged his first solo gig at Small's Paradise in Harlem, New York. He developed most of his shtick there, portraying a nutty, demented persona (see Figure 1-3). He often burned himself onstage with exploding fuse boxes. Although his backup musicians changed frequently, he had one mainstay: a cigarette-smoking, flaming skull named Henry. He recorded his most successful single, "I Put a Spell on You," in 1956. The song was written as a ballad, but after a night of boozing, Hawkins added screams, yells, and groans. Although the tune was strangely appealing to some, several radio stations banned it because, they said, it sounded cannibalistic.

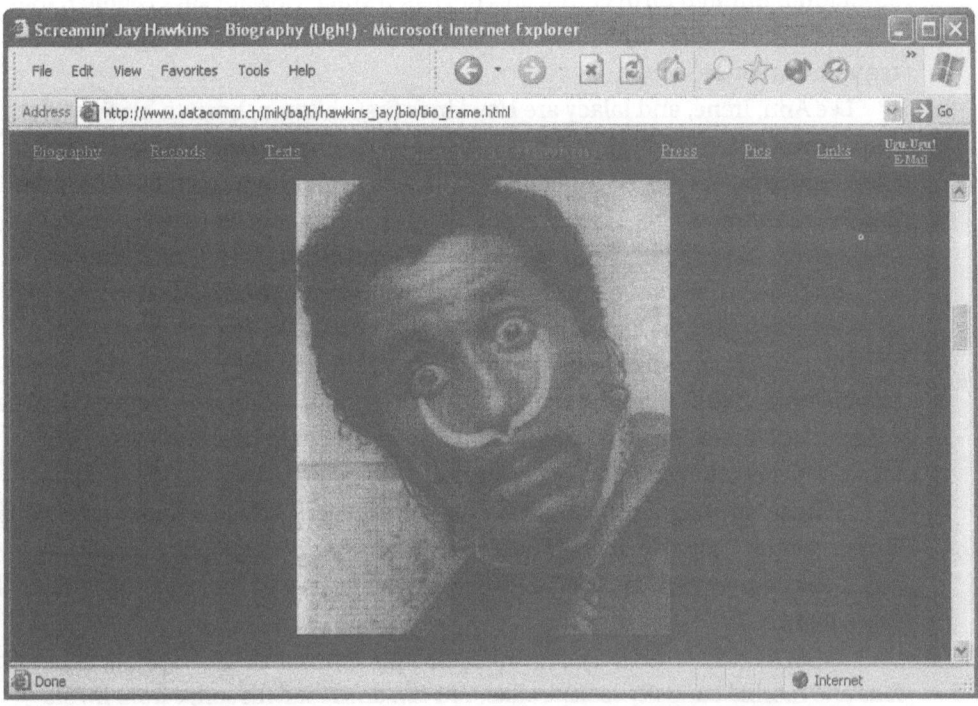

Figure 1-3. This excellent fan Web site contains many photos of Hawkins doing his shtick.[4]

Throughout the '50s, Hawkins spent most of his time in Harlem and Philadelphia, Pennsylvania. But when he was at the Brooklyn Paramount Theater in December 1956, Alan Freed bribed him with $2,000 to start his show by rising out of a coffin. Hawkins received such an overwhelming response that he kept the stunt in his act until he died.

Hawkins never sold a lot of records ("I Put a Spell on You" didn't even go Top 40), but his stage show earned him a place in the history books. In later years, he moved into film and had acting parts in Jim Jarmusch's *Mystery Train* in 1989 and Bill Duke's *A Rage in Harlem* in 1991; Jarmusch had already used "I Put a Spell on You" throughout his 1984 *Stranger Than Paradise*.

With his outlandish outfits and macabre stage props, Hawkins has also been recognized as a precursor of the horror-metal of Alice Cooper, Ozzy Osbourne, and Marilyn Manson. His personal life was no less extreme. In addition to having six wives, he claimed to have had sex with thousands of women all over the world, and many of the children who resulted never knew their father. Just how many children are there? One newspaper story claims that Nigolian was able to verify more than

4. http://www.datacom.ch/mik/ba/h/hawkins_jay/bio/bio_frame.html

33 children through birth certificates or DNA testing. Howard says Nigolian told her the number was only "in the teens." Nigolian herself did not respond to requests for interviews.

Lee Ann, Irene, and Jalacy are Hawkins's first children, born to his first wife Anna Mae Vernon, and they all knew Screamin' Jay well. They still live in the Cleveland area. Sporting Screamin' Jay's own cape and wedding band and other jewels, Irene made a life-sized puppet of her dad from pillows, drapes, and old clothes. She has used it in puppet shows in Cleveland and on local TV shows.

Hawkin's prominent nose and wild laugh has been passed down to many of his children, as has his love of performing and musical ability. Howard's own daughter is a singer, and Howard herself used to do stand-up comedy. Her son is tall and attractive like his father and has attracted much attention from his female college classmates. In fact, many of the offspring seem to have inherited their father's strong interest in the opposite sex.

"When one of my sisters, Helen Perez, became seriously ill, I went to New York City to see her," says Howard. "There she was, on her hospital bed, and all she could talk about was, 'I am seeing three different guys, and I am thinking about all these men.'"

Today, Hawkins's memory lives on in the Web browsers and MP3 players of music fans and morbid curiosity seekers alike. You can download his songs from music-sharing sites or purchase CDs and albums from music stores. Fans publish biographies of Hawkins, but when he is mentioned on Web pages or in newsgroups, much of the time people are talking about all the children he had and how many of them found one another online.

The children themselves—who have as yet received no inheritance from Hawkins's estate—seem happy to know their father and accept his prolific tendencies. "I think of all the years I would look out into space wondering where my father ways," Howard says. "Now I know I have a father who made it into the history books, and I have my brothers and sisters. When they do my family history, I can tell people where I came from. It makes me feel great."

Lookin' for Love in All the Right-Wing Places—Online

Whatever you think of Rush Limbaugh's viewpoints, you have to admit that he talks a good game. The right-wing radio commentator has made a successful career pushing patriotism and conservative values on syndicated radio programs. But when it came to finding his third wife, he went online. Specifically, he used CompuServe to motor-mouth his way into a romance with a then-married woman he met through e-mail and a discussion forum called a *bulletin board*—which seems a very unconservative thing to do.

The relationship started on an inauspicious note. In 1990 Marta Fitzgerald, a former aerobics instructor who was a student at the University of North Florida, sent a message through CompuServe to Limbaugh, asking for some advice. It seems one of her professors had criticized President Ronald Reagan (whom Limbaugh has frequently described as the greatest president in American history). Limbaugh at first failed to reply.

When Marta heard him respond on his radio show to some flight attendants who had written to him claiming they wanted to meet him, Marta was offended. She fired off an angry letter to the pundit. This time she became the focus of his attention. An e-mail correspondence ensued. In 1992, Marta and her husband divorced; in 1994, she and Limbaugh (see Figure 1-4) were married by no less than U.S. Supreme Court Justice Clarence Thomas.

Figure 1-4. Photo published on the Cape Girardeau, Missouri, Web site tribute to its hometown boy[5]

On his official Web site (http://www.rushlimbaugh.com/), shown in Figure 1-5, Limbaugh makes frequent references to his "lovely and gracious" wife, whom he has

5. http://rosecity.net/rush/photo5.html

been known to call the Jacksonville Jaguar. Together, they hold an annual telethon to fight cancer. As of this writing, they have been married for nearly a decade.

TIP   The Cape Girardeau site A Rush Limbaugh Hometown Page (http://rosecity.net/myweb1/rush/) includes a photo of a mural of Limbaugh in the city's downtown area and a virtual tour of sites associated with his youth.

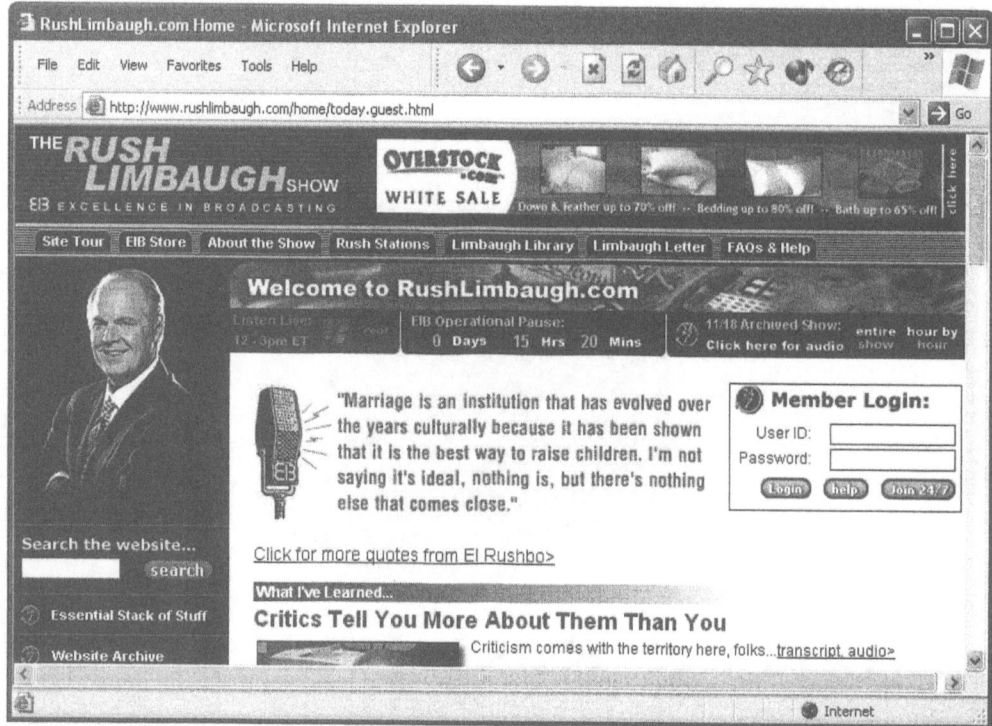

Figure 1-5. Rush Limbaugh: a significant presence both online and on the air[6]

---

6.   http://www.rushlimbaugh.com/home/today.guest.html

Giving Family Members a Voice

In the Andy Hardy movies of the 1940s that starred Mickey Rooney, the family would gather around the dinner table and hash out their disagreements. Everyone would get a chance to bring up issues and air their opinions. These days, society's great dinner table is the Internet. Everyone with the ability to create a Web site and exchange e-mail messages can be heard—no matter what they have to say, no matter whether anyone wants to hear it. The following are some of the cyberspace dinner table's more unlikely debaters and the messages they want to convey.

Manson Family Values

Many people find criminals and murderers repulsive. Just as many find them utterly fascinating. The more notorious the criminal, the more attention the gawkers devote to him (or her). In the annals of crime, one of the most notorious criminal "families" is the so-called family of the followers of Charles Manson.

In August 1969, five individuals were murdered in the secluded home of film director Roman Polanski. The victims included film star Sharon Tate, best known for her role in the movie *Valley of the Dolls*. She was eight months pregnant with Polanski's son. Another victim was an heiress of the Folger family of Folgers Coffee fame. The gruesome, ritualistic killings included the words "Pig" and "Helter Skelter" being written on the front door and wall of the home in the victims' blood. Several days later, two more people were found stabbed to death in their Hollywood Hills home.

TIP Manson's story, and the story of the murders and other crimes in which he and his followers took part, is recounted on many Web sites. One of the best is at http://www.cielodrive.com/.

Manson and three of his female followers were eventually sentenced to death for the murders. Although the Manson murder case seems far removed, a marker of the end of the "hippie" era of the 1960s and a series of crime scenes limited to Los Angeles, the eerie thing is that the Internet has actually brought the Manson family closer to us in the present day. Because a California law was passed in 1972 that briefly outlawed the death penalty, neither Manson nor the other followers who were convicted were put to death. They all remain in various prisons, serving life terms. Their sympathizers continually mount campaigns to get parole hearings for them, and the victims' families continually have to attend those hearings to argue that the prisoners should remain incarcerated. (At this writing, Manson is 68 years old and up for parole in 2007.)

The Internet actually gives the Manson cult a new forum for expounding their views on the environment, overpopulation, and the need to do away with as many as 50 million people. A Web site that was created by one of Manson's friends and that serves as a more-or-less official mouthpiece for Manson, Access Manson (http://www.atwa.info/), hasn't been updated in a while, but it gives you insight into the passion his supporters still feel for him (see Figure 1-6).

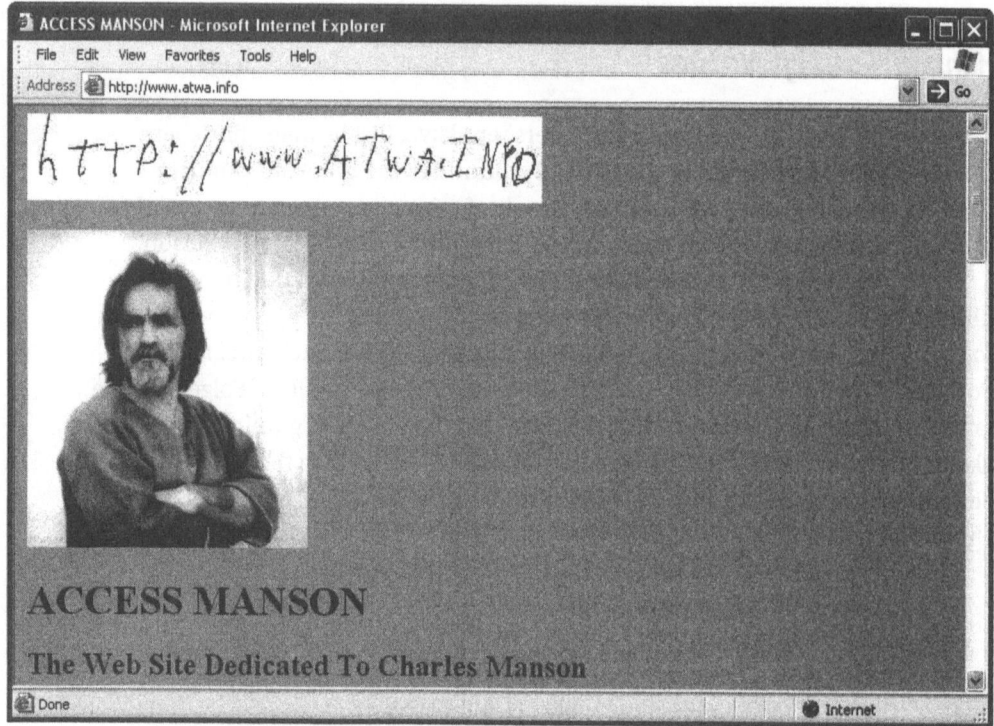

Figure 1-6. Web sites run by Charles Manson's followers still seek his release from prison.[7]

TIP You can hear a group of songs written by Manson and recorded by the family at http://www.geocities.com/SunsetStrip/Cabaret/4359/family.html—if you dare.

---

7. http://www.atwa.info/

Preacher Is Master of His Domain (Name)

Former Vice President Dan Quayle may have popularized the term "family values," but the fundamentalist preacher Jerry Falwell has long been associated with espousing them. In a traditional, mom-and-apple-pie family, people are supposed to work out problems amicably without bullying people into submission. Right?

Tell that to the Reverend Falwell. In early 2003, he became embroiled in a dispute over the domain names jerryfalwell.com and jerryfallwell.com. At the time, these two domain names were owned by Gary Cohn, a resident of Highland Park, Illinois. Early in 2003, news reports stated that Falwell was protesting Cohn's use of the domain name to publish a parody of Falwell (who himself owned falwell.com). On various Internet sites, Cohn published copies of letters he received from Falwell's representatives, who contended that jerryfalwell.com was part of Jerry Falwell's trademark and should legally belong to him.

In summer 2003, the site at http://www.jerryfalwell.com/ was suddenly taken over by Falwell and his religious organization. The parody was gone. You can still see the parody (see Figure 1-7) and a link leading to Falwell's official home page at http://www.internetparodies.org/.

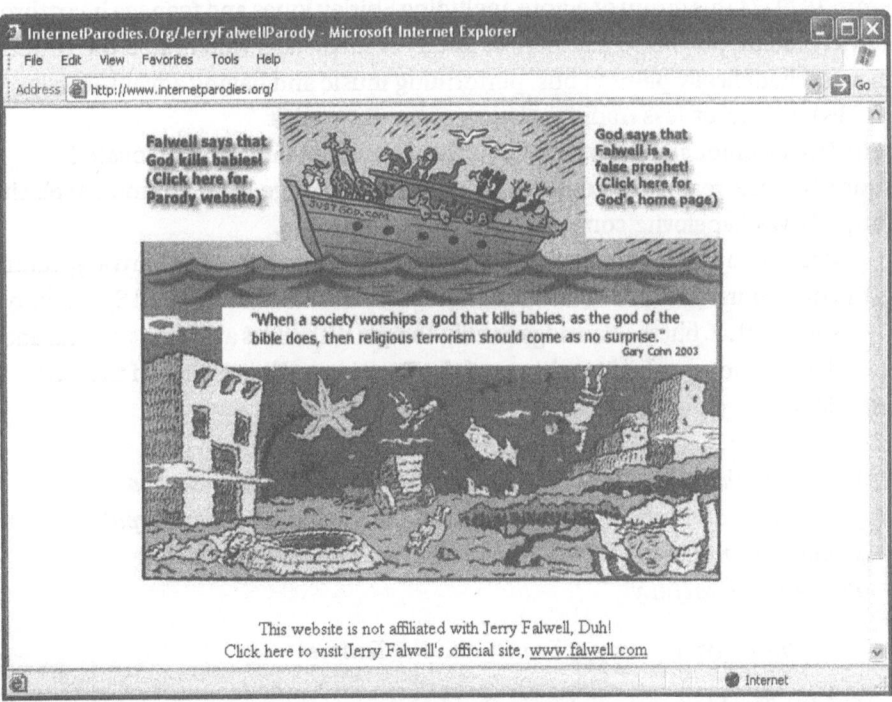

Figure 1-7. The king of "family values" bullies domain name owner into submission.[8]

---

8.   http://www.internetparodies.org/

What happened? A federal judge in Virginia dismissed Falwell's attempt to gain control of the domain name because the court did not have jurisdiction over the case. Earlier, Falwell had tried unsuccessfully to get the domain name through the Uniform Dispute Resolution Procedure, which is designed to settle domain name disputes. Cohn says, "I won the case in federal court. So I proved my point about the legality of real name parodies, and I just gave him the names. I can expose his hate preaching again in some future date."

NOTE   Cohn owns at least one other noteworthy domain name: oj.com. He uses the site's home page (http://www.oj.com/) to publish a "cutting" jibe at O.J. Simpson.

The Partridge Family Temple: C'mon, Get Happy!

"C'mon, get happy!" was a recurrent phrase in one of the hit songs foisted upon the tender ears of children subjected to the televised antics of the Partridge family. From 1970–74 this group of actors, including Shirley Jones and teenage heartthrob David Cassidy, portrayed a fatherless family of musicians who toured the country in a psychedelically painted bus, performing music and having adventures.

For a more-or-less traditional view of the show, visit http://www.cmongethappy.com/. But the view of the family that's located squarely in the realm of Internet Babylon is the Partridge Family Temple Web site (http://www.kapelovitz.com/pft/), shown in Figure 1-8.

Most TV shows are just shows. But according to this site, "The Partridge family is the most pure example of the mix between Television, Reality, and Spirituality."

Not only that, but the Partridge Family Temple Web site is a religious organization founded on the so-called teachings of the Partridges. This is part of the site's manifesto:

We believe that each of the members of the Partridge family is a god or goddess. We also believe that each element of the show has archetypal symbolic significance. Some of the major symbols are the following. Please study carefully:

The Genealogy: A history of Reality and the Temple

Shirley: The Mother Earth Virgin Goddess

Keith: The Male Sex God

Laurie: The Whore of Babylon

Danny: The Trickster God

Chris: The Cosmic Drummer

Tracy: The Virgin Nymph

The Bus: The Spiritual Chariot

Get the picture? The site is a hilarious take on the show and a must-visit for anyone who remembers it. Just don't take it too seriously—and get happy!

Figure 1-8. This site deconstructs the Partridge family and proposes that they are gods to be worshipped.[9]

---

9. http://www.kapelovitz.com/pft/

Saddam and His Sons

Before the U.S. armed forces silenced him permanently along with his brother, Saddam Hussein's eldest son Uday had a home page as well as e-mail accounts with Yahoo! and with Microsoft Passport.

A page on the U.S. State Department's Web site says Uday has a "history of extreme violent behavior including murder, torture, and rape of women and girls." He has also been reported to send death threats using e-mail. Although Yahoo! ran the risk of violating U.S. trade sanctions against Iraq by allowing Uday Hussein to have the e-mail address udaysaddamhussein@yahoo.com, it's quite possible the U.S. intelligence services were monitoring his activities by snooping on his account.

In case you need to ask Saddam Hussein about his sons' e-mail activities, you can attempt to send a message to the dictator's e-mail address: press@uruklink.net. But don't expect a response anytime soon.

Keeping Up with the Bin Ladens

A 30-year-old Los Angeles Web designer named Christopher Curry purchased the domain name that was once used by the family of Osama Bin Laden in October 2001. That fact in itself is interesting. But why was the domain name available in the first place? Believe it or not, Saudi-binladin-group.com was registered on September 11, 2000, and had a predetermined expiration date of September 11, 2001 (the date of the attacks on the World Trade Center and the Pentagon). A coincidence? No one seems to know for sure.

Curry's reasons for purchasing the domain name were simple enough. Besides being a Web designer, he is active in the field of domain name speculation. He originally planned to purchase the binladin-group.com and saudi-binladin.com names and other related names, thinking he could sell them for a profit and donate the proceeds to the Red Cross disaster relief fund. But rather than creating the usual portal to a site awaiting a sale, Curry decided to turn the site (see Figure 1-9) into a clearinghouse of information about the Bin Laden family, which includes 50 children, among them the notorious terrorist Osama Bin Laden.

 **NOTE** *Domain name speculation* is the practice of purchasing a domain name in the hope that someone will pay more to purchase it from you. For instance, the domain name loans.com was auctioned off to the Bank of America for $3 million in 2000 by someone who registered it in 1994; such stories keep domain name speculators on the hunt.

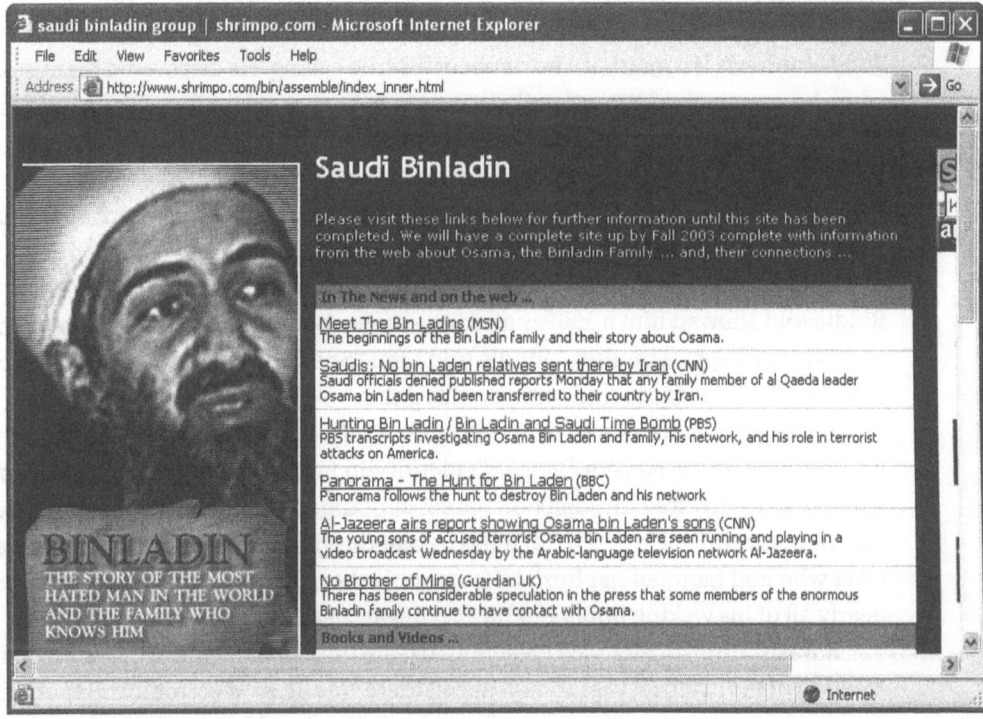

Figure 1-9. An American designer is the owner of the Web domain name once owned by the family of Osama Bin Laden.[10]

Long-Lost Family Members Get IDed Online

What's that you say? Don't know who your real parents are? Wish you could have another conversation with that girlfriend who dumped you during sophomore year? You say your husband went out for groceries one day and never returned? Don't fear: Ever-increasing numbers of the missing, the dead, and the forgotten are all being identified online. Some of these stories aren't pretty, especially the ones having to do with the dead whose remains are found and need to be identified. But others have a happy ending. The following is just one example.

---

10. http://www.shrimpo.com/bin/assemble/index_inner.html

"Tent Girl" Identified After 29-Year Obsession

Todd Matthews is a man with no doubt of his true calling. He discovered his mission when he encountered a mystery about a woman known only as Tent Girl. A resident of Livingston, Tennessee, Todd heard about Tent Girl from his father-in-law Wilbur Riddle, who had discovered her body near I-75 in Kentucky in 1968—before Todd was even born. What was left of her was wrapped in a canvas shroud resembling a tent, so a local newspaper dubbed her Tent Girl.

When Matthews became engaged to marry Riddle's daughter Lori in 1988, Riddle told showed him a 1969 magazine article about the discovery of Tent Girl.

"This girl's got a mother," Riddle told him. "She's got a Daddy. She could have a husband. We've got to find out who this girl is."

Todd became fascinated by the story. Actually, despite his marriage, the truth is he became obsessed with Tent Girl's identity. In fact, his young marriage became strained as he scoured through newspaper clippings and lab reports. He contacted the county coroner. He drove 200 miles to visit the girl's grave. He visited the undertaker who had handled her burial. He not only thought about the case during nearly all of his waking hours but he also began sleepwalking.

It wasn't until former Vice President Al Gore implied he had participated in the creation of the Internet that Todd realized there was a new electronic medium that could help in his quest. "He (Gore) lives about 40 miles from me," says Matthews. "And he's my cousin. I knew when I heard of the 'Information Superhighway' that it was the only way this case could be solved." Todd saved up and bought a computer. He searched countless missing-person Web sites. His wife began to complain that he spent so much time on the Tent Girl mystery that he was ignoring his own family. His response was to create a Web site devoted to Tent Girl, shown in Figure 1-10. You can also find the site at http://www.tentgirl.com/.

NOTE   You can find out more about Vice President Al Gore's "creation of the Internet" remarks and how they affected the 2000 presidential election in Chapter 11.

Figure 1-10. The Internet helped the Tent Girl to be identified after 29 years.[11]

---

11. http://www.angelfire.com/tn3/masterdetective2/

One night, after his wife and child had gone to bed, he was surfing yet another missing-person Web site when he found a posting from Rosemary Westbrook about her sister Barbara Ann Hackman-Taylor:

My sister Barbara has been missing from our family since the latter part of 1967. She has brown hair and brown eyes, is around five feet two inches tall, and was last seen in the Lexington, Kentucky, area....

The details matched what Todd already knew. He woke up his wife to announce that he had finally identified the Tent Girl. He still had to convince authorities to exhume the girl's body and conduct DNA tests. But eventually Tent Girl was given a name, and her family was able to have closure. It was never determined for certain whether Hackman-Taylor was the victim of a homicide. Police wanted to question her husband, but he had died of cancer years before.

Todd Matthews started his own Web site for missing-person cases, and he now works for an organization that helps identify the remains of missing persons, the Doe Network (http://www.thedoenetwork.com/), as their media director. And, presumably, he spends more time with his family.

Changing Lives with One Click

Because phone numbers, street addresses, and e-mail addresses are now so readily available, the Internet has become "a giant worldwide telephone directory," said A. Michael Noll, a professor at the University of Southern California's Annenberg School for Communication.

With unaccustomed ease, people looking for adopted children, lost lovers, and other missing people can in many cases quickly track them down. Dora Luna is an example of a person who used the Internet to fill the gaping hole in her life. She was always among the tallest girls in her class, which made her feel ugly— especially when she compared herself to her mother's slight frame. She went so far as to tell the nuns at her East Los Angeles school that she was adopted.

Her mother's response was that her daughter was not adopted but rather that she looked like her father who left before she was born. Refusing to be comforted, Luna would stare enviously at the girls whose fathers dropped them off at school. "I really missed my dad," she said in an article in the *Los Angeles Times*. "I would cry at night and wish so hard he would come. All the other girls had their dads, and I always wondered about mine."

Three decades later, she found him with the click of a button. While aimlessly surfing the Internet for the first time one afternoon in a friend's office, Luna stumbled across a site that enables computer users to search for people. On a whim, she punched in the name "Uriel Medina"—that of the father who left a month before she was born. She clicked the search button. Seconds later, she was staring at an address and phone number. Within a month, the East Los Angeles activist and the ranch hand from Ciudad Juarez, Mexico, were reunited. Luna marvels at the power of technology. Her father, who had never even heard of the Internet, calls it miraculous. They both agree that they have a new chance to be together.

"It's so amazing," she said. "My life has changed completely. There's all this negative press about the Internet, but nobody talks about the good things you can do with it."

Looking Over Your Kids' Shoulders, Virtually

Ever wonder what your kids are doing when they spend hours in front of the computer? You can "spy" on them, in the virtual sense, using a product called FamilyCAM from Silverstone Software. The software takes a series of screen images at specified intervals; you can review it later when they're away from the machine. As shown in the following figure,[12] the images are displayed in miniature format within a Web browser. Now if they could just come up with CarCAM, DateCAM, and so on.

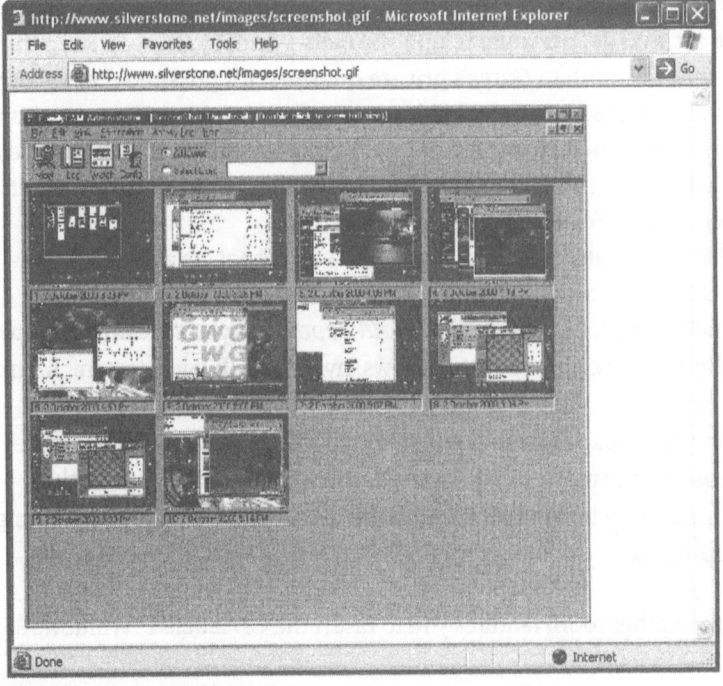

---

12. http://www.silverstone.net/images/screenshot.gif

Home Sweet Home Page

Much has been written about the "wired home" and how having a home computer network that includes an Internet connection will make family life easier. You won't have to carry floppy disks or CDs from one room to another. And sharing an Internet connection means your kids will be able to go online from the comfort of their own rooms where you won't be able to see what they're doing. Hmmm.... The following are two families who are taking advantage of technology to improve the little places they call "home."

Family Living, Bill Gates-Style

Poor Bill Gates. The multibillionaire chairman of Microsoft is the butt of endless jokes and the subject of a myriad of unofficial home pages and hoaxes that plague the Internet. But what about Gates the family man?

The $53 million residence near Seattle, Washington, in which Bill and his wife Melinda raise their children is a showplace of technology both old and new. The dining room is rumored to seat 150 guests. Visitors reportedly wear lapel pins that allow them to be followed throughout the house so they can hear music, see examples of their favorite art, and get personal telephone calls—and, by the way, keep to the more public rooms rather than Gates's private quarters. It's possible that visitors will find high-tech sensors placed alongside a $36 million Winslow Homer painting that reportedly hangs outside Gates's personal library as well as ancient marvels such as Leonardo da Vinci's handwritten notebook, the Codex Leicester, which Gates purchased in 1994 for $30.8 million.

You don't have to gawk at the mansion from a tour boat, as a *Seattle Times* columnist did (http://seattletimes.nwsource.com/html/sherrygrindeland/135155829_grin03e.html). *U.S. News and World Report* lets you take an online tour of the estate at http://www.usnews.com/usnews/nycu/tech/billgate/gatehigh.htm (see Figure 1-11).

A page called Jim's Joke Repository (http://www.jimpoz.com/jokes/) pokes fun at the Microsoft chairman's home sweet home with remarks such as the following, which readers who are familiar with the quirks of the Windows operating systems will appreciate:

- Walking to another room requires you to insert the CD labeled "Windows 95."

- The doormat reads "Start" instead of "Welcome."

- Buying new furniture requires you to use the Add New Hardware Wizard.

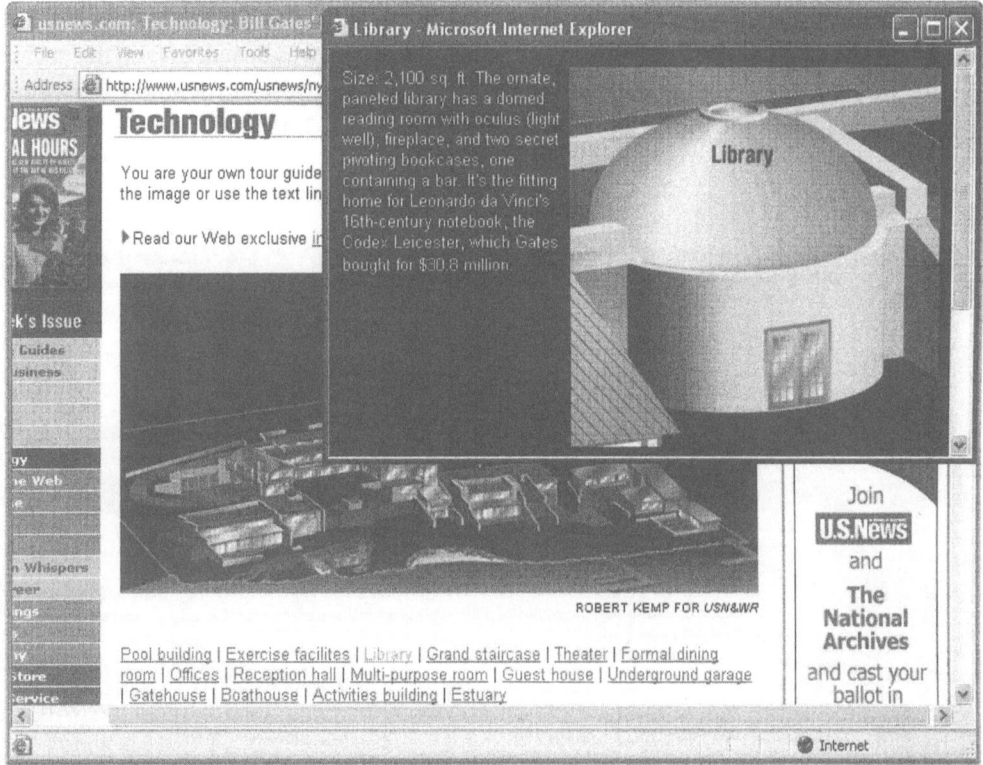

Figure 1-11. Bill Gates's library, a room you can view on an online virtual tour[13]

Don't go looking for Bill's own home page at http://www.billgates.com/. At this writing, that domain name is owned by a Texas company called motherboards.com. Bill apparently hasn't done a "Jerry Falwell" yet (see the "Preacher Is Master of His Domain (Name)" section about Falwell earlier in this chapter) and fought to retrieve his own domain name—not yet. You can find his official online home at http://www.microsoft.com/billgates/default.asp.

The Hills Are Alive...with the Sound of Marketing

When I first saw the Trapp Family Lodge's Web site (http://www.trappfamily.com/), I thought the lodge was in Austria. Then I realized that it was not in the European Alps depicted in the movie *The Sound of Music* but in the White Mountains of Stowe, Vermont. Ah, a marketing gimmick thought up by someone trying to make

---

13. http://www.usnews.com/usnews/nycu/tech/billgate/gatehigh.htm

a buck off the movie, my skeptical mind thought. When I explored the site, however, it quickly became clear that marketing is being done, all right, but by the members of the original von Trapp family on which the movie was based. In fact, the current president of the lodge is Johannes von Trapp, the youngest son of Maria, the woman portrayed in the movie by Julie Andrews (see Figure 1-12).

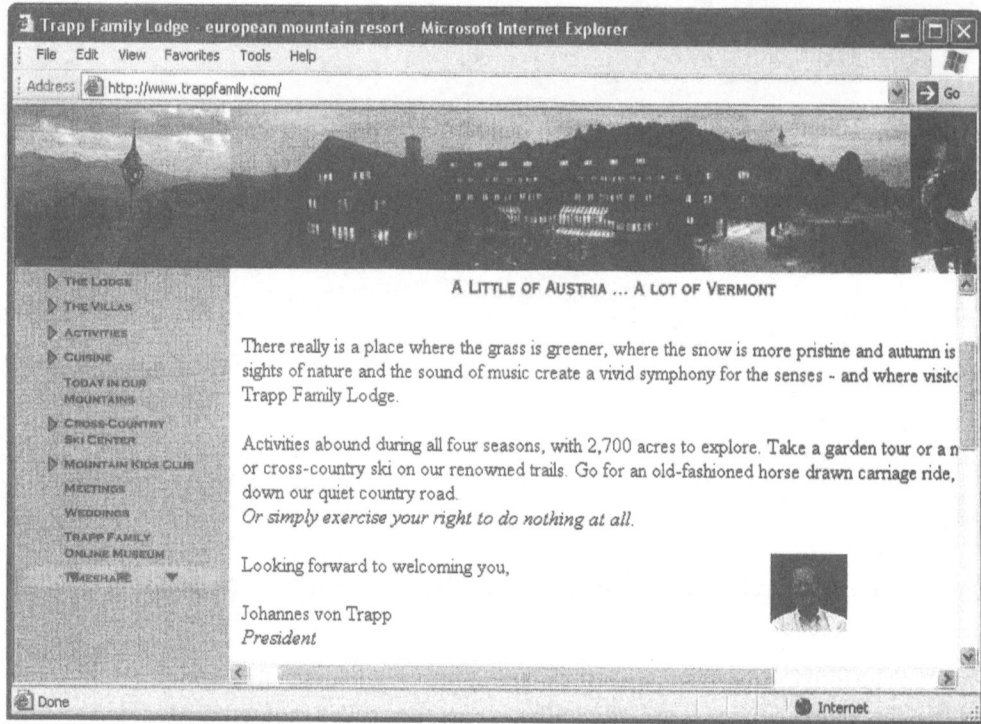

Figure 1-12. This Web site has got to be one of the Trapp family's newest "favorite things."[14]

It turns out that the Trapp family has been in Vermont since 1939 and their lodge has been open since 1950, but their home on the Web gives them a new way for their voices to be heard. The Web site for the lodge includes recipes such as Maria's Favorite Linzertorte and Venison Loin on Schupf Nudles with Ligonberry, among other "favorite things."

---

14. http://www.trappfamily.com/

Point, Click, Order a Child

Not so long ago, the question of whether to have a child was the most personal of decisions. Here, too, computers and the Internet have made the family bedroom just another node in the worldwide network. Some Web sites enable women to conceive, and others deliver products that stop a pregnancy from progressing. Couples who have children can take control of the adoption process by going online—as long as they make sure they get the right child.

Boy or Girl? You Decide

Computers take the mystery out of so many things. The Boy or Girl Web site (http://www.boyorgirl.com/) claims it can predict whether you will have a boy or girl with 92 percent accuracy. If you are already pregnant, it can tell you the gender of the child. If you want to become pregnant, it can tell you the best days on which to conceive.

The method used is highly scientific: a mixture of the Chinese lunar calendar, astrology, and psychic prediction. All you have to do is sign up, provide some pertinent personal information, and pay a modest fee (ranging from $2.99 to $4.99), and the Web site will do the rest.

Sperm Banks Take Online Withdrawals

You can verify your checking account online, pay your bills, and transfer funds from one account to another. Why not withdraw sperm from a sperm bank? It's an option being pursued by many who are, for one reason or another, missing that vital component of the reproductive process.

Prospective parents aren't the only ones using the Net for sperm-related activity. The Sperm Bank of California (http://www.thespermbankofca.org/) recruits sperm donors online, offering $50 per donation and a $200 bonus for passing an exit blood test. It's possible to do the donation process online, but you do have to visit the sperm bank's Berkeley offices to make the actual "deposit."

Both the Sperm Bank of California and Fairfax Cryobank in Virginia maintain a database of sperm donors. As shown in Figure 1-13, you can search the Cryobank's database by donor blood type or other characteristics such as ethnic origin, hair color (black, brown, auburn, blond, red), or hair type (straight, wavy, or curly). At some sperm banks, you can even listen to audio recordings of donors or find photos of donors who have the physical characteristics for which you are looking.

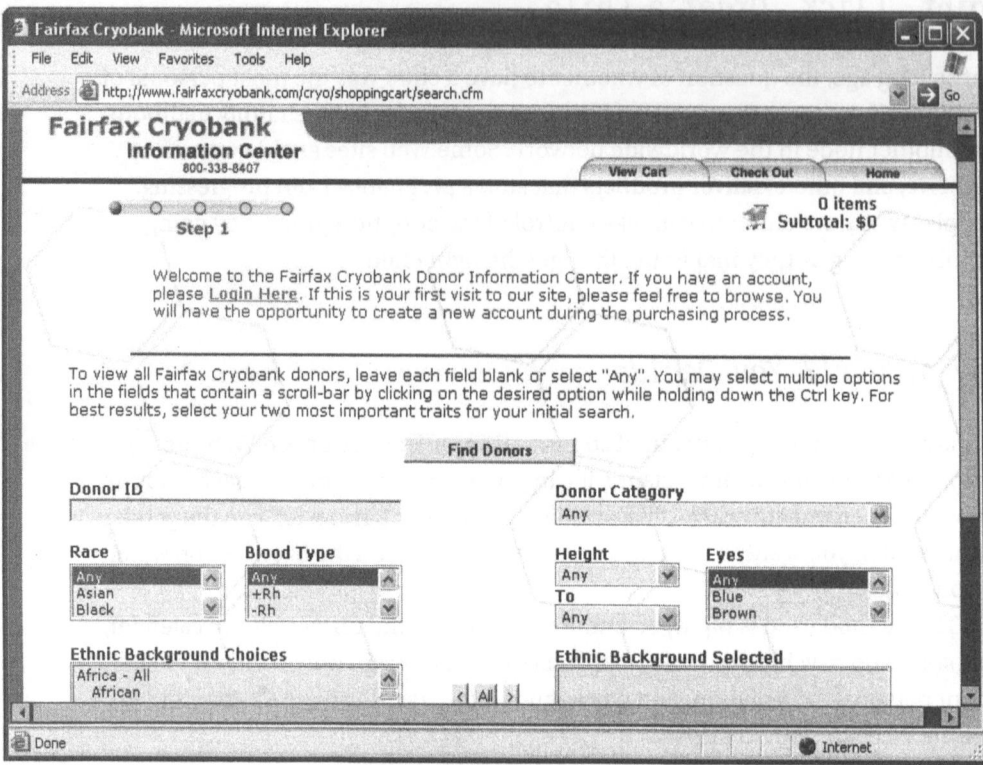

Figure 1-13. Although many Web surfers are looking for sex online, others only want sperm.[15]

An article in Wired News (http://www.wired.com/news/medtech/0,1286,57020,00.html) tells the story of a woman named Chloe Ohme and her female partner, Jane Duxbury, who found the right donor after browsing the databases of several online sperm banks. They requested and received the registration forms for the sperm bank by e-mail. Following the policy observed by many sperm banks, they had their doctor sign the forms and fax them back to the company.

Once they finished registering, Ohme and Duxbury waited for the right time of the month. Then, they placed their online order with the sperm bank and had FedEx ship the sample overnight right to their door. Frozen sperm is shipped in a thermos-like canister that is cooled with liquid nitrogen or packed with dry ice.

The final step in the process, the actual insemination, was a low-tech affair aided by the fact that Ohme is a trained midwife. She let the vial of sperm defrost and then "put it in her armpit" to warm it up. "It's the best way to bring it up to body temperature," she commented. A simple 1-milliliter syringe did the rest.

---

15. http://www.fairfaxcryobank.com/cryo/shoppingcart/search.cfm

Where to Go the "Morning After"? Just Log On

Few sights generate more anxiety more quickly than a torn, dripping condom. Passionate moments quickly deteriorate into a heated discussion: Now what?

You've got 48 to 72 hours to take one of the so-called morning-after pills, your best bet for preventing pregnancy. But first you need to talk to your doctor (assuming you have one), get a prescription, and find a pharmacy that carries the drug. But what if it's Friday night and your doctor is not available or your conservative pharmacist refuses to dispense the drugs?

Just turn to one of several Internet sites to make a house call and provide you with prescriptions for the emergency contraception. At least one will ship the pills directly to you.

At VirtualMedicalGroup.com (http://www.virtualmedicalgroup.com/), you can make a "virtual office visit" and order Plan B, a pill that can prevent pregnancy if taken within 48 hours of unprotected sex.

There are two hormone pills designed to prevent pregnancy after accidents: Plan B and Preven. Doctors may also prescribe higher doses of birth control pills as they've done for decades for rape victims. The methods reduce risk of pregnancy by 75 percent.

Clients fill out an online medical survey, which is forwarded to physicians in the client's state for prescription approval. They pay $49 for the virtual visit and $53 for two of the pills.

Planned Parenthood of Georgia has created a Web site devoted solely to online emergency contraception (http://www.ecconnection.org/). The clinic offers prescriptions through its Web site for a $40 a consultation, not counting the cost of the drugs (Plan B or Preven). The catch is that the drugs are shipped only to pharmacies in the state of Georgia itself.

B-Commerce: The "Internet Twins" Adoption Scandal

If you order the wrong drapery online, you can simply return it and exchange it for the correct variety. But what happens when you order the wrong babies for adoption, and you are induced to return them?

That's what happened to a California couple, Richard and Vickie Allen. In late 2000, they obtained twins, Belinda and Kimberley, through an Internet adoption agency. The girls' natural mother had just split up from her husband and was willing to have the twins adopted. She went to a California "baby broker," who sold them to the Allens.

But when a couple in North Wales, Alan and Judith Kilshaw, offered double what the Allens paid (about $13,300), the broker and the natural mother, Tranda Wecker, tricked the Allens into giving them back. They then transferred them to the Kilshaws.

The Kilshaws quickly drove across country to Arkansas, which has less strict adoption laws than California, where they adopted the twins. (A court in Arkansas later nullified the Kilshaw adoption.) Just to complicate things even further, a third couple emerged to say that they, too, were offered the twins for about $10,000.

In January 2001, the Kilshaws were reportedly considering the possibility of turning their story into a film. A judge later ruled that the Kilshaws had an "overriding preoccupation with the media" that overshadowed their concern for the twins' welfare and ordered that they give up custody. Tawdry tales of the Kilshaws unconventional lifestyle, including visits from paranormal investigators, caused them to be vilified in British tabloids. The girls were eventually sent to a foster home in Missouri. The Kilshaws developed their own theater show, *Meet the Kilshaws*, in an effort to tell their side of the story to the public.

NOTE   A tongue-in-cheek story on SatireWire (http://www.satirewire.com/news/0101/btail.shtml) reported that this adoption scandal was not expected to hurt the sales of other babies by online "b-tailers" working in the burgeoning "b-commerce sector," according to an expert study.

Family Stress, Internet-Style

The Internet is famous for bringing people together. It's also a place where people can split up faster than you can type a username and password. If you need to cope with the stress of your online divorce, you can find sage advice from a psychotherapist who works out of an office in cyberspace—you provide your own couch.

Log In, Split Up, Move On

Lots of people go on the Internet looking for individuals to marry. A growing number, however, are looking to get unmarried and finding that online divorces are relatively quick and easy compared to going to a traditional lawyer and paying $1,500 or more. The completecase.com Web site has stripped the process down to a matter of $300, and 20,000 people have reportedly signed up for it and the rival service LegalZoom.com.

The Divorce Wizards organization likens the process to shopping at a supermarket. Part of its Web site (http://www.divorcewizards.com/divorcemart.html) is labeled "Welcome to Divorcemart: Your online stop for legal documents and more." The Dissomaster online tool enables you to estimate your child support payments.

The trend toward online divorce works well for those who are looking at an uncontested split-up. "For me, it was a purely economic decision," John Chang, of South Pasadena, California, told Wired News. "When you don't have children or a lot of assets, it's the way to go."

NOTE   If you are considering online divorce because of the trend toward online infidelity but you need some information to back you up, check out Infidelity Check (http://www.infidelitycheck.org/). The online service specializes in detecting instances of "online infidelity"—visits to chat rooms and Internet pornography that could result in real-life encounters or, at the least, breakdowns of intimate relationships.

Virtual Marriage Counseling

Getting unmarried can be every bit as stressful as getting married—or, if you have already tied the knot and are having problems, simply staying married. If you need some counseling and don't want to see someone in person, consult social worker Jacqueline Gay at Marriage Matters (http://www.marriagematters.com/).

Gay provides online counseling to people by e-mail, phone, or instant messaging. Who would share their most intimate marital secrets over the worldwide computer network? "I have found the people I work with either have very busy schedules or want to maintain their privacy," she explains. "People who use online counseling comment that the format suits their personalities and is easier emotionally and physically than 'going' to a therapist. Often the response time is quicker, and they are able to write when they are in the middle of the crisis or emotion."

The Internet Saved My Mind

My friends joke with me that the amount of time I spend writing and working at the computer will prevent me from getting Alzheimer's disease, which destroys memories and other brain functions. But this is no joke to some real-life people who are using computers and the Internet to cling to their memories and their families.

Blogs—online diaries that pundits, artists, and just plain folks use to record their daily thoughts and activities—are all the rage these days. You don't think of blogs as forums for retirees who are in their "golden years." But some recent studies have reported that keeping your mind active can delay the onset of the dementia that makes Alzheimer's disease (AD) so devastating. Whether you have been diagnosed with AD or know someone who has, you can read people's attempts to use blogging to keep their minds sharp and active and hopefully delay the dementia. AD has no known cure, and there is no proof that blogging, or any other form of cognitive exercise, can slow its progress. But those who blog believe it helps, and their thoughts and beliefs are the whole point, aren't they?

NOTE   Actually, a study of a group of nuns conducted by the University of Kentucky suggests that keeping mentally active does delay the onset of the dementia that accompanies AD. Read about it at http://www.mc.uky.edu/nunnet/.

At age 62, Mary Lockhart (see Figure 1-14) is a patient diagnosed with AD who suffers mild to moderate memory loss. Mary says her blog and the rest of her Web site (http://www.angelfire.com/ok4/mari5113/index.html) has greatly improved the quality of her life by helping her recall tasks completed and milestones passed. "I just share some of the things I do each day. Some of them are my slip-ups. My journal tells me when I've paid the bills, bathed the dogs, and fed my flowers," she says.

Not only do Lockhart and other blogging seniors publish photos of their family and friends on their Web sites, but Lockhart often writes about the friends she has made online in the course of live chat events she has hosted for the Dementia Advocacy and Support Network International (http://www.dasninternational.org/). The feeling of having an extended family and a network of friends not only helps improve cognitive functioning but is nice in its own way, too.

"When I am working on my Web site, it helps keep my mind occupied and makes me use my brain," she explains. "Also, I don't think about my problems when I am busy. I am able to reach out to people all over the world who have been diagnosed with dementia and their care partners. When I get an e-mail from someone who has read my Web site and is patting me on the back, it sure does make my heart smile."

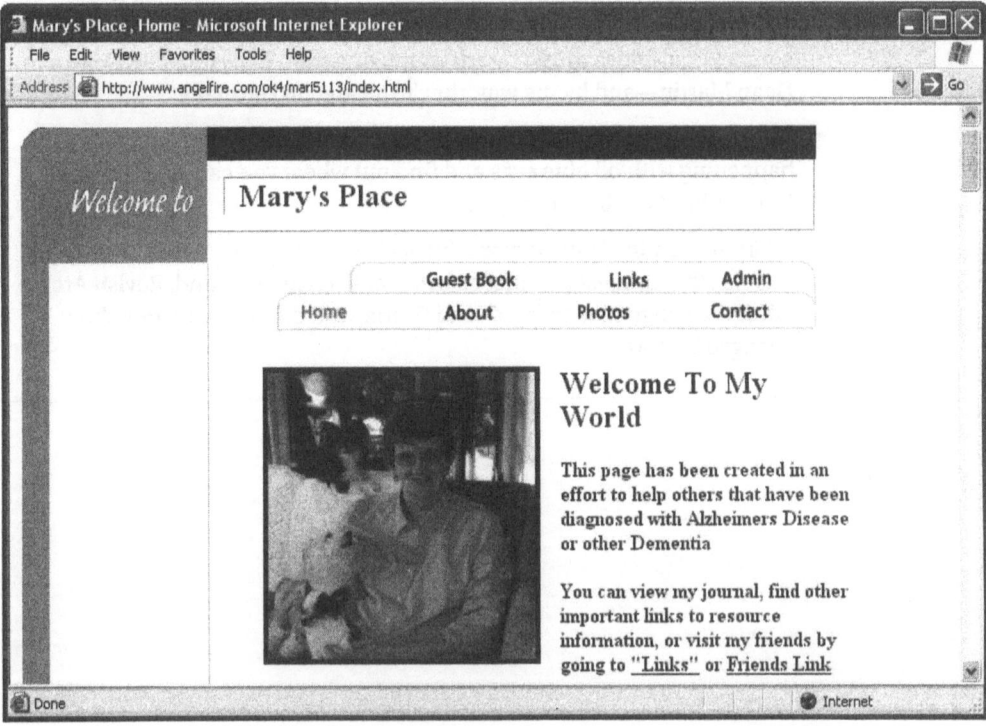

Figure 1-14. Mary Lockhart keeps a blog (a Web log) to improve brain function and make friends.[16]

Random Googling

The Internet contains countless Web sites, chat rooms, newsgroups, and other resources related to families and family life. The following list contains a few I found noteworthy—a random sampling of sites that turned up after searching for the term "family" on the search service Google (http://www.google.com/):

- **The Official Web Site of the British Monarchy (http://www.royal.gov.uk/output/Page1.asp)**: With 645 household employees, at least five palaces, and millions of dollars in income, you'd think they could buy themselves something the rest of us mere mortals have: a last name.

---

16. http://www.angelfire.com/ok4/mari5113/index.html

- **Bear Family Records (http://www.bear-family.de/):** This small record label, started by a former wine trader, reissues classic American bluegrass, country-and-blues music by artists ranging from Elvis to Willie Nelson to Dean Martin—and by the way, they're located in Germany.

- **SinatraFamily.com (http://www.sinatrafamily.com/):** Find out what's happening with ol' blue eyes and find out where you can let daughter Nancy's boots walk all over you.

- **All in the Family (http://www.allinthefamilysit.com/):** When I was a kid, this was the funniest and most controversial family around. Revisit Archie, Edith the Dingbat, Meathead, and Gloria, and discover why this show changed TV forever.

CHAPTER 2

Washed Up in Babylon

THE BETTER HORSES are put out to pasture—or, for the lucky few, out to stud. The also-rans end up at the glue factory, or so the story goes. Where do actors go when their time in the limelight is over? They don't go to rehab. Instead, they get a Web site.

It's fascinating to check in on the people we grew up watching on TV or in the movies. In many cases, they have taken on a new identity thanks to the Web. Sometimes (as in the case of Bob Crane) you learn that there was a dark side hidden behind a sunny public persona. In other cases, people who were famous (or almost famous) have found a new life through their Web sites.

From the Small Screen to the Small Monitor

The most hilarious rebirths that have taken place on the Internet have to do with celebrities who never made it to the top echelon of stardom. You would think that members of this group wouldn't have so far to fall. Ah, but you would be wrong, dear reader—surprisingly wrong.

The Rise and Mysterious Fall of Bob Crane

Bob Crane was best known in the 1960s as the star of a TV series about World War II called *Hogan's Heroes*. In the show, which ran from 1965–1971, Crane played the leader of a group of Allied soldiers who were imprisoned in a German POW camp called Stalag 13.

Hogan was hardly a model prisoner. He always had some kind of secret scheme in progress. Rather than trying to escape, though, he used the POW camp as a base for intelligence operations against the Germans. His men regularly went underground, headed into town, and somehow obtained gourmet foods and other supplies. Crane and his fellow cast members, including his second wife (who played a character in *Hogan's Heroes*), are depicted in Figure 2-1 in an image from Morty's World of TV, one of the many fan sites that provides facts about the show (http://mortystv.com/showcards/hogans_heroes.shtml).

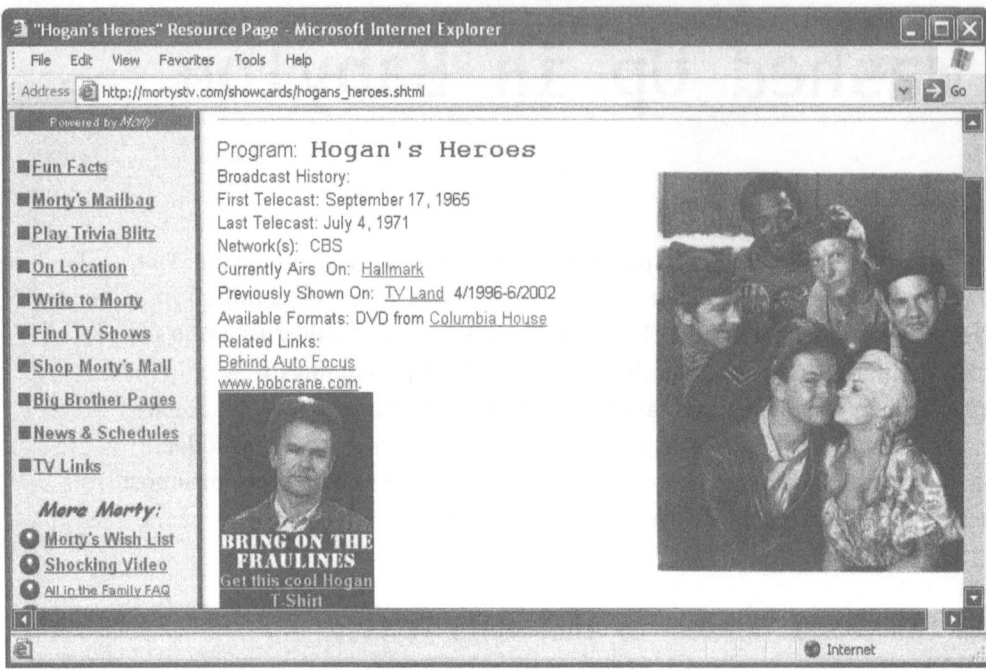

Figure 2-1. The public face of Bob Crane: with the Hogan's Heroes cast[1]

In the 1950s, Bob Crane was a successful radio host on radio station KNX in Los Angeles, California. His real ambition was to be an actor, however. He began to get parts in various TV shows of the early '60s, including *The Dick Van Dyke Show* and *The Twilight Zone*. He briefly had a role on *The Donna Reed Show* but was dismissed by the show's producers because his character, Dr. Dave Kelsey, was "too suggestive."

In 1965 he landed the lead role in *Hogan's Heroes*, for which he was twice nominated for an Emmy. During the run of the show, he met Sigrid Valdis (also known as Patti Olsen), who played Hilda on the show. Crane divorced his wife of 20 years and married Olsen in 1970 on the set of *Hogan's Heroes*. For several years, Patti Crane ran a discussion group on Yahoo! Groups devoted to Bob Crane and dispelling the many myths about him (see Figure 2-2). She recently had to abandon the group for health reasons.

After *Hogan's Heroes* was cancelled in 1971, Crane found a few acting roles, but nothing that gave him the notoriety and satisfaction of the TV show. He was in Scottsdale, Arizona, in 1978, starring in a play called *Beginner's Luck*, when he was found murdered in his motel room. He had been beaten with either a lamp or his

---

1. http://mortystv.com/showcards/hogans_heroes.shtml

own camera tripod and strangled with an electrical cord. His murderer has never been charged, and the death remains a mystery.

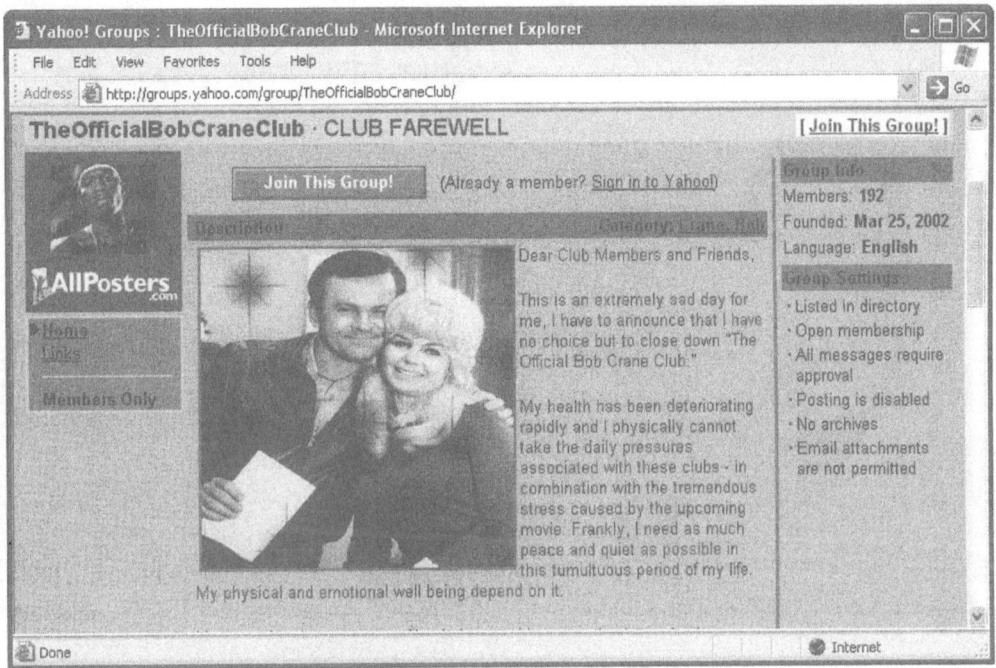

Figure 2-2. Crane and his wife Patti, who worked to defend his name long after his death[2]

Everything you've read to this point is the public side of Bob Crane's life. But it's hardly the whole story. Much of the rest of Crane's private life revolved around sex and photography. He is known as the "King of Stag Films," a title promoted by his son, Scotty, who has given interviews to radio talk show host Howard Stern and others regarding the elder Crane's sexual proclivities. Crane was one of the earliest amateur pornographers. He was making porn films, starring himself and others, as early as 1956. When actors such as Carroll O'Connor (*Archie Bunker*) and John and Patty Duke Astin visited, they got a tour of the home and were routinely shown Crane's porn videos. You can become a member of Bob Crane's Web site (http://www.bobcrane.com/, shown in Figure 2-3) and view him in some of the films he made.

---

2. http://groups.yahoo.com/group/TheOfficialBobCraneClub/

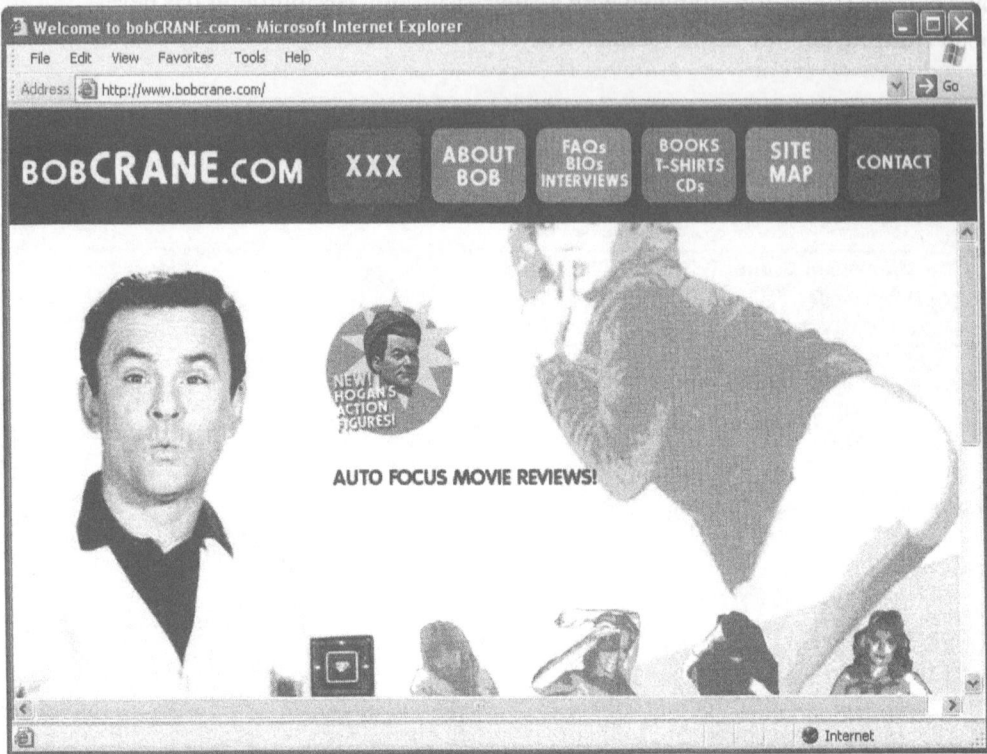

Figure 2-3. Crane's family celebrates his love of sex and shows his self-made "stag films" on his Web site.[3]

It might seem surprising that Bob Crane's official Web site, which is run with the participation of his family, pays so much attention to his X-rated pursuits. The Crane family celebrates all parts of Bob Crane's life; they say the "sex stuff" was a part of that life and needs to be acknowledged as well. He was open about his movie making with his family (Crane showed photos to his son as a child; his wife built him a studio in their home). They object to Crane's portrayal in the film *Auto Focus*, which suggested that he might be gay, had a penile implant, and had a dark, sinister side.

---

3.   http://www.bobcrane.com/

TIP Larry Hovis, who played Sergeant Carter on *Hogan's Heroes*, died in 2003 but lives on through his Web site (http://larryhovis.com/). Amazingly, Leon Askin, the Viennese actor who played the minor character General Burkhalter, has his own Web site as well (http://www.askin.at/english.htm). Askin describes Beverly Hills, California, schoolchildren who used to mistake him for the better-known character Colonel Klink (played by Werner Klemperer, http://www.angelfire.com/celeb/werner/) and who would raise their arms in the Nazi salute, which would stop traffic.

Bill Mumy: Not Lost in Cyberspace

All too many people, actors or not, create Web pages that serve more or less as a "Hi there" poster. They don't realize that the best Web sites need as much content as possible to support them. They post a few photos, a few favorite links, and maybe an online diary called a *blog*. They're as boring in cyberspace as they are in real life.

Bill Mumy, who is best known as one of the stars of the 1960s TV show *Lost in Space*, shows how to do the Web right on his personal Web site (http://www.billmumy.com/, shown in Figure 2-4). He uses the site to "reflect back on the past and look ahead to the future," as he says on his home page.

Luckily for Mumy, he has a lot of career material to talk about. He not only played Will Robinson in *Lost in Space*, but he starred in episodes of *The Twilight Zone*, *Babylon 5*, and many other TV shows and movies. He uses the site to present a visual résumé of his past work, talk about current projects, and promote his rock band. There's also a link to his fan club plus links to Web sites devoted to other stars of *Lost in Space*:

- **Guy Williams (http://www.zorrofx.com/dads_pg.htm)**: Williams's son has created a Web page in his memory.

- **June Lockhart (http://www.junelockhart.com/)**: A static Web page with photos from the actress's long career.

- **Marta Kristen (http://www.martakristen.com/)**: The gorgeous blonde on *Lost in Space* has an online shop where you can purchase videotapes of her movies, including *Beach Blanket Bingo* and *Battle Beyond the Stars*.

- **Angela Cartwright (http://www.angela-cartwright.com/):** She not only played the little girl in *Lost in Space* but was one of the kids in the movie *The Sound of Music*. She uses her Web site to promote her photographs and an artisans' boutique.

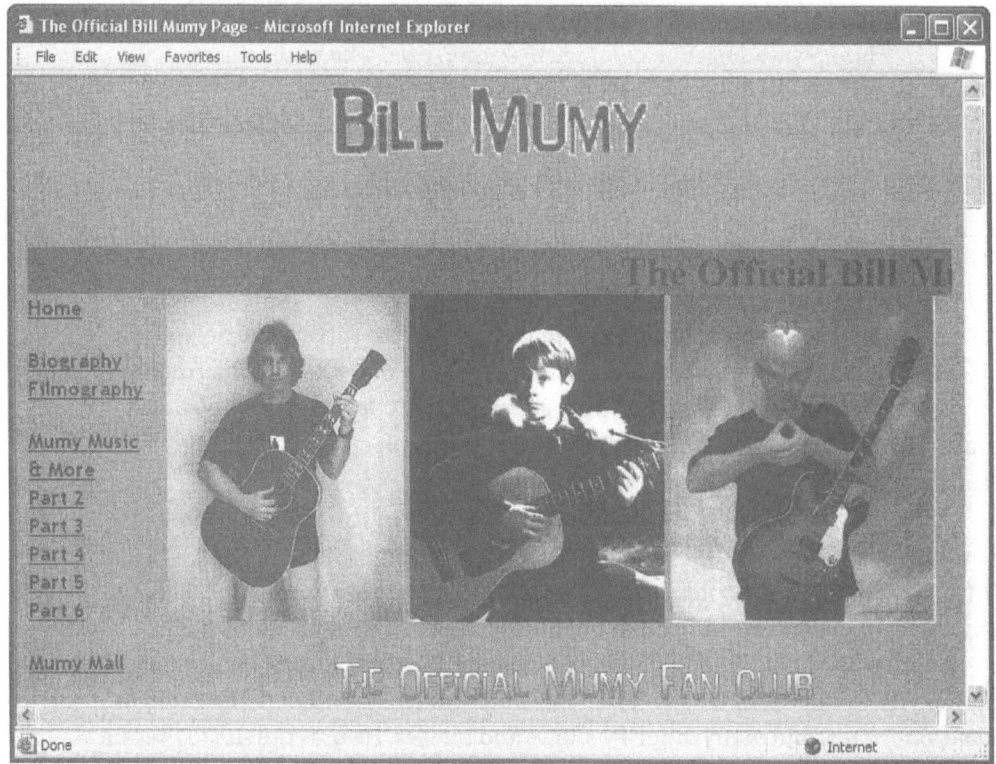

Figure 2-4. He was lost in space, but now has a home in cyberspace.[4]

There was once a site devoted to the man who was condemned to wear the Robot B9 suit, Bob May. I couldn't find the site online at this writing. I did find a site devoted to May and the robot at Robot Web (http://www.aboyd.com/robots/lis3.html, shown in Figure 2-5). The robot, after spending many years in storage, has found a new career as a spokesman for Altoids mints (http://www.altoids.com/).

---

4. http://www.billmumy.com/

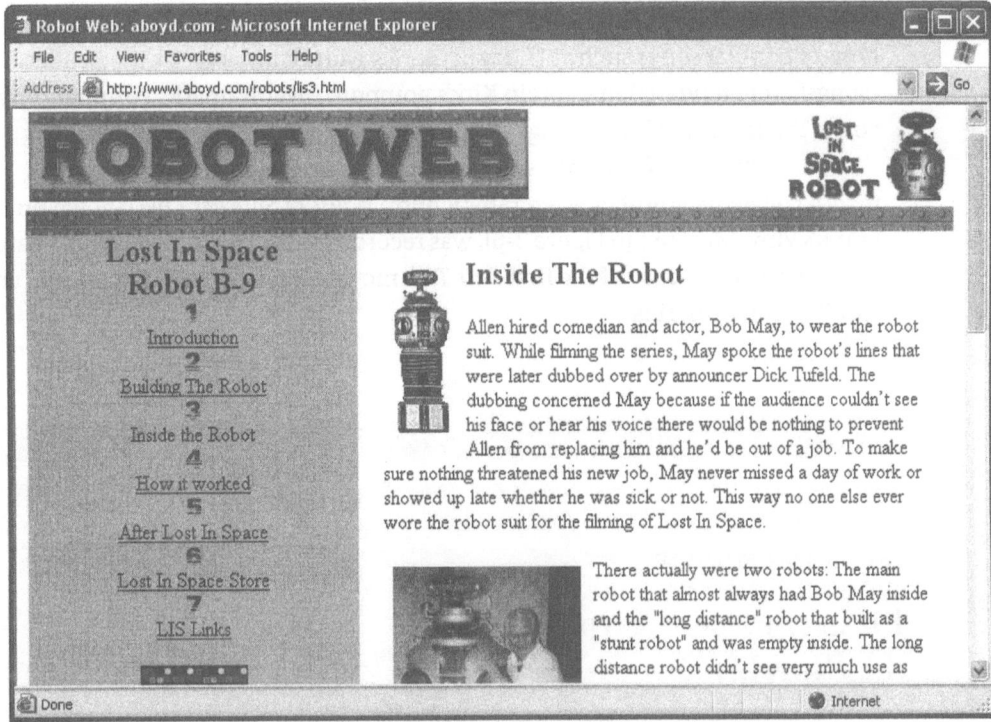

Figure 2-5. "Danger, Will Robinson!" Robot B-9 now pushes Altoids mints.[5]

Star Trek: The Washed-Up Generation

In the annals of the Internet, no TV show has received as much attention as *Star Trek*. In the earliest days of the Web, in 1994, I remember standing at a coworker's computer and listening to sound clips of William Shatner, the original Captain Kirk, singing one of his unforgettable (or should I say, unforgivable) songs. Since then, several generations of *Star Trek* actors and actresses (including members of *Star Trek: The Next Generation*) have gone online. The following are some examples of what you might find, should you decide to boldly go where no one has gone before.

Unforgettable Song Stylists

What ever gave *Star Trek* actors the notion they could sing? What prompted them to come out with their own record albums? Was it all those hours they spent zooming around at warp speed that warped their judgment? William Shatner started the

5. http://www.aboyd.com/robots/lis3.html

sorry trend with a 1968 album called *The Transformed Man*. He didn't sing, exactly. Rather, he did "spoken word" recordings of works by Shakespeare as well as renditions of popular songs such as "Lucy in the Sky with Diamonds" by the Beatles. The "songs" were rendered in Captain Kirk's pompous, overdramatic, commanding voice: You imagined him saying, "Beam me up, Scotty" at any moment.

The Transformed Man has since become a cult classic, eagerly sought by record collectors. Another, even rarer album, *William Shatner Live* (shown on Frank's Vinyl Museum in Figure 2-6), was recorded at the nadir of the actor's career (just before the release of the first *Star Trek* movie) as he answered questions at a *Star Trek* fan gathering.

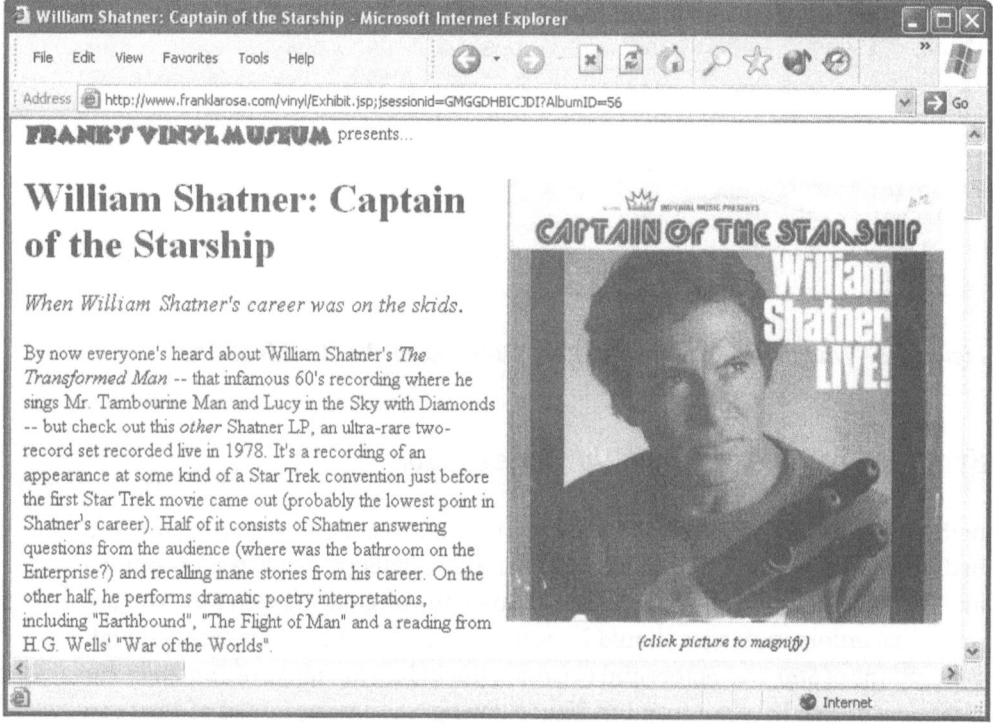

Figure 2-6. A transformed man: William Shatner, singer and entertainer[6]

Shatner has good-naturedly poked fun at his own attempts as a singer in recent years. He gave a recitation in one commercial for the online service Priceline. He also "sang" Color Me Badd's "I Wanna Sex You Up" at the 1992 MTV

---

6. http://www.franklarosa.com/vinyl/Exhibit.jsp;jsessionid=GMGGDHBICJDI?AlbumID=56

movie awards. You won't find any of Shatner's albums on his own Web site (http://www.williamshatner.com/), but he does sell his novel *Shadow Planet* there, as well as a VHS tape entitled *William Shatner's Star Trek Memories.*

Leonard Nimoy, who is at least as well known as Shatner, if not more, played Mr. Spock on the original *Star Trek* series. One of his catchphrases from that series, "highly illogical," became the title of his own album (see Figure 2-7). On it, he tackled such songs as "The Ballad of Bilbo Baggins," "Ruby, Don't Take Your Love to Town," and "If I Were a Carpenter."

Figure 2-7. The thought of Leonard Nimoy making his own album seemed highly logical at the time.[7]

---

7. http://www.daisyplanet.com/st/info/Leo_High.html

TIP   Look up Nimoy's *Highly Illogical* on Amazon.com
(http://www.amazon.com/). Scroll down to the reader reviews. They
are some of the funniest I have ever read. You can also find Nimoy's
"Y2K Family Survival Guide" on Amazon.com.

One of the strangest titles for a *Star Trek*–related album (and that's saying
something) was recorded by Brent Spiner, who did a great job as Data, the yellow-
eyed android, in *Star Trek: The Next Generation*. The album was called *Ol' Yellow
Eyes Is Back*. You can't see it in Figure 2-8, but Spiner's eyes were bright yellow, and
the rest of the album cover was black-and-white; see Star Trek: Variations
(http://www.daisyplanet.com/st/actor-e.html) for the original cover.

*Figure 2-8. Worf, Captain Picard, and other character-actors sang backing vocals
on Brent Spiner's album.[8]*

---

8.   http://www.daisyplanet.com/st/actor-e.html

The album featured classic songs such as "Embraceable You," "Carolina in the Morning," and "Zing! Went the Strings of My Heart." One song included backing vocals by the Sunspots, who were Spiner's fellow *Star Trek* actors Patrick Stewart, Jonathan Frakes, LeVar Burton, and Michael Dorn.

Last but certainly not least is someone who can actually sing, write, and entertain: Nichelle Nichols, best known for her role as Lieutenant Uhura on the original *Star Trek* series. Nichols's story is full of surprises. The Hip Surgery Music Guide (http://www.hipsurgerymusic.com/Nichols/) reports that she was discovered by jazz legend Duke Ellington at age 15, and that she toured with Ellington as his band's singer. In her early days on *Star Trek*, she had to deal with various types of racial prejudice, such as withheld fan mail and unequal pay. When she was about to quit the show, no less a person than Dr. Martin Luther King convinced her to stay. She and William Shatner had TV's first interracial kiss in 1968. She calls her Web site Uhura.com (see Figure 2-9).

Figure 2-9. Nichelle Nichols keeps in touch not with her transporter but with her Uhura.com Web site.[9]

---

9. http://www.uhura.com/

After the TV series ended, Nichols appeared in several films and worked for NASA, helping to recruit females and minorities into the astronaut program. She helped launch the careers of Sally Ride (the first American woman in space) and Guion Bluford (the first African American in space) and was an inspiration for black female astronaut Dr. Mae Jemison.

Nichols' LPs include *Down to Earth* (Epic, 1967), *Dark Side of the Moon* (R-Way, 1974), and *Out Of This World*, (R-Way, and shown in Figure 2-10). She has also published two novels.

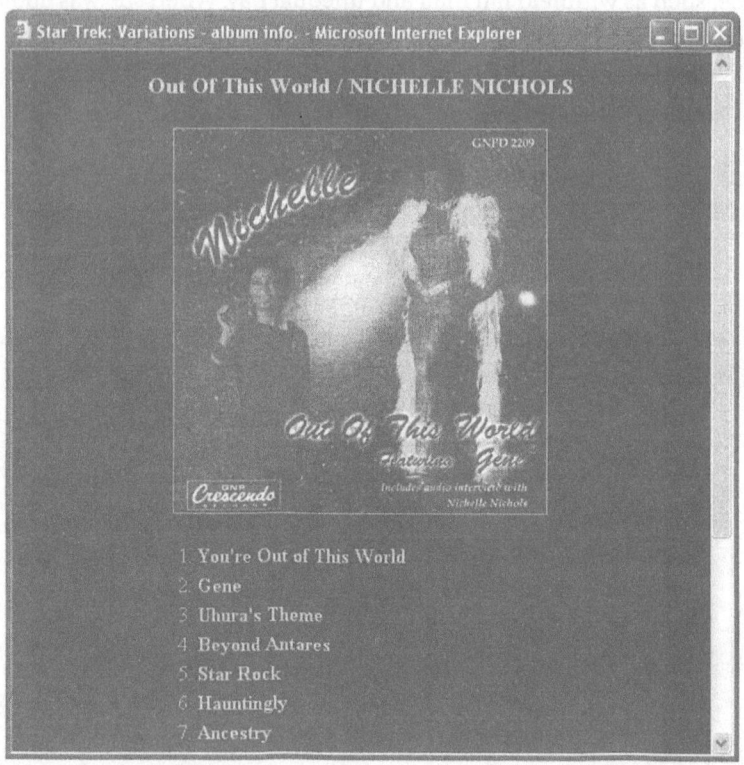

Figure 2-10. This album included a vocal version of the Star Trek theme: Who knew there were words to it?[10]

Coping with Life After the Next Generation

Wil Wheaton, who played young Wesley Crusher on *Star Trek: The Next Generation*, says he created his first Web page only after someone told him a Wil Wheaton

10. http://www.daisyplanet.com/st/info/Nic_Out.html

discussion group had been created on Yahoo! Groups. He made it as simply and quickly as he could. After quickly getting 700 visitors, he decided to create a "real" Web site. The result: Wil Wheaton Dot Net (http://www.wilwheaton.net/).

This book's editor suggested mentioning Wheaton as an example of "one of the worst actors of our time" ending up with his own Web page. Wheaton is an example of a young actor (he was 16 when he got the part of Crusher) who now has to cope with life after getting his Big Break. I find it difficult to be harsh on Wheaton because his online blog indicates that he is a fellow die-hard Chicago Cubs fan.

Cindy Brady Voted Alter Ego Off Survivor Island

Susan Olsen told an interviewer for the online magazine KAOS2000 that she cringed when she first saw her character, Cindy Brady, on the popular show *The Brady Bunch*. You probably have to think a moment to remember Cindy: She was the youngest daughter, the one with a lisp, the one who looked a bit like Shirley Temple. The photo in Figure 2-11, taken from Brady World Web site (http://www.bradyworld.com/brady.htm), should refresh your memory. That's Olsen in the bottom-left corner.

"I loved my job, but I really wasn't fond of Cindy," Olsen told the magazine (http://www.kaos2000.net/interviews/susanolsen00.html). It should come as no surprise, then, that Olsen booted her own character off a desert island in a special *Brady Bunch* edition of the TV show *Survivor*.

Back in 2000, a Web site called Zap2It.com held a *Brady Bunch* edition of *Survivor*. The show attempted to explore what would transpire should the oh-so-lovable members of one of TV's best-known families be stuck on an island having to eat rodents and bugs. The real-life actors from the original show were given the opportunity to vote off their characters.

For those of you who don't remember or who didn't watch the original show, *The Brady Bunch* told the story of two divorcees who married and created a "blended" family. The father had three sons, the mother three daughters. They all went on the honeymoon together, and the show followed their "growing pains."

The virtual *Brady Bunch Survivor* show was hardly Olsen's first foray into cyberspace. For years, she had to endure rumors circulating on the Internet and on TV shows such as *Big Brother* claiming she had a secret life as a porn actress. Interestingly, in the aforementioned KAOS2000 interview, she admits contributing some sound effects to a porn movie (spaceship sound effects, not *those* sounds) but says she never appeared in front of the camera.

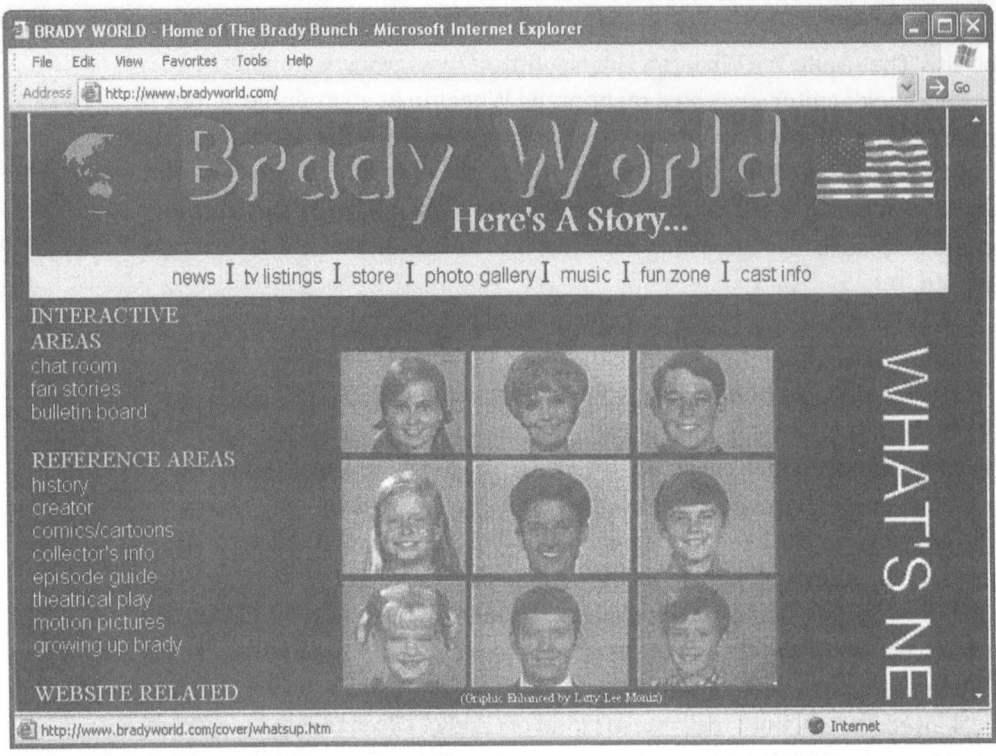

Figure 2-11. Cindy Brady: Voted off a desert island by her real-life alter ego, Susan Olsen[11]

NOTE   Another member of *The Brady Bunch* achieved a dubious sort of fame on the Internet. The Church of the Sub-Genius, which is described in Chapter 17, promoted a subgroup called The Clan of the Recycled Head of Marcia Brady among its many strange beliefs.

For a while, Olsen was the cohost of an Internet radio show on a now-defunct Web site, ComedyWorld.com, where she interviewed a host of illustrious guests, including the bizarre Broccoli Man (http://www.madmartian.com/broc/broctalk.htm). Most recently, she has served as a spokesperson against migraine headaches—the very maladies that were probably induced by the voice of Cindy Brady from 1969 to 1974.

11. http://www.bradyworld.com/

TIP   Once again, you'll have no trouble finding the original actors from this TV show on the Web. Florence Henderson (Mom Brady) is at http://www.flohome.com/; you'll find links to the other actors' Web sites at http://www.bradyworld.com/cover/links.htm. You won't find one for Christopher Knight, who played Peter Brady and who has since gone on to serve as a spokesperson against Attention Deficit Disorder as well as acne. See Buck Wolf''s Wolf Files column for a summary of Knight's work against acne (http://abcnews.go.com/sections/us/WolfFiles/wolffiles191.html).

Whatchu Talkin' 'Bout, Gary Coleman?

The child stars of the TV show *Diff'rent Strokes* appear to have encountered some seriously bad karma. Dana Plato had several run-ins with the law and died of a drug overdose. Todd Bridges was arrested several times and was acquitted after he was accused of shooting a crack dealer.

Gary Coleman, probably the best-known star from the show, earned millions from it, but he accused his parents of making off with the fortune. He was eventually forced to declare bankruptcy and had to take a $7-per-hour job as a security guard on a movie set. After getting into a fight with a fan who wanted his autograph, he was fined $400. He could not pay the fine and subsequently declared bankruptcy. That's when a Web site called Underground Online (UGO) got involved.

UGO created the Gary Coleman Web-a-Thon to auction off celebrity memorabilia and raise money for the diminutive actor. The site, which is preserved on the Internet Archive (see Figure 2-12), might look at first like it was making fun of Coleman. But all indications are that it was motivated by genuine concern over Coleman's plight. The auction offered such items as a tiny pimp suit tailored for Coleman, his 8-pound bowling ball, and items offered by New York Yankees players Derek Jeter and Chuck Knoblauch, among others.

From the Public Eye to Public Service

As I write this, Arnold Schwarzenegger has just been elected governor of California. That may be hard to believe, but his election looks (almost) sensible compared to those of other actors who have made their way to Washington as publicly elected representatives and who occasionally turn up on the Web.

Figure 2-12. A Web auction was held in 2000 to help bankrupt child star Gary Coleman.[12]

For example, take Fred Grandy, who is best known for his role as the ship's purser Gopher Smith on the TV series *The Love Boat*. He was also educated at Harvard University. And he was elected to the U.S. House of Representatives as a Republican from Iowa. He served four terms but left to run for governor of Iowa, a race he lost.

This juxtaposition of banal and high-minded has an odd effect on the Internet. It makes such people seem more interesting and pretty much guarantees that they'll end up in some unusual places online. In Grandy's case, you can find him in the following locations:

- On the Dynamic Biorhythms Web site (http://www.greenline-soft.com/dscr.php?CB=1247), you can discover Grandy's current biorhythms.

- He turns up on the Web site for Washington, D.C., radio station WMAL (http://wmal.fimc.net/showdj.asp?DJID=16433), where he has his own show.

---

12. http://web.archive.org/web/20011116021505/http://webathon.ugo.com/

- For $5,000 to $10,000, you can hire him as a speaker through the Leading Authorities Speakers Bureau (http://www.leadingauthorities.com/search/biography.htm?s=3369).

- On the Web site for *Mother Jones* magazine (http://www.motherjones.com/coinop_congress/stock_congress/fred_grandy.html), you can read a critical look at a stock deal involving Grandy.

- You can read a brief biography of him along with other politicians in the Political Graveyard Web site (http://politicalgraveyard.com/bio/grainger-gransback.html).

- On the Dead or Alive? Web site (http://www.deadoraliveinfo.com/dead.nsf/gnames-nf/Grandy+Fred/), you will discover that he is, indeed, still alive.

The same goes for Ben Jones, who gained fame as Cooter the mechanic on *The Dukes of Hazzard* and who served two terms as a U.S. representative from Georgia. But Jones has tended his own Web presence and developed a Web site called Cooter's Place (http://www.cootersplace.com/, shown in Figure 2-13).

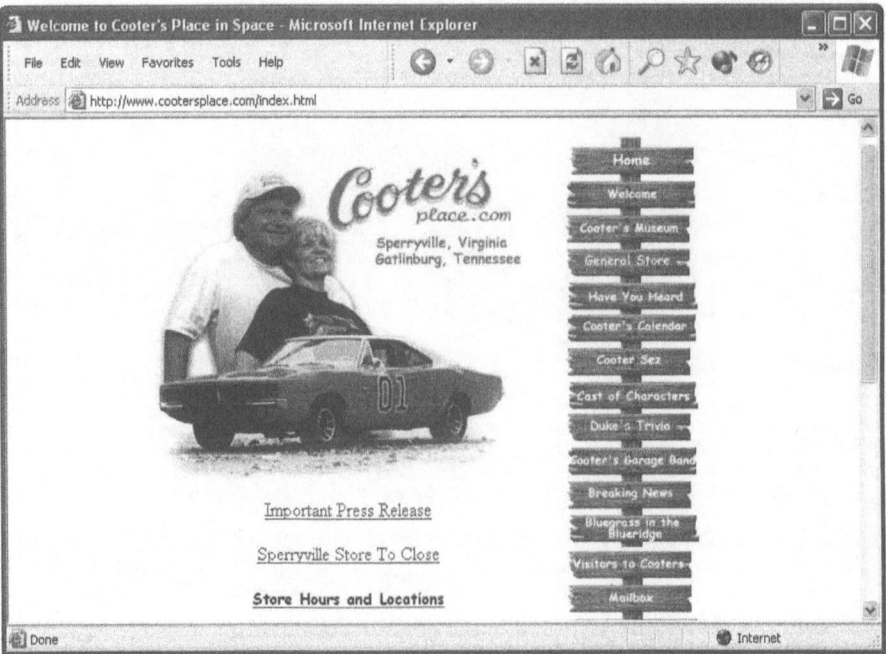

Figure 2-13. Ben Jones: actor, Congressman, and ongoing celebrity[13]

---

13. http://www.cootersplace.com/index.html

She Will Survive, in Bigger Form

In the 1970s, Gloria Gaynor strutted her stuff down the runway at Studio 54 and other discos, singing her big hit "I Will Survive." These days Gaynor, like the rest of us who gyrated to the phrase "burn baby burn" from "Disco Inferno" during the 1970s, are more concerned with burning excessive fat and surviving into our sunset years.

In an effort to add some luster to her once-shining career, Gaynor has become a full-figure model. She signed a contract with the Wilhelmina modeling agency and plans to appear in TV and magazine ads endorsing products that appeal to "women of substance."

Gaynor, who has her own Web site at http://www.gloriagaynor.com/ (see Figure 2-14), had the typical career breakdown prior to her resurrection. She lived the high life, chose the wrong friends, and got involved with drugs. In 1978, she fell from the stage of New York's Beacon Theater. When she awoke the next morning, she found that she had narrowly missed being paralyzed.

Figure 2-14. Gloria Gaynor: Disco queen turned full-figure model[14]

---

14. http://www.gloriagaynor.com/main.htm

She turned to religion and found work in European countries where the mirrored disco ball never stopped twinkling. Now she's hitting the nostalgia circuit in the United States, teaming up with K.C. & the Sunshine Band, and occasionally Sister Sledge and The Tramps, on the '70s Flashback tour.

"I'm looking to promote anything a woman my age might be interested in, except tobacco or alcohol," Gaynor says. "I have a message of hope."

What Do You Do After You've Changed the World?

Steve Wozniak and Steve Jobs are credited with helping launch the personal computer revolution in the late 1970s, when they created the Apple I and then the Apple II computers, forerunners of the Macintosh. While Jobs has been visible as CEO of Apple Computer and Pixar, the animation studio, Wozniak has kept a relatively low profile.

Woz, as he likes to be called, made Wired News in early 2003 when he moved out of his multimillion-dollar mansion in Los Gatos, California. He was forced to move out because the home was in a wireless "black hole," an area that did not receive wireless communications signals. He moved into his other mansion a couple of miles away.

Woz spent many years out of high-tech pursuits. After leaving Apple in the mid-1980s, he taught at a local grade school. Each summer, he taught computer classes in the garage of his mansion, which was turned into a computer lab. In an interview with the Tech Museum of Innovation (http://www.thetech.org/exhibits/online/interviews/woz.cfm), he said teaching was "a ball all the time" and explained that "I kind of wanted to teach somebody things that are easy to learn. A few kids could get inspired—might change their life. At least their homework will look better."

Woz is now founder and CEO of Windows of Zeus (http://www.woz.com/), an end-to-end wireless platform for communications.

Random Googling

The Internet contains countless Web sites and other resources related to celebrities who have had their day in the sun. The following list contains a few I found noteworthy—a random sampling of sites that turned up after searching for the terms "celebrity" and "washed up" on the search service Google (http://www.google.com/):

- **Celebrity Kidz (http://www.celebritykidz.com/):** There's something wrong with this site, and it's not just a spelling problem. Check it out, and see if you, too, aren't left with an uneasy feeling about the photos and the attention being given to child actors.

- **The Poseidon Adventure (http://www.theposeidonadventure.com/intro2.htm):** A tribute to one of the campiest movies of all time. The Links page includes a link to a tribute (http://www.theposeidonadventure.com/intro2.htm) to an actor named Fred Sadoff, who played a character named Aristotle Linarcos in the movie. One can only ask: Why?

- **The Hall of Washed-Up Celebrities (http://www.julianjowl.co.uk/):** Some of the people celebrated on this site, such as Madonna, are very much active and not quite washed up. Others are people who were only ever famous in the United Kingdom. The author's profiles seem preoccupied with a certain part of the human body and are surreal. In other words, it's a wacky site worth a brief visit.

- **Washed-Up Celebrity Dunking Booth (http://angelfire.lycos.com/doc/arcade/dunk.html):** An interactive game that requires the Shockwave plug-in for your browser. If you have Shockwave, you click your mouse and dunk a washed-up celebrity. When they sink into the water, you get to read brief biographies with pathetic details describing their current activities.

CHAPTER 3

The Babylon Enquirer

YOU CAN STILL ORDER groceries online from a few markets, despite the demise of the grocery service Webvan. It only stands to reason, then, that you should be able to look over a few of the so-called supermarket tabloids when you surf the Web. Sure enough, the Web is full of gossip, photos, rumors, and sensational stories about many of the figures you know from the entertainment industry—along with some you don't know but whose deeds are just as notorious.

Sometimes, those in the public eye get more than they bargain for when they venture into cyberspace. The Internet, it turns out, is a place where people can exercise little control over their public image. It's a place where fans indulge their obsessions and where critics sling slander and criticism without mercy. Actors and sports stars who carefully tend their public images with the help of agents and publicists discover that cyberspace is a space where anything goes, and not just in a "cyber" or "virtual" way. Bloggers can spread any wild rumors they find and are protected by the First Amendment. Web sites publish photos of naked celebrities as well as gory autopsy photos of famous people (see Chapter 9 for examples of the latter).

In this chapter, you'll find some of the more memorable misadventures of well-known sports, entertainment, and radio figures on the Internet. Like anyone else, celebrities lose their temper, make fools of themselves, break the law, and otherwise distinguish themselves online.

Titillating Television Tidbits

Television is all about personality. Even news programs are built as much around current events as the journalists who deliver them. Writers and producers occasionally develop their own followings and have message boards devoted to them—where else could that happen but on the Net? The small screen is home to some big egos, and those egos make their presence felt on the Web. The following are just a couple of examples.

West Wing *Creator Goes Ballistic on Chat Boards*

Aaron Sorkin is the creator of some well-respected television shows, including *Sports Night* and *The West Wing*. He's also known as being a workaholic and a prolific writer. Sorkin, who is shown in Figure 3-1 on a site that bears the name of a campaign slogan in the show—Bartlet4America (http://www.bartlet4america.org)—got in a feud with a former writer for *The West Wing*, Rick Cleveland. The two didn't have their dispute backstage or in a private room—their dispute took place in a message board on the Web site MightyBigTV.com (now known as Television Without Pity).

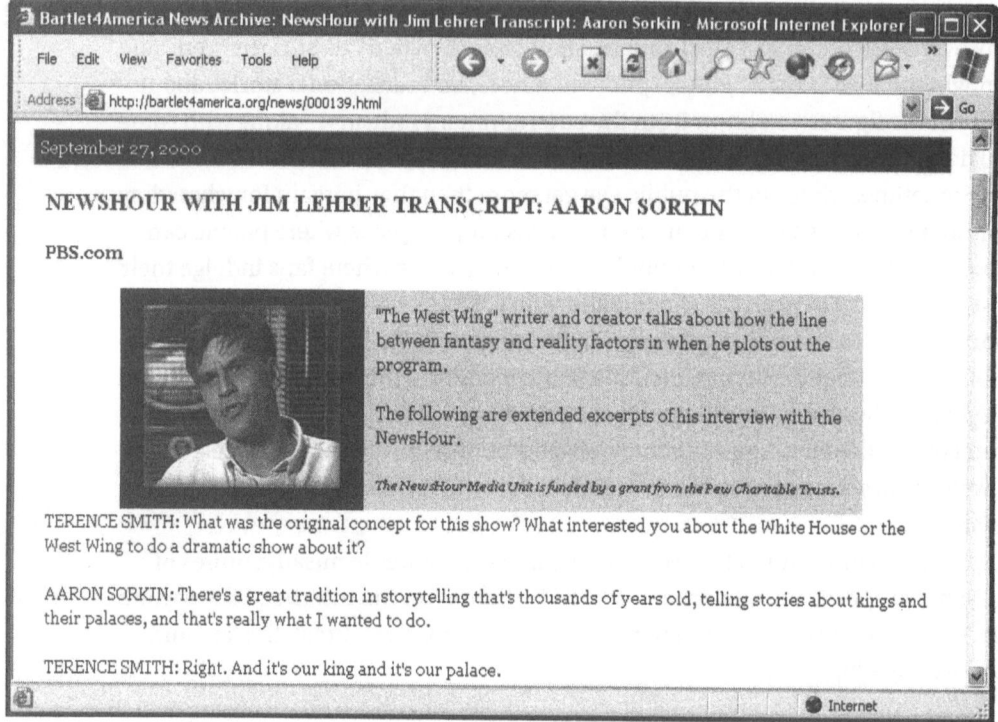

Figure 3-1. Aaron Sorkin and a cowriter exchanged barbs on a public message board.[1]

The odd thing is that Sorkin and Cleveland had won an Emmy award together. Earlier, writers for the show had complained that Sorkin was claiming undue credit for their work. Cleveland commented on the message board that Sorkin had snubbed him when they were called onstage to collect their Emmy award. Sorkin charged back that he had thrown out Cleveland's original script and that Cleveland was later fired.

---

1. http://www.bartlet4america.org/news/000139.html

After reporters learned of the dispute and began to publicize it, Sorkin posted an apology on the message board: "I deeply regret not having thanked you that night [the night of the Emmy Awards]." The dispute quickly died down. But as Slate columnist Mickey Kaus commented: "How weird is it that a big celebrity macher like Sorkin bothers to defend himself (and attack others) on what is basically a fan site?"

NOTE   *The West Wing* has an enthusiastic following on the Web. Web sites have been created that bear the domain names of individual characters: leomcgarry.net and joshlyman.com, for example. Aaron Sorkin also has a discussion group devoted to him on Yahoo! Groups (http://groups.yahoo.com/group/AaronSorkin).

American Idol *Contestant Bumped for Online Porn Photos*

For several months early in 2003, the second season of the reality TV show *American Idol* held the attention of much of the country. The final episode, which aired in May 2003, saw a heavyset singer named Ruben Studdard eke out a narrow victory over wiry singer Clay Aiken.

Early in the second season, a woman named Frenchie developed a huge fan following. Frenchie (whose real name is Franchelle Davis) was listed by an entertainment magazine as one of the top six contenders for the top prize. But Davis had some skeletons in her closet that the *American Idol* producers found offensive. As reported in one of the leading Internet gossip sites, the Smoking Gun (http://www.thesmokinggun.com, shown in Figure 3-2), Davis once posed topless on the X-rated Web site Daddy's Little Girls. When the news came out, Davis was not only thrown off the show, but all references to her were removed from the Fox Television Web site devoted to the program.

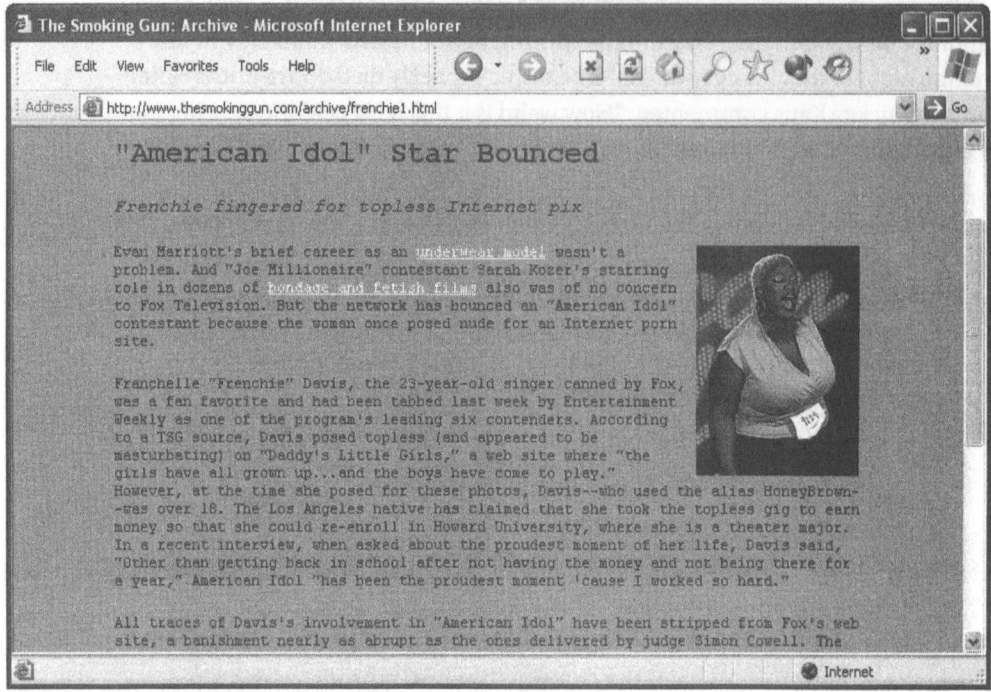

Figure 3-2. An X-rated job cost Davis her moment of fame on American Idol.[2]

The fan sites developed by followers of *American Idol* were flooded by protest over Davis's removal. And, as the Smoking Gun pointed out, at least one contestant on shows such as *Joe Millionaire* had starred in X-rated films. Davis herself explained that she was older than 18 at the time the photos were taken, and she took the job to help pay for her college education. But no matter: Frenchie was gone. Eventually, Studdard and Aiken were left as the last two finalists—which brings us to the next Internet-related controversy surrounding the program.

When the final voting was held and Studdard was chosen over runner-up Aiken, *American Idol* host Ryan Seacrest announced on live television that only 13,000 votes, and later only 1,335 votes, had separated the two. Fox subsequently claimed the true difference was actually 134,000 votes. Matt Drudge, the well-known Internet gossip columnist and owner of the Drudge Report (http://www.drudgereport.com/idol1.htm) said "serious questions" were being raised about the integrity of the vote. It was later revealed that many would-be voters received busy signals and never got through. A whopping 240,000 wrong-number votes went to a company called Cinergy Communications in Evansville, Indiana; only 72,000 were for Studdard—not enough for Aiken to win but more than enough to remind

2. http://www.thesmokinggun.com/archive/frenchie1.html

everyone of the voting problems in the presidential election just a few years before in 2000.

Scandalized Sports Stars

The Internet has given sports fans new ways to follow their favorite teams and athletes. You can follow games on your Web-enabled cell phone to get the latest scores, for instance. News that might be censored on TV or radio finds its way into the wild world of the Internet, along with some things that could only happen online.

Tennis Beauty Gets Virus Named After Her

Anyone who follows pro tennis knows about the Russian star Anna Kournikova, who is known as much for her smashing good looks as her smashing forehand. Kournikova gained some attention in online gossip columns when some fake nude photos identified as her were published in *Penthouse* magazine. But Kournikova is best known in cyberspace for having a virus named after her. A virus, as you probably know, is a piece of malicious computer code. Viruses make their way into the computer systems of individual users by being made to look like something harmless— even desirable. The more desirable the virus seems to be, the more likely it will be downloaded by users. Once downloaded, the virus starts performing whatever task its maker has programmed into it.

The Anna Kournikova virus was sent to unsuspecting users via e-mail in early 2001. It purported to be a photo of the Russian tennis star. Eager recipients who clicked the file instead activated a program that enabled itself to be spread by e-mail to any e-mail addresses contained in the user's Microsoft Outlook address book.

NOTE Technically, the Anna Kournikova virus is called a *worm* because it does not actually cause damage to the user's computer; it replicates itself in great quantities, however, and the resulting heavy traffic can slow down traffic on the Internet.

Kournikova is no wallflower when it comes to the World Wide Web. She has her own Web site (http://www.kournikova.com) on which she publishes an online diary, also called a *Weblog* or *blog* (see Figure 3-3). Look closely at Figure 3-3: At the top, you see an advertisement that pretends to be a utility used to scan for viruses, which seems more than a little ironic.

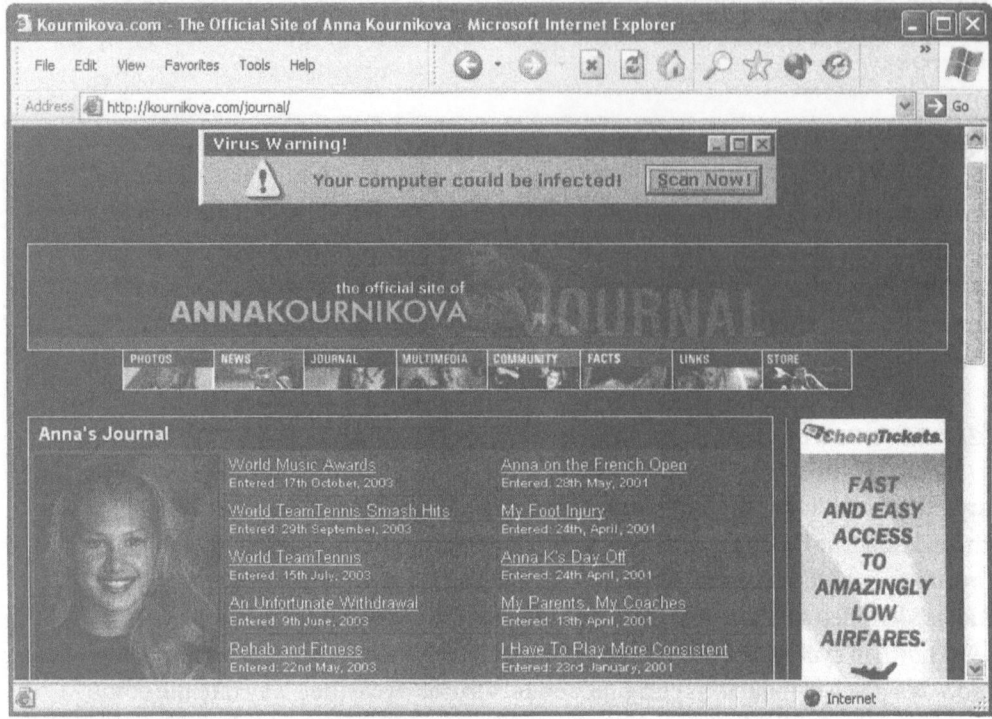

Figure 3-3. Anna Kournikova uses the Internet—and has been misused by it, too.[3]

On her blog, you can discover that Anna likes reading Chekhov and Tolstoy and find other fascinating statements such as, "When I'm not playing tennis, most of my time is taken up with doing photo shoots and interviews. The rest of the time I like to lay by the pool and relax a little bit, maybe go the beach and read a book."

Kobe Bryant's Accuser Revealed

In cases of rape and sexual assault, the news media keep the name of the accuser private. Correction: the *traditional* print, radio, and television media keep the name quiet. On the Internet, however, this and other such rules are commonly broken.

---

3. http://kournikova.com/journal/

Take the case of Kobe Bryant, the superstar player for the professional basketball team the Los Angeles Lakers. Bryant was charged with one count of felony sexual assault after a female employee of a Colorado resort charged that he sexually assaulted her on June 30, 2003. The judge in the case warned Bryant's defense attorney not to reveal the name of the 19-year-old alleged victim in open court; yet she did so several times during pretrial hearings. The name was not reported by the media. But one talk show host on radio station WRVA, Michael Graham, published a link to a Web page that identified the woman by name and contained several photos as well. Graham was called a "scumbag" by another talk show host, but he asserted that protecting the victim's identity was the equivalent of presuming the guilt of the accused.

AskOJ.com: Why?

In 1995, when former football star, TV commentator, and sometime movie actor O.J. Simpson was charged with murdering his wife Nicole Brown Simpson and Ronald Goldman, the World Wide Web was still relatively new. It was far from the mainstream source of news, gossip, and commentary that it is today. Many people had Internet connections only at their office, if at all.

Yet, those of us who were transfixed by the trial of Simpson turned almost every day to a site called Pathfinder, an early news and entertainment site run by Time Warner. The high number of visits the O.J. Central site received during the trial was an early clue that the Web could be a legitimate source of news. Millions of visitors clicked the diagrams of the murder scene and read all they could about the case.

As the trial wound down and a verdict was eagerly anticipated, Pathfinder decided to cover all the bases. It prepared two separate Web pages—one announcing that Simpson was found guilty, the other announcing he had been acquitted. It's a strategy frequently followed by news organizations when an important story needs to get out to the public right away. But someone at the Pathfinder Web site made a huge mistake: When, on October 3, 1995, the verdict was announced stating that Simpson was not guilty, the page shown in Figure 3-4 appeared online.

Figure 3-4. Guilty or not? Pathfinder initially published this decision.[4]

The error was quickly repaired, and the page with the correct verdict (or should I say, the correctly *reported* verdict) appeared on Pathfinder (see Figure 3-5).

The damage had been done, however. Someone in the Far East apparently stored the original Web page on a computer and, when the mistake was discovered, spread the incorrect page around the world. Rupert Murdoch used the page to ridicule Time Warner's journalistic credentials, claiming the mistake was as big as the infamous "Dewey Defeats Truman" headline in the presidential election of 1948.

O.J. Central garnered such a large percentage of Pathfinder's Web traffic that it kept the site alive even years after Simpson was set free. The two pages are preserved for posterity on Ghost Sites (http://disobey.com/ghostsites), which preserves many long-dead Web sites, including Pathfinder.

---

4. http://disobey.com/ghostsites/show_exhibit/pathfinder6/

Figure 3-5. That's better...or is it? The verdict correctly reported.[5]

 TIP   An online museum has been set up to commemorate Pathfinder and O.J. Central. To find out more about this groundbreaking Web site, go to http://www.geocities.com/SiliconValley/Station/4122/slide1.html.

The verdict was not the end of O. J.'s forays into cyberspace, however. For several years, he stayed out of the public eye, giving few interviews (except for a notable televised argument with Nicole Brown's sister Denise). Then, in 2000, it was announced that Simpson would make himself available on the Web through a Web site called AskOJ.com (see Figure 3-6). People with questions to ask him could do so—as long they were willing to pay $9.95 for becoming a member, which included the privilege of posing one question.

Entertainment Network, the developer of the site (as well as a previous site that used 55 Webcams to follow a dormitory full of coeds around), used the home page to offer a $100,000 reward for information that might lead to the arrest and conviction of the killer of Nicole Brown and Ronald Goldman. It said it was impartial

---

5.   http://disobey.com/ghostsitesshow_exhibit/pathfinder7/

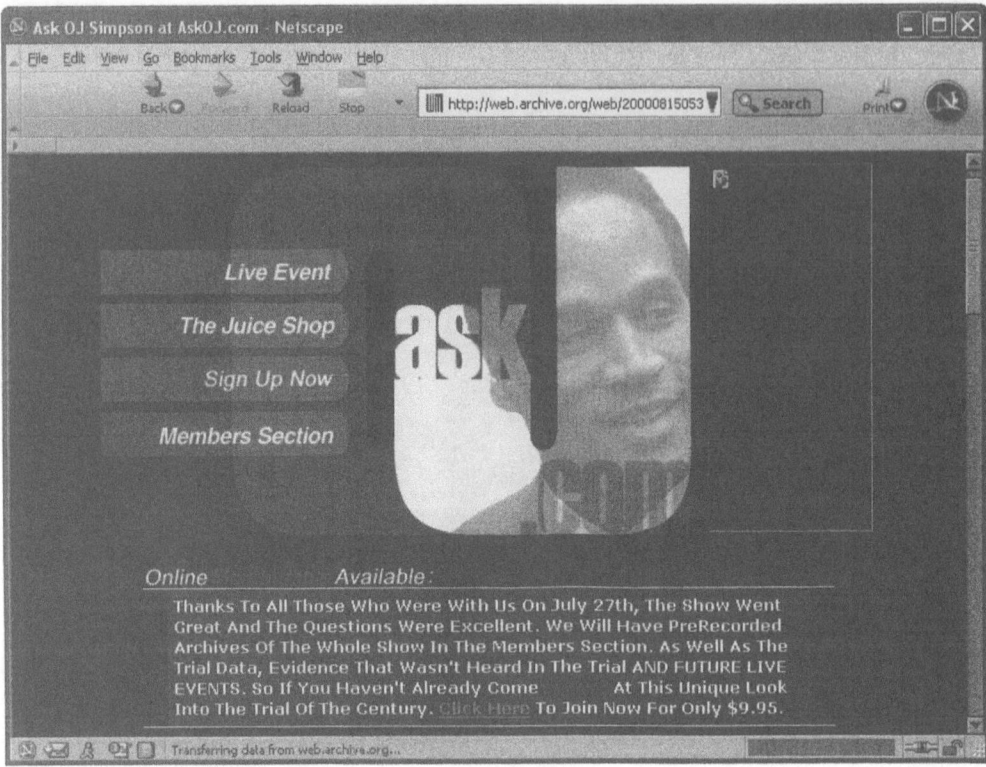

Figure 3-6. O.J. Simpson held an online chat with the paying public on this Web site.[6]

in the "Simpson matter," however. The Juice Shop part of the site also gave visitors the chance to buy footballs autographed by Simpson for $59.95 as well as jerseys and other football memorabilia. Reportedly, AskOJ.com was eventually going to include video of Simpson taking a lie detector test. I don't know if this actually went online, however. And as far as I know, that $100,000 reward has never been claimed.

NOTE A parody site, Ax OJ.Con (http://dangernauts.com/axoj/ home.html) was created to poke some very pointed fun at AskOJ.com. Although AskOJ.com was offline at this writing, Ax OJ.com was still alive and kicking dirt at Simpson.

6. http://web.archive.org/web/20000815053647/http://www.askoj.com/

Tarnishes on the Silver Screen

Hollywood has a long history of high jinks and strange behavior among its movie stars and the many others who crank out the films we all flock to each year. After all, a book called *Hollywood Babylon* was the inspiration for the book you're reading now. How does Hollywood come out on the Internet? Pretty much the same as other media: You get obsessed fans arguing over every detail of your work; stars who attract minute attention from people who love them; stars whose missteps are explored and blown up for all the world to see and then preserved forever in Web archives and on hard disks around the world.

Fans Feel the Force, Figure Out Future Star Wars Plots

The *Star Wars* series of movies and other works of science fiction have always been a staple of discussion on the Internet among obsessed computer programmers who need to know every detail about characters such as Luke Skywalker, Jar Jar Binks, and Jabba the Hut.

One of the earliest Web sites to indulge the *Star Wars* phenomenon, TheForce.net (http://www.theforce.net) was digging up secret details about *Star Wars* movies back in 1996 and is still going strong today. Longtime contributors to the site delight in working out the plots of *Star Wars* films that George Lucas has not yet completed. They either guess the twists and turns or find crew members who give out details about what costumes the characters are wearing or what they appear to be doing before the camera. The fans who contribute to TheForce.net put together these tidbits of information in an area called Virtual Sequels (see Figure 3-7).

They call them *spoilers*—bits of information about movies that leak out before the movies have been released. They're snapshots of the costumes the characters will wear or bits and pieces of dialogue they will supposedly say. If you take the Virtual Sequels site seriously, the information sometimes comes from screenwriters and crew members who work on the actual movies. There's no guarantee that the news will actually come to pass on the big screen because the filmmakers can change their minds at any moment. It's just another example of how the Internet gives fans the place to indulge their passion about a subject as fully as they wish, even to the extent of spoiling their own suspense about future works of art.

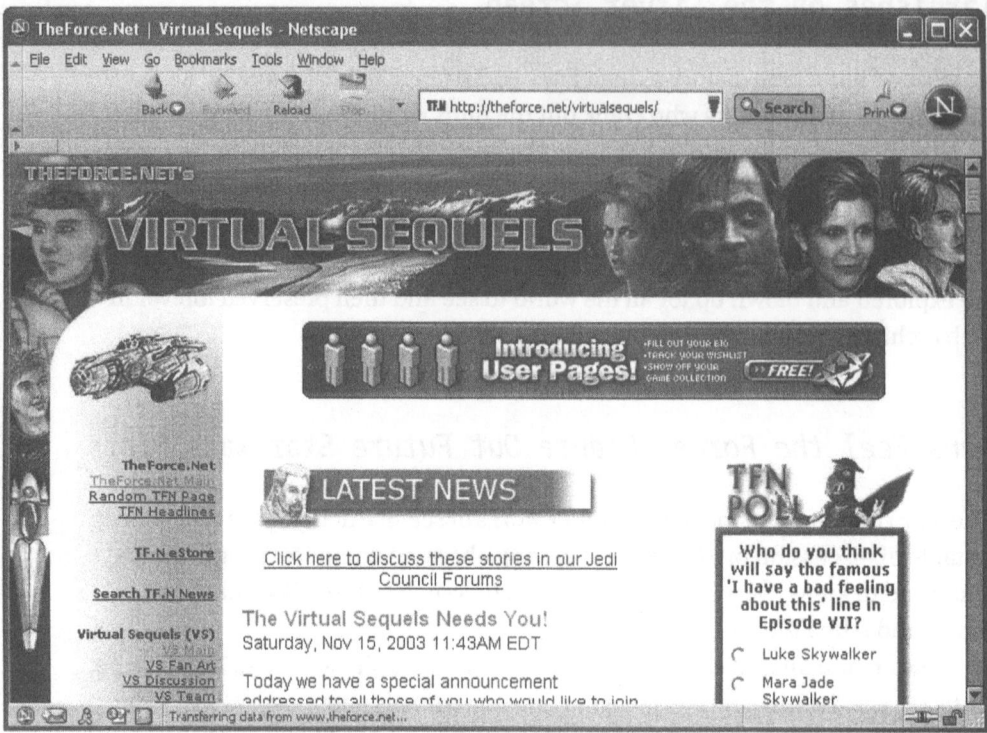

Figure 3-7. Star Wars enthusiasts use this site to work out plots of future movies before George Lucas finishes creating them.[7]

NOTE   The television show *Celebrity Justice* reported on one of the ways movie and TV stars are abused online. The story, which aired in October 2003, alleged that a man named Jeff Martin had bought domain names referring to black entertainers such as Victoria Rowell, Angela Bassett, and Vanessa Williams. All of the domain names direct visitors to an X-rated Web site featuring black women. Martin reportedly purchased the domain names for as little as $15, then forced the stars such as singer Natalie Cole to buy back the own domain names for much more. "If they thought their domain name was so important, they should have trademarked it and registered it themselves," Martin said on the televised report.

---

7.   http://www.theforce.net/virtualsequels/

Kids Rush to Defend Harry Potter Series

The series of books by J. K. Rowling about the young wizard Harry Potter is a publishing phenomenon and among the most popular books of all time. But the Harry Potter stories have also been among the most frequently banned books in recent years. Conservative Christians charge that the books trivialize the conflict between good and evil, saying that they glorify witchcraft.

Young people, of course, adore Harry Potter and his friends. They eagerly awaited the release of the first movie in the series, *Harry Potter and the Sorcerer's Stone.* That was around the time (in 1999) when Gary Feenstra, the superintendent of schools in Zeeland, Michigan, issued a memo prohibiting the Harry Potter books from being read in class in fifth through eight grades and banning the books from school library displays; a group of Zeeland school kids rushed to Harry's defense. They started the Muggles (Humans) for Harry Potter site, which was later renamed kidSPEAK! Where Kids Speak Up for Free Speech! (http://www.kidspeakonline.org, shown in Figure 3-8).

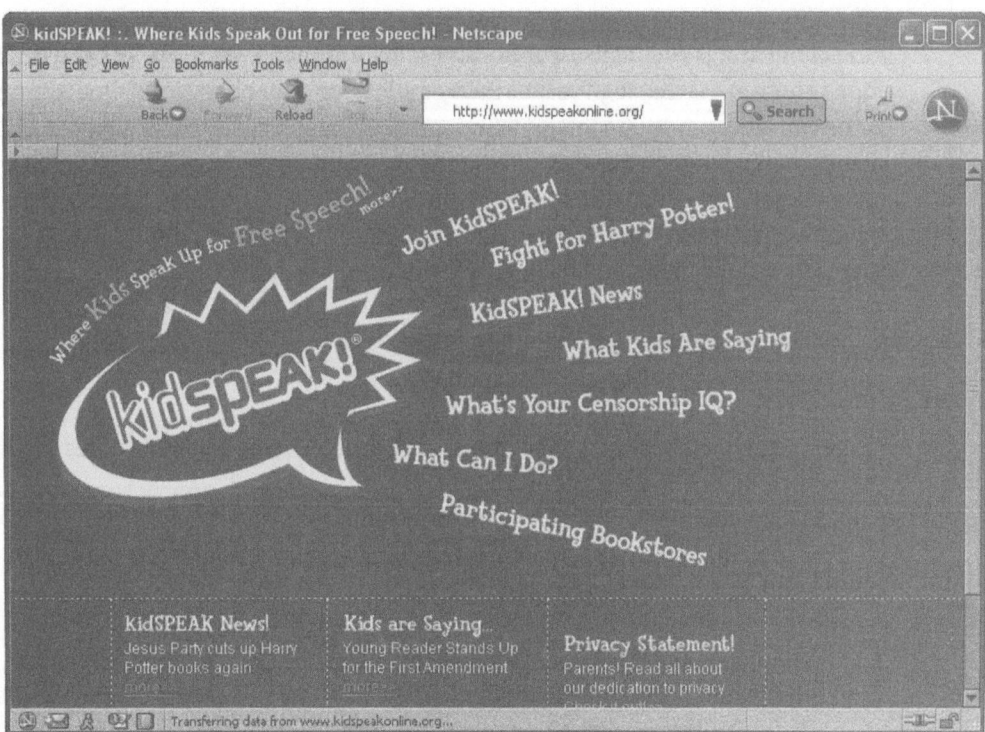

Figure 3-8. A group of students created this site to fight censorship of the Harry Potter books.[8]

---

8. http://www.kidspeakonline.org/

Before long, more than 18,000 students around the United States had joined the site. The school district eventually reversed nearly all of the superintendent's rulings. kidSPEAK! later worked to reverse censorship of the Harry Potter books in Cedarville, Arkansas. The site remains online with the broader mission of educating kids about censorship and keeping them informed about other free speech controversies, ranging from the Captain Underpants series of books to the Pledge of Allegiance.

 TIP   You can read the original text of Feenstra's memo at http://www.kidspeakonline.org/fighthp_zeeland.html. Criticism of the Harry Potter books still rages: You can purchase a video called *Harry Potter: Witchcraft Repackaged* for $24.95 from a Web site at http://www.theharrypottervideo.com/.

OmniLeonardo

One of the things you realize quickly about the Internet, even if you've been online for a short time, is that it gives fans many outlets for their obsessions. One example is the OmniLeonardo site (http://www.omnileonardo.com/) that is devoted to the activities of one actor: Leonardo DiCaprio. I picked this site at random; I could have chosen one of the dozens of Web sites devoted to DiCaprio or one of the countless other fan Web sites devoted to other movie stars. OmniLeonardo is a typical example of the kind of devotion you see all over the Web:

- The owner of the site is unnamed although uses the word "I" throughout the site.

- The owner liberally copies photos and articles from other Web sites to provide this site with content.

- The site is flooded with articles (in this case, more than 2,300) and photos of the actor (more than 6,000).

- The site includes a message board, which gives fans a place to exchange gossip about the actor's personal life (Is Leo going to get married? Does Leo have a Yorkshire terrier?) and possible future movie deals.

One wonders what DiCaprio himself feels about such attention, if he thinks about it at all. An article by the UCLA Online Institute for Cyberspace Law and

Policy (http://www.gseis.ucla.edu/iclp/manship1.htm) estimates that there are as many as 500 fan Web sites devoted to this particular actor. "As the Internet provides a greater outlet for the exploitation of celebrity images, the legal community must carefully examine the consequences of the application of the right of publicity to fan Web sites in particular," the article observes.

 NOTE   In 1999, lawyers for Fox Television sent letters to the owners of 50 fan Web sites, ordering them to stop the unauthorized publication of copyrighted material. One fan of *The Simpsons*, the popular cartoon show, was ordered to stop using sounds that Homer Simpson frequently emits, including the famous "Doh!" and "Woohoo!" exclamations. The owner started a new fan site, but this time taking care to follow Fox's strict usage guidelines.

Making Waves on the Airwaves

Radio personalities use their voices to portray a particular point of view that, in turn, promotes a particular image. Often, they come off as smart, holier-than-thou figures who are somehow qualified to criticize others for behavior of which they do not approve. When they do so, they open themselves to scrutiny about their own personal activities. With increasing frequency, the Internet is playing a role in the downfall of such personalities.

Radio Celebrity Arrested in Chat Room Sting

Jim Fox was one of Cincinnati's best-known radio personalities. Back in 2000, Fox (whose real name is Alan Pruett) hosted the morning country music program on radio station WUBE. Xenia, Ohio, police lieutenant Dan Donhue told the *Cincinnati Enquirer* that Fox chatted with an undercover police officer posing as a 14-year-old girl in a chat room named "Curious 'N Cute." He allegedly dedicated a song by Shania Twain ("Honey, I'm Home") to the "girl" on the air.

When Fox drove to Xenia to have sex with the fictitious girl, he encountered police, who arrested him. He was reportedly apprehended in his Ford Explorer with "a box of condoms, beer, and quilts to cover the vehicle's floor," the *Cincinnati Enquirer* reported. Fox pleaded no contest to a fourth-degree misdemeanor charge of soliciting a minor. He was ordered to pay a $250 fine, given a suspended sentence of 30 days in jail, and placed on probation for five years. The next day, he was fired by WUBE. But he was hired to serve as a talk show host on another local radio station, WLW. "Given a second chance, I can be a useful member of society again," he told the *Cincinnati Post.*

Rushbo's E-Mails Scanned for Drug Clues

The single most influential and successful radio personality of recent years, Rush Limbaugh, often railed against drug use. When Grateful Dead guitarist Jerry Garcia died in 1995, Limbaugh said the singer "destroyed his life on drugs."

But a few years later, Limbaugh made a surprising about-face on drug use. Suddenly, he began to advocate legalizing drugs and taxing drug users. Why the switch? Only in 2003 did a possible answer emerge. It first appeared in the publication that gave its name to this chapter, the well-known and much maligned *National Enquirer* (see Figure 3-9).

Figure 3-9. E-mail messages supposedly showing Rush Limbaugh trying to obtain illegal drugs were published in this notorious tabloid.[9]

---

9. http://www.nationalenquirer.com/stories/feature.cfm?instanceid=59485

The *Enquirer* published a series of e-mail messages from Limbaugh to various drug suppliers, trying to illegally obtain prescription painkillers such as OxyContin and other medications. "You know how this stuff works...the more you get used to, the more it takes," one of the e-mails allegedly sent by Limbaugh read. "But I will try and cut down to help out." But could one actually believe anything printed in this tabloid?

In this case, the allegations turned out to have some basis in fact. On October 10, 2003, Limbaugh announced during his radio program that he was addicted to painkillers and was checking into a rehab center. "I want to ask for your prayers because I look forward to resuming our excursion into broadcast excellence together again," he told his listeners.

Limbaugh used his own official Web site (http://www.rushlimbaugh.com/) to put a positive spin on his misfortunes. The site published links to columnists such as Matt Drudge who defended Limbaugh and invited fans to send e-mails to Limbaugh voicing support for him. The site even reproduced Limbaugh's on-air statement about prescription pain medications.

Sex and Porn and Rock 'n' Roll

When it comes to strange behavior, you can hardly get stranger than rock stars or their fans. Rock stars used to trash hotel rooms (and I presume they still do). Now they have the chance to act naughty on the Internet as well. Their fans have been known to do some crazy things, too, as you'll read in the sections that follow.

Justin Timberlake's French Toast Fetches Fortune

So, like, you know, Justin and all those cutie hunks from *NSYNC, they like, stopped by the Zoo—you know, the Zoo, Z100, WHTZ-FM, this, like, radio station in New York, back in 2000. And, like, they wanted some breakfast, you know. So, like, they gave the boys this French toast, right? And, like, Justin, he's so thin he's phat—he's such a hottie—he, like, only half-finished his French toast. And what do ya think happened? Those crazy dudes from the Zoo, they found Justin's half-eaten piece of French toast, and they, like, decided to put it up on eBay! You know, eBay (http://www.ebay.com,), that narly big auction site?

So, like, it started out as this big, huge joke, but, man, you know how many crazy folks bid on the toast? That toast was, like, *toast*, when they got done with it! This student at the University of Wisconsin, this *NSYNC, like, fanatic named Kathy Summers, she won it with a bid of—get this—$1,025! She paid $1,025 for this French toast that Justin got his cute little mouth into! And she was gonna freeze-dry it and keep it in her room. Well, wouldn't you? And the money went to charity! If I had known, I would have bid $1,026! No lie!!

The Who's Pete Townshend Pays Price for Visiting Porn Site

Soliciting sex in chat rooms is one thing. Menacing young people on X-rated Web sites is another. But simply visiting X-rated sites and viewing some naughty photos...you can hardly help doing that, whether you want to or not, considering the number of fake domain names, X-rated pop-up ads, and unwanted software that's around to attract people to the "blue" areas of the Web.

Pete Townshend, founder of the British rock group The Who, admits he visited a certain U.S. Web site and that he submitted his credit card information to the site to view photos. Unfortunately for him, the site was being monitored by Scotland Yard. He was one of 1,600 people charged with possessing indecent photos downloaded from the Internet. Police searched his London home and removed his computers.

Townshend was eventually cleared of the charge and released with a warning, but only after he had been fingerprinted and photographed and made to submit a DNA sample. His name was also placed on the British Sex Offenders Register for five years.

Townshend, who has explored sexually risqué themes in songs such as "Pictures of Lily" and "I'm a Boy," insisted to reporters that he was not a pedophile. He claimed he was doing research for a book he was writing, investigating the kind of abuse he believes he experienced as a child. In a statement he released, he criticized the "mentally ill people" who were guilty of child abuse.

NOTE A related story on the BBC Web site (http://news.bbc.co.uk/2/ hi/entertainment/548548.stm) describes the first complete broadcast of Townshend's work *Lifehouse*, which is said to have predicted the Internet. "I thought the Internet was inevitable," he told the BBC, adding that he was uneasy about the reach of the new medium, which he feared would reduce the power of the arts.

KISS Star Promotes His Own Cartoon Show Online

Remember KISS, the band that hit it big in the '70s and was known for wild makeup, pyrotechnics, and loud, loud music? KISS is still around (they toured with Aerosmith at the time this book was being written, in 2003). Gene Simmons, the leader of KISS, reports on his Web site that as many as 355,000 Web sites mention the rock band KISS and 188,000 mention him.

Simmons, who's now preoccupied with managing the KISS brand and associated merchandising empire, tells his story on a surprisingly interesting Web site (see Figure 3-10). The site also promotes a KISS cartoon that just began to air in fall 2003. The cartoon, called *My Dad the Rock Star*, follows the adventures of a boy who wants to live a quiet, normal life and has to deal with the antics of his "larger than life, Heavy Metal dad named Rock Zilla."

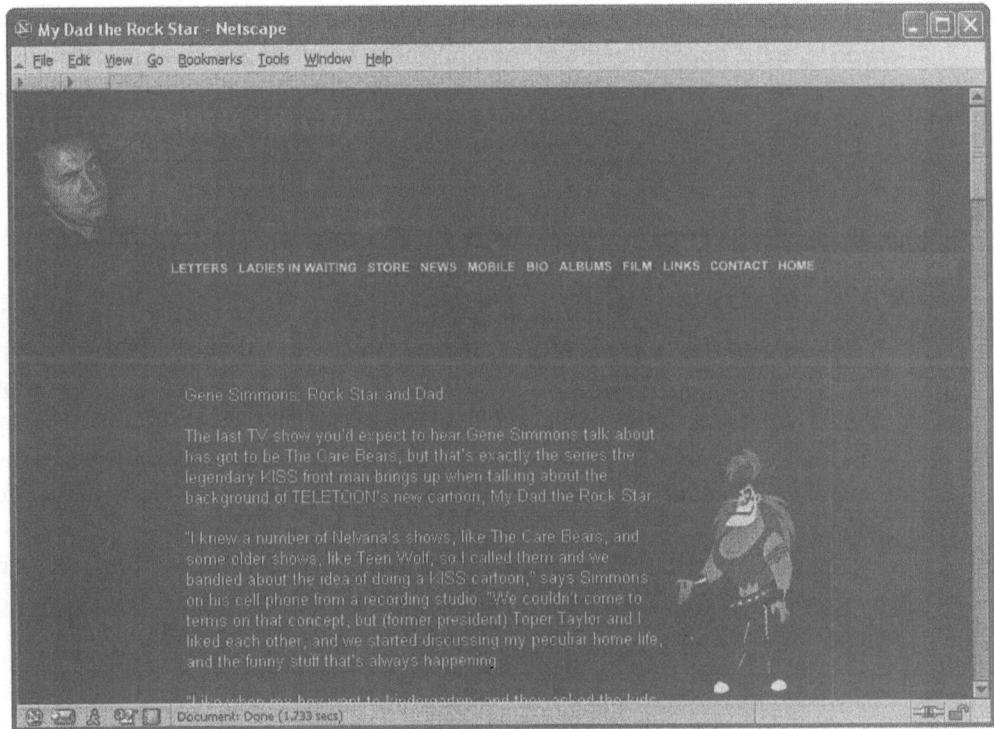

Figure 3-10. Heavy-metal rock star, tongue wagger, cartoon developer, and father: Gene Simmons brings it all together on his Web site.[10]

As Simmons describes it, "...The real truth is that my son Nick has a mom and dad who are especially weird...his mom's a Playmate, that's Shannon Tweed, and his dad is seven feet tall with Godzilla boots who sticks out his tongue for a living."

Simmons, you learn on the site, was born Chaim Witz in Haifa, Israel, the son of a Holocaust survivor. He and his mother immigrated to New York, where he

---

10. http://www.genesimmons.com/

attended the local yeshiva, high school, and community college before changing his name and beginning his career as a rock musician in 1972. Find out more at http://www.genesimmons.com/pages/rockstar.html.

Celebrity Garbage Picking

Some celebrities sell objects that have been associated with them in an effort to raise money for charity. Rosie O'Donnell is well known for her charity auctions on eBay, and, as I write this, Oprah Winfrey is auctioning furniture that's been on her TV show as well as other objects. Not all of the objects that turn up online are associated with the upper echelon of show business, however. Some semicelebrities actually need the money, and they take their own cast-off clothing and possessions to the online auction block.

Buy Joey Buttafuoco's Boots, Please

For a short time in 2000, a Web site called Scandalagency.com tried to make money off anyone who was involved in a scandal. Joey Buttafuoco, who gained a sort of notoriety in the "Long Island Lolita" case when his teenage lover Amy Fisher shot his wife, offered his boots on the site. They weren't just any boots, of course—they were size 10½, double-E rattlesnake boots. Buttafuoco claimed he was wearing the boots when he was arrested for allegedly soliciting a prostitute in Hollywood. The opening bid was $600.

The site also tried to pawn such strange items as the red, lycra, stretch top and pleated skirt that Divine Brown was wearing the night she was arrested with Hugh Grant on Hollywood's Sunset Strip. It attracted a bid of $5,000.

Auctioning Off Celebrity Bric-a-Brac

The practice of collecting garbage from the trash bins outside the homes of celebrities hit its peak in the '70s and '80s, until such treasures as Bob Dylan's unsent letter to Johnny Cash's and Cher's bank receipts began to be offered for sale by scavenger collectors. These days, celebrities shred their garbage or keep it out of reach of dumpster divers. But sites such as eBay frequently offer bric-a-brac associated with well-known people and events.

When I checked, Startifacts (http://www.startifacts.com/) was offering a variety of goodies on eBay, including pink slippers owned by Angelina Jolie (minimum bid $450); a small piece of a scarf worn by Jimi Hendrix; three words cut from a letter written by George Washington; an unused ticket to a 1994 concert by the rock group Nirvana; a section of fence from Elvis Presley's Memphis home, Graceland; and on and on. Many of the items come with a certificate of authenticity.

Random Googling

From rumor to humor, when it has to do with celebrities, you'll have no problem finding it on the Web. The following list contains a few I found noteworthy—a random sampling of sites that turned up after searching for the term "celebrity" on the search service Google (http://www.google.com/):

- **Popped Clogs (http://www.poppedclogs.co.uk/):** This site sends subscribers an e-mail obituary the moment anyone famous kicks the bucket. The shameless home page attempts to predict who will be the subject of the next announcement.

- **Celebrities Eating (http://www.celebrities-eating.com/):** Some sites depict celebrities in various states of undress. Others show off the mug shots of famous people who've been arrested. This one actually publishes unflattering photos of supermodels, singers, actors, and the latest actor-turned-governor-of-California in the process of chowing down.

- **Celebrity Dead Pool (http://www.stiffs.com/index.html):** A well-known and popular game in which participants guess various celebrities whose demise they think is imminent. The one with the most correct guesses wins prizes.

- **They Died in Florida (http://www.yuckles.com/fldead.htm):** Guess which famous people died in Florida, and click each image to find out more about them. Contestants include Lobster Boy, Al Capone, and Marilyn Manson. (In Chapter 20, you'll find out that Manson is still alive and still painting at the time of this writing, however.)

Part Two
The Afterlife

CHAPTER 4

Unsolved Mysteries
in Babylon

EVERYONE LOVES A MYSTERY. When the mystery either occurs or is explored online, it assumes new proportions. For one thing, there is almost no limit to the amount of time you can spend trying to unravel a mystery. The information you can research online is there all of the time, day or night, for years. For another, trying to solve a mystery on the Internet is more private than going to a library. You are in control of what you want to look for and how many bits information—or "clues"—you want to absorb at any one time. You can do it without your spouse looking over your shoulder, which means you can choose the venues where you want to hunt.

Some mysteries could occur only online, such as the search for a hacker or a cyberstalker. Others began in the real world, such as the search for the Zodiac Killer, but they have taken on a second life on the Internet. Others, such as the identity of the person who created a song about Russian President Vladimir Putin, are every bit as silly as they would be offline. This chapter explores a few of the frivolous as well as the deadly serious mysteries you can explore on the Net.

To Catch a Criminal

As everyone knows from stories in the news media (and from reading Chapter 7 of this book), the proliferation of computers with valuable storehouses of information has bought a new type of criminal to the surface: the hacker. Hackers try to break into networked computers by "cracking" passwords or by fooling their victims into giving out sensitive information. Sometimes the hunt for such criminals turns up surprising details. You can go online to explore facts surrounding "real-world" criminals and share opinions with other fascinated amateur criminologists.

The Chase of the Phantom Dialer

From March 1991 to December 1992, a hacker known as Phantomd or Phantom Dialer hijacked hundreds of computers connected to the Internet. He assumed control of the U.S. Defense Department's Ballistic Research Laboratory, the Massachusetts Institute of Technology, and the National Institutes of Health, among others. But the identity and motives of the amazingly successful attacker turned out to be a surprise.

He turned out to be a young man known publicly by the pseudonym Matt Singer. (He was given the false name at the request of his parents, who wanted to protect his identity.) Singer was not a criminal or computing genius. He was, in fact, ridiculed by his fellow hackers for his lack of competence as a programmer. But he had a level of dogged determination that outdistanced his peers. Singer would type random combinations of letters for hours, trying to find the right password "with bread-mold tenacity," in the words of one systems administrator.

He was eventually able to gain access to nearly every system he attacked. When he was able to invade the Bureau of Land Management's dam control system for Northern California, the FBI realized that someone like him could easily create a monumental disaster either by design or by mistake. But once inside, Singer didn't do anything. It was all about gaining access.

Singer was eventually captured and was subsequently diagnosed as being either learning disabled, mildly retarded, or schizophrenic. He was confined in his home because of bad eyesight, asthma, and chronic hepatitis, so he had plenty of time to pursue his obsession with breaking into important computer networks. Surprisingly enough, federal authorities declined to prosecute him. He remains free but presumably has his name on a watch list for hackers.

TIP   The case of the Phantom Dialer and its implications for security on the Internet are recounted in the book *At Large: The Strange Case of the World's Biggest Internet Invasion* by David H. Freedman and Charles C. Mann (Simon & Schuster, 1997). You can order it at http://www.amazon.com/exec/obidos/tg/detail/-/0684824647/002-3505406-0984031?v=glance.

Searching for the Zodiac Killer

The most notorious unsolved murders are probably those attributed to Jack the Ripper in London in the late 19th century. But another unidentified serial killer operated right here in the United States and not so long ago, either. Tom Voigt, a Web designer based in Portland, Oregon, is obsessed with finding the notorious Zodiac Killer. Voigt faces several obstacles, none of which deters him in the least: Many investigators believe the killer is dead, the murders attributed to the killer occurred in the 1960s and 1970s, and many others have investigated the case and written about it and failed to conclusively identify the murderer.

NOTE See Chapter 9 for more on Jack the Ripper and online resources related to his exploits.

Thanks to Voigt's Zodiackiller.com Web site (http://www.zodiackiller.com/) as well as books about the case, the number of individuals who are aware of the Zodiac Killer and interested in "decoding" his identity appears to be growing, not shrinking, with the passage of time. The site presents lots of information about the killer and the clues he left behind—including his many letters to the press taunting the police and boasting of his deeds, the code he devised and used in some letters and which was only partially cracked, and harrowing accounts from a few lucky survivors.

Voigt's Web site is a prime example of what makes a Web site popular and how the Internet can contribute to solving a mystery (though it's still an open question whether this one will ever be solved). First, there are plenty of juicy details (more than 550 Web pages worth) to keep visitors fascinated for hours: police reports, gory crime scene photos, and big reproductions of the chilling letters and cryptograms sent by the murderer to local newspapers (see Figure 4-1 for an example).

Second, the site is interactive. Not only can people with information about the murders contact Voigt, but there's a message board where those interested can exchange comments. On September 27, 2003, Voigt even held a picnic at the site of one of the murders for the people who have contributed to his site and to his investigation over the years. He quipped to a reporter that he wouldn't have been surprised if the killer himself stopped by to pick up some souvenirs.

Ten Most Wanted List Hits Cyberspace

It's no surprise that the FBI's famous Ten Most Wanted Fugitives list has its own Web site (http://www.fbi.gov/mostwant/topten/fugitives/fugitives.htm). The list has traditionally been posted in public places—most notably, postal facilities—to solicit leads from the public. Now, though, the FBI is taking a more active role in publicizing its most wanted fugitives. It has arranged with Terra Lycos to display virtual "wanted posters" on Web sites that are part of the Terra Lycos worldwide network.

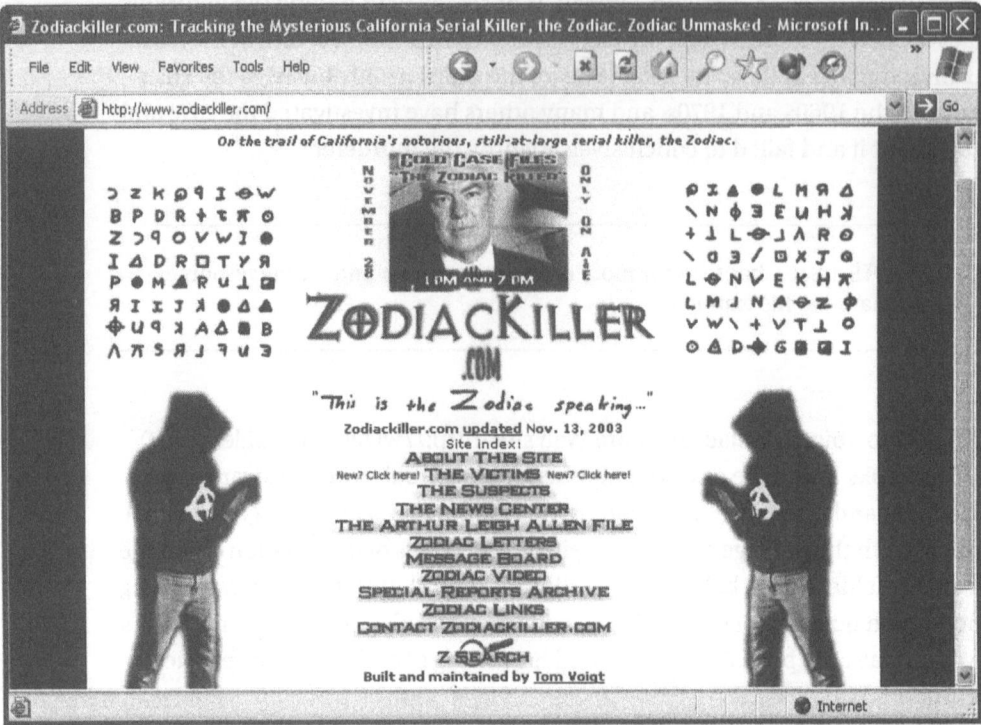

Figure 4-1. Keeping interest alive decades after the killings: the Zodiackiller.com Web site [1]

Terra Lycos reportedly will not charge the FBI for the ads, which seek information regarding one James "Whitey" Bulger, who is wanted in connection with 21 murders since 1995. As of October 2003, Bulger was still included on the list, along with Osama Bin Laden (see Figure 4-2).

The Ten Most Wanted list went on the Internet in 1995. In 1996, an anonymous 14-year-old Guatemalan citizen was surfing the Web when he recognized a neighbor's photo on the list. When Leslie Rogge was brought through the gates of the U.S. embassy in Guatemala, he was the first fugitive on the list to be captured with help from the Internet. Rogge had escaped from jail 11 years before and had been featured five times on the TV show *America's Most Wanted,* which is shown on cable television in Guatemala. The teenager who identified Rogge had just obtained a connection to the Internet.

---

1. http://www.zodiackiller.com/

Figure 4-2. The FBI's Ten Most Wanted list heads into cyberspace.[2]

What Happened to the Brink's Gold?

The Brink's security company has a reputation for being able to protect large sums of money as they are transported from place to place in armored cars. But that isn't always the case. Back in November 1983, a gang of armed, masked robbers burst into a warehouse near Heathrow Airport one November night, beat up and poured petrol over the security guards, and made off with three tons of gold: 6,800 bars loaded in 76 cardboard boxes, worth 26 million British pounds.

The thing that usually happens with such robberies is that the perpetrators are caught, and most, if not all, of the gold is returned. In this case, once again, things went differently. Although authorities believe as many as 15 members of a South London gang took part in the robbery, only a handful of bandits were ever caught. And 10 million pounds' worth of the fortune remains missing. At the time, it was the biggest theft in British criminal history.

---

2. http://www.fbi.gov/mostwant/topten/fugitives/fugitives.htm

Kenneth Noye, who is believed to have "laundered" the gold so it could be turned into cash, was jailed for 14 years for the crime. He lived off the fortune in luxury homes both in the United Kingdom and in the south of Spain. Noye was eventually sentenced to a jail term for helping to launder the proceeds.

Despite determined police work spanning two decades, it seems that most of the robbers have gotten away with it. Many believe that most of the gold will never be recovered. It is claimed in some quarters that anyone wearing gold jewelry bought in the United Kingdom after 1983 is probably wearing some gold taken in robbery.

What's the connection to the Internet? You can read about the theft and the killings and arrests that have followed it in archived articles on the Web sites of British media such as the *Guardian* (http://observer.guardian.co.uk/uk_news/story/0,6903,958307,00.html) and at http://www.thisisthewestcountry.co.uk/the_west_country/archive/2001/03/05/SOMERSET_NEWS_NEWS06ZM.html.

Who Was Deep Throat?

The identities of notorious criminals are always a source of fascination. But some other figures fascinate the public, too. One such person is known only by the name he gave himself, Deep Throat. He was a critical source for the series of stories that appeared in *The Washington Post* in 1972 and '73 and that played an important role in the downfall of President Richard Nixon. In the film *All the President's Men*, Deep Throat appears as a chain-smoking, shadowy figure who met reporter Bob Woodward in a parking garage and pointed him toward the source of the conspiracy.

In 1998, Professor Bill Gaines of the University of Illinois gave his journalism students a challenge: Determine the identity of Deep Throat. It took four years of research but, in 2002, Gaines's students reached their conclusion and released their conclusions on a Web site (http://deepthroatuncovered.com/).

The front page of the site, shown in Figure 4-3, wastes no time in identifying the person: Fred Fielding, who worked as an assistant to White House Counsel John Dean at the time of the Watergate break-in and the subsequent cover-up.

Fielding has denied being Deep Throat. Reporter Carl Bernstein has sharply criticized the investigation and said Gaines should be "spanked" (see http://www.cleveland.com/news/plaindealer/index.ssf?/base/news/1051263572302521.xml). But his criticism focused on the students' attempt to reveal reporters' confidential sources. He refused to comment on whether the students had made the right guess.

Figure 4-3. This Web site attempts to prove the identity of the man known as Deep Throat.[3]

Strange Events

Sometimes, mysteries you encounter on the Internet don't concern any one individual. Rather, they focus on odd events or places that could only occur online. The following are a few examples.

Did the Internet Suicide Take Place?

Rock stars of the past have done all kinds of things to gain attention. They have been known to bite the heads off chickens and roll around on broken glass. These days, a poor rock group has got to go an awfully long way to get in the news. And because it's the 21st century, the Internet has got to play a role somehow. Right?

---

3. http://deepthroatuncovered.com/

In September 2003, a group with the provocative name Hell on Earth announced a sure-fire way to gain attention for its act: One of its fans, who was suffering from a terminal illness, planned to commit suicide on stage during a concert that would be broadcast—you guessed it—on the Internet. The fan (who had to remain anonymous for legal reasons) reportedly wanted to raise awareness for physician-assisted suicide. The fan issued a press release that stated, "I thank the Lord that Hell on Earth is giving me this opportunity to end my suffering. I just want to say as my last will and testament that this is my God-given choice to end my life."

The group's lead singer, Billy Tourtelot (shown in Figure 4-4), told *Rolling Stone* magazine that he had received an e-mail message from the fan, who stated an interest in dying at one of the group's concerts (thus giving new meaning to the phrase "to die for"). The combined suicide/concert was planned for October 4 at the State Theatre in St. Petersburg, Florida. When the news got out, the city council of St. Petersburg hurriedly obtained an emergency court injunction that blocked Hell on Earth from holding the concert, suicide or not. If a suicide did take place, the band could face felony charges for assisting in a "self-murder," a crime that carries a 15-year penalty. The group found another venue for the concert, but that theater's owner cancelled it for fear others would copy the fan's act and commit suicide as well.

Hell on Earth next decided to publicize the location of the concert on its Web site (http://www.hellonearth.net/) and continue to broadcast it live online. However, the suicide would take place at a separate, undisclosed location. Then, the next strange thing happened: It was reported that a group of computer hackers in Korea staged a Denial of Service attack on Hell on Earth's Web site. In such an attack, a Web site is flooded with large numbers of simultaneous requests for connections, rendering it unable to process any other requests.

Subsequent reports speculated that the "attack" was simply the site being overloaded by too many people trying to connect at the same time. Whatever the reason, the Internet broadcast was canceled. Hell on Earth reportedly did hold the concert—but Tourtelot claimed he did not know whether the suicide ever took place. Other reports said the *concert* may or may not have taken place. The only thing that did take place was an effective publicity stunt because stories about the group and the suicide were carried around the world.

Figure 4-4. After the live suicide was canceled, the lead singer decided to run for St. Petersburg City Council.[4]

 TIP   If you visit the *other* Hell on Earth Web site (http://www.hellonearth.com/), which has nothing to do with the rock band of the same name, you can read about the tired Webmaster's adventures with a toothache. You can also learn how he coped with his site being inundated with e-mail and visits from curious fans wanting to find out about the "Internet suicide."

---

4.   http://www.hellonearth.net/

Who Caused the Diablo "Genocide"?

For those who are video game enthusiasts, the life and death struggles of virtual characters can seem all too real. The unpredictability of cyberevents is heightened when players connect on the Internet to play the game together. The game Diablo II attracts devoted players from around the world who assume different roles as they move through fictitious lands.

The most popular video games also tend to be the most realistic. But usually, the kinds of disasters that plague the "real" world, such as mass murder and genocide, don't occur in the cyber-environments. So, on December 31, 2000, when the virtual alter egos of the Diablo II players began dying off en masse, it must have been a shock. Even the best players went down without knowing why their characters had died.

By the time the smoke cleared on January 1, 2001, speculation raged as to the cause of the disaster. Was it a bug in the software? An attack by a hacker? Some speculated that it was virtual "genocide." The game's manufacturer was never specific about the cause of the incident. But it did issue a statement that the "problem" had been repaired. The players who had been wiped out got something they never would in real life—they were brought back to life, and precious objects such as amulets and axes were restored to them.

 NOTE Amazon.com is running a singular "mystery box" promotion that is proving strangely popular with consumers. Amazon's free Goodie Box is a box of unidentified "goodies" from unidentified "software publishers."

Who's Puttin' the Putin Song Online?

In summer 2002, Russian citizens were just crazy for their president, Vladimir Putin. They liked Putin so much that they started puttin' the name Putin on just about anything. Web site domain names bearing some form of his name sold for high prices. And a song called "A Man Like Putin" became popular on Russian radio stations. The problem was that people who wanted to buy "A Man Like Putin" couldn't find it anywhere in stores. It could only be downloaded as an MP3 file from file-sharing services such as Morpheus and Kazaa.

An article in Wired News speculated that "A Man Like Putin" was created by a Russian band formed especially to record the song "Singing Together." In the song, a woman tells her drunken boyfriend that she wishes he was more like Putin:

Someone like Putin, full of strength

Someone like Putin, who doesn't drink

Someone like Putin, who doesn't hurt me

Someone like Putin, who won't run away

It was never very clear who exactly created this song, however. And the fact that the song was never put up for sale at a traditional music store raised suspicions: Was the song actually an elaborate public relations campaign, an attempt to make Russia's president more popular? If so, that goal was achieved. Although Putin himself was reported to disapprove of his newfound "cult status," such objects as Putin watches, "nesting dolls" bearing Putin's face (shown in Figure 4-5), and even a Putin tomato were reported to be selling in Russia.

Figure 4-5. *Nesting dolls bearing his face were just one of the ways in which Russians honored their president, Vladimir Putin (shown with a doll of U.S. President Bill Clinton).*[5]

---

5. http://www.spacedaily.com/news/bmdo-00zi.html

Mysterious Deaths

The Internet enables people from all around the world to get caught up with tragedies that may have occurred decades in the past and thousands of miles away. It doesn't matter if you're halfway around the world; it's like you're there on the premises. It's like it's happening again in your living room. You can, in fact, view television coverage of the JFK assassination and the subsequent murder of Lee Harvey Oswald (I know this from experience).

What Happened to Paul Wellstone?

Sometimes, an event occurs that just *has* to be the result of a conspiracy. It must be a conspiracy, or else it would have never happened. On Friday, October 25, 2002, U.S. Senator Paul Wellstone, his wife, daughter, and three campaign workers were all killed in a plane crash north of Duluth, Minnesota. The tragedy occurred less than two weeks before the senatorial election was to take place in Minnesota. At the time, Wellstone was reported to be leading his Republican challenger, Norm Coleman.

Millions of Minnesotans were upset by the deaths; that's to be expected. But a Web site in England called the Truth Seeker (http://www.thetruthseeker.co.uk/article.asp?ID=271) raised questions about the crash, even drawing parallels with the attacks on the World Trade Center. It's hardly the only Web site to raise the question of some sort of conspiracy or foul play. A variety of alternative news outlets have published stories speculating that the proverbial "vast right-wing conspiracy" was at work. It's just one example of conspiracies blossoming all over cyberspace simply by word of mouth. Because Wellstone was an outspoken Democrat, and because the balance of power in the Senate was probably changed by his death, there had to be more to it than a simple accident.

For example, consider a story on Conspiracy Planet (http://www.conspiracy-planet.com/channel.cfm?channelid=78&contentid=652), which bills itself as the Alternative News & History Network, entitled "Is This What Killed Sen. Paul Wellstone's Plane?" (as though a plane is a living being that could be killed); the story suggests that a mysterious high-energy pulse emitted by the U.S. Air Force might have brought about the disaster. The same site reports on British soldiers who have been equipped with microchip implants in their brains. Any suspicious death is likely to be identified as a vast conspiracy by sites all over the Web; be sure to take any such comments with a huge grain of salt.

The Hunt for Elvis

In some ways, Elvis Presley is just as powerful, if not more, than he was in life. His life and legacy cross boundaries of age and geography and only grow stronger in cyberspace. Elvis lived a real rags to riches story; he transformed himself from a poor teenager into a rock icon. Now, his fans on the Internet transform him from a corpse to a living creature who is seen periodically around the world. Just check out the Elvis Hunter Web site (http://www.elvishunter.8k.com/, shown in Figure 4-6).

Figure 4-6. Anything and everything is possible on the Internet—just ask Elvis.[6]

Don't take the "Elvis is alive" rumors too seriously. That's what Elvis Hunter says, at least. The site's creator, Thom Britain, shows Elvis meeting with Bigfoot and suspicious crop circles in Tupelo, Mississippi (the King's birthplace), that show he is now working for an "evil alien empire." It also suggests offering him bacon or other pork products to calm him down, in case you happen to run into him.

---

6. http://www.elvishunter.8k.com/

TIP Read about the Elvis Is Alive Museum in Wright City, Missouri, on the Missouri Life Web site (http://www.missourilife.com/muse010.shtml).

Assassination Debates

We all have an Achilles heel, and this is mine. From the moment I first began surfing the Web, I was scouring Web sites for photos and rumors surrounding the death of President John F. Kennedy. JFK was killed when I was six years old, and his death affected me strongly. I couldn't get it out my mind, in fact. Now, I don't have to. Photos of his assassination, eyewitness accounts, and the Sixth Floor Museum Web site (http://www.sixthfloormuseum.com/) enable me to continually revisit and replay the awful events of just a few seconds in Dallas, Texas, on November 22, 1963. I can even look out the window of the so-called sniper's nest in the Texas School Book Depository building, where the museum is now located because a Web cam points out the window, broadcasting live images round the clock (see Figure 4-7).

Many assassination buffs consider JFK's death to be the greatest unsolved murder mystery ever. But just as many consider the case to be closed. The raging debates between conspiracy theorists (CTs) and "lone nut" proponents (LNers) keep the event alive many decades after the fact. Unfortunately, the useful research that some people are trying to do tends to get drowned out by backbiting, bickering, and baiting as CTs and LNers go at one another, apparently without end.

The other big political assassinations of the sixties—those of Senator Robert F. Kennedy and Martin Luther King, Jr.—also attract buffs who can't accept the conclusion that lone individuals did the killings or that they acted alone. Any event that causes a dramatic outpouring of grief and/or outrage is sure to live on online.

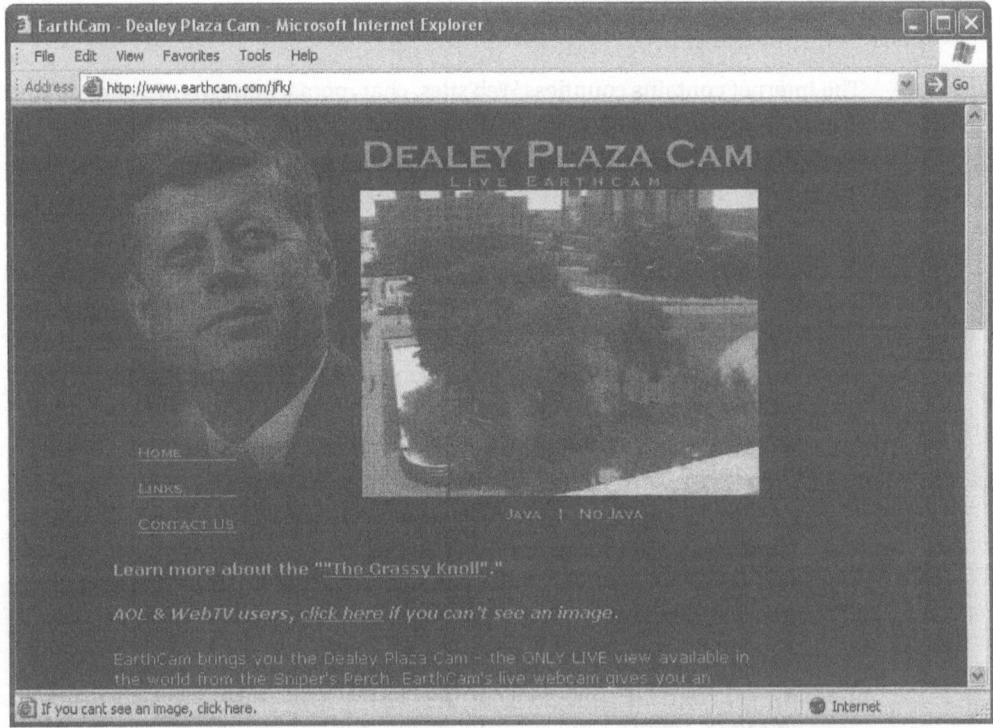

Figure 4-7. Site of an assassination: A live Web cam keeps watch on Dealey Plaza four decades after JFK was killed there.[7]

---

7. http://www.earthcam.com/jfk/

Random Googling

The Internet contains countless Web sites, chat rooms, newsgroups, and other resources related to mysterious deaths, murderers, and treasure hunts. The following list contains a few I found noteworthy—a random sampling of sites that turned up after searching for the term "mystery" on the search service Google (http://www.google.com/):

- **The Mystery Spot (http://www.mystery-spot.com/):** The Mystery Spot is a 150-foot-wide area in the redwood forests west of Santa Cruz, California. Visitors to the spot report strange gravitational effects as well as visual phenomena. The cause? "Flying saucer fans speculate that cones of metal were secretly brought here and buried in our earth as guidance systems for their spacecraft." Or perhaps it's carbon dioxide seeping from the earth or something called *radiesthesia*....Well, that explains it!

- **The Virtual Cyclorama of the Museum of UnNatural Mystery (http://unmuseum.mus.pa.us/cyclar.htm):** There are many cool features on this Web site, but the cyclorama stands out for me. You can use your mouse to pan around huge circular images of mysterious sites such as Stonehenge and the Temple of Zeus.

- **Mystery Date: One Gal's Guide to Good Stuff (http://members.tripod.com/~Mystery_Date/):** Lynn Peril admits that she is obsessed by "old sex and dating manuals, etiquette, and self-help books," and the like. This is an online *'zine* (an electronic magazine) devoted to feminine instructional manuals and products of the 1940s and '50s.

- **Cosmic Mystery Tour (http://archive.ncsa.uiuc.edu/Cyberia/Cosmos/CosmicMysteryTour.html):** The University of Illinois provides this look back—way back—at the origins of the universe as modern science sees it. Creationists will probably prefer the Great Dinosaur Mystery (http://www.christiananswers.net/dinosaurs/home.html).

CHAPTER 5

Death in Babylon

"O Death, where is thy sting? O Grave, where is thy victory…. Thanks be to the Great God Internet who giveth us victory over death with a DSL connection."

—*1 Cor. 15.55–56, liberally paraphrased by the author*[1]

YOU'VE ALWAYS BEEN TOLD there's an afterlife. But who knew you could find life after death on the Internet?

Millions of individuals look at the Internet as a place to change their lives. Countless others look at it as a place to die. I mean that literally: People who are considering suicide will find instructions on the various ways to end it all online. They'll also find people who want to counsel them to stay alive. A few creative souls have proposed that the Web can be a place to document the actual process of death and decomposition in order to demystify the subject.

In the hope of finding some sort of life after death, some people have sought to have themselves or their loved ones frozen. The idea is that they can be brought to life at a later date when medical discoveries have advanced to a level that permits them to be cured of whatever illnesses they had to endure previously. There's a town in Colorado that has adopted its own "frozen dead guy" and holds a festival in his honor each winter.

The Web has always been a place to bring people together, and funeral directors have discovered the Web's potential as a place for posting online memorial tributes to their clients as well as broadcasting memorial services live to relatives. A number of sites exist to preserve (whether planned or not) the last utterances of people before their deaths. Other sites memorialize loved ones who have passed, including stillborn babies who never even had a chance to live outside the womb.

Humor and death go together naturally. By looking death in the face and finding humor in it and in how we handle it, it loses much of its power. That's what a 50-year-old Texas woman and cancer patient has found. And a Web site that proposed a series of amusement parks for the dead and their families caused humor and controversy for its creator and many others.

---

1. The real 1 Cor. 15.55–56 reads like this: "O death, where is thy victory? O death, where is thy sting? The sting of death is sin, and the power of sin is the law."[56]

NOTE   The Internet abounds with sites that contain photos of dead people, accidents, and disasters. Some of them charge visitors to view such content, and others don't. This chapter doesn't point you to any of these sites. You won't have any trouble finding them on your own.

Documenting the Dead

By creating Web sites devoted to someone who has died, or even documenting our own deaths, we say goodbye in a public way. A number of individuals have explored, or at least proposed, just what it would be like to document their own deaths on the Internet. In part, they are fueled by an imaginative curiosity. At the same time, they seek to demystify death so people can deal with it in a realistic, rational way.

Death on the Internet, or, Timothy Leary Reaches an Ultimate Altered State

Timothy Leary was all about shattering the taboos that society imposes on most of its members. He is best known as a Harvard psychologist who advocated the use of LSD in the 1960s and urged a generation to "turn on, tune in, and drop out." When it came time for Leary to drop out permanently, in 1996, he decided to break another rule—the one that says death has to be a private affair and that one should passively submit to the process.

Rather than simply dying in a room surrounded by a few friends, Leary (shown in Figure 5-1) decided to design his own death and—not only that—to document it on the Internet. In the book *Design for Dying* (HarperCollins, 1997), which was written during the last months of his life and published after his death from prostate cancer, he suggested that people dispel their fear of death by letting technology help them take control of how, where, and when we die. He reportedly said, "How you die is the most important thing you ever do."

He decided to shun conventional hospital care in favor of dying at home. When he announced that he would broadcast his death live on his Web site and then be cryogenically frozen, he got lots of media attention. News about the event spread quickly throughout the Internet community.

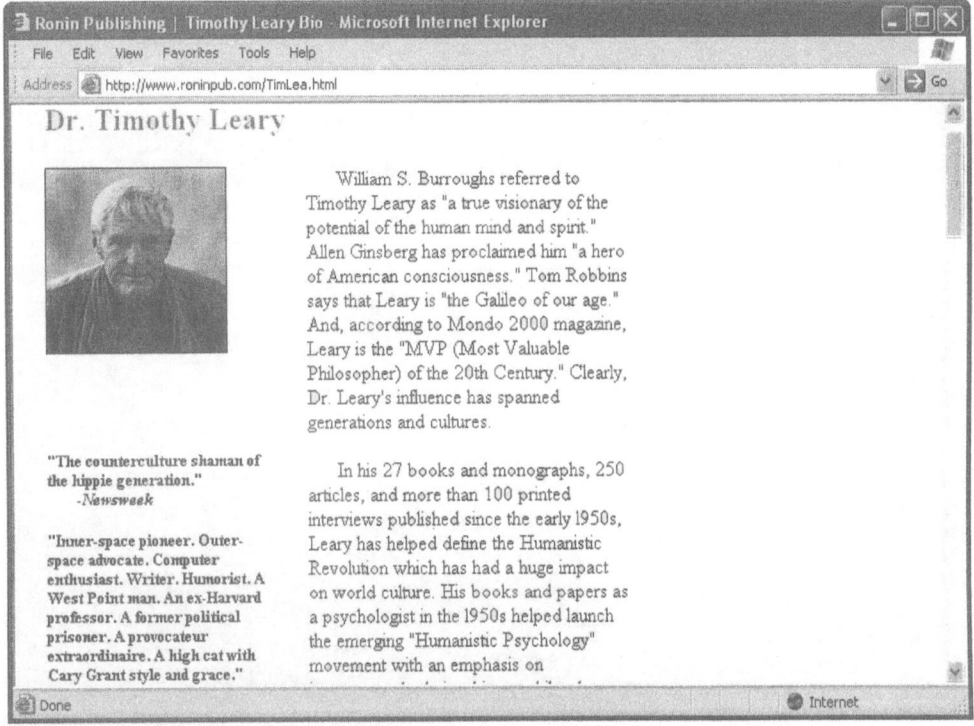

Figure 5-1. Leary's publisher maintains a biography online as well as a tribute to his "ultimate trip."[2]

A few days before his death, Leary learned that 7 grams of his remains would be shot into space on a Spanish satellite, alongside those of *Star Trek* producer Gene Roddenberry. He was reportedly "jumping up and down in his wheelchair" at the news.

Leary's plans to broadcast his "cybercide" on the Web never happened; he died quietly in his Beverly Hills home on May 31, 1996, surrounded by a few friends. On the day he died, the Web was flooded with announcements and online discussions about his passing. His Web site (http://www.leary.com/), shown in Figure 5-2, reports that his final hours were documented on videotape, but that footage was never publicly shown.

---

2.   http://www.roninpub.com/TimLea.html

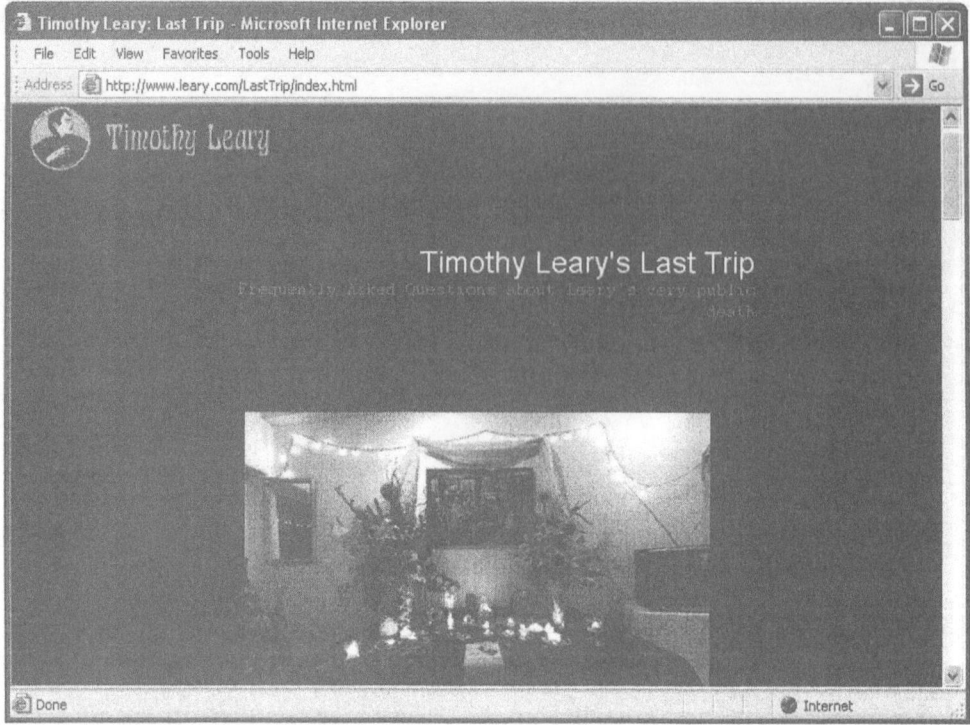

Figure 5-2. Leary's Web site documents the scene of his death, but the actual event did not appear online.[3]

A television documentary, *Timothy Leary's Last Trip*, was produced. Leary himself wrote a book entitled *Design for Dying* (HarperCollins, 1997). One chapter title, "Death Is the Ultimate Trip," perpetuates his image as a drug-crazed "out-there" philosopher. But the book actually focuses on the use of drugs as a way to better understand what happens after death. Leary was one of the first to use the Web to preserve his own legacy: his Web site was set up as a virtual tour of the home where he spent his last years, complete with a library where visitors could access some of his written works. His final words, as reported by his friends, were "Why not?"

Smile, You're on Necrocamera

Cameras are everywhere these days it seems. Spy cameras abound at the Sturgis motorcycle rally (http://www.sturgisrally.net/). EarthCam

---

3. http://www.leary.com/LastTrip/index.html

(http://www.earthcam.com/) includes links to Webcams at Ground Zero, in dorm rooms, in an SUV driving around South Florida, in a beehive, and at Loch Ness. Why not put a camera in a coffin?

That's the premise of *Necrocam*, a 50-minute film made in 2001 for VARA, the Dutch public broadcasting network (see Figure 5-3). In the film, Christine, a teenager suffering from cancer, tells her friends that upon her death she wants a digital camera with an Internet connection installed in her coffin. Images of her decaying remains will then be transmitted to a Web page for all to see, making her virtually immortal. The friends pledge to install a Webcam in the coffin of the first one to die, and they seal their pact with an oath to what they see as the highest power in cyberspace: "This we swear on Bill Gates's grave."

Figure 5-3. The Necrocam Web site vividly portrays the process of a body's decomposition.[4]

---

4. http://www.omroep.nl/vara/necrocam/

When one of the teenagers dies, the survivors must decide whether to fulfill their high-tech pledge and if so, how. One stipulation moves the story into the gothic realm of Edgar Allan Poe. The coffin is to contain a heating element that will speed or reduce the body's rate of decomposition. The temperature will then be controlled by online visitors who can adjust an interactive thermostat on the Web site.

 TIP   A version of *Necrocam* with English subtitles is available on the VARA Web site at http://vara.nl/necrocam/. You'll need RealOne Player (http://www.real.com/) to watch it on your computer.

The notion of a Webcam in a coffin almost came to pass during the production of the film. In 1998, Ine Poppe, an Amsterdam artist, was reading when Zoro, her tech-obsessed 15-year-old son, sat down next her and said, "Mom, when I die, I want a Webcam in my coffin, and I'm serious about it."

A week later Ine Poppe saw a newspaper ad soliciting screenplay ideas. With Zoro's approval she drafted a two-page proposal for "Necrocam," a word coined by her son. Jan Rutger Achterberg, an executive with the Dutch public broadcasting channel VARA, was on the jury and liked her idea enough to want to produce the film for VARA.

As part of her research process for the script, Poppe received a grant from the Amsterdam Art Foundation to study the feasibility of installing a Webcam in a coffin. After talking to a technical expert and an undertaker, she concluded it would be possible, as well as legal, in the Netherlands. She finished the script, and the film went into production in late 2000.

During that time Poppe learned that Zoro's father, her ex-husband, the Austrian artist Franz Feigl, was diagnosed with cancer and was given less than two years to live. Death imitates art. Ms. Poppe said, "Franz said to me, 'If you want to do a real Webcam, you can use my body.'" Poppe seriously considered the idea but resisted, she said, "because it would put such a strain on the family emotionally."

But the final decision was not made until Achterberg invited them to a private screening of the completed film, which ends with a vivid, horrendous shot of a decomposing face. Feigl continued to volunteer his services, even though there were tears all around him as the lights came up. Ultimately, his family declined his offer. Mr. Achterberg said, "Ine told me, 'With this film, I have shown what I want to show, so why should I do it in reality?'" (Feigl died in 2002.)

Tracking Ghosts on the Web

Some individuals with Webcams to spare have figured out another way to track the dead. Rather than filming a body in a coffin, they attempt to capture a spirit on the Web. June Houston has a very personal reason for ghost watching: She says it helps her get to sleep at night.

Since 1995, the artist has had Webcams installed at strategic places (under her bed, in the basement, in her closets). At this writing, she had 32 Webcams scattered around her New York City apartment. Thousands of visitors, many of whom visit the site on a regular basis, report on any signs of ghosts. Figure 5-4 shows a sample report.

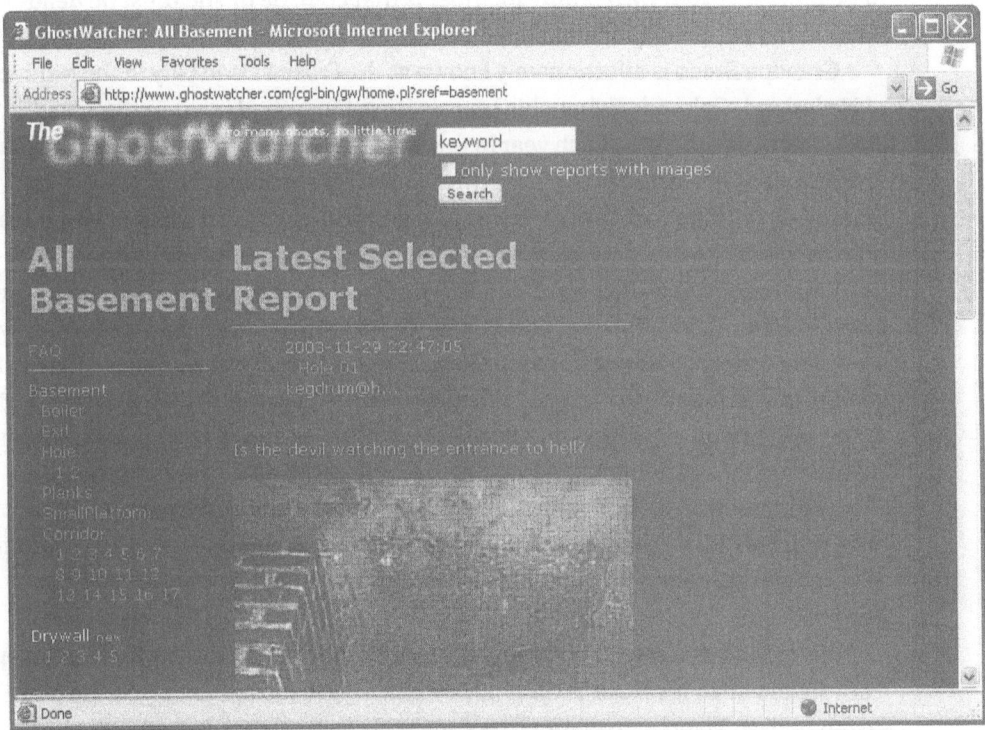

Figure 5-4. Which is scarier, seeing ghosts or having 32 Webcams in your apartment? [5]

---

5. http://www.ghostwatcher.com/cgi-bin/gw/home.pl?sref=basement

Preserving the Dead

Timothy Leary, who is mentioned earlier in this chapter, planned at one time to have his body (or at least his head) cryogenically frozen. He decided not to do this, according to his Web site, because he was afraid of waking up at some point in the future, surrounded by men holding clipboards and studying him intently. This feat hasn't stopped others from having their earthly remains put in deep freeze. The problem is, if the facility that is supposed to cryogenically preserve someone goes out of business, you're stuck with a frozen corpse. That's just what one Colorado town discovered and subsequently decided to celebrate online.

So you think *your* grandfather is cool? That may be true, but chances are he's not as cool as Grandpa Bredo Morstoel. Grandpa Bredo is –90 degrees Fahrenheit to be precise. If your own family member is that cool, he or she must be dead—as is the case with Grandpa Bredo.

Grandpa Bredo is affectionately known as the Frozen Dead Guy to the residents of Nederland, Colorado, where his body is stored in a shed in an undisclosed location outside of town. Each year in the dead of winter, the town holds an annual Frozen Dead Guy Days festival. Activities include a parade, a "coffin race" (see Figure 5-5), a "blue ball," and a "polar plunge," which is a swim in a nearly frozen body of water.

Who, exactly, is the Frozen Dead Guy and how did he come to live—or, rather, *reside* in Nederland? Morstoel was born in Norway in 1900; he died in his family's mountain retreat in Norway. His grandson, Trygve Bauge, was interested in cold in general and in cryogenics in particular. He first came to the United States in 1980 to "be safe from nuclear war" and was widely known as a wild-eyed nonconformist. He believed that bathing in ice water could prolong one's life and founded the Boulder Polar Bear Club. Trygve's own home page (http://www.powertech.no/~trygveb/TMP.html) proclaims his interest in "life extension" through ice bathing as well as "entrepreneurial liberty and livable survival of nuclear war and lesser dangers."

When Morstoel died, Trygve and his mother had the old man's body cryogenically frozen at an institute in California while Trygve looked for a place to store frozen bodies. They built a large structure in Nederland that resembled a castle and that was designed to withstand earthquake, bomb, fire, flood, and other disasters. They moved Grandpa Bredo and another frozen dead man, Al Campbell of Chicago, Illinois, from the California institute to a shed in back of the house.

Figure 5-5. A person in a makeshift coffin is carried through Nederland, Colorado, during the annual Frozen Dead Guy Days festival.[6]

 **NOTE** The story of Morstoel and his grandson Trygve is too detailed to be included here in its entirety. I highly recommend you read the full version at http://www.frozendeadguy.com/fdg/saga.htm.

Eventually, Trygve ran out of time on his visa, and, after a time when he declared himself to be a "fugitive from justice" and hid from the authorities, the U.S. Immigration and Naturalization Service deported him to Norway. His mother Aud, who was left behind, received an eviction notice because the home had no electricity or plumbing. She told her story to the local paper and mentioned matter-of-factly that she was afraid the two frozen bodies in the shed would melt. When the local reporter conveyed this bit of information to the town clerk, all hell broke loose. The mayor, police, and press raced to the property. They opened the

---

6. http://www.frozendeadguy.com/fdg/P1010056.JPG

shed and discovered the bodies stored on ice. The story became an international event, one that attracted reporters from all over the world.

At a town meeting, an emergency ordinance was passed that made it illegal to store frozen bodies on local properties. However, the ordinance did not cover the bodies already in the shed, and Grandpa Bredo was thus "grandfathered in." His daughter was deported, and Al Campbell was sent back to Chicago. But Grandpa Bredo remained. A local company was hired to maintain his temperature at –90 degrees Fahrenheit(see Figure 5-6). A new-and-improved shed was donated by a builder and a local radio station. A documentary film was made and shown at the Telluride Film Festival. Over time, the town began to embrace its frozen resident.

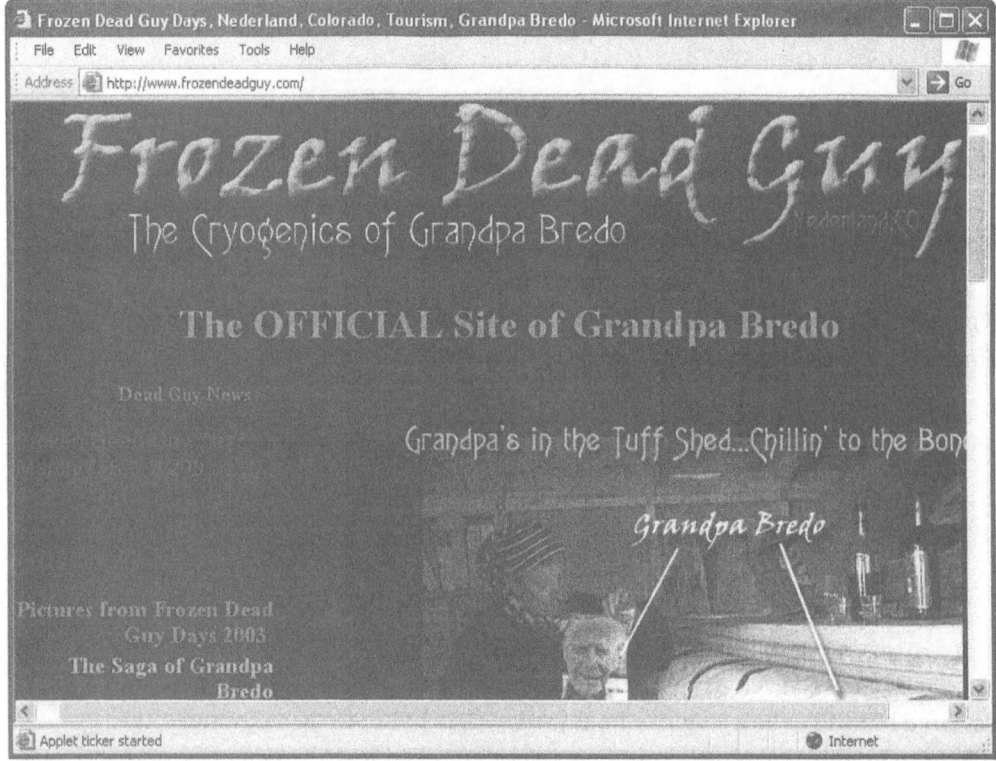

Figure 5-6. Grandpa Bredo gets a visit from his caretaker in his shed.[7]

---

7. http://www.frozendeadguy.com/

NOTE An Oregon company, Rogue Brewery, created a beer called Dead Guy Ale to celebrate the Mayan Day of the Dead (http://www.rogue.com/brews.html#deadguy). But it participates in the Frozen Dead Guy Days festival and advertises on the Frozen Dead Guy Web site.

Remembering the Dead

After the attacks on the World Trade Center on September 11, 2001, walls and light poles became covered with makeshift posters created by individuals looking for their loved ones. Those posters eventually became memorials to those who perished that day. The World Wide Web provides an obvious medium for anyone wanting to provide information about those who have died and who want to share the details with loved ones or anyone else who is interested. A growing number of funeral homes and other services offer Web page tributes as part of their memorial services. The following are some other ways in which the dead are memorialized online.

Online Undertakers Bring Wakes to the Web

At a time when fears of terrorism are making people think twice about flying, the Web is bringing people together. Teleconferencing is helping businesses save money on travel. The Internet is even bringing the dead and the living together: A few funeral homes have started to transmit memorial services over the Internet so that those who are unable to attend can participate from afar.

EulogyCast.com (http://www.eulogycast.com/) works with several funeral homes to Webcast memorial services as they occur. The broadcast is also recorded so it can be played back either on the Web or in DVD or VHS format. Figure 5-7 shows an example.

E-Mail from the Dead

It seemed like a great idea: a Web site where individuals could submit e-mail messages that would be stored online until their deaths, at which point they would be sent to family and friends. The idea came to Todd Michael Krim the way it comes to many people: During a transatlantic flight to London that was experiencing a lot of turbulence, he realized that he hadn't properly said goodbye to those he loved. He obtained $500,000 in seed money and started a FinalThoughts site at http://www.finalthoughts.com/. Like so many Web sites created during the boom years of the Internet, it sought to make revenue by attracting banner advertisers and by collecting commissions on purchases made by visitors who clicked other ads.

The site was set up so that each user chose a "guardian angel." The designated "angel" would notify FinalThoughts when the user had died. About 10,000 customers signed up for the "e-mail from the afterlife" service, which, like so many online services of the day, was free.

Figure 5-7. EulogyCast.com brings memorial services to family and friends with computer access.[8]

The problem was that, after all those individuals had prepared their messages for the afterlife, it turned out that FinalThoughts went to that great network in the sky before they ever did. Like so many startups, it went belly-up. Luckily, another Web site (InternalMemos.com) was able to function as FinalThoughts' "guardian angel" and published Krim's own farewell memo:

---

8.   http://www.eulogycast.com/cgi-bin/accounts/authorized/final_cablesl.cgi?ayfewy

January 14, 2003

Dear Friend,

I regret to inform you that the FinalThoughts.com website (www.finalthoughts.com) will be shutting down on January 31, 2003, for an indefinite period of time. The market downturn of the last two and a half years has made it increasingly difficult for our company to stay in business and cover the costs of operating the website. We apologize for any inconvenience this may cause you...

Finally, please note that any email messages or online forms that you have completed and stored on the FinalThoughts.com website are available for you to print out and save for future reference. After the site shuts down, however, this information will no longer be available....

NOTE   You can read this message from beyond the grave at http://www.internalmemos.com/memos/memodetails.php?memo_id=1252.

Last Words Online

Rebecca Kris was a typical 18-year-old college freshman at Central Michigan University. She was active in sports, she was thinking of being a political science major, and she loved to stay up late partying and talking to friends online. And she kept a *blog* (a Web log) on the LiveJournal Web site (see Figure 5-8).

She loved having a boyfriend, too. Her blog entry for January 23, 2002, reads "this magical concept of a boyfriend decreases the idea of 'spare time.'" The entry left in the morning of January 25 reads simply "hehehehehe." That night, she and her boyfriend were killed in a car accident. Her blog turned into a tribute site as friends left messages describing how she had touched their lives.

Another young person, Brian Faughnan, who disappeared during a hiking trip in 2002, kept a blog. After his disappearance, members of his family used a blog (http://faughnan.blogspot.com/) in order to provide status reports for friends and interested members of the public.

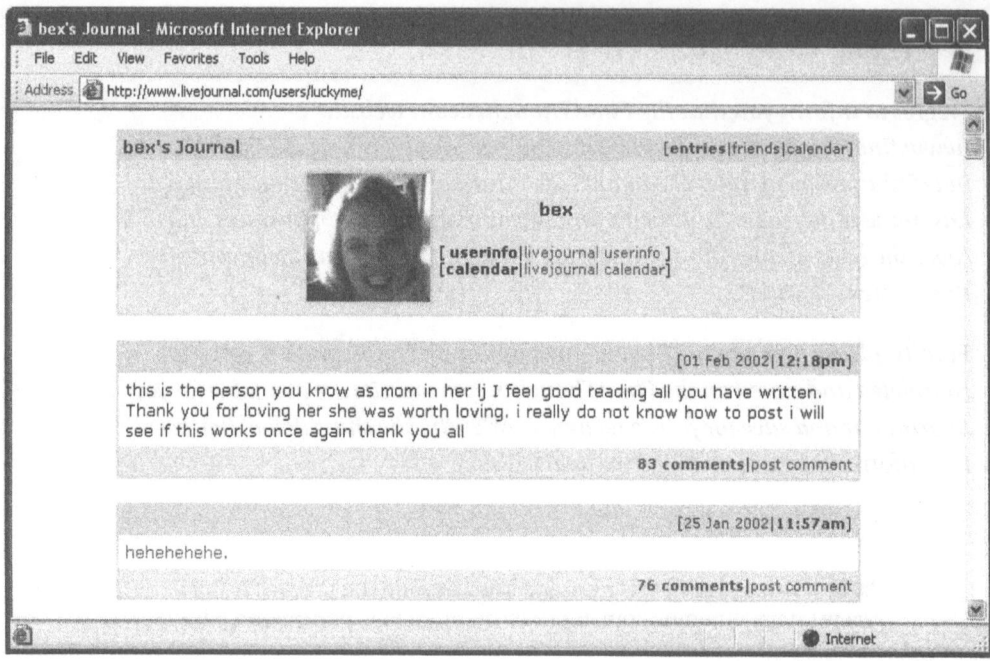

Figure 5-8. This college freshman left some of her last thoughts online in her blog.[9]

September 11 Morbid History

The events of September 11 are so overwhelming that it's difficult to find crazy, odd stories about it. But you can find a few online. Crazy News (http://www.crazynews.net/dp/1-12.htm) reports on a man who had an office on the 103rd floor of one of the World Trade Center towers. However, on the morning of the attacks, he was not at work but at his girlfriend's apartment with his cell phone on. When his wife called his phone, hysterically asking if he was all right, he said calmly that, of course, he was all right; he was at his office. This was reported to be the first divorce directly related to the terrorist attacks.

A Web page entitled the Strange Pop Culture Coincidences of 11 September 2001 (http://septterror.tripod.com/coincidence.html) reports on movie plots, proposed CD covers, video games, and other pop culture references that seemed to prefigure the terrorist attacks. The idea of the towers exploding or being attacked in some way seemed to be "in the air" before the terrible events themselves.

---

9. http://www.livejournal.com/users/luckyme/

Making Hay from Others' Pain, Online

Ah, those pesky domain name speculators. Nothing deters them. After thousands of people died on September 11, their thoughts immediately turned to domain names related to the attacks that they could sell. The following domain names were reported to be for sale:

- wtcnot.com: $500,000

- asiawtc.com: $50,000

- biowtc.com: $50,000

- eurowtc.com: $50,000

- taipeiwtc.com: $50,000

- taiwanwtc.com: $50,000

- attacksonworldtradecenter.com: $21,000

- theworldtradecenternewyork.com: $10,000

- wtcdeathcount.com: $5,000

- pentagona.com: $1,950

Castor Oil, Day in the Bathroom: An Online Wake

Writer Shoba Narayan didn't want to hold a wake for her Aunt Sheila. First, she and her family are Hindu, and it's not part of their religious tradition. Second, her relatives were scattered from New Zealand to India to the United States.

Last and hardly least, Narayan's memories of her aunt were hardly positive. As reported on her Web site, her fondest memory of her aunt was forcing her and her siblings to drink spoonfuls of castor oil.

However, she did have 36 cousins online participating in their own family newsgroup from five different continents. And her cousin Vikram was all for the idea. So one night she went online and typed her eulogy to her aunt. She wrote that her aunt may not have been able to recall any of the children's names and the kindest thing she said was, "Child, get out of my way." Yet, she meant well...you can read the rest of what Narayan found to say during her online musings on her Web site at http://www.shobanarayan.com/papers/nytarticles/nyt_main.htm.

Baby Photos Memorialize Parents' Beloved "Angels"

Everyone likes looking at baby photos. Lying in bed, surrounded by teddy bears and pillows, babies look so cute. Even with their eyes closed, they are appealing. But when you look closely at some of the photos of the children, you soon realize that those babies are never going to open their eyes.

Parents who lose children in childbirth or because of miscarriage, SIDS, or neonatal illness can create memorial Web pages to the infants. Many of those pages are linked on a Web site called Angel Babies Forever Loved (http://www.angels4ever.com/). This site brings together members of a club that no one really wants to join if they can help it. It provides a message board, a chat room, and a newsletter containing articles with titles such as "Holidays: They Come Whether We Like It or Not."

Not all of the memorial pages contain actual photos of dead infants. In those that do, the children sometimes look like they're alive—dressed in sleepers, surrounded by stuffed animals. Other images can be upsetting, especially if the babies died in the womb before delivery. Being able to have a tangible reminder of the lost children apparently helps parents with the grieving process.

Embracing Death

Death is something we learn to avoid thinking about. We don't deal with it until we have to do so. Even if they are seriously ill, people begin to think about their own death and funeral plans with reluctance. Even though you can find information online about how to make a bomb and how to commit suicide, it's sometimes difficult to find information about what happens when we die. The auction giant eBay (http://www.ebay.com/) has banned sales of videos that depict death with titles such as *Faces of Death*.

Cancer Patient Deals in Death—Literally

In 1999, Sterling Silver Rose (also known as Toni) was told that she had an aggressive form of breast cancer and that she might want to make funeral arrangements. When she began to investigate options and asked questions about embalming and other mortuary practices, she found funeral directors reluctant to answer her questions. She is an ardent admirer of the author Jessica Mitford, who is best known for her exposé of the funeral trade, *The American Way of Death*. Rose decided to follow Mitford's example by talking openly about funeral practices on the Web:

I found that funeral directors in my area did not like me asking questions about embalming. In fact, I was told that I "shouldn't be asking about it" and that "you will be dead, so you don't really need to know." Why would I give consent to be embalmed without knowing what it entails? Would you consent to having a vital part of your body removed while you were alive without knowing the risks and benefits? I think not. So why should things be any different when we are dead? Anyway, I got mad and decided that if it was this big secret that it needed to come out of its secrecy.

Rather than avoid the subject, the 50-year-old Texas resident decided to deal with her own mortality by delving into all aspects of undertaking, autopsy, and burial. Not only that, but she started the e-commerce Web site Death Becomes You (http://bluelips.net/, shown in Figure 5-9) that deals in death.

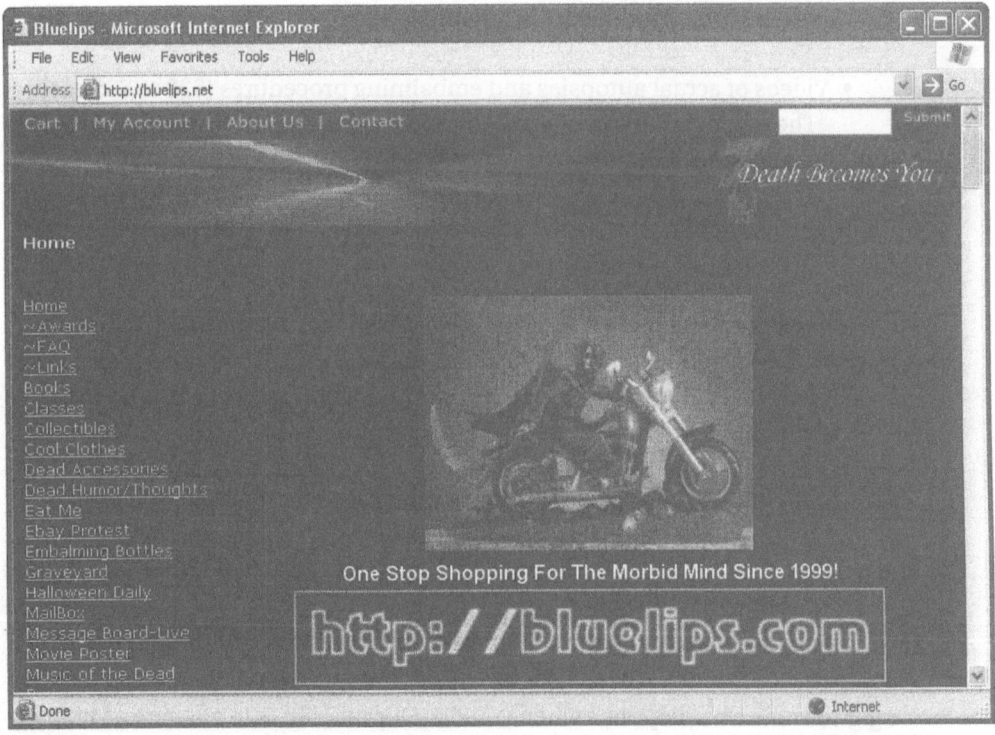

Figure 5-9. This Web site, started by a seriously ill cancer patient, sells death-related items with a sense of humor.[10]

---

10. http://bluelips.net/

Customers who are curious about funeral homes and autopsies can purchase books and videos on the subject through the Death Becomes You site. Most of the sales items include humorous remarks about how each item might be used in the home. Just a few examples of Rose's extensive selection of morbid merchandise include the following:

- Embalming bottles obtained from a funeral home ($20 for two): "I even have one of these sitting on the bar in my home."

- A paperweight in the shape of a casket ($27): Cute!

- Orifice plug ($10): Please, don't ask me to explain.

- Toe tags of the sort used by funeral homes and coroners ($12.50 for a bag of 25): "Put one of these on someone who has passed out from too much partying").

- Videos of actual autopsies and embalming procedures ($20 to $35 each): "The editing in this video is poor; however, the graphic embalming that takes place will leave you cringing."

In the FAQ for her site, Rose explains in detail just how advanced her breast cancer is. She added the following:

I am a Stage IV breast cancer. My prognosis with advanced cancer was 3–5 years. Year 5 is in 2004. My medical records scare people; they can't figure out why I am still alive. I think much of it has to do with my strong constitution as a person: You knock me down, I get back up. You cut off my boobs and within a few days I'm riding my motorcycle again (and at the time I did that I still had a drain sticking out of me). I feel the cancer in me, but every day when I get up I have a little chat with my body and I tell it, "I'm not ready for you today, please leave me alone." It always seems to work for me and I get things done.

She also explains why she sells hard-to-watch videos of embalming and autopsies that are otherwise difficult to find: "People want to know and have a right to know what happens when you die. Our mission is to educate as many people as possible about the process of embalming and funeral customs."

In an ironic twist, representatives from the funeral industry have actually approached her about being a funeral director. "I think what makes me unique is that I am laughing at death really. I have no interest in doing the embalming, but I do think I'd be a great grief counselor. Who knows, maybe death will begin a new career for me?"

 TIP   Rose and her Death Becomes You site are included in a documentary by Patrick Shen called *Flight from Death: The Quest for Immortality.* You can find out more about the film and view a short trailer about it at http://www.flightfromdeath.com/.

Learning How to Die in Babylon

A famous poem by Dorothy Parker goes like this:

Razors pain you;
Rivers are damp;
Acids stain you;
And Drugs cause cramp.
Guns aren't lawful;
Nooses give;
Gas smells awful;
You might as well live.

It's true: Many methods of doing away with oneself are, as my daughters would say, "yucky." That's one reason why many Web sites provide instructions on various methods of suicide. The obvious issue, the "how-to," is only one aspect to be considered. Others include leaving notes and tying up loose financial ends so as not to burden relatives. One of the best-known online documents, "A Practical Guide to Suicide," is published by the pro-suicide Church of Euthanasia and is at http://www.satanservice.org/coe/suicide/guide/. The Web site associated with the ASH newsgroup (http://www.ashbusstop.org/pg_practical.html) presents a more balanced view. Just as many Web sites present alternatives to suicide or ways to cope with suicidal thoughts, such as Suicidal.com (http://www.suicidal.com/) and the Suicide Crisis Center (http://suicidecrisiscenter.com/).

Mickey Mouse and the Lighter Side of Suicide

For 16 days in 1930, cartoonist Floyd Gottfredson created a series of cartoons depicting Mickey Mouse trying various ways to kill himself. Gottfredson worked with Walt Disney and created many Mickey Mouse comics in the 1930s and '40s.

It seems Mickey was in despair over losing Minnie to another, bigger mouse. In the end, of course, Mickey concluded that he "might as well live" and went on to a thriving career in TV, film, radio, video, and so on.

"Please Help Me Kill Myself"

The traditional greeting for newcomers to the alt.suicide.holiday newsgroup, commonly known as ASH, goes like this: "Welcome to ASH, sorry you're here." This newsgroup (plus another, alt.suicide.methods) is guaranteed to depress anyone no matter how good they're feeling. ASH has gained quite a bit of publicity in recent years—so much so that participants are wary of talking to the media.

ASH was the subject of a documentary by Dutch filmmaker Walter Stokman. The film featured interviews with individuals who posted messages on ASH—including one woman who reportedly married another person she met online.

ASH was critically observed in a series of articles in Wired News dealing with young people who committed suicide after posting messages to the newsgroup.

 NOTE If you are familiar with newsgroup software that's built into e-mail programs such as Outlook Express and Netscape Messenger, you can access alt.suicide.holiday directly. Otherwise, you can read newsgroup postings through a Web-based interface at http://ashbusstop.org/cgi-bin/webboard/ikonboard.cgi.

One story (http://www.wired.com/news/culture/0,1284,57480,00.html) focused on a 24-year-old computer programmer named Michael Benjamins, who reported that he was looking for a "fast, reliable way to kill myself." He further reported that he had spent time in a mental institution and might not be able to obtain a gun. Subsequent postings focused on his years of depression and mental turmoil. In one posting he then reported that he had purchased a shotgun at a Wal-Mart and was eager to die.

Michael Benjamins did kill himself by placing his shotgun in his mouth and pulling the trigger on October 17, 2000. The article questioned why no one in the newsgroup had sought to help him, to contact police, or to dissuade him from suicide. However, Benjamins' father was reportedly not critical of ASH, but even thought it was "real positive in that you can find someone who understands where you come from."

ASH's philosophy is to provide a place for participants to speak freely about their feelings and find support. They aren't interested in intervention. They accept where participants are coming from, even if they are on the verge of ending it all. You can connect to the group, read posts with titles such as "Catching the bus," "Jumping," and "Request info. on hanging," and develop your own opinion.

Laughing at Death

The Internet has a reputation for being outrageous and over the top. Media outlets and writers such as yours truly are only too happy to perpetuate that image. It's not surprising, then, that a seemingly crazy idea such as a real estate development company's quest to build a Disney-style memorial theme park and mall for the dead should fool some reputable media outlets.

That's just what happened with the Final Curtain: a Web site created by well-known hoaxster and performance artist Joey Skaggs (see Figure 5-10). *The Los Angeles Times* and other publications were only too happy to purvey a story that portrays another crazy, off-the-wall Web site.

Like Sterling Silver Rose (see "Cancer Patient Deals in Death—Literally" earlier in this chapter), Skaggs is outraged by how the funeral industry makes people purchase things they don't need in order to memorialize the dead. In 1998, he assembled a group of writers, artists, and designers to create the Final Curtain Web site. The fictitious development company that was purported to run the site planned to start a chain of theme parks for the dead. The parks would include adventure rides such as the "roller coaster of life and death," playgrounds where children would play atop gravesites, and even a time-sharing program for the dead. A giant Etch A Sketch would be filled with ashes of the dead mixed with iron filings.

Then there was the proposal for a giant tombstone that served as an ant farm, made from soil and cremated remains. That prompted a letter from an attorney for the makers of Uncle Milton's Ant Farm, protesting the use of the term "ant farm" as a violation of its trademark.

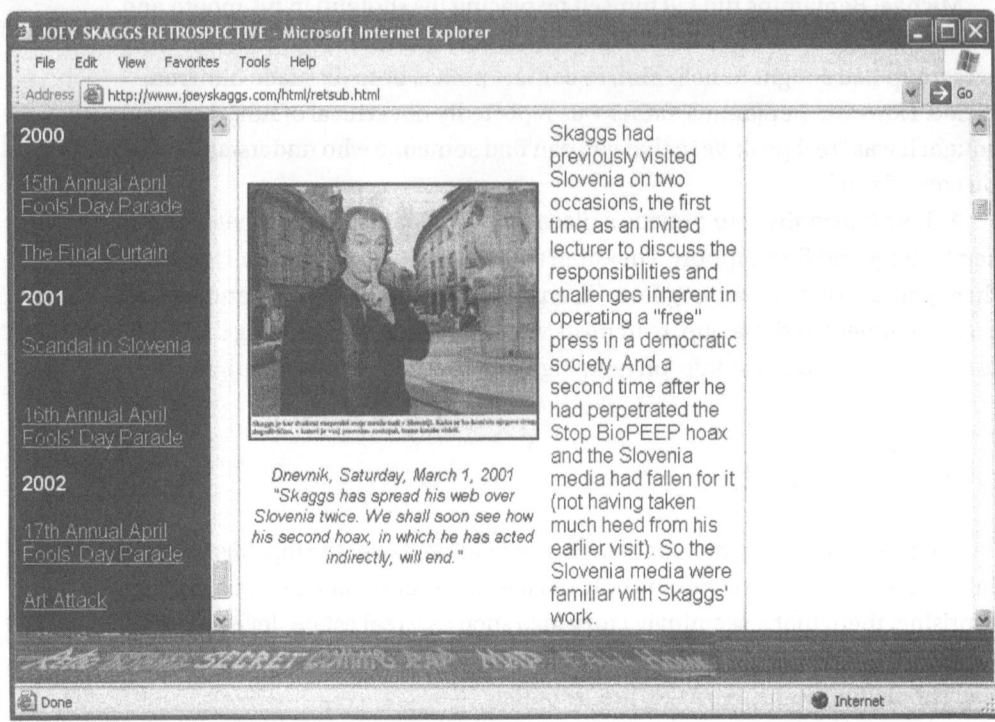

Figure 5-10. Joey Skaggs's Web site looks back on three decades' worth of hoaxes.[11]

Even though the hoax took place in 1999–2000, the Final Curtain is still online, so you can check out the timeshare greenhouse, the wall emblazoned with the names of "innumerable art critics," and much more (see Figure 5-11).

---

11. http://www.joeyskaggs.com/html/retsub.html

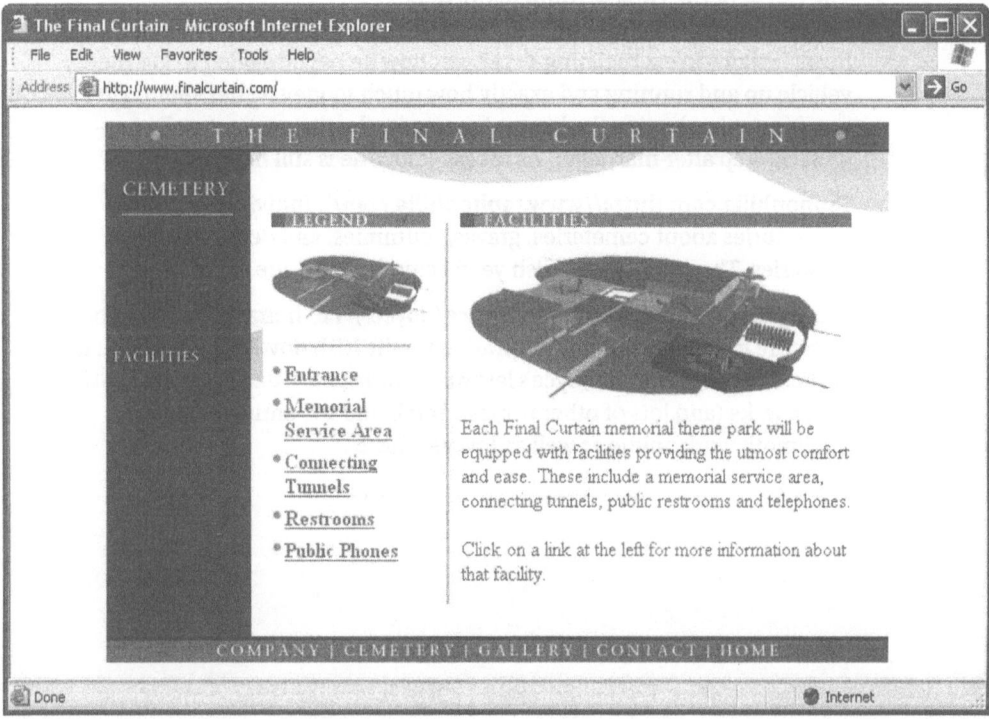

Figure 5-11. An amusement park for the dead, an amusement for its creator: the Final Curtain[12]

Random Googling

The Internet contains countless Web sites, chat rooms, newsgroups, and other resources related to death, suicide, and associated topics. The following list contains a few I found noteworthy—a random sampling of sites that turned up after searching for the term "death" on the search service Google (http://www.google.com/):

- **The Death Clock (http://www.deathclock.com/):** Enter your vital statistics in the handy Web page calculator, and the site pops up a friendly little window that reports exactly how many seconds you have left to live. Have a nice day!

---

12. http://www.finalcurtain.com/

- **The Curse of the Hearse Named Morticia**
  (http://www.morticiathehearse.co.uk/): The owner of an old British hearse relates in excruciating detail just how he has struggled to get the vehicle up and running and exactly how much money he has spent. He comments that buying the hearse "seemed to be the next naturally progressive step after marriage." As far as I know, he is still married.

- **Taphophilia.com (http://www.taphophilia.com/):** Individuals submit news stories about cemeteries, graves, mummies, and death-related mysteries. The result: a ghoulish yet fascinating Web site.

- **Finnegans Web (http://www.trentu.ca/jjoyce/):** I'm betraying my love of literature in general and my admiration for the Irish novelist James Joyce in particular, I suppose, but Joyce's last work *Finnegans Wake*, does have to do with a wake (and lots of other things). You'll find the entire text of this mammoth work online as well as Joyce's *Ulysses*.

CHAPTER 6

God in Babylon

God bless the Internet!

—*A character named Paul Finch, in the movie* American Pie

HUMAN BEINGS HAVE BEEN seeking a way to communicate their spiritual beliefs to other human beings for just about as long as human beings have been around. For the Northwest Native Americans, totem poles were a sort of Web site carved in wood, with layers of symbols stacked atop one another. The ancient Egyptians built pyramids and other monuments that had visual "hyperlinks" that provided details about their gods, members of their royal families, or events in their past.

These days, if a religious group has a message, it's likely to have a Web site, making the Net a veritable smorgasbord of the spirit world. The Internet is practically heaven-sent for declaring your version of the higher power. You can use a Web site to worship your chosen deity or simply to experience fellowship with like-minded souls.

It's lots of fun to meet the angels and devils who inhabit the realms of the Net, whether you want to sign on as a true believer or just want to find the next Heaven's Gate. You'll have no problem locating resources that lead to the more mainstream systems of belief on the Internet. You can read holy texts online, you can find columns and columns by religious leaders ranging from His Holiness the Dalai Lama to the Pope, and you can view the artwork of the Vatican. But because we're exploring Internet Babylon, in this chapter you'll encounter sites where it's hard to tell whether they are tongue in cheek or for the really out-there seeker. You can take your pick of digital gods, would-be saints, and visions that purport to purvey the meaning of life itself.

Gods, Saints, Sisters, and Singers

God frequently shows up where you least expect Him (or Her, or It). In fact, if you enter "God" into a search box on Yahoo! (http://www.yahoo.com/), you'll find millions of forms of divinity. God is omnipresent on the Internet, in other words. The next sections focus on individuals who declare themselves to be gods, have been called gods, or seek to get close to God in some way. The thread that ties them all together is the Internet—which enables mere mortals like you and me to commune with deities in whatever way we choose. You'll enjoy adoring God's wacky countenance as it is presented and interpreted online.

Digital God Creates Digital Life

'Fess up: Like most kids, you probably tried to play God once in a while. Perhaps your attempts at ultimate power over creation focused on the ability to take life away: You may have caused a grasshopper to part company with its legs, dissected a worm, or poured salt on a slug to see what would happen.

As any amateur god will tell you, it's much easier to cause death than to breathe life into inanimate objects. The British scientist Steve Grand has set himself a much more difficult goal—to create a robot that will one day possess its own intelligence and will grow and develop in much the same way as a human being.

Grand, who is the author of the book *Creation: Life and How to Make It* (Harvard University Press, 2001), describes himself as a "digital god" on his personal Web page. Some intelligent organizations have given him a vote of confidence as well. In 2002, Grand (shown in Figure 6-1) received a Dream Time Fellowship of £40,000 from Britain's National Endowment for Science, Technology, and the Arts (NESTA). He has been called the most intelligent man in Great Britain (apparently beating out the well-known scientist Stephen Hawking) as well as one of 18 scientists most likely to change the world during the 21st century.

On Grand's Web site (http://www.cyberlife-research.com/) he presents different views of Lucy, an artificial life form that has been under development since 2000. Lucy is not Grand's first venture into creating life forms, however. He was the architect and lead programmer for the computer game Creatures, which enabled players to follow the development of virtual life forms called Norns (see the "Norns: You, Too, Can Play God" sidebar).

While raising his own biological son, Grand had time to explore the development of organisms and muse about simulating the evolution of the human brain on a computer. He set about trying to develop machines that would have a sort of consciousness. His first version of Lucy resembled an orangutan. His second version, which was under development at the time of this writing, was expected to have a stronger and more mobile body as well as better eyesight and a more powerful brain. At the core of this Frankenstein-like vision is Grand's belief that the key to developing artificial intelligence is in a group of neurons in the cerebral cortex of the brain. If he can decode how those neurons are wired and how they function, he may be able to create an artificial brain that can learn and display creativity.

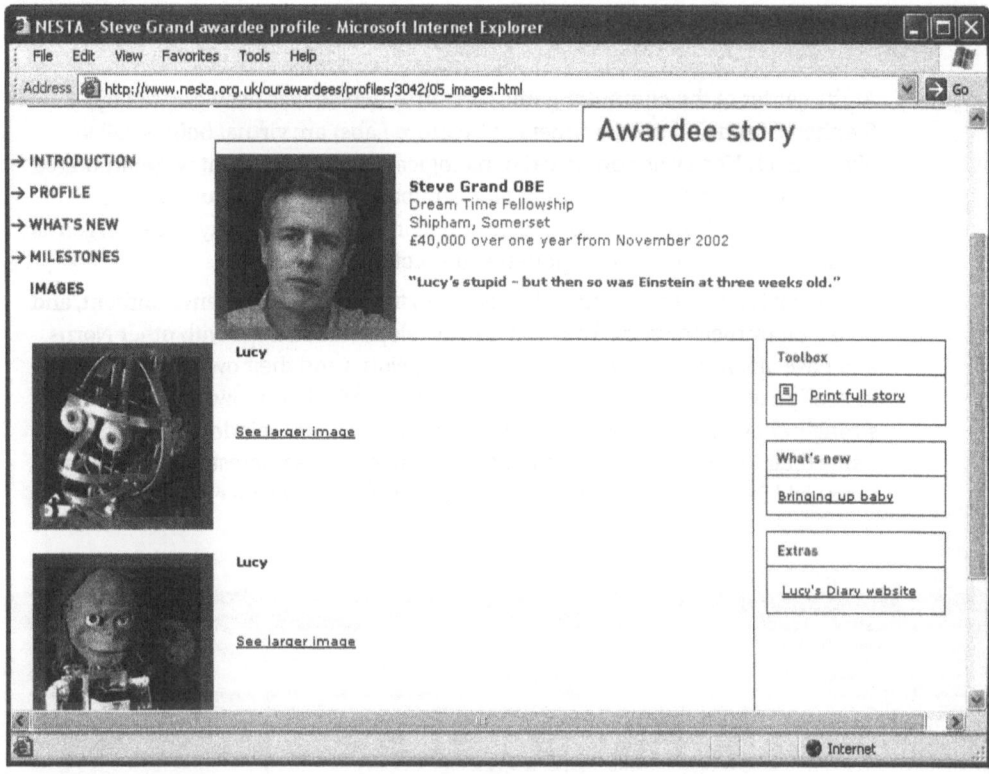

Figure 6-1. Stephen Grand and two views of his intelligent robot, Lucy[1]

Grand's ability to help his artificial life form develop doesn't extend to all aspects of his life, however. He admits that six years of being a househusband and primary caretaker of his son while his wife worked to support the family convinced him that, although he might be a digital god, he wasn't cut out to nurture perpetual infants. Grand hopes that Lucy will develop just as a child does and that he will be able to guide her through nursery school. She may learn to crawl before taking her first steps and repeat rudimentary sounds in much the same way that human toddlers learn.

---

1. http://www.nesta.org.uk/ourawardees/profiles/3042/05_images.html

Norns: You, Too, Can Play God

At the center of the computer game Creatures (which was itself created by Stephen Grand and programmers at Creature Labs) are virtual beings called Norns. Each Norn was composed of biological components that were simulated by computer programs, including biochemicals, genes, and neurons. The behavior of the Norns was not programmed in a predictable way but emerged as a result of the way those components interacted.

Norns can learn from their mistakes, adapt to their surrounding environment, and be taught by their owners. They can also develop relationships with other Norns and have offspring. The connection between Norns and their owners has resulted in nearly a million Norn enthusiasts around the world. Norn "owners" often feel as strongly about their virtual beings as pet lovers do about their dogs and cats. They name their Norns and follow their antics with passionate interest, taking delight in their vivid facial expressions; the following figure[2] shows some examples.

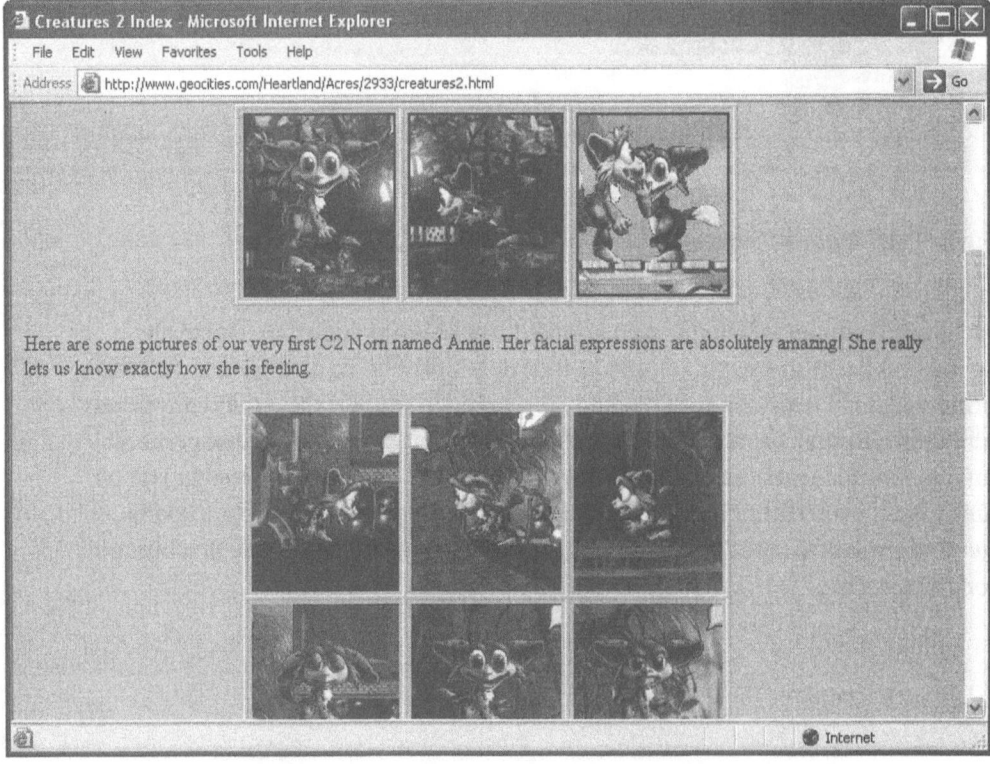

---

2. http://www.geocities.com/Heartland/Acres/2933/creatures2.html

Is owning a Norn the same as "playing God?" I'm not exactly sure. But when you create creatures such as Norns (or those more recent and more sophisticated virtual beings, the Sims, who have a virtual home at http://www.eagames.com/official/thesimsonline/home/index.jsp), you can watch watch them grow, get married, have children, run into problems, and struggle through their virtual existences, so whose perspective are you taking? Isn't it a godlike perspective? You be the judge.

Looking for Jesus in All the Wrong Places

Maybe it's a good thing that there are no photographs of Jesus. That way, the object of worship can evolve to meet specific needs. The problem is that some of us have overactive imaginations. Others have too much time on their hands. Whatever the reason, countless people devote time and energy to discovering new ways of depicting Jesus or creating their own strange fantasies about him.

The Web site Jesus of the Week (http://jesusoftheweek.com/), run by the alternative publisher New Times, gives Jesus hunters a place to submit statues, paintings, or other images they've spotted. One of my visits featured the Jesus of the Week as a scene of the Last Supper that someone allegedly spotted in an Olive Garden restaurant. It shows Jesus overeating (presumably unable to resist the temptation of Italian food) in the company of his equally sinful apostles (see Figure 6-2).

It's difficult to pick a single image of Jesus that sums him up...my favorites include the Black Velvet Jesus, the Barbie/Ken Jesus, and the bizarre Joe Millionaire Jesus, who gives new meaning to the phrase "the laying on of hands."

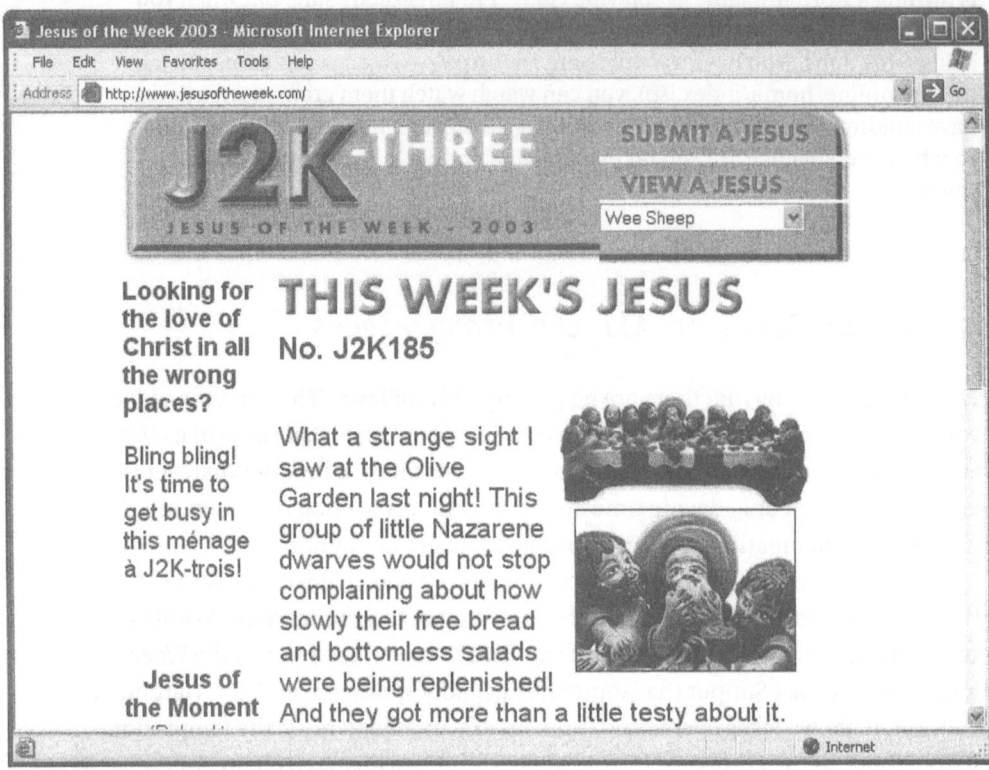

Figure 6-2. Jesus as a Barbie doll, Jesus in butter, Jesus in an Italian restaurant—you'll find them all on this Web site.[3]

Elvis: Not Just King; He's God

Millions of fans around the world worship Elvis Presley. But one Web site really, *literally* worships Elvis today. The First Presleyterian Church of Elvis the Divine puts the "fun" back in "fundamentalism" and celebrates the King's life and career at the same time. You can see this from the rather provocative splash page shown in Figure 6-3.

---

3. http://jesusoftheweek.com/

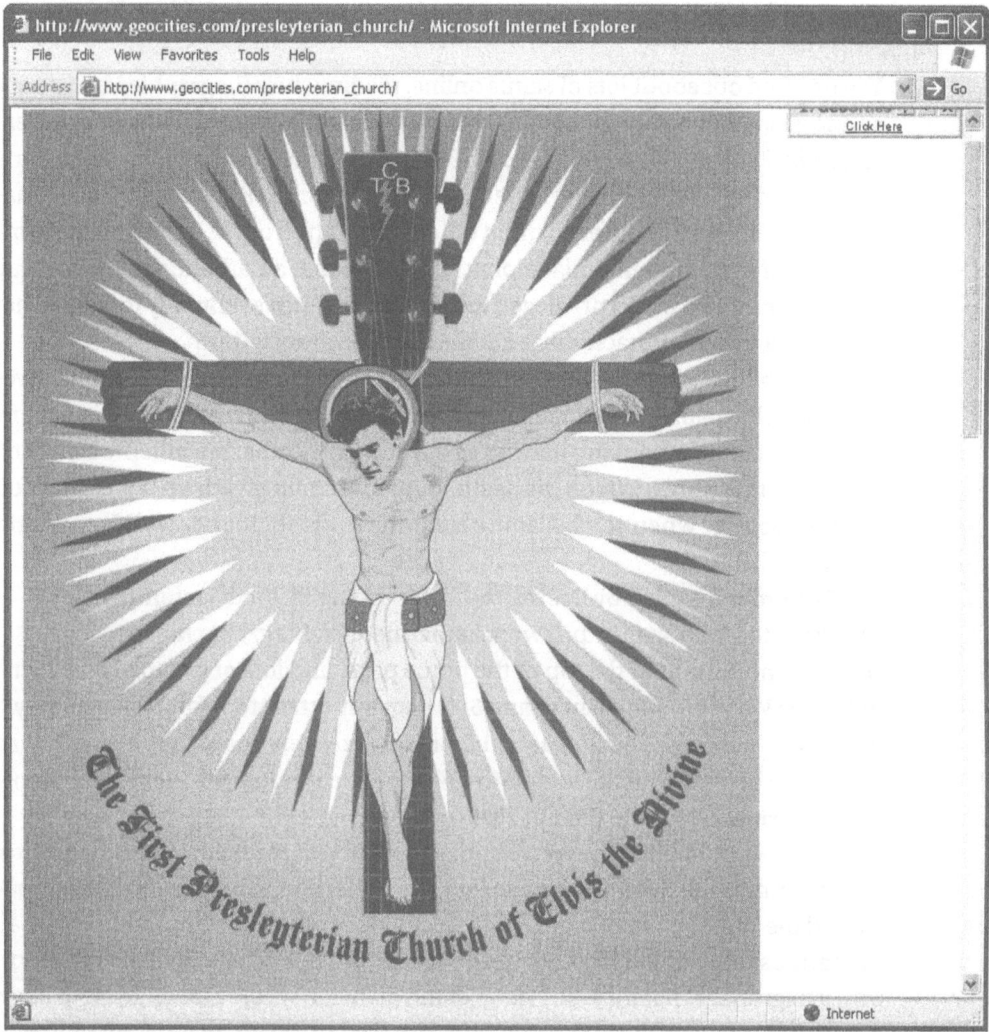

Figure 6-3. Elvis's spirit lives on in this worshipful Web site.[4]

The first ordained minister of the church, Minister Anna, tends the site with tender loving (or as she would probably say, "Love Me Tender") care. She has developed a stringent set of guidelines for those who want to be members—they must make a pilgrimage to Elvis's home, Graceland, at least once in their lives. Plus, they must face Las Vegas daily. Most importantly, Presleyterians are "required to overindulge in worldly pleasures." For these church members, Elvis is their rock and their roll.

---

4. http://www.geocities.com/presleyterian_church/

The Heiress and Socialite Who Became a Saint

You can find out about lots of saints online, reading their biographies in sites such as Encyclopedia.com and Biography.com. But few other saints have a Web presence as detailed as Saint Katharine Drexel. Drexel died in 1955, long before the Internet was created by God (see the story later in this chapter). But her story is tailor-made for online exploration. After all, what other saint started out as a millionaire-heiress member of a prominent Philadelphia family, became a Catholic nun, gave away her millions to aid underprivileged minorities, and was eventually judged to have performed the two miracles that entitled her to canonization?

As a child, Katharine saw the poor when they were invited three times a week to her family's mansion in Philadelphia for handouts. Her father, Francis, accumulated a fortune as a banking partner of J. P. Morgan. Katharine inherited a good portion of that portion upon his death. But rather than giving up her money for a vow of poverty when she became a nun, she decided put her worldly materials to work.

The order founded by Drexel, the Sisters of the Blessed Sacrament, has a sophisticated Web site (http://www.katharinedrexel.org/), including a logo, a scrolling message near the top of the home page, and lots of photos and hyperlinks. The Web site (shown in Figure 6-4) is an important tool for raising money for the order—although Drexel was a millionaire and spent more than $20 million on projects to help the African and Native American communities, her wealth went to other charities when she died in 1955.

The church deemed miraculous the cures of two seriously ill children whose relatives prayed to Saint Katharine. She was declared a saint in 2000. The sisters started the Web site in anticipation of the floods of pilgrims who came to visit Saint Katharine's tomb at the "mother house" of the order. The site invites visitors to take a pilgrimage that includes views of the mansion where Drexel grew up as well as her shrine and artifacts from her life. The Web site even includes an online newsletter, Peacemaker. The online souvenir shop contains a varied array of sacramental items: You can purchase everything from the usual books and portraits to a Katharine Drexel coloring book and a Katharine Drexel icon refrigerator magnet.

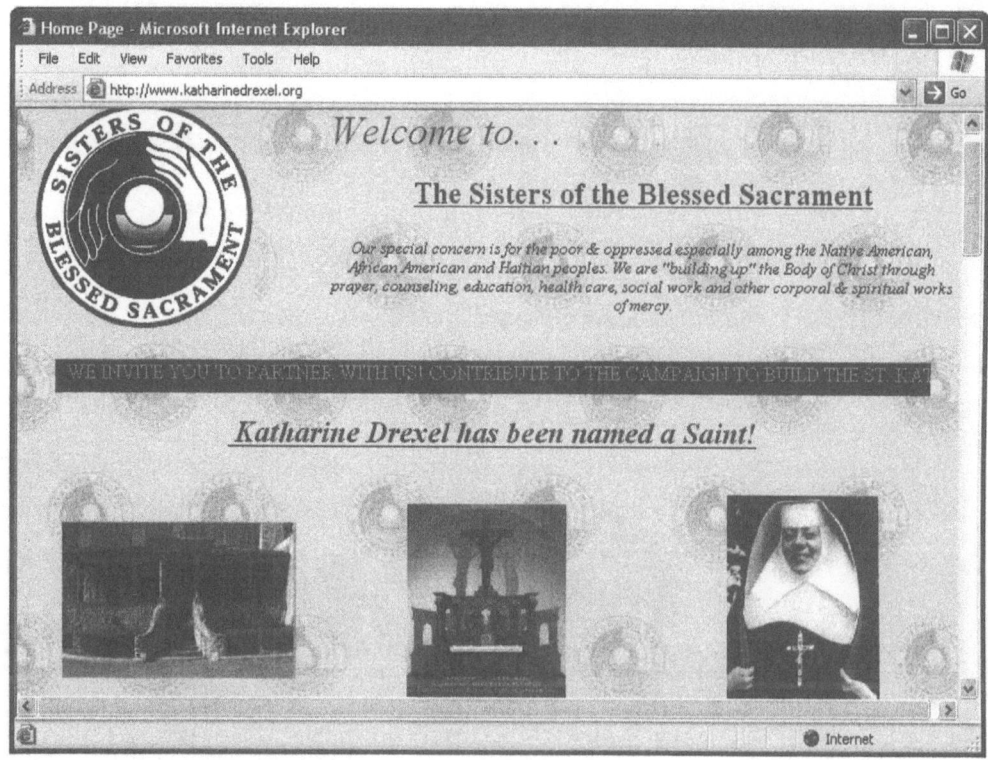

Figure 6-4. Hyperlinks and JavaScript can promote prayers and charity.[5]

Inspired by a Vision, Sustained by Almighty Dollar

I found HuggyJesus.com on the Jesus of the Week site mentioned earlier in this chapter. The product itself is good in its own right: Huggy Jesus is a plush doll that comes with a certificate of authenticity and a scripture verse. He also has bare feet, realistic fingernails, and (though you can't see them in Figure 6-5, take my word for it) toenails.

5. http://www.katharinedrexel.org/

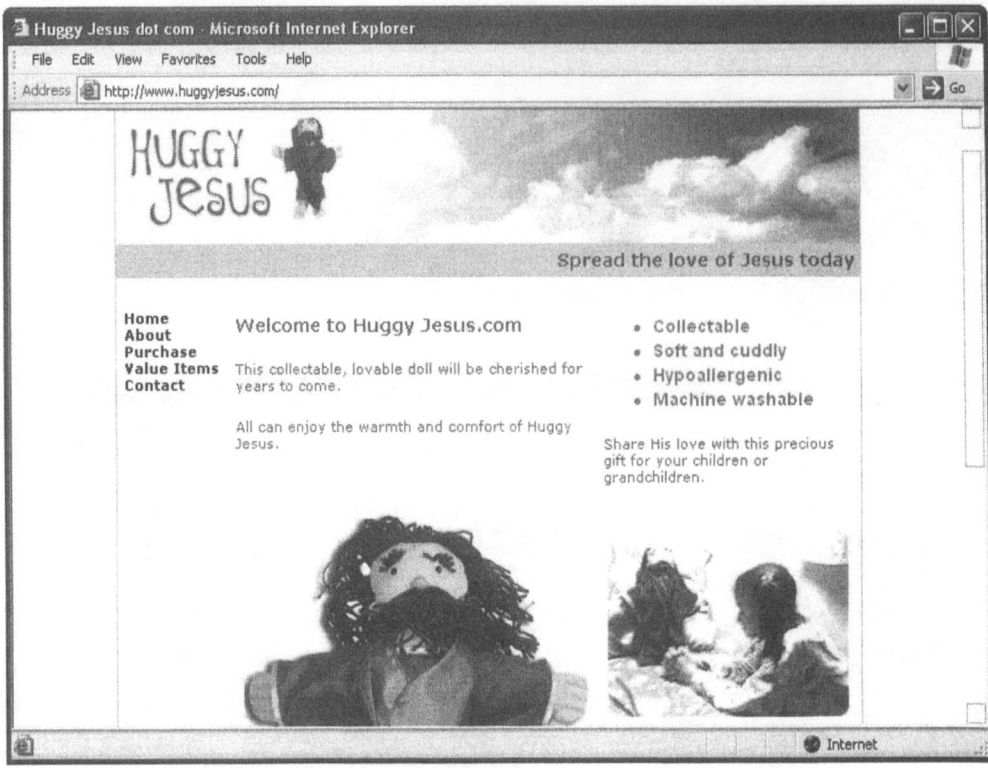

Figure 6-5. Coming to a kid's Christmas tree near you—it's Huggy Jesus! [6]

But as those TV infomercial pitch people would say, "Just wait! That's not all." Huggy Jesus, it turns out, is the result of a vision experienced by a Seattle, Washington, man named Sean Pinkerton. Pinkerton lost his job as a machinist in the economic downturn of 2001. He found himself without a home and depending on food banks for his meals. One rainy night (as the story is presented at http://www.huggyjesus.com/about.htm) he stumbled into a church and began to pray. You can pretty much guess the rest or read about it online. He was drawn by a powerful force to the altar, hugged the statue of Jesus that seemed to be beckoning to him, and, well, the rest is e-commerce history.

Keeping Demons Away with the Wolf

There are Web sites that use Java applets and other gimmicks while focusing on their message, such as the one described in the preceding section. Then there are

---

6. http://www.huggyjesus.com/

Web sites that seem to drown in ads, pop-up windows, and gimmicks, such as Ishaah.com.

A 60-year-old woman named Ishaah who calls herself Wolf Sister, has set up a Web site (http://www.ishaah.com/) that provides visitors with her pronouncements about Love, Light, and Native American spirituality. This site, which is built around inspirational poems and sayings—some by Ishaah, some borrowed from other authors—is inspirational from an e-commerce standpoint as well. Ishaah has managed to get links to her site all over the Internet. In a list of the most popular religious Web sites once maintained by *USA Today*, Ishaah.com was found to be more popular than the venerable publication *Christianity Today*.

Ishaah.com has a variety of messages to convey to its visitors, only one of which has to do with peace and love. Along the way you'll find pop-up ads for car insurance, debt relief, plasma TVs, and a dating service. The barrage of ads, plus the never-ending background music, will want to start you on a wolf hunt right away. Listen closely for other sounds that aren't so melodic and that apparently have to do with a graphic labeled "Diarrhea" at the bottom of one of the site's pages. If you can figure out what kind of spirituality is being offered here, please tell me.

Places and Ways of E-Worship

One of the great things about the Internet is that it enables individuals to do things they could never accomplish otherwise because of geographic or other boundaries. They can purchase things from sellers around the world, and they can take virtual visits to churches, temples, and sacred sites where they can worship for a day or for a lifetime.

The following sections describe some online places of worship that shatter geographic boundaries and enable people to connect with God and others who have similar beliefs.

TIP   Beliefnet.com, which provides a clearinghouse of online information about many different religions, has an online locator that will help you find a place to worship. You can use it to find a church, a Sikh temple, a wiccan coven, a Mormon ward, and much more. Try it at http://www.beliefnet.com/index/index_10060.html.

A Web Site That's a Real Mecca

One of the tenets of Islam is that members are required to journey to the city of Mecca, the birthplace of the prophet Muhammad, at least once in their lifetimes. This pilgrimage is known as the Hajj. But why go only once? You can visit Mecca any time of the day or night simply by connecting to the Hajj Information Center on the Web site IslamiCity.com (http://www.islamicity.com/mosque/hajj/).

This site (see Figure 6-6) lets you hear prayers from Mecca or other cities five times a day via live Webcam. However, you need to pay a $59.95 annual membership fee to access the content. Membership also entitles Muslims to services such as an online tool designed to help them learn the Koran; a Memorial Park to eulogize loved ones; screen savers with antique images of the Hajj; and news from the Arabic TV channel Al Jazeera, which has been criticized by the administration of U.S. President George W. Bush.

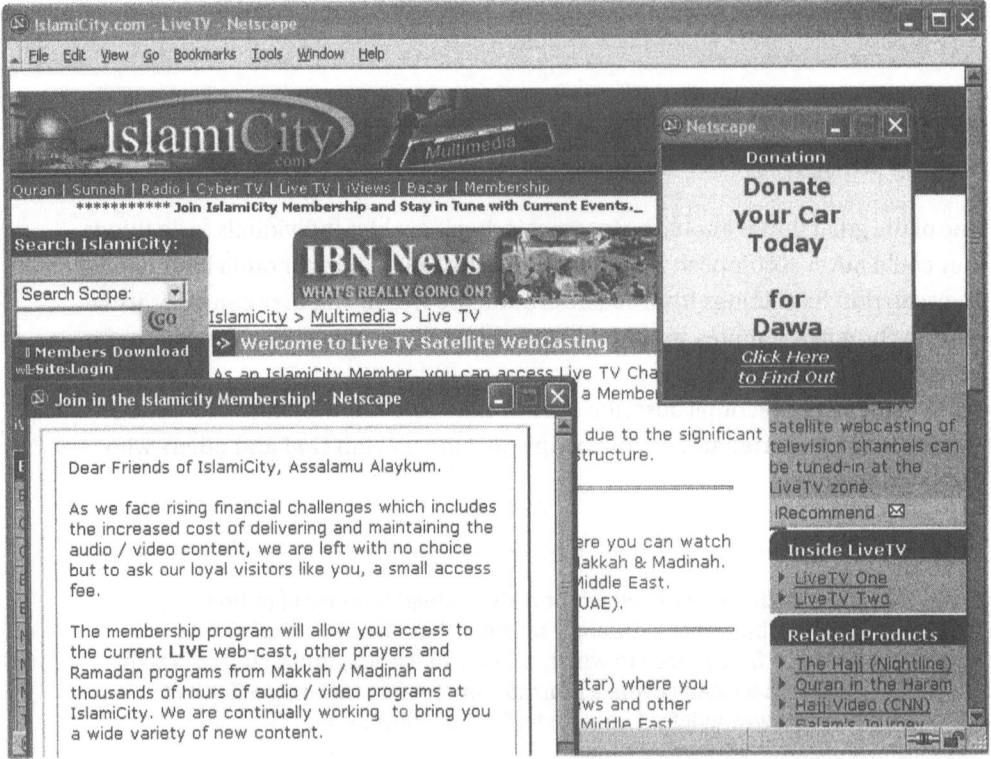

Figure 6-6. Live pilgrimages mix with pitches for donations on this Web site. [7]

---

7. http://www.islamicity.com/mosque/hajj/

This Church Conducts Real "Web Services"

When I was growing up in the Chicago, Illinois, area, local television stations used to broadcast a version of Sunday services called "Mass for Shut-Ins." Now they only broadcast news and cartoons on Sunday mornings. However, everyone from folks in the hospital across town to Inuits in Alaska to Zen monks in Japan can tune in to live services from Peachtree Presbyterian Church in Atlanta, Georgia. Each Sunday at 9, 10, and 11:30 a.m. Eastern Standard Time, a live Webcast broadcasts on the church's Web site (http://www.peachtreepres.org/). The term "Web services" gets a new meaning on this site.

Buddhas Reborn—Online, at Least

Those pesky Talibans. They thought they were ridding themselves of some vile religious symbols that were offensive to Muslims when they blew up two of the biggest freestanding statues of the Buddha known in the world. Little did they know that not only were the U.S. armed forces heading in their direction, but the Internet was going to rebuild the statues they eradicated in the blink of an eye in March 2001.

The statues are considered significant not just because of their age but because they were a link between East and West. It's believed that the descendants of Greek artists, who came into the region along with the army of Alexander the Great, created the monuments in the fourth century A.D. The New 7 Wonders Web site (http://www.new7wonders.com/) has taken on the task of giving the statues a virtual rebirth online.

Not Your Average Baptist Church

Landover Baptist Church has a harmless, legitimate-sounding name. But the moment you connect to the home page of its Web site (http://www.landoverbaptist.org/, shown in Figure 6-7), you know immediately that this isn't the usual church—in fact, it can't be a real Baptist church at all.

The moment you scan the page entitled "What We (God) Believes," you realize just how much of a farce this site is. Landover Baptist Church makes fun of the huge fundamentalist church complexes sweeping the country by boasting that its site in Freehold, Iowa, includes a Christian Amusement Park (Landover Bible Theme Park and Red Sea World), a PGA 18-hole golf course, Exodus Acres (a Silver Gated Community), a Christian Circus Camp, Retreat Center for Republican Candidates, and much, much more. If you don't take Christianity too seriously, you're sure to get a kick out of this site.

Figure 6-7. Irony, not piety: Landover Baptist Church[8]

Take a Virtual Bath in the Ganges

Hinduism's biggest holy festival, in which as many as 30 million pilgrims journey to bathe at the spot where the Ganges, the Yamuna, and the Saraswati rivers come together, is getting an online presence. Already, pilgrims heading to the Kumbh Mela festival are greeted by huge television screens and big hot air balloons advertising everything from Internet access to soap ("You've bathed in the Ganges, now bathe with Ganga," reads the ad for Ganga soap). Now, a variety of Internet-related companies have joined in. Festivalgoers can stop at computer kiosks where they can send and receive e-mail. They can visit a number of cybercafés as well. However, Internet connectivity in the Indian countryside is so unpredictable that just getting online at any of the kiosks, which are covered by tin sheets, is "in God's hands," according to one of the kiosks' own operators.

Much of the business at the kiosks involves printing astrology charts that can be taken to one of the swamis who come to Kumbh and who are believed to have

---

8. http://www.landoverbaptist.org/

mystical powers. The swamis, who sit on or near the path leading to the bathing spot, used to have to draw the astrology charts by hand. Now, they prefer to have supplicants bring computer-drawn charts to them so they can focus on predicting what is in store for their visitors. Some of the healers who frequent the festival have their own Web sites; Shri Mahadev (http://www.mahadev.org/) includes no images of the holy man but RealAudio files of him speaking.

Stonehenge Will Take You Higher

The Stonehenge Organisation Web site (http://www.stonehenge.org.uk/, shown in Figure 6-8) includes a Shockwave animation depicting how the mysterious set of huge stones was constructed.

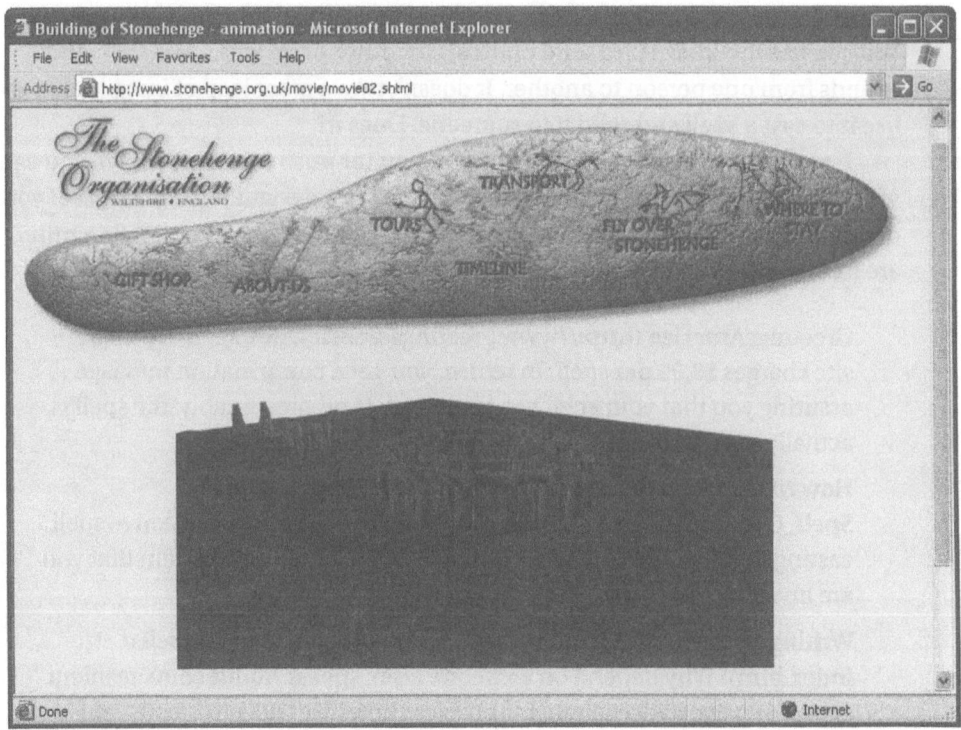

Figure 6-8. Stonehenge, one of the world's most famous ancient sites, is reputed to be a place where Druids worshipped.[9]

---

9. http://www.stonehenge.org.uk/movie/movie02.shtml

Of course, if you can't afford to travel to England, you can always view the one-half scale model of Stonehenge created with "water jet technology" and located at the University of Missouri's campus in Rolla, Missouri (http://www.ohwy.com/mo/u/umrstone.htm). Or you can discover America's own version of "Stonehenge," a 4,000-year-old stone complex that is also an astronomical observatory.

TIP   You can read about myths and legends associated with England's Glastonbury Abbey, which is the oldest above-ground Christian church in the world and reputed to be the burial place of King Arthur and Lady Guinevere, at http://www.glastonburyabbey.com.

Spelling It Out for a Special Someone

You can use the Internet to send photos, computer programs, messages, and sounds from one person to another. It doesn't take a great leap of imagination to use it to cast a spell and send it to someone. Does it?

If you want to draw someone closer to you (or push someone away), you can visit a variety of sites that purport to send a spell to a designated individual of your dreams (or nightmares). Some of the sites charge a fee for the service, but others are free, however. Here are some suggestions:

> **GreetingsAmerica (http://www.greetingsamerica.net/spell.asp):** This site charges $3.99 per spell. In return, you get a confirmation message assuring you that your spell has been sent. (And presumably, the spell is actually sent, too.)

> **How to Cast a Spell (http://www.geocities.com/jkarrah/Spell_Casting.html):** A good introduction to the basics of effective spell casting that includes the admonition to make absolutely certain that you are invoking the correct deity before you get started.

> **Writing Spells (http://paganwiccan.about.com/cs/writingspells/index.htm):** Why depend on someone else's spells? About.com's resident expert in pagan/wiccan religious topics shows you how to create your own spells here.

Love Spells (http://members.lycos.co.uk/ravenwitch487/ newpage12.html): This site presents you with love spells that are guaranteed to attract a lover. Some of them are complicated, however. You'll need rose petals, rose quartz, apple seeds, red candles, and more. For instance, Love Potion Number 9 calls for the following:

- 9 ounces of sweet red wine
- 9 basil leaves
- 9 red rose petals
- 9 cloves
- 9 apple seeds
- 9 drops of vanilla extract
- 9 drops of strawberry juice
- 1 ginseng root, cut into 9 equal pieces

Be sure to place these nine ingredients into a cauldron on the ninth hour of the ninth day of the ninth month of the year. Stir the potion nine times and, if you haven't developed a grade-9 headache by this time, say the magical incantation presented on the Love Spells Web site.

Pass the Virtual Collection Plate, Please

A *tithe*, according to that venerable resource Dictionary.com, is "a tenth part of one's annual income contributed voluntarily or due as a tax, especially for the support of the clergy or church."

One association of churches may not be asking for a tenth of its parishioners' income, but it has found a new way to ask for whatever people are willing to give. The Diocese of Baton Rouge in Louisiana has installed an electronic kiosk in one of its offices that is designed to alleviate the guilt of anyone who forgets to contribute during a religious service.

The kiosk (which is shown on the Web site of its creator, PlannedLegacy, and shown in Figure 6-9) provides a touch screen that can be used for e-tithing: donating by cash, check, or credit card. In return, the kiosk immediately provides a printed receipt. Along with the receipt, parishioners also receive a prayer. The program, instituted in 2003, is considered experimental; there are no plans to install kiosks in any of the churches—at least not yet.

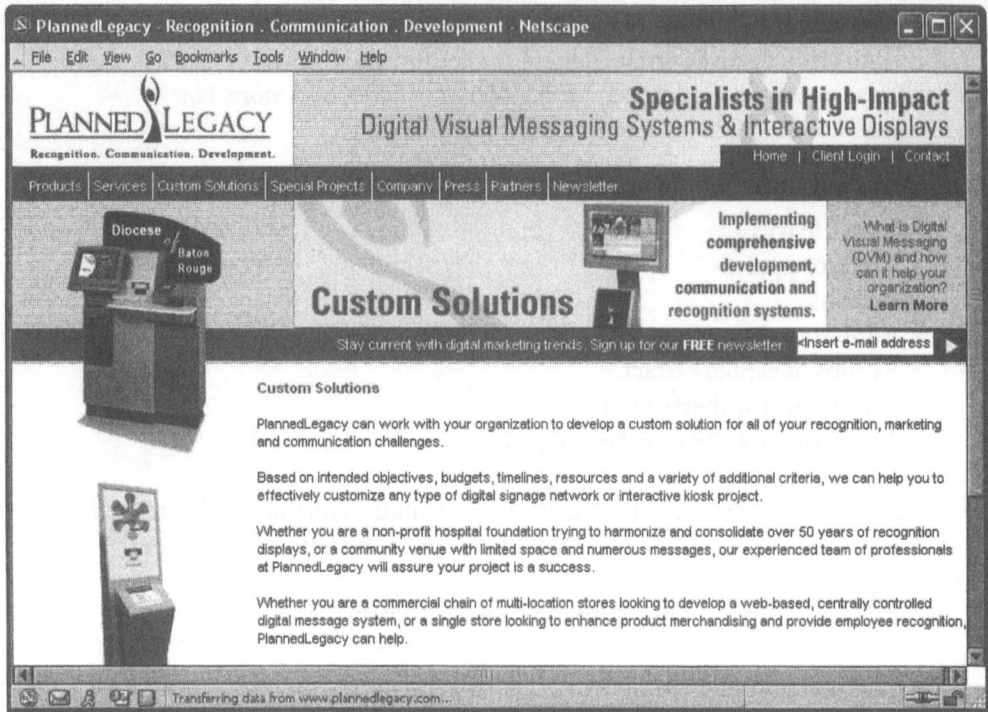

Figure 6-9. Interactive kiosks give parishioners a chance to get in touch (touch screen, actually) with God.[10]

A Psalm a Day Keeps the Devil Away

Too busy to pray between checking your e-mail, sending that text message, and fielding that cell phone call? Never fear; even the most harried high-tech worker can get a reminder to say a prayer in the form of a message transmitted to your cell phone or pager.

Alan Wostenberg, who is Catholic, sought a way to send a reminder to himself as a way to keep a promise. He and his wife had promised to pray for one another at 3 p.m. each day. At the time, Wostenberg was unemployed. The prayers were, in part, to help him find a job. With a background in computer programming, Wostenberg sought a high-tech solution. He programmed a computer to send a "reminder psalm" to him and his wife at 3 p.m. each day.

Wostenberg knew there were many others who offered a prayer at 3 p.m., so he decided to offer the same service on a subscription basis. For a $4 setup fee and $19.95

10. http://www.plannedlegacy.com /

per year, members of the PsalmWeaver service (http://www.psalmweaver.com/) would receive daily psalms in their phone, pager, or e-mail inbox.

After several months, 176 "psalmweavers" joined up, many of them praying for the unemployed. At least one member's prayers were answered: Wostenberg reports that he found part-time work as a church programmer in early 2003.

Find Yourself a Coven to Call Your Own

You say you're a witch, but your spells just aren't working quite right? You need to compare notes with your fellow witches and get together once in a while for some tarot card readings or some good old-fashioned pagan earth worshipping?

Never fear: Wave your wand, light up your computer, and head over to the Witch's Voice (http://www.witchvox.com/), where a database called Pagans/Witches of the World is waiting to match you up with the witch, or group of witches, for which you are looking. Listings are broken down by state and include groups of teen wiccans, families of wiccans, college wiccans...you can also find witches with particular specialties, such as divination, healing, massage therapy, and handfasting (pledging or betrothing).

Worshipping with a Very Special Member

People around the world worship all kinds of things. In Japan, there are a few Shinto shrines where people pay homage to one of the fundamental elements in creation: the male phallus. At the Tagata Jinja Shrine in Komaki, the central object of devotion is a two-meter-long (about six-feet-long) male reproductive organ. It is made of wood and is at least 200 years old. It attracts the faithful who are hoping to have a child. The phallus actually plays a central role in an annual fertility festival held March 15 that is intended to guarantee a good harvest.

You can read about this and other shrines to fertility in an article on the *Mainichi Daily News* Web site (http://mdn.mainichi.co.jp/waiwai/0207/020712holiness.html). Better yet, see the phallus for yourself in a short video at http://www.yamasa.org/japan/english/destinations/aichi/tagata_jinja_video.html (when I visited, only the Windows Media versions were working, however).

Divine Spam Didn't Go Down Well

Back in 1999, it seemed like the prayers of e-commerce entrepreneurs were being answered all over the Internet. You could come up with any way to make money— even if it purported to be sending prayers to heaven.

The PrayerWheel Web site charged members $19.95 per month to send prayers from mail server to mail server around the world in a gigantic loop—in other words, to send divine spam to e-mail addresses that didn't necessarily ask for it. The site's founder reportedly said the service was intended to help busy people alleviate their guilt about forgetting to say their prayers in a fast-paced high-tech world. Though PrayerWheel got lots of attention from the media and visitors who wanted to read the prayers posted on its site, few signed up for the monthly service. When the Day of Judgment came and the Internet e-commerce bubble burst, PrayerWheel was cast into the depths along with sites for home grocery delivery, sock puppet pets, and many sites mentioned elsewhere in this book.

Beliefs That Inspire Disbelief

Inspirational messages are perfect for distribution on the Internet. They're short, easy to digest, and easily distributed by e-mail or other methods.

It's a validation; it's cheap and easy way to comparison shop. You don't have to check out a book, visit a temple, or listen to a drawn-out spiel by someone trying to convince you that their system is the best. People can express their beliefs almost in the form of personal ads, such as for a date; you can initiate a serious relationship without ever leaving your desk. Humans are creators of fantasy games. The Internet is perfect for the "what if" games that people love so much. It's kind of a fill-in-the-blank belief system. If you keep clicking long enough, chances are you'll find something that comes close to your own beliefs. And no matter how odd or offbeat they are, they are likely to be validated.

When the Force Is with the Census

Jedi, the league of knights made famous by the *Star Wars* series of movies, were never intended to be a religion. But thanks to the Internet, they're not only a system of belief—they have suddenly become the fourth most popular religion in Great Britain.

Before the 2001 British census, a campaign was launched on the Internet (the Internet being the natural place to launch such frivolous quests) to get Jedi listed by the British government as an official religion. An e-mail message that circulated far and wide across Britain claimed (falsely) that the government would have to recognize Jedi as a religion if 10,000 Britons declared it on the census forms.

It turned out that some 390,000 Britons followed the e-mail message's instructions. That's 0.7 percent of the country's population. Jedi was thus ranked ahead of Judaism and Buddhism. However, the Bureau of National Statistics (obviously acting under the influence of the Dark Force) ruled that Jediism still didn't qualify to be a religion. Luke Skywalker was reportedly heading to the British Isles to lead a protest.

NOTE   If you count yourself as a fan of that other science fiction series, *Star Trek*, you can translate everything from recipes to declarations of love into science fiction languages, including Klingon, Romulan, and Vulcan at the Universal Translator Assistant Project (http://hometown.aol.com/JPKlingon/uta/).

Yes, Virginia, God Did Create the Internet

If you really believe that God created everything and knows everything, it's not a huge leap to say that God created the Internet as well. Right? That, at least, is what a single article published on a religious satire Web zine called Detox claims. The zine, which is described by its creator Dov Wisebrod as a "religious recovery webzine," includes a tongue-in-cheek explanation in which the organization the Paley Institute supposedly announces that the "Internet was created by God."

In the article, a Dr. Ian Cleanthes claims, "We are very excited by our proof of the worldwide computer network's divine origin." The article very plausibly claims that the institute used one of the proofs created by Paley (1743–1805), an Anglican priest and philosopher to prove that God created the Internet. The article (http://www.catalaw.com/detox/reverse/21.shtml) is a creation of Dov Wisebrod, but it was, predictably, reprinted on other Web sites as though it was true.

NOTE   If you hear the phrase "net dot god," chances are it does not refer to the ultimate being. It's actually online lingo for someone who has been online since the beginning, one who "knows all" and has "done all."

Seeing the Light Changes Web Designer's Life

Reata Strickland had a quiet, predictable life with its own personal dramas. She was a Webmaster at the University of Alabama and taught Sunday school in Tuscaloosa, Alabama. She overcame a drinking problem after joining the church; she sang in the choir and spoke to churchwomens' groups. One of the texts that had touched her was a short story called "Interview with God." The anonymously written story inspired her, and she made a promise to turn it into a Web page presentation using the Shockwave software program.

When she had some time, Reata (pronounced "Rita") spent two days putting the presentation together, presenting different segments of the text with backgrounds showing peaceful, inspirational scenes from nature. "What surprises you most about humankind?" God is asked. God's answer: "That they get bored with childhood. They rush to grow up and then long to be children again. That they lose their health to make money and then lose their money to restore their health."

On Memorial Day 2001, Reata posted the pages on a Web site run by her local United Methodist Church. She felt good that she had kept her promise to herself and thought no more about it—that is, not until four days later the church's Internet Service Provider (ISP) contacted her. They complained they were going to have to take the site down because it had received 500,000 visitors and was consuming too much bandwidth. Reata moved Interview with God to her own Web site (http://www.reata.org/, shown in Figure 6-10) where traffic continued to grow.

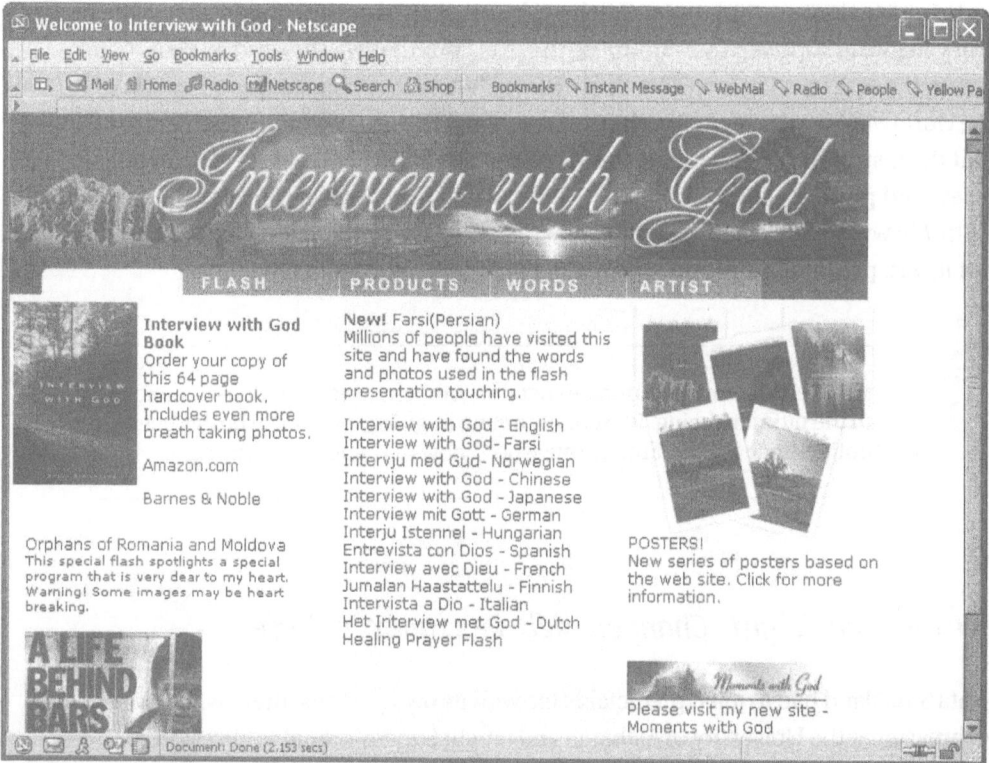

Figure 6-10. The Interview with God site—an inspirational phenomenon that has changed many lives.[11]

---

11. http://www.reata.org/

In June 2001 alone, Jupiter Media Metrix reported that Reata.org had attracted 2.4 million visitors. To keep her creation online, Reata had to figure out how to pay for the 40 gigabytes of bandwidth that were being consumed as viewers around the world connected to it and enjoyed the presentation.

Reata's husband, Steve (see Figure 6-11), who had just become a Methodist minister (and who had also been a heavy drinker during his previous career as a construction worker), was chagrined to find that his wife was attracting far more attention from spiritual devotees than he was. Although he preached to congregations of a dozen or more, she was soon giving talks to far larger groups and getting tens of thousands of e-mail messages from thankful visitors telling her how Interview with God had changed their lives.

"A woman wrote and told me she lived in New York City just blocks from the World Trade Center," Strickland says. "She said that for the several past weeks she had no hope, that all seemed lost. Then she said her husband made her sit at the computer and watch Interview with God. She said she watched it over and over, and as she watched it, hope returned. She thanked me for my site and for helping her get back to living."

Figure 6-11. Steve and Reata Strickland[12]

12. http://www.momentswithgod.com/artist.html

Today, Interview with God and a related site, Moments with God, attract as many as 500,000 visitors each month. The site stays afloat thanks to donations as well as the sale of T-shirts, screen savers, and other items. In some ways her life has changed dramatically; in others not at all.

"I still do the things I have always done," she explains. "I clean the house, shuttle the girls, and get up every day and go to work. In other ways, perhaps internally, I have been changed greatly. I was shocked at the number of people—one million each month on both sites—who are touched by something I created. It is hard to imagine that something like Interview with God would be seen by people all over the world. Then the e-mail from people telling me their stories and asking for prayers was life changing. Once someone drove from another state just to meet me and say hello."

In 2002, Strickland turned Interview with God into a 64-page book sold on Amazon.com and in brick-and-mortar bookstores. It might sound like there was a design to all of this, but it wasn't one that Strickland prepared. "I did not have a marketing plan or strategic plan on producing Web sites and books. It just happened. I try not to touch the beauty of Interview with God by checking how many 'hits' the Web site gets. Interview with God has a life of its own. It is my job to help keep it alive and share it with others."

Hell: It's What You Make It

Who says Hell has to be only one way (hot) and provide sinners with only one type of experience (really unpleasant)? In *The Divine Comedy*, Dante envisioned many levels of Hell. Buddhists believe that there are hells where beings are continually hot, cold, or hungry, among other things, and that the deeds you perform throughout your life determine the area of Hell to which you'll go.

That's the idea behind the online utility Design Your Own Hell (http://www.gaydeceiver.com/misc/hell/), which is based on the belief that Hell is what you make it.

Created by Jason and Heather Steiner, the utility is presented as an online form you fill out. First, you select specific individuals who need to be relegated to the fires of eternal damnation. At this writing, possible selections covered practically the entire sociopolitical spectrum, including Militant Vegans, Goths, Rednecks, and Libertarians. You have a chance to redeem some of the miscreants if you want to do so. Then you assign them to nine levels of hell. The resulting graphic, which presents nine layers growing progressively redder, is intended to be a supplement to a Weblog, though it can be pasted into any Web page as well.

Random Googling

The Internet contains countless Web sites, chat rooms, newsgroups, and other resources related to God and religion. The following list contains a few I found noteworthy—a random sampling of sites that turned up after searching for the terms "God" and "religion" on the search service Google (http://www.google.com):

- **Beliefnet (http://www.beliefnet.com/):** This site provides news, columns, and stories about many different religions. If you're not sure which religion you belong to, or should belong to, you can take the site's Belief-O-Matic quiz. Answer 20 questions about your concept of God, the afterlife, and other topics, and the service reports back what religion you belong to—whether or not you were aware of it.

- **Disturbing Auctions (http://www.disturbingauctions.com/ view.pl?item=23):** This site contains strange auctions of all sorts; this specific Uniform Resource Locator (URL) lists links to a black velvet painting entitled *God Bless Our Truckers*.

- **First Church of Jesus Christ, Elvis (http://jubal.westnet.com/ hyperdiscordia/sacred_heart_elvis.html):** The First Presleyterian Church, mentioned earlier in this chapter, is hardly the only online shrine dedicated to the worship of the King of Rock. Visit the First Church of Jesus Christ, Elvis; you can also make pilgrimages to http://www.churchofelvis.com/.

Part Three
Bad Boys and Naughty Girls

CHAPTER 7

Hackers and Other Internet Heroes

CONSIDER THE MANY STORIES and legends of the Wild West. The good guys such as Wyatt Earp get our admiration. But it's the bad guys, the Jesse Jameses and Billy the Kids, who really attract a morbid fascination and who are admired by many. Even in more recent films and books, we love the people who break the rules and use technology to accomplish things that "mere mortals" such as us cannot do—think about *Mission: Impossible, Spy Kids*, and the *Terminator* series of movies.

Some of the biggest "stars" in cyberspace are typically portrayed as ingenious tricksters who wreak havoc, take down Web sites, steal personal and confidential information, and generally cause trouble.

Before you write off hackers and say they are the ones who do everything wrong on the Internet, however, remember that many of the people who developed the software you use every day were essentially hackers—people who tried out new programs or who tried to do things that hadn't been done before or that they weren't "supposed" to do. Their desire to share information or accomplish tasks in a new-and-improved way resulted in much of the software we take for granted today. Even without trying to be helpful, hackers do help improve security on the Net by breaking and entering systems and uncovering weaknesses that need to be strengthened.

The problem with reading (and writing) about hackers is that, in order to fully understand what they have accomplished, some knowledge of computers and networks is helpful. I'm not saying it's mandatory to know what terms such as "buffer overflow" and "public key encryption" mean. I'll do my best to explain what's going on without having to get overly technical. But be aware—this chapter ventures dangerously close to "geek" territory. The geeks, after all, are the ones who created the Internet in the first place and who keep us on our toes even as we take its infrastructure for granted and try to make it part of our everyday lives.

NOTE The term "hacker" is used in a very broad sense in this chapter. Here, it's a catchall term that includes all kinds of people who gain unauthorized access to networked sources of data. In fact, hackers and crackers take different approaches. *Hackers* are typically programmers who like overcoming challenges and using their expertise to solve problems and uncover information. *Crackers* are primarily interested in discovering protected or sensitive information by guessing or decoding passwords or breaking into networks.

The White Hats and the "Hacker Ethic"

The "hacker ethic," according to that authority on all things techno-speak called the Jargon File (http://www.tuxedo.org/jargon/), is defined as "the belief that information sharing is a powerful positive good and that it is the ethical duty of hackers to share their expertise."

Early "hackers" were more interested in breaking new ground technically and developing new software than in breaking into systems and causing destruction. To most people, the following names may leave you scratching your head. But to programmers and network administrators, this first generation of pioneers is as well-known as Guglielmo Marconi to radio, Alexander Graham Bell to the telephone, or Chuck Yaeger to supersonic flight.

The Legend of Mel, the "Real Programmer"

Computer programmers and technical experts are a persnickety bunch. They tend to admire people who do things no one else can do. They especially admire programmers who can solve problems as elegantly and efficiently as possible. The ultimate programmer may not have actually existed. But the legend about Mel the "Real Programmer" is one of the most frequently circulated on the Net.

NOTE To understand the story of Mel, it helps to know that FORTRAN is a computer programming language.

Erik Brunvand, in an essay about legendary hackers, attributes this particular legend to a fellow named Ed Nather, who posted the following story online on May 21, 1983:

A recent article devoted to the macho side of programming

made the bald and unvarnished statement:

Real Programmers write in FORTRAN.

Maybe they do now,

in this decadent era of

Lite beer, hand calculators, and "user-friendly" software

but back in the Good Old Days,

when the term "software" sounded funny

and Real Computers were made out of drums and vacuum tubes,

Real Programmers wrote in machine code.

Not FORTRAN. Not RATFOR. Not, even, assembly language.

Machine Code.

Raw, unadorned, inscrutable hexadecimal numbers.

Directly.

Lest a whole new generation of programmers

grow up in ignorance of this glorious past,

I feel duty-bound to describe,

as best I can through the generation gap,

how a Real Programmer wrote code.

I'll call him Mel,

because that was his name.

It goes on from there. You get the idea, though: The programmer is so good that he doesn't need to use a human-created language; he writes directly in the complex system of 0s and 1s that computers understand. You can read the full version at http://www.cs.utah.edu/~elb/folklore/afs-paper/node4.html.

From Hacker to Crusader

Richard Stallman started out as a programmer at the Artificial Intelligence Laboratory (AI Lab) of the Massachusetts Institute of Technology. He could be called a hacker because, like other programmers in the innovative lab, he was adept at improving existing programs and making hardware such as printers work better. One of his innovations involved an improvement in the code that allowed one of the first network laser printers to run smoothly. In that environment, programmers commonly worked on each other's code, improving it by sharing their work freely with one another. This ethic—the notion of sharing work freely so it can be improved cooperatively—is one that Stallman has held onto his entire career. Instead of working as a lone hacker, however, Stallman (shown in Figure 7-1) became an activist. Ever since, he has crusaded for "open source" content in computing, whether it's software, text, or whatever.

As you can tell from his personal Web site (http://www.stallman.org/), Stallman feels strongly about a lot of issues, and he is not afraid to do something about them. He founded the GNU's Not Unix (GNU) Project, which is dedicated to distributing software freely and which created the General Public License (GPL), a legal device used to keep computer software owned by the community of its users rather than a for-profit company. He is also the original president of the Free Software Foundation and winner of the 1990 MacArthur Fellowship (commonly known as a "genius grant"). He represents one type of hacker: the one dedicated to keeping information freely available.

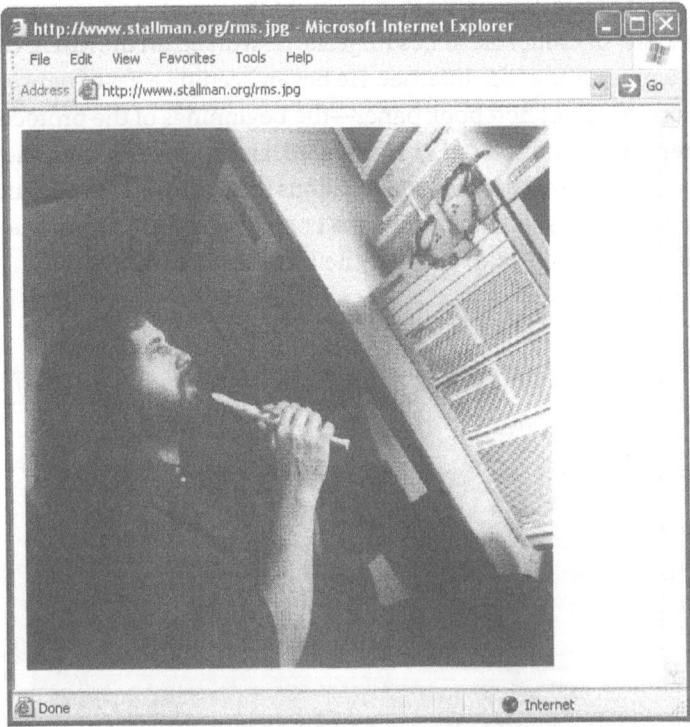

Figure 7-1. Richard Stallman: Hacker turned open-source crusader[1]

The Internet's "Heavenly Father"

Jonathan Postel, another figure regarded with reverence by Webmasters, network administrators, programmers, and anyone associated with the infrastructure of the Internet, was hardly a "hacker" in the destructive sense. He was an innovator and a pivotal figure in the development of the Internet. He was called by the *Economist* magazine "the Heavenly Father of the Internet" because of his flowing beard (shown in Figure 7-2) and sandals, which recall another, much earlier heavenly Father.

It's hard to explain why Postel was an important figure in the history of the Internet without starting to throw around the kinds of jargon that will put most people to sleep—words such as "IP addresses" and acronyms such as "TCP/IP." But you don't really need to get lost in the details. Think of someone such as James Madison, who wrote much of the U.S. Constitution but doesn't get a lot of credit for it. Postel, similarly, wrote or edited many of the proposals called Request for Comments (RFCs) that created the Internet and the features that enable it to operate more or

---

1. http://www.stallman.org/rms.jpg

less the same way, from network to network, all around the world. As a graduate student at the University of California at Los Angeles, he worked on the ARPANET project, which was a precursor of the Internet. He began keeping a list of network protocol numbers on a scrap of notebook paper—the beginnings of the protocol system that the Internet depends on today. He created, among other things, the Domain Name System (DNS) that enables organizations to have their own domains on the Internet, such as microsoft.com and apress.com. Vinton Cerf, one of the early developers of the Internet, said, "He was the Internet's Boswell and its technical conscience."[2]

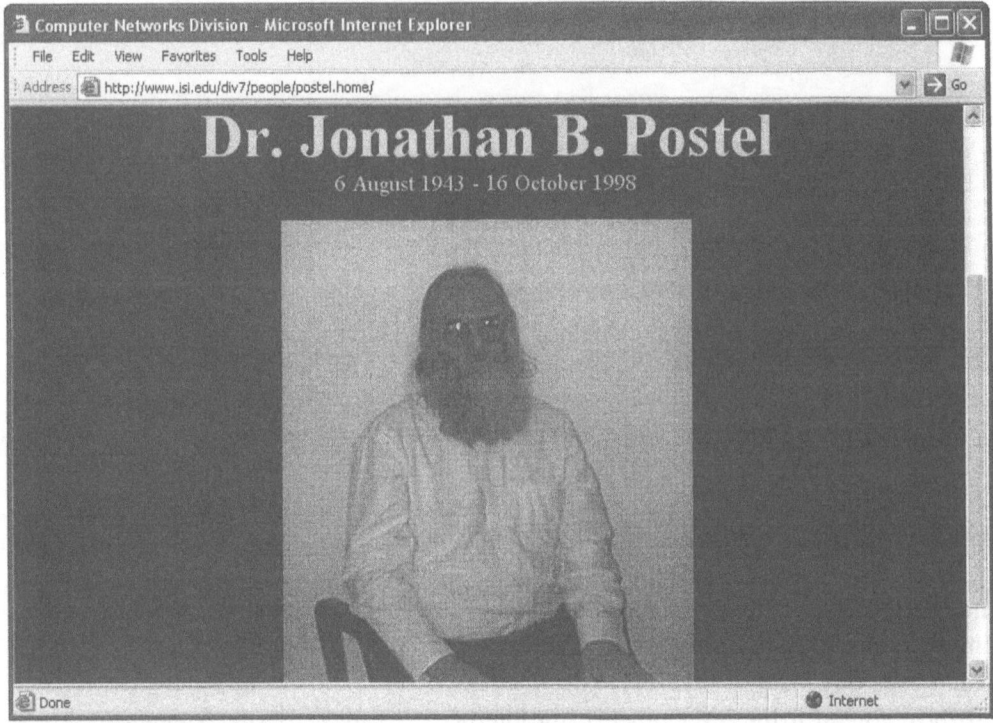

Figure 7-2. Heavenly Father of the Internet: Jon Postel [2]

Linus Offers Software Minus the Cost

If you've ever had to trudge to the computer store to lay down the big bucks for the latest version of Microsoft Windows or the newest edition of Mac OS, you know that operating systems are big business. They are developed by lots of programmers

---

2. http://www.isi.edu/dv7/people/postel.home/

who work for corporations. Those programmers work under Non-Disclosure Agreements (NDAs) that prohibit them from telling anyone outside the corporation about their work. The programmers are paid for their work by consumers like us, who are (presumably) happy to purchase the new-and-improved software in return for all the work the corporation's employees have done.

That's how the software distribution system works most of the time. A 21-year-old college student in Helsinki, Finland, had a different idea that ended up turning the software world upside down, however. He had just purchased his first personal computer, which ran Microsoft's MS-DOS operating system. He quickly grew dissatisfied using a system that seemed to be incapable of running his favorite programs without crashing.

Just for fun (that's the title of his biography, by the way), Linus Torvalds wanted to see if he could improve on one of the operating systems that was already widely in use, Unix. Torvalds (shown in Figure 7-3) sat down and wrote his own operating system. Rather than employing a team of programmers and forming a corporation that would make him lots of money, however, Torvalds posted his entire operating system in the open, on the Internet. He invited other programmers to improve his operating system. And they did. The improvements were also posted online.

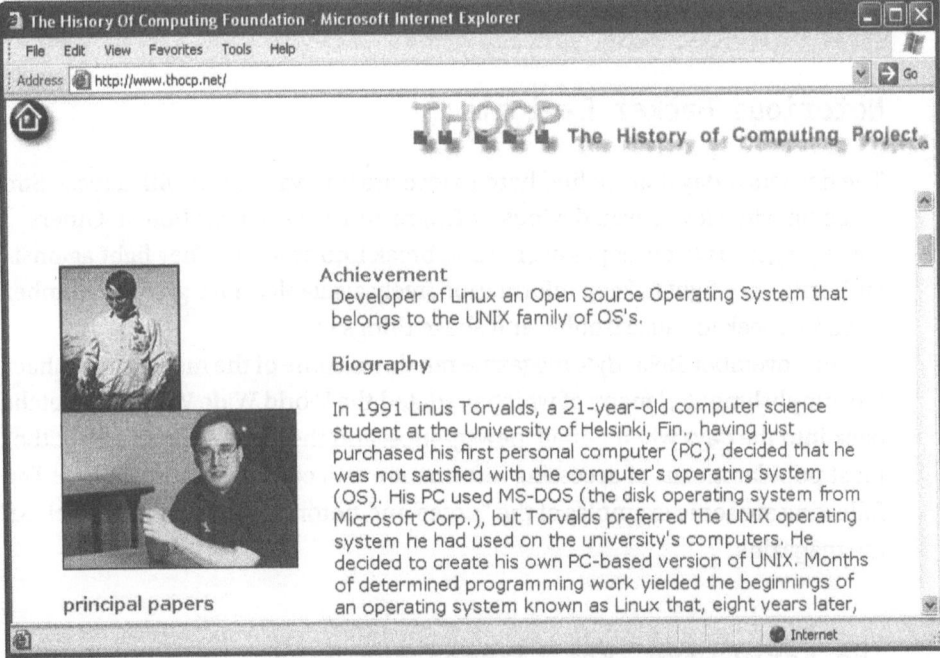

Figure 7-3. Linus Torvalds has a page in the biographies of computer pioneers presented on the History of Computing Foundation Web site.[3]

---

3.   http://www.thocp.net/

NOTE The History of Computing Foundation's Web site is at http://www.thocp.net/.

The Linux operating system, as it came to be known, was developed by a loose committee of volunteers sharing their work online—a system of software development and distribution that has come to be known as *open source*. Linux spread like wildfire around the world and is now a legitimate competitor to Windows. (The version of Linux known as Red Hat looks more like Windows all the time, as a matter of fact.)

By sharing his initial work and maintaining a low-key attitude, Linus Torvalds is revered by programmers everywhere. And he ended up doing all right financially, as well, especially after he moved to the San Francisco Bay Area to work for Transmeta, a company cofounded by Microsoft cofounder Paul Allen. The Linux operating system is regarded as secure and efficient, and it rarely crashes because it has been developed and improved by a huge army of volunteers working together. Torvalds has been portrayed as a sort of David who is out to slay Bill Gates, the Goliath of Microsoft, but he has always said he is a programmer who simply hates to use poorly written computer code.

Notorious Hacker Exploits

The hackers today that we find hard to love are innovators but with a twist. Some come up with clever, even devious, software and ways to distribute it. Others use their genius to crack passwords and break into systems. They fight against authority, they fight to keep information freely available, and a growing number of them just seek to cause trouble and shake things up.

In November 1995, *Byte* magazine ran down some of the more notable hacker "accomplishments," many of which predated the World Wide Web and stretched back into the days when e-mail, newsgroups, and the Gopher service were the most popular means of accessing information and communicating online. The following are some examples of the "noted and notorious" hacker feats as cited by the magazine.

The Early Worm That Flipped the Bird

On November 2, 1988, at 8 p.m., a graduate student at Cornell University named Robert Tappan Morris sent an application that he had written out into the Internet.

The program was called a *worm*—a program that could act on its own, performing functions that Morris had designed into it. The worm also did one other thing that worms have been known ever since—it kept duplicating itself over and over, taking up disk space and slowing down network traffic.

The Morris worm, as it has come to be known, was one of the first instances of a malicious program that proliferated by means of the Internet. As the worm multiplied, it began filling up memory space and consuming computer resources until computer systems began failing. Days of work were required in order to remove the worm and undo the damage. A newly formed security organization called CERT (which stands for Computer Emergency Response Team) was formed to deal with any future security threats. This group, and others, are kept busy with a constant stream of viruses, worms, and other harmful programs that circulate online.

Unfortunately for Morris, he became the first individual to be tried and convicted by means of the computer Fraud and Abuse Act of 1986. However, he was sentenced to three years of probation, 400 hours of community service, and a $10,000 fine.

After the storm of negative publicity and trouble that resulted from the release of the worm, hackers got back at Morris, in a subtle way, by changing his network username from RTM to RTFM. The acronym RTFM is well-known among computer professionals; it stands for Read the F***ing Manual.

Morris, by the way, has gone on to do extensive research on routers and switches—hardware that is designed to do the opposite of the Morris worm and keep traffic flowing smoothly from machine to machine on a computer network. It's unfortunate that his name is continually associated with the worm he created; he went on to earn a doctorate degree from Harvard University and is on the faculty at the Massachusetts Institute of Technology.

Hacker Quest Starts When Things Don't Add Up

Clifford Stoll wasn't an accountant. He was a systems administrator at Lawrence Berkeley Laboratory. He noticed a 75-cent discrepancy in a computer account. The gap bothered him because the account was supposed to be defunct; yet it was being used by someone who appeared to be unauthorized—a hacker. The intruder was creating accounts on the system. Stoll could have ended the exploit by changing passwords and tightening access privileges. That would have been the easy way out. He decided to let the hacker continue to infiltrate the system to determine what was going on. Before long, Stoll realized that the hacker was using the account to gain access to military computer networks, including some run by the U.S. Department of Defense. Stoll could see that the hacker was a spy, apparently looking for classified military information.

Because the hacker would only strike sporadically, the tracking process took months, even years. Doggedly, Stoll was able to follow the hacker by setting up programs that would cause him to be paged whenever the intruder entered the system. Stoll tracked the connection to a network in McLean, Virginia, and ultimately to West Germany. When Stoll set out some harmless files as bait and induced the intruder to provide a name and an address, the FBI and CIA joined the hunt. A group of young German men was originally apprehended. Stoll wrote about the hunt in *The Cuckoo's Egg: Tracking a Spy Through the Maze of Computer Espionage* (Doubleday, 1989), an early and entertaining tale of hacking and computer security. The book was on the *New York Times* bestseller list for four months and prompted hackers to attempt to break into his computer. The entertaining book contains lots of useful information, including the following recipe for chocolate chip cookies:

- 2 eggs.

- 1 cup brown sugar.

- ½ cup regular sugar.

- 2 sticks softened butter.

- Fold in 2 ¼ cups flour, ½ teaspoon salt, 1 teaspoon baking soda, and 1 tablespoon of vanilla (and 3 tablespoons of cocoa if wanted).

- Add 2 cups of chocolate chips.

- Bake at 375 degrees for 10 minutes.

A truly colorful character, Stoll is also known for manufacturing Klein bottles (shown in Figure 7-4), amazing structures that are described as "a single-sided bottle with no boundary. Its inside is its outside. It contains itself." Find out more at http://www.kleinbottle.com/.

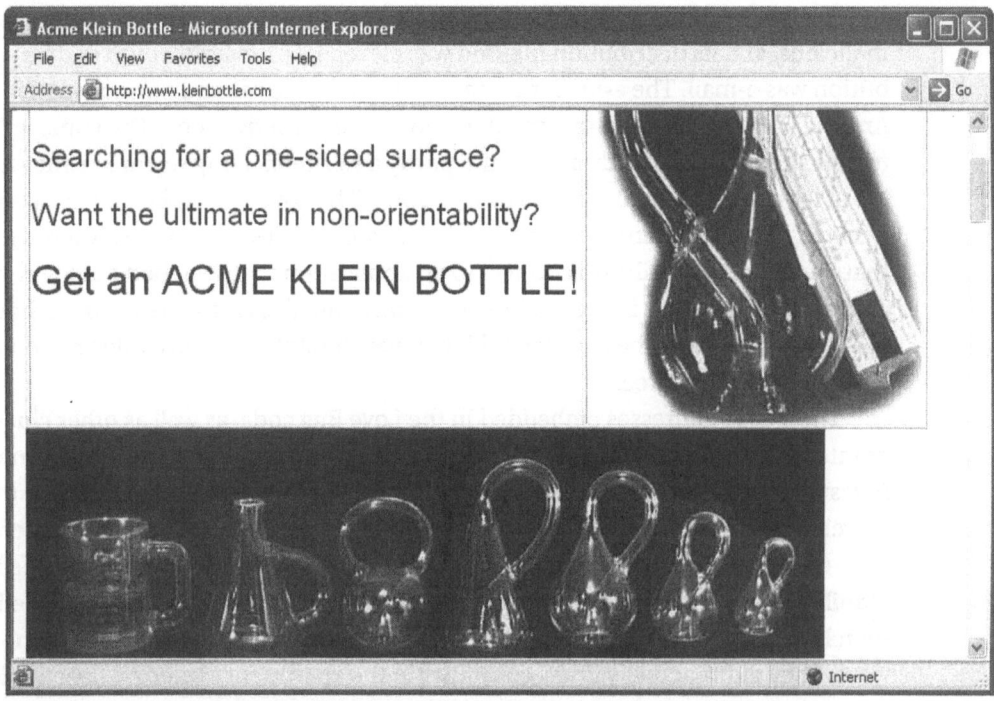

Figure 7-4. Clifford Stoll is a bottle maker as well as hacker tracker, astronomer, and author.[4]

How Do You Say I Love You? V-I-R-U-S

What would you do if you received an e-mail message bearing the subject line ILOVEYOU and if it appeared to come from someone you know personally? You would open the attachment it bore just out of curiosity if nothing more, wouldn't you? That's what millions of unsuspecting victims did beginning in early May 2000. By doing so, they infected their own computers with the single most destructive and virulent virus ever released on the Internet, which came to be known as the Love Bug. Those infected included computer users in the Pentagon and British Parliament, as well as millions of individual users around the world. It cost billions of dollars in lost business and computer repair, and yet its author was never prosecuted.

---

4. http://www.kleinbottle.com/

The Love Bug virus wasn't especially complex or even well written, but it was malicious, and its distribution method was clever. Its primary method of distribution was e-mail. The e-mail message contained a file called an *attachment*. Anyone who clicked the attachment let loose its destructive code. The code, in technical terms, was partly a virus and partly a self-replicating worm like the Morris worm mentioned earlier in this chapter. The Love Bug replicated itself on a network like a worm and destroyed and manipulated files like a virus. Not only that, but it had the ability to connect to an application that searched out login names and passwords in the victim's own computer files and e-mailed them back to the virus's author. The hacker could then use the stolen account information to surf the Internet for free.

The e-mail addresses embedded in the Love Bug code, as well as other clues, pointed to an individual who was a member of a computer club in the Philippines. Investigators traced the dial-up phone numbers used to upload the viruses to the servers used by Internet Service Provider (ISP) Sky Internet. The phone numbers were traced back to an apartment using Caller ID. Before long, a bank employee in Manila was taken into custody along with his girlfriend. Investigators had obtained a search warrant to look for the computer that they thought was the source of the virus. They didn't actually find a computer in the apartment shared by the couple, however.

But authorities were hampered by the lack of any Philippine law that covers computer crimes. One was soon passed, but it didn't apply to the Love Bug's creator. Later that year, the girlfriend's brother, Onel de Guzman, admitted that he may have "accidentally" released the virus. But he maintained that he was not its author. Ultimately, the individual responsible for the most costly virus in history went unpunished because of the difficulty of definitely determining that a particular individual was the author of a particular bit of computer code. Polls taken in the Philippines discovered that the majority of the population expressed pride at being citizens of the country where the Love Bug was born. Asiaweek.com interviewed de Guzman (shown in Figure 7-5) and named him one of their "Top 50," reporting that his friends had taken to calling him the Terminator.

Figure 7-5. Onel de Guzman said he may have "accidentally released" the Love Bug.[5]

De Guzman was charged with theft and credit card fraud, but the charges were eventually dropped. Worse, the success of the Love Bug quickly spawned copycat versions with names such as Joke and Mother's Day. The next year, another virus was disseminated by e-mail with a memorable come-on: The message purported to have an attachment that was a photo of the 19-year-old Russian tennis star Anna Kournikova. When curious people clicked the attachment, they saw no photo, but they unleashed a virus. A Dutch hacker was later arrested on charges of damaging property and computer programs for that prank. Today, computer users around the world are admonished not to open attachments borne by e-mail messages they don't recognize and didn't ask for, thanks to the Love Bug and its descendants.

---

5. http://www.asiaweek.com/asiaweek/features/power50.2001/p11.html

Script Kiddie Brings Down Internet Giants

Hackers come in many different varieties. A special variety called the *script kiddie* is a young person who breaks into computer systems to wreak havoc. One of the most serious ways to cause trouble on the Internet is to flood a computer called a *server* with thousands of connection attempts, causing it to slow down and eventually cease to function. It's the digital equivalent of a telephone switchboard being flooded with more phone calls than the operators can handle. If enough computers try to connect to a single Web site all at the same time, it, too, can overload and stop processing requests. Some hackers are able to place software on computers they are able to infiltrate around the Internet. The software causes those computers to attack a Web server by trying to connect all at the same time: It's called a Denial of Service attack.

 NOTE Most Web servers have firewalls and other security systems installed that are able to detect Denial of Service attacks and cut them short.

In February 2000, one of the most severe Denial of Service attacks recorded stopped traffic on many of the biggest Web sites, including those of Amazon.com, eBay, and Yahoo! The culprit turned out to be the 14-year-old Canadian script kiddie known only as MafiaBoy, who was arrested in April 2000. In January 2001, he pleaded guilty to 58 charges related to the attacks. During his sentencing hearing, his lawyer argued that he was attempting to help the companies that were attacked by exposing security flaws in their systems. He was eventually sentenced to eight months in a juvenile detention center.

"Cyberterrorist" Wanted to Really Shake Up the System

Digital cash, encryption, and anonymity: They sound like some of the security-related topics that many individuals were concerned about after the September 11, 2001, terrorist attacks. But Jim Bell was thinking about these concepts nearly a decade before. He reached the conclusion that they could be used not to preserve things such as government but to destroy it.

In a notorious Internet essay called "Assassination Politics," Bell proposed the idea that if people could anonymously send digital cash to a central organization, they could cause the death of officeholders with whom they were dissatisfied. The concept seems "out there," but the government took it seriously. They labeled him a techno-terrorist, and, in 1997, he pleaded guilty to charges of interfering with IRS agents and using false Social Security numbers. In 2000, he was arrested again for stalking a federal agent. In 2001, he was sentenced to serve ten years in federal prison.

 TIP   You can read a version of "Assassination Politics" at http://www.jya.com/ap.htm.

Now They're on Our Side...Aren't They?

They achieved a sort of notoriety by using their expertise. But natural gifts can be used for good or not-so-good purposes. They got in trouble by finding new ways to make money or break into networks. Instead of being on the lam or on the witness stand, they're now on the Web—and you can send them your money if you want to buy their books or take their advice.

Hacker No. 1 Makes a Comeback

A few lucky people are so prominent in their chosen fields of endeavor that they are associated with them. Think serial killer, and the names Jack the Ripper and John Wayne Gacy come to mind. Think terrorist, and the words Osama Bin Laden pop into your consciousness, whether you like it or not. When asked to name a hacker, most people in the know will immediately name Kevin Mitnick—a legacy he may or may not be proud but one that he'll have to live with until he does something else just as notable.

The world's most notorious hacker, Mitnick has a long and storied history. Much of his story was documented in a book called *Takedown* (Warner Books, 1996), which was written by computer security expert Tsutomu Shimomura. After Mitnick infiltrated Shimomura's own computer, Shimomura helped authorities track down Mitnick. You can read that very entertaining book for details about Mitnick; a brief summary follows.

TIP Shimomura's story about Mitnick's capture is the subject of its own Web site at http://www.takedown.com/. For the other side of the story of Mitnick's pursuit and eventual arrest, read *The Fugitive Game: Online with Kevin Mitnick* by Jonathan Littman (Little Brown & Company, 1996). This book was based on more than 50 hours of phone conversations with Mitnick while he was hiding from authorities.

Mitnick was sentenced in 1989 for stealing the VMS operating system from Digital Equipment Corporation, software that was valued by DEC at $1 million. He served a year in jail and was then sentenced to three years of probation. He then attacked the San Diego Supercomputer Center systems. Mitnick was arrested by the FBI on February 15, 1995, in Raleigh, North Carolina. He was held without bail for more than four years. He spent some of that time in solitary confinement because authorities feared he could manage to hack into a phone or other electronic device and wreak havoc. He was finally released from jail in January 2000.

He has long been rumored to have cracked into the North American Air Defense (NORAD) Command computer, which supposedly inspired the movie *War Games*. (He has denied this allegation.)

He has a talent for social engineering—disguising his identity and inventing a plausible tale to fool network administrators and other personnel into giving out passwords and other confidential details needed to access network resources. During his jail term, he was forbidden to dial the telephone himself because of his history of misusing cellular phones, turning conventional phones into pay phones, and performing other phone pranks. Mitnick was banned until January 2003 from using a computer or acting as a consultant. What's he doing now that he's free to be online once again?

He's been pretty busy: He played the role of a CIA computer expert in an episode of the ABC television series *Alias*. He hosted a radio show and wrote a book called *The Art of Deception: Controlling the Human Element of Security* (John Wiley & Sons, 2003) that tells people how to protect against a subject he knows well: social engineering.

And We Have a Winner: Kevin Poulsen

Kevin Poulsen, who called himself Dark Dante, had clearly defined motives for his telephone network hacking. Unlike hackers whose motives seem unclear, Poulsen was always goal oriented. For instance, in 1990 he hijacked Pacific Bell's telephone switching network. Why? He wanted to ensure that he would be the 102nd caller to a radio station in Los Angeles so he would win the Porsche sports car they were giving away—and he did win. He used the same trick to win a trip to Hawaii and thousands of dollars in cash. When he was caught, he was sentenced to prison for five years. He had been the first hacker charged with espionage, but those charges were eventually dropped.

Poulsen was the subject of a book by Jonathan Littman called *The Watchman: The Twisted Life and Crimes of Serial Hacker Kevin Poulsen* (Little Brown & Company, 1997). He became a writer for online publications such as ZDNet and SecurityFocus, where he kept track of the exploits of hackers and products designed to thwart them.

Teenage Stock Whiz Trades Way to Consulting Gig

As a teenager, Jonathan Lebed was an overachiever. The problem was, he did his achieving outside of class, connecting to stock exchanges using his father's stock trading account. At the tender age of 15, the New Jersey teenager didn't just buy and sell stocks, either. After buying some stocks, he would visit online chat rooms and leave comments and rumors about how well those same stocks were expected to do. When others purchased the stocks he had talked up, he would then sell them for a profit. And it was quite a profit for a high school student: It was estimated that he made as much as $800,000 in stock market trades. He took to carrying a black briefcase to his high school classes, and his friends consulted him for stock recommendations. He may not be a hacker, but many regard him as a sort of Internet hero.

The U.S. Securities and Exchange Commission didn't approve of Jonathan's hobby. They made him return $280,000—which still left him with a tidy profit. He also gained some notoriety for his exploits. Debates raged online as to whether he had actually violated the law. The BBC did a news story on him, as did the CBS news show *60 Minutes*.

Lebed has also been able to parlay his reputation for stock market success into a consulting business. The home page of his Web site Lebed.biz (http://lebed.biz/, shown in Figure 7-6) contains a link to what it calls a "book that was written about Jonathan Lebed." Actually, the book by Michael Lewis, *Next: The Future Just Happened* (W. W. Norton & Company, 2002), discusses Lebed as well as other Internet-related stories. Lebed.biz charges members a $200 annual fee to get profiles of stocks that Lebed recommends as having growth potential. You can consult him yourself—and by the way, at this writing he is only 18.

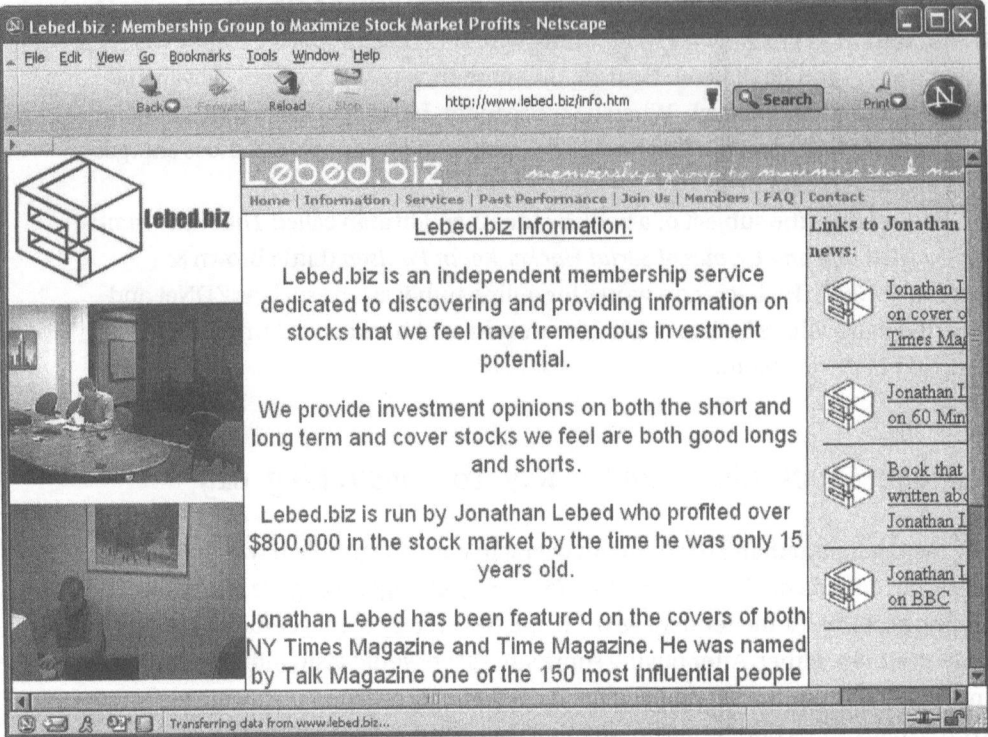

Figure 7-6. This teenage stock trader will give you "buy" and "sell" recommendations for a fee.[6]

Of Cyberpunks and Cyberhavens

Steve Jackson Games is an Austin, Texas, company that makes computer games, including the popular Hacker series of packages (see Figure 7-7). In 1990, the company made only board games that simulated various computer activities and experiences, and it published books. One of their early games, GURPS Cyberpunk, attracted attention from an unlikely source. The company's offices were, in fact, raided by armed agents of the U.S. Secret Service on March 1, 1990. The Feds confiscated several computers, printers, hard disks, and the game and associated book-in-progress because they considered them a threat to national security.

---

6.   http://www.lebed.biz/info.htm

Figure 7-7. The Hacker game creator was accused of being one by the U.S. Secret Service.[7]

NOTE   You can read about the story in detail at http://www.sjgames.com/SS/.

Initially, news reports about the raid said the Secret Service had raided a ring of computer hackers. Only months later did the company receive an affidavit stating that the author of the program had discussed it with computer security experts who described themselves as computer crackers. After three years, a federal court ruled that the raid had been illegal and unjustified and awarded damages and attorney fees to the game company.

7. http://www.sjgames.com/hacker/

Steve Jackson Games went on to produce some highly successful games that use computer hacking as the theme. And as a result, the Electronic Frontier Foundation (EFF) was formed to guard against just this sort of infringement of civil liberties.

The word "freedom" comes up a bit in connection with hackers, programmers, and a peculiar category of techno-geeks called *cyberpunks*. Cyberpunks aren't hackers, exactly; they're people who live, eat, sleep, and breathe computers and computing. And they just want to be free. Well, a group of American cyberpunks has set up the world's smallest "data haven," a place where anyone who wants to store sensitive information can do so free of the Internet-related regulations and taxations being imposed (or at least considered) by countries around the world.

HavenCo (http://www.havenco.com/) is located on Sealand, a grandiose-sounding name for a former fortress the size of a basketball court that rests atop two cement caissons in the North Sea. The facility was originally erected about six miles off the coast of England for the purpose of shooting down Nazi aircraft during World War II. HavenCo is intended to be a place where organizations can locate their e-mail or other servers without having governments scrutinize the traffic that passes through them. In an era where the U.S. government is scrutinizing all sorts of databases in the hunt for potential terrorists, this is a real concern.

Sealand (see Figure 7-8) has a storied history for such a tiny island. The platform was abandoned until 1966 when a onetime British Army major named Roy Bates landed on and claimed it as an independent nation that would have its own flag, stamps, and currency. A 1968 court decision in England recognized the island as a sovereign nation. The founders of HavenCo had to reach an agreement with Bates, who is otherwise known as the "crown prince" of Sealand. Bates's son and heir apparent of Sealand, Michael, is the chief logistics officer for HavenCo.

"The Sealand Government is ideal for Web business, as there are no direct reporting or registration requirements," boasts the HavenCo Web site. In other words, it's a place that extols one of the ultimate hacker goals: freedom.

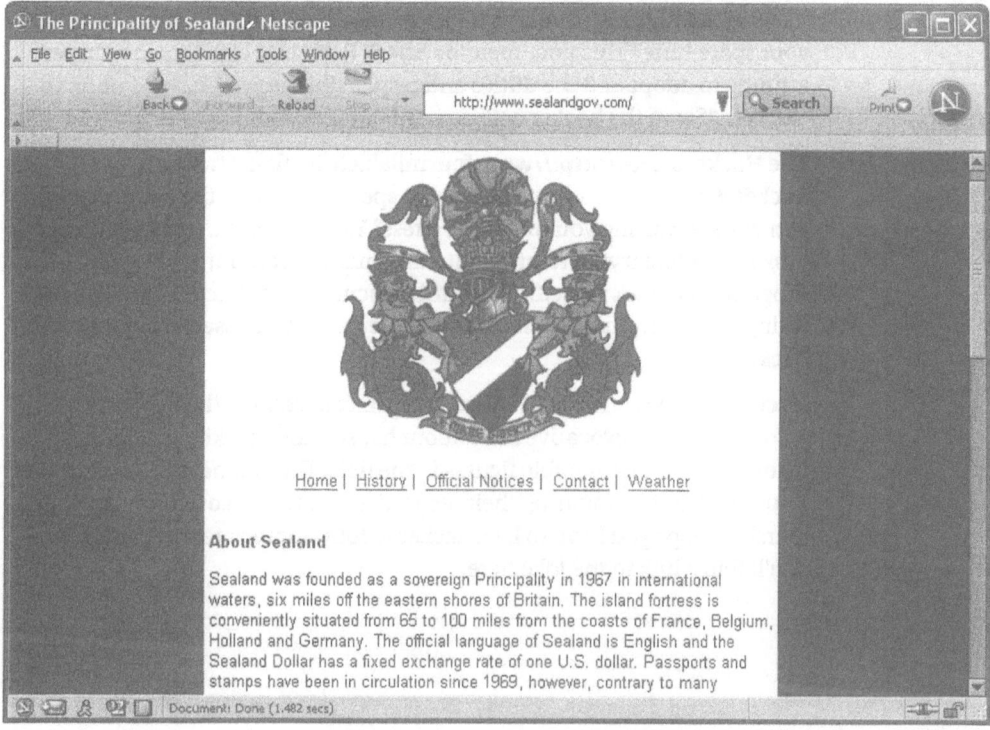

Figure 7-8. The coat of arms of Sealand bears the motto that means "From the sea, freedom."[8]

Random Googling

The Internet contains countless Web sites, chat rooms, newsgroups, and other resources related to hacking and hackers. The following list contains a few I found noteworthy—a random sampling of sites that turned up after searching for the term "hacker" on the search service Google (http://www.google.com/):

- **The Hacker House Legend (http://www.hackerhouse.com/legend1.htm):** Okay, it has nothing to do with computers, but it's a great story about a haunted house in North Carolina that has been the scene of disappearances and mishaps for several centuries.

---

8.   http://www.sealandgov.com/

- **How to Become a Hacker (http://www.catb.org/~esr/faqs/ hacker-howto.html):** Looking for a new career or just something to do in your spare time? This document by Eric S. Raymond explains the proper attitude to adopt and the duties and responsibilities you have to observe (such as "Serve the hacker culture itself").

- **The Hacker's Diet (http://www.fourmilab.ch/hackdiet/www/ hackdiet.html):** You say the hours you spend in front of the computer late at night are causing you too much stress? You say you can't help eating junk food while trying to break into that military computer network? " Programmer, hack thyself," this quirky document instructs—it's all about losing weight, from the perspective of the harried, stressed-out computer hacker.

- **Hacker's Wisdom (http://www.ee.ryerson.ca:8080/~elf/hack/):** A collection of provocative links about hackers and hacking, including jokes, legends, and notable figures in the field. Did you hear the one about Jesus and Satan comparing their respective abilities as computer programmers? Perhaps you have to be a hacker to fully appreciate the humor, but you'll find a link to the joke here.

CHAPTER 8

Spam and Other E-Mail Follies in Babylon

EVER HAVE THE DESIRE to open your eyes first thing in the morning and immediately have some folks you've never met tempt you with hot sex, allergy cures, a smaller waistline, and (whether you are male or female) a 12-inch penis, guaranteed? That's the glory of spam, a stream of unwanted e-mail that moves as swiftly, floods us as frequently, and is as constant (and, many fear, as unstoppable) as the mighty Mississippi.

Spam, as you probably already know, refers to the unwanted, unasked-for e-mail offers sent to anyone with a valid e-mail address. It's frequently referred to as UCE, which stands for Unsolicited Commercial E-Mail. Spam gets its name from the canned meat product created by the Hormel Foods Corporation in Austin, Minnesota, in 1937. SPAM (the meat product, that is) was immortalized in a sketch by the British comedy group Monty Python. In the sketch, a couple enters the Green Midget Café and are unable to order anything to eat without getting multiple helpings of SPAM along with it. It often seems like e-mail works the same way. You can't sign up for an e-mail account, or for any service or product you see advertised on the Web, without having tons of spam sent to your inbox.

Plenty of books (some written by yours truly) explain what spam is and how to reduce it. If you're like me, you don't pay any more attention than you have to when you select and delete the message. This chapter gives you a safe, entertaining way to examine some colorful spam e-mail you'd probably ignore otherwise. You'll find out who sends spam, why they do it, and discover some of the creative ways artists are putting spam to good use.

 NOTE   Don't use the term "e-mail" in France lest you run afoul of the language police. In June 2003, the French Culture Ministry banned the use of the term "e-mail" in government documents in favor of the new French word "courriel." Not everyone has embraced the new term, however. Some French Internet service providers said they would not change their own references to the term "e-mail" because "e-mail" is now too thoroughly assimilated to be changed.

...But First, a Word About the "Other" Spam

The story of SPAM began in 1937, when a Minnesota food processing plant executive named Jay C. Hormel created a canned meat product composed of pork shoulder and ham and literally spiced up with a set of secret spices. He then held a contest to name the product. Kenneth Daigneau, a relative of a Hormel executive as well as an actor, was awarded a $100 prize for coming up with the immortal term "spam." (It's not a very imaginative creation, however, when you consider that the product's previous name was Hormel Spiced Ham.)

NOTE A very entertaining non-Hormel SPAM page (http://www.modernsurf.com/spam/) posits the theory that SPAM was actually created in 1927 when the Hormel company had to find a way to deal with tons of unused pork shoulder on its hands; the site claims they decided to can it and encase it in gelatin to preserve it, which led to what we know today as SPAM.

Over the years, SPAM has gained a lot of notoriety—some positive, some poking fun at it. Russian Premier Nikita Khrushchev credited SPAM with helping to keep his troops alive during World War II. According to the SPAM FAQ (http://www.spam.com/sp/sp_fq.htm), Hawaiians love SPAM and eat more of it than any other U.S. state (it goes really well with pineapple rings, don't you know?).

You can show your love of SPAM in many ways. You can enter an annual Best SPAM Recipe competition at your local state fair. You can attend events such as the SPAM Jam, which was held on Waikiki Beach in 2003 (see Figure 8-1). Find out more by joining the official SPAM Fan Club at http://www.spam.com/fc.htm.

TIP Don't miss the chance to take a virtual tour of the SPAM Museum in Austin, Minnesota (home of the Hormel Foods Corporation). Visitors to the real brick-and-mortar (or more likely, aluminum, in keeping with SPAM's container) museum enter through a doorway that's been painted to look like a huge can of SPAM. The entrance is depicted on the museum's home page at http://www.roadsideamerica.com/attract/MNAUSspam.html.

Figure 8-1. The Hormel Foods Corporation presents buckets full of entertaining information about their spiced ham product on the official SPAM Web site.[1]

The Hormel Foods Corporation appears to be tolerant when it comes to the use of the term "spam" to describe e-mail messages offering "hard-core porn and the like. But the company (which holds the trademark to the food product name SPAM) objects to anyone attempting to trademark a SPAM-related term. In 1997, Hormel protested when bulk e-mailer Sanford Wallace began taking publicity photos of himself with cans of SPAM and attempted to register the domain names spamford.com and spamford.net. In 2002, Hormel attempted to block trademark applications by a company called SpamArrest.

A statement on the Hormel Web site (http://www.spam.com/ci/ci_in.htm) reads as follows: "This slang term does not affect the strength of our trademark SPAM. We do not object to use of this slang term to describe UCE (unsolicited commercial e-mail), although we do object to the use of our product image in association with that term."

---

1. http://www.spam.com/

TIP SPAM, the processed meat product, is the subject of virtually endless attention on the Internet. Dan Garcia's Spam Homepage (http://www.cs.berkeley.edu/~ddgarcia/spam.html) is a good place to start. It contains links to the Spam Carving Contest and includes poems celebrating SPAM, photos of Cream of SPAM soup, a NASCAR race car advertising SPAM, and much more than you probably ever wanted to know about everyone's favorite gelatinized canned meat delicacy.

Kings and Queens of Spam

The title "King of Spam" seems to be in high demand among entrepreneurs. Over the years, a variety of individuals have been called the King or Queen of Spam because of their propensity in sending as many unsolicited commercial messages as possible to as many individuals as possible. *USA Today* estimated in 2003 that as many as two million spam e-mail messages would be sent that year—roughly 300 for every individual on earth. About 90 percent of those messages are believed to come from 150 big-time spammers. The problem with spam, though, is that it is accepted by a small number of consumers. But e-mail is so inexpensive to transmit that, even if a few individuals respond to a pitch that was sent to millions of recipients, it becomes profitable for the sender and his or her advertisers.

Big-time spammers have a particular image, which may or may not be deserved. The image calls for them observe the following questionable behavior patterns:

- Gather as many legitimate e-mail addresses as possible by obtaining the e-mail addresses of people who have taken out online subscriptions, buying e-mail lists, or using programs to scour the Web for e-mail addresses openly published in the body of Web pages.

- Hide behind fake e-mail addresses that "bounce back" e-mail when someone tries to contact them.

- Conceal their geographic location by routing bulk e-mail through foreign servers, making it difficult or impossible to trace.

- Do not give consumers the chance to "opt out" of mailing lists.

Although I don't want to give these people any more attention than they deserve, it is worth studying them in order to learn about their motives and to determine why spam is so prevalent. The following are stories about a few individuals who have either dubbed themselves spam "royalty" or who have been given that dubious distinction.

Early Spam King Reappears in New Guise

One of the early individuals to be dubbed the King of Spam, Sanford Wallace, gave up his throne not for the woman he loved but because he was bankrupt. Originally, Wallace pioneered the dubious field of junk fax solicitation. When this practice was outlawed by the U.S. Congress, Wallace moved to junk e-mail solicitation. His companies, Promo Enterprises and the infamous Cyber Promotions, used to send out as many as 30 million pieces of junk e-mail every day.

For a while, Wallace (shown in Figure 8-2) was defiant about criticism of his activities. In response to being called "spamford" by antispam protestors, he registered the domain name spamford.com. But his ventures also piled up more than $3 million in debts. EarthLink alone won a $2 million judgment against Wallace for using its servers to distribute unsolicited e-mail advertisements. That was in 1998. In 1999, Wallace returned with a new ploy that he claimed was legal. After portraying himself as an antispam activist, Wallace started an opt-in e-mail solicitation service SmartBot. But SmartBot disappeared, and with it, Wallace did too. At least for now.

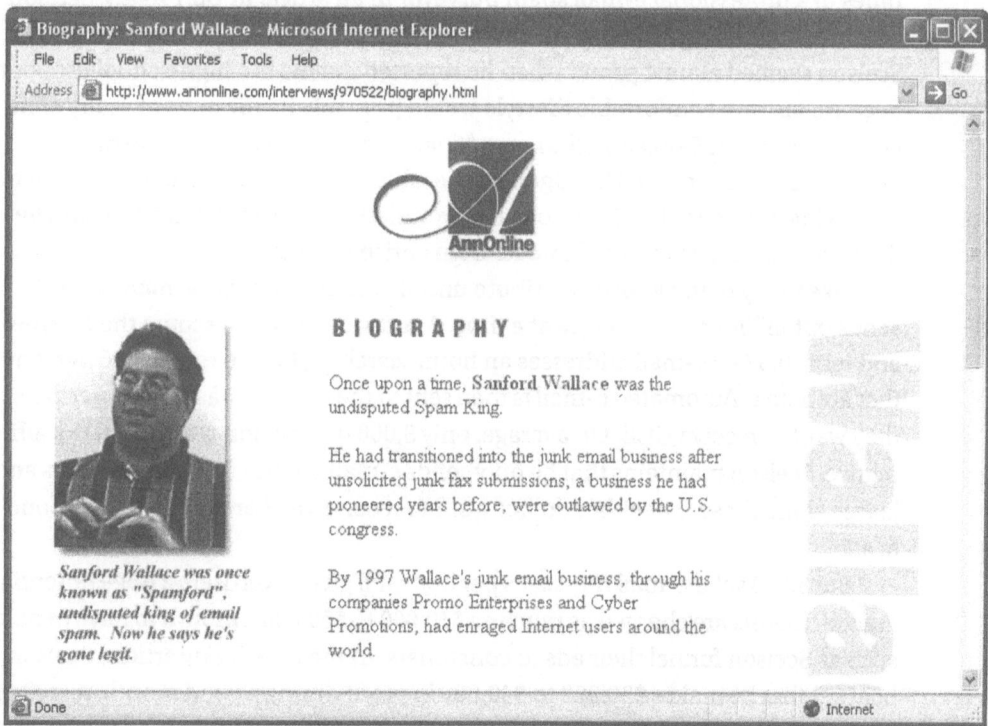

Figure 8-2. An early spam king who supposedly went straight: Sanford Wallace [2]

---

2. http//www.annonline.com/interviews/970522/biography.html

NOTE The Internet service provider EarthLink has been one of the biggest opponents of spam. EarthLink won $16.4 million in federal court against Howard Carmack, dubbed the Buffalo Spammer, who allegedly used stolen credit cards, stolen identity information, and other illegal activities to purchase hundreds of e-mail accounts that he then used to send out spam. In 2002, EarthLink won a $25 million judgment against K. C. Smith, who allegedly used EarthLink servers to send out as many as one billion spam e-mails.

"Cajun King of Spam" Speaks Out

Ronnie Scelson works out of his home in Slidell, Louisiana. He claims he does not purvey spam because he does not send out ads for sex, Viagra, or get-rich-quick schemes. The talkative Scelson, who apparently can't keep his mouth shut when given the chance to talk at length about himself, gave a rare insight into the life and times of a professional e-mail spam purveyor in an article in *USA Today*. Scelson admitted to sending out 60 to 70 million ads a day and two billion each month. Scelson seemed almost proud when he reported that he is a high-school dropout because his very comfortable lifestyle would probably be the envy of many of his classmates today. Being a well-known "Spam King" does have its drawbacks, however. He keeps a small handgun on the table next to his computer whenever he is working, for one thing. He also carries a variety of guns for protection, and he does have to field a variety of threats from antispam activists.

Like many of those who distribute unsolicited commercial e-mail, Scelson sends out millions of messages at a time. A software program scours the Internet and tests 165,000 e-mail addresses an hour, searching for the roughly 16 percent that are active. Automated e-mail is then sent to the accounts, asking subscribers if they want to receive UCE. On average, only 3,000 of 5 million respond in the affirmative. Scelson maintains that he only sends e-mail pitches to those accounts and leaves alone those that either do not want to receive UCE or that do not respond at all.

But 3,000 valid e-mail messages per hour still give advertisers a huge potential market. Clients are charged as much as $10,000 to $50,000 a month to have people such as Scelson funnel their ads to consumers. In the *USA Today* article, Scelson boasted that he makes $30,000 to $40,000 in profit during a good month. A staff of 16 part-time technicians helps Scelson fend off hack attacks from antispammers and maintain his far-flung operations.

Alan Ralsky, who has actually described himself as the King of Spam, doesn't maintain the pretense that he sends unsolicited e-mail in an "ethical" way.

He's quite upfront about many of his tactics. In 2002, he bragged to a *Detroit Free Press* reporter that he uses aliases, reroutes his e-mail through foreign servers, and reaps huge profits. The article, however, revealed details about his $740,000 mansion in the upscale Detroit suburb of West Bloomfield. The information enabled antispam activists to post his address online. Others signed Ralsky up for tons of junk mail to be sent to his home. It hasn't deterred Ralsky from continuing his highly profitable e-mail operations; at this writing, he was still listed as one of the Spamhaus Project's ROKSO database of "hard-core spam offenders" (http://www.spamhaus.org/rokso/index.lasso) when this was written.

The Spam That Reaches into Browser Toolbars

Here's a test: Open your copy of Microsoft Internet Explorer right now. Click the View menu, and then click Toolbars. Scan the various toolbars that are listed, and look for one called Xupiter. What, you ask, is Xupiter? It's a peculiar and, many would say, particularly insidious form of unsolicited advertising that worms its way into many users' copies of their Microsoft-created browser.

Xupiter makes its way into the browser interface in at least one way. When you visit certain Web sites allegedly run by a father and son team named Saeid and Daniel Yomtobian, you encounter a dialog box asking if you want to download the Xupiter toolbar. If you respond in the affirmative, you get the toolbar. Some, however, believe that the toolbar can somehow be downloaded without any participation by the user. Simply having the word Xupiter appear constantly in the View menu provides free advertising for Xupiter.com, a site that purveys gambling and the usual assortment of diet products and men's health "enhancements" that typically appear in spam. The toolbar can allegedly damage some versions of Windows XP, making it impossible to use My Computer or to browse directories on the file system. At the least, Xupiter's toolbar is regarded as an example of *spyware*—software that tracks what you do online to build a marketing profile that can be sold to advertisers.

 TIP Just in case you do find Xupiter in your View menu, you can remove it (and other spyware you may not even be aware you have) using a program called Spybot, which is available at http://www.safer-networking.org/.

The Yomtobians, who reportedly live in California, are well-known spammers who specialize in sending out advertisements for X-rated Web sites. They have also been charged with setting up "stealth" Web sites—sites that appear when people make a small spelling error in the Uniform Resource Locator (URL) they legitimately want to visit. They are shuttled to a gambling site or one with sexually explicit content. According to a decision published by the World Intellectual Property Organization in Geneva, Switerland, Saeid Yomtobian registered www.altabista.com and www.altaista.com in 1997, for instance.

The Best and Worst E-Mail Pitches

Most e-mail spam pitches are forgettable. Mortgage rates seem to always be at an ALL-TIME LOW! Online pharmacies want to send you all kinds of substances to help you live a LONGER and HEALTHIER LIFE! You can view SEXY PICS, make $$ surfing the Web, and make money in your sleep!

Once in a while—a great while—someone comes across unsolicited commercial e-mail that actually makes you chuckle or smile. Here's a quick example:

> *DEAR RECEIVER,*
>
> *You have just received a Taliban virus. Since we are not so technologicaly advanced in Afghanistan, this is a MANUAL virus. Please delete all the files on your hard disk yourself and send this mail to everyone you know.*
>
> *Thank you very much for helping us.*
>
> *—Taliban hacker*

 NOTE I've taken care to preserve the misspellings and grammatical errors to preserve the full flavor of this message. Others are presented in the sections that follow.

The Best

In December 1998, the television show *Saturday Night Live* aired a sketch called "Christmas Balls." Actor Alec Baldwin played Pete Schweddy, owner of the holiday bakery Season's Eatings. Schweddy brought a selection of his Christmas Balls over to a radio talk show hosted by two women; a hilarious set of double entendres about "balls" resulted. The following e-mail message, originally published in 1995 on the Web site of the legendary e-zine simply called Suck, reminds me of that sketch.

It purports to be a "real" IBM internal message sent to field engineers in all of the company's branch offices:

Abstract: Mouse Balls available as FRU (Field Replacement Unit)

Mouse Balls are now available as FRU. Therefore, if a mouse fails to operate or should it perform erratically, it may need ball replacement. Because of the delicate nature of this procedure, replacement of mouse balls should only be attempted by properly trained personnel.

Before proceeding, determine the type of mouse balls by examining the underside of the mouse. Domestic balls will be larger and harder than foreign balls. Ball removal procedures differ depending upon manufacturer of the mouse. Domestic balls are replaced using the twist-off method. Mouse balls are not usually static-sensitive. However, excessive handling can result in sudden discharge. Upon completion of ball replacement, the ball may be used immediately.

It is recommended that each replacer have a pair of spare balls for maintaining optimum customer satisfaction, and that any customer missing his balls should suspect local personnel of removing these necessary items.

To reorder, specify one of the following:

P/N 33P8468 - Domestic Balls P/N 33P8461 - Foreign Balls

"Good Luck, Mr. Gorsky"

A particular variety of spam, one that is well-known in offices and organizations around the world, is the e-mail joke. A series of jokes is circulated among office members so frequently that no one has any idea where the e-mail originated. The jokes are sent only because they are funny—and often, they are. The following is one unsolicited joke that actually made me chuckle:

When Apollo Mission Astronaut Neil Armstrong first walked on the moon, he not only gave his famous "One small step for man, one giant leap for mankind" statement, but followed it by several remarks—the usual com traffic between him, the other astronauts, and Mission Control. Before he re-entered the lander, he made the enigmatic remark "Good luck, Mr. Gorsky."

Many people at NASA thought it was a casual remark concerning some rival Soviet cosmonaut; however, upon checking, there was no Gorsky in either the Russian or American space programs.

Over the years, many people have questioned him as to what the "Good luck, Mr. Gorsky" statement meant. On July 5, in Tampa Bay, Florida, while answering questions following a speech, a reporter brought up the 26-year-old question to Armstrong. He finally responded. It seems that Mr. Gorsky had died, and so Armstrong felt he could answer the question. When he was a kid, Neil was playing baseball with his brother in the backyard. His brother hit a fly ball that landed in front of his neighbors' bedroom window. The neighbors were Mr. and Mrs. Gorksy. As he leaned down to pick up the ball, he heard Mrs. Gorsky shouting at Mr. Gorsky, "Oral sex? Oral sex you want? You'll get oral sex when the kid next door walks on the moon!"

I know what you're wondering: Did this story really happen? Nope. The joke has been circulating so long, though, that NASA has actually denied it. You can read more about it—and follow a link leading to transcripts of the actual Apollo moon mission—on the Truth or Fiction Web site at http://www.truthorfiction.com/rumors/armstrong-gorsky.htm.

Abort, Retry, Ignore

The following refers to the alert message that Windows users see when a program crashes. It should be read to the meter of the poem *The Raven* by Edgar Allen Poe:

Abort, Retry, Ignore?

Once upon a midnight dreary, fingers cramped and vision bleary,

System manuals piled high and wasted paper on the floor,

Longing for the warmth of bed sheets, still I sat there doing spreadsheets.

Having reached the bottom line I took a floppy from the drawer,

I then invoked the Save command and waited for the disk to store,

Only this and nothing more.

Deep into the monitor peering, long I sat there wond'ring, fearing,

Doubting, while the disk kept churning, turning yet to churn some more.

But the silence was unbroken, and the stillness gave no token.

"Save!" I said, "You cursed mother! Save my data from before!"

One thing did the phosphors answer, only this and nothing more,

Just, "Abort, Retry, Ignore?"

Was this some occult illusion, some maniacal intrusion?

These were choices undesired, ones I'd never faced before.

Carefully I weighed the choices as the disk made impish noises.

The cursor flashed, insistent, waiting, baiting me to type some more.

Clearly I must press a key, choosing one and nothing more,

From "Abort, Retry, Ignore?"

With fingers pale and trembling, slowly toward the keyboard bending,

Longing for a happy ending, hoping all would be restored,

Praying for some guarantee, timidly, I pressed a key.

But on the screen there still persisted words appearing as before.

Ghastly grim they blinked and taunted, haunted, as my patience wore,

Saying "Abort, Retry, Ignore?"

I tried to catch the chips off guard, and pressed again, but twice as hard.

I pleaded with the cursed machine: I begged and cried and then I swore.

Now in mighty desperation, trying random combinations,

Still there came the incantation, just as senseless as before.

Cursor blinking, angrily winking, blinking nonsense as before.

Reading, "Abort, Retry, Ignore?"

There I sat, distraught, exhausted, by my own machine accosted.

Getting up I turned away and paced across the office floor.

And then I saw a dreadful sight: a lightning bolt cut through the night.

A gasp of horror overtook me, shook me to my very core.

The lightning zapped my previous data, lost and gone forevermore.

Not even, "Abort, Retry, Ignore?"

To this day I do not know the place to which lost data go.

What demonic nether world us wrought where lost data will be stored,

Beyond the reach of mortal souls, beyond the ether, into black holes?

But sure as there's C, Pascal, Lotus, Ashton-Tate and more,

You will be one day be left to wander, lost on some Plutonian shore,

Pleading, "Abort, Retry, Ignore?"

—Author unknown

The Worst

The Craig Shergold e-mail scam is one of the best known of a genre. It goes like this: A young person has a life-threatening illness; if you can just make a donation to his or her charity organization, the young person might have a chance at life. Often, there's more than a germ of truth in the e-mail. The campaign might start with a real child who is really sick. (Then again, it might not.) The campaign might really help the child to improve. The problem is that no one tells the people who circulate the e-mail that the campaign is over. The e-mail continues to circulate and takes on a life of its own. This one is perhaps the most pervasive and best known:

> *To Whom It May Concern:*
>
> *We are participating in a request that business cards be sent to Craig Shergold at the address below.*
>
> *Seven-year-old Craig has a brain tumor and has little time to live. Craig turned in his wish to the Children's Make-A-Wish Foundation and has expressed his desire to have an entry in the* Guiness Book of World Records *for the largest collection of business cards received by an individual.*
>
> *Please take time to send a copy of this note to another twenty (20) addresses of your choice. Let's help to make Craig's dream come true.*
>
> *This will only take a few minutes of your time and will mean so much to Craig.*
>
> *Thanks for your help.*

As you might expect, Brit Shergold was flooded with get-well cards when this e-mail started to circulate around 1990—16 million of them, in fact, which did allow him to make the *Guinness Book of World Records*. Shergold was seriously ill from a brain tumor when his doctor noticed that he was getting lots of get-well cards and teased Craig that he should try to get the record. Craig's mother (who had been told by doctors to take Craig home to "die in peace") thought this would be a good way to pick up her son's spirits after he missed a planned meeting with Princess Diana. The British press took up Shergold's quest, and the Children's Wish Foundation notified its U.S. offices.

When a Virginia billionaire named John Kluge heard about the story, he paid to bring Shergold to the United States for an operation. Doctors at the University of Virginia Medical Center removed almost all of the tumor in March 1991, and to date, the cancer has not returned. Shergold is now a healthy young English man in his 20s.

But on the Internet, Shergold perpetually remains seven years old, dying of cancer, and in need of get-well cards. His name is typically misspelled, and letters and cards are sent to the Make-A-Wish Foundation, which is not the name of the organization that originally took up Craig's cause. But every time a sympathetic employee gets a chain e-mail letter about Craig, it is distributed to a dozen more locations, and the Make-A-Wish Foundation receives more cards. Craig's parents and even the newspaper columnist Ann Landers put out notices asking people to stop sending cards, but nothing seems to stop it. Sympathy, it seems, is timeless.

NOTE   Another child who has been the subject of e-mail prayer solicitations, Amanda Bundy, really exists and really had a cancer scare. The growth that was found in her body, however, was not cancerous. But by the time this was discovered, e-mail messages (and presumably, prayers) were continuing to circulate around the Internet. Read about it on the Truth or Fiction Web site (http://www.truthorfiction.com/rumors/a/amandabundy.htm).

The Great Pyramid Continues Online

Another type of e-mail scam is a variation on the pyramid scam, which has been victimizing people for decades. Someone who has supposedly made a fortune by mailing out requests for money suggests you do the same. E-mail turns out to be perfect way to deliver such bogus requests.

You, Too, Can Be Scammed from the Comfort of Your Own Home

The following is one of the most egregious examples I found of this particular offensive missive:

> *PLEASE READ AND ANALYZE THE FOLLOWING AND DETERMINE IF $5 IS WORTH KNOWING IF THIS IS REALLY POSSIBLE!!!!!*
>
> *Dear Friends,*
>
> *My name is Dave Rhodes. In September 1988 my car was reposessed and the bill collectors were hounding me like you wouldn't believe. I was laid off and my unemployment checks had run out. The only escape I had from the pressure of failure was my computer and my modem. I longed to turn my advocation into my vocation. This January 1989 my family and I went on a ten day cruise to the tropics. I bought a Lincoln Town Car for CASH in Feburary 1989.*
>
> *I am currently building a home on the West Coast of Florida, with a private pool, boat slip, and a beautiful view of the bay from my breakfast room table and patio. I will never have to work again. Today I am rich! I have earned over $400,000.00 (Four Hundred Thousand Dollars) to date and will become a millionaire within 4 or 5 months. Anyone can do the same. This money making program works perfectly every time, 100% of the time. I have NEVER failed to earn $50,000.00 or more whenever I wanted. Best of all you never have to leave home except to go to your mailbox or post office.*

You can guess where this classic "pyramid scam" is going. If you can stand it, you can read the rest at http://www.suck.com/daily/95/11/15/money.txt.

The Nigerian E-Mail Grifters

Nigeria, one of the poorest countries in Africa, has embraced the Internet in a wholehearted way. At the least, the enterprising people who have been purveying scams by mail or fax for years have now turned to the Internet as a new, low-cost, high-volume medium for cheating people out of their money. You have probably received spam e-mail solicitations from them at one point or another.

The story usually goes like this: Someone of significance in Nigeria—a high-ranking government official or a widow—urgently needs your assistance to transfer a large amount of money out of the country. You will receive a substantial reward for your help. The amount of money involved might be as much as $20 million dollars. The actual amount is unimportant because it does not exist. What is important is a temptation for the e-mail recipient. If you will only let the Nigerian official make use of your bank account, you'll get 20 percent of the proceeds. Just send your name, address, telephone, fax numbers—and oh, by the way, your bank name and account numbers.

"Please note that this transaction is 100% safe and free and we will commence the transaction from the date of receipt of the following information via the telefax number above," the letters typically read.

In an article in Wired News (http://www.wired.com/news/culture/ 0,1284,53818,00.html), reporter Michele Delio actually interviewed a Nigerian who admitted to writing such letters as part of his family's business. Such "business" is referred to by law enforcement officials as "419 fraud," referring to the section of the Nigerian penal code that outlaws it. If you see such a letter, run to Nigeria before you respond to it.

Great Spam E-Mail Hoaxes

E-mail is known for being a convenient means of legitimate communication as well as delivering hoaxes about viruses and other disasters that people should guard against. The Urban Legends Reference Pages (http://www.snopes.com/ computer/virus/virus.htm) include a long list of virus hoaxes as well as legitimate viruses that have been distributed by mass e-mail. The sections that following mention a few them.

The Good Times Virus

This fictitious virus is one of the best-known e-mail hoaxes ever. It spawned a number of variations, with names such as Penpal Greetings and Join the Party. The e-mail message that caused all the trouble went like this:

Thought you might like to know...

Apparently, a new computer virus has been engineered by a user of America Online that is unparalleled in its destructive capability. Other, more well-known viruses such as Stoned, Airwolf, and Michaelangelo pale in comparison to the prospects of this newest creation by a warped mentality.

What makes this virus so terrifying is the fact that no program needs to be exchanged for a new computer to be infected. It can be spread through the existing e-mail systems of the InterNet.

Luckily, there is one sure means of detecting what is now known as the "Good Times" virus. It always travels to new computers the same way—in a text e-mail message with the subject line reading simply "Good Times." Avoiding infection is easy once the file has been received—not reading it. The act of loading the file into the mail server's ASCII buffer causes the "Good Times" mainline program to initialize and execute.

The program is highly intelligent—it will send copies of itself to everyone whose e-mail address is contained in a received-mail file or a sent-mail file, if it can find one. It will then proceed to trash the computer it is running on.

The bottom line here is: If you receive a file with the subject line "Good Times," delete it immediately! Do not read it! Rest assured that whoever's name was on the "From:" line was surely struck by the virus. Warn your friends and local system users of this newest threat to the Internet! It could save them a lot of time and money.

That's nothing. A variant of the Good Times virus allegedly stepped over the laws of physics. Simply viewing the message with your feeble little human eyeballs would destroy your computer by causing it to initiate something called an "nth complexity infinite binary loop." Whatever that is. Good Times was a good joke for its creators—the Federal Communications Commission was forced to issue an official denial that it had ever sent an alert out about Good Times (http://www.fcc.gov/Bureaus/Miscellaneous/Public_Notices/1995/pnmc5036.txt).

The Klingerman Virus: E-Mail That Really Hurts

Viruses can be harmful to your computer. But you have to admit that they are not as scary or destructive as some of the viruses that can make you very sick, such as the West Nile virus or AIDS. You can imagine how alarming it would be if a computer virus could be passed from machine to human being and somehow make someone physically ill.

That's not quite the premise behind the Klingerman virus, another fictitious virus that was publicized heavily by e-mail. The Klingerman virus was supposedly a real virus sent to people via their physical mail. The message went like this:

Very scary. Be careful. This is an alert about a virus in the original, one that affects your body, not your hard drive. There have been 23 confirmed cases of people attacked by the Klingerman virus, a virus that arrives in your real mail box, not your e-mail inbox.

The Klingerman virus is among a half-dozen hoaxes described on the Centers for Disease Control and Prevention Web site (http://www.cdc.gov) under Current Health Related Hoaxes and Rumors. The Klingerman e-mail message, which purports to emanate from "Schwab corporate headquarters," claims that the Centers for Disease Control and the U.S. Postal Service are trying to track down the sender of randomly mailed blue envelopes that carry a sponge containing the virus. All pure fiction—but oddly, they foreshadowed the all-too-real Anthrax murders that really occurred a few years later.

But what is all too real in the e-mail message is what is described as an information phone number that is in reality a number at Yale New Haven Hospital, which received so many calls it has had to record a special message: "Thank you for calling the employee assistance program. For an appointment, or if you have an emergency, press 1. If you're calling about the Klingerman virus, it's a hoax. Please do not forward it."

Turning Spam into Art

Sometimes, the best way to neutralize something is to transform it. Some very clever people have taken the most mindless, intrusive, least imaginative of objects— UCE—and transformed it into something completely different. The following are just two of the ways in which spam e-mail can be turned into art.

Spamradio: Background Music for Your Ears

The music is hypnotic, even sleep inducing. The voice that accompanies the music is a computerized voice synthesizer, speaking in a monotone, with no inflection or expression. After a minute or two, when you get used to the strangeness of the sound, you suddenly pay attention to what the voice is reading: the text of real spam e-mail messages. Welcome to Spamradio (shown in Figure 8-3), one of the strangest and most imaginative ways ever of turning what one person would call detritus into what many would call art or at least an odd form of entertainment.

Richard Airlie, a Scottish computer programmer, and Ian Morrison, a computer security specialist from London, received spam in their own e-mail inboxes for years. Like everyone else, they deleted the e-mails without even reading them or thinking about them very much. One day, a lightbulb came on. They realized they could actually use this free material and turn it into something larger, better, and even stranger. Airlie and Morrison started Spamradio as a way of protesting the ultimate cost of Spamradio: The consumer ultimately pays for getting the message. The original idea was to have real human beings read the spam, but it would represent a full-time job for some unfortunate person—something they couldn't ask anyone to do, says Morrison. The synthesized voice read the processed e-mail text automatically, but by itself, it seemed too spare. So to spice things up, ambient music was added, which Morrison himself helped record with a local London band.

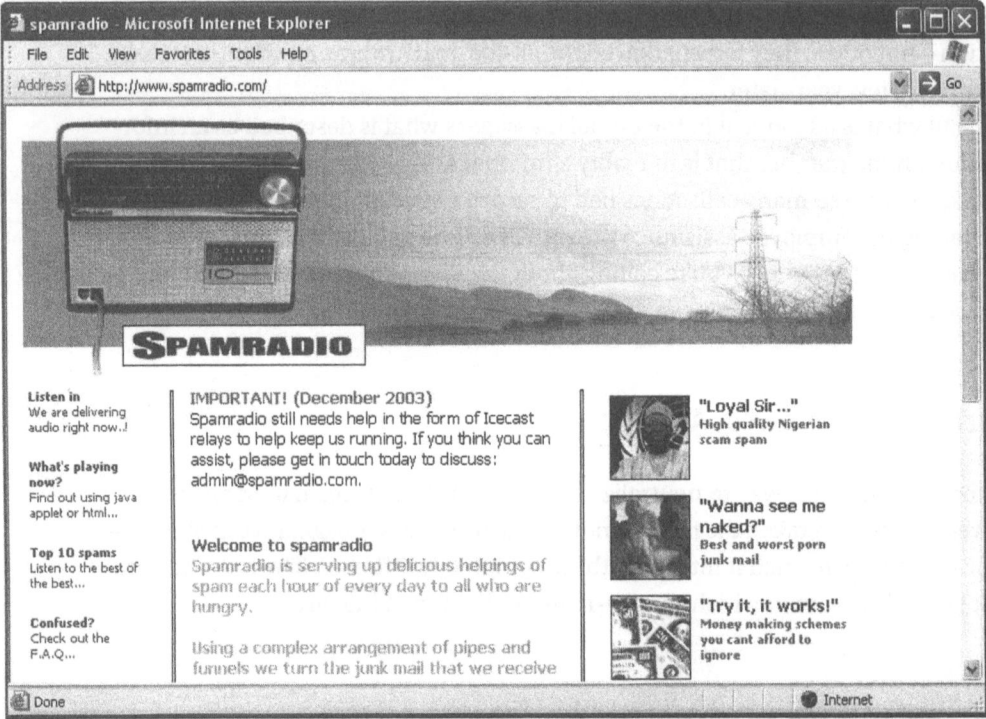

Figure 8-3. An astonishing and probably ineffective way to fight spam: Spamradio[3]

The voice reads, "...Free life insurance quotes from companies nationwide... no cost or obligation on your part...the most advanced Bible software available today...take advantage of this sizzling summer special...." Some of the more bizarre spams are preserved in a sort of Spam Hall of Fame. These include the offer to become a "real, fully ordained minister in just 24 hours."

Even though my experience of Spamradio had me staring blankly into space in hypnotized fascination after a few minutes, Spamradio is an interactive rather than passive experience. You can customize the stream to listen to a particular type of spam: X-rated, Nigerian scam, or general "junk mail," for instance.

---

3. http://www.spamradio.com/

Morrison even took Spamradio live on stage, appearing at a meeting of the Dorkbot group (a group of electronic artists and technically minded individuals) in London in Spring 2003.

 TIP Spamradio is streamed over the Internet in MP3 audio format. To listen, you need a player that can handle MP3 files, such as Winamp or Audioactive Player (Windows/Mac) or iTunes (Macintosh).

Spamagrams: Turning Pure Drivel into...Artful Drivel

An Australian fellow named Larry Brash is heavily into anagrams—words and phrases that are created when you turn around and reuse the letters available in other words and phrases. For instance, if you turn around the letters in the word *spam*, you get *maps, amps, samp*...you get the idea. Well, Larry Brash loves anagrams so much that he maintains the FAQ for the newsgroup alt.anagrams, runs the Anagrammy Awards, and wrote the Anagrammy FAQ.

On most newsgroups, when you see postings with headings such as "LONG DISTANCE FOR 3.85 CENTS A MINUTE" or "THIS IS ABSOLUTELY LEGAL," you ignore them. When you see them on alt.anagrams, don't ignore them—chances are Larry or another of the newsgroup participants has turned the spam heading into a clever anagram in the body of the newsgroup message.

The brainpower needed to turn a phrase such as "THIS CAN MAKE YOU EASY MONEY" into "Eh, it's a really key scam. You annoy me!" is considerable. Some anagram software programs are available to turn long spam headings into something completely different. But whether the anagrams make sense depends on the judgment of the anagram creator. The best "spamagrams" turn out to be statements against spam itself. Table 8-1 lists some examples taken from Brash's Best Spam Anagrams page (http://members.ozemail.com.au/~lbrash/anagrams/best2.html). Many of the examples published on this page could not be repeated in polite company, and you should check them yourself.

Table 8-1. Spam Anagrams

Original Phrase	Anagram
Money Making Opportunities	You're into inept spamming. OK?
Free & Unlimited Web Space	Spam: We benefit? Crude lie!
Home schooling (guitar, computer music) over the Internet	I contrive to circle more spamming throughout Usenet, eh?
EARN $100,000 PER YEAR SENDING E-MAIL	100,000 are reeling. I yearn: End Spam!
TURN YOUR COMPUTER INTO A 24 HR. A DAY CASH MACHINE!!	A rich spammer (a nut) 24; I hurry to con and cheat you.
Looking for Serious Writers	Solution: forgeries work, sir.

After the spam e-mails are turned into spamagrams, Larry recommends mailing them right back to the spammer from whence they came.

Other E-Mail (Mis)Adventures

There's more to e-mail than just spam, of course. E-mail, in fact, is the most popular service on the Internet, ranking higher in popularity than even the World Wide Web. The Meta Group, one of those research organizations that purveys statistics about the Internet, reports that 30 billion e-mail messages were sent in 2002 and projects that 60 billion will clog cyberspace in 2006.

E-Mail Entertainment: Remember ASCII Art?

ASCII art, a form of computer art that used to adorn e-mail messages and newsgroup postings all over the Internet, is rapidly going the way of Egyptian hieroglyphs, cave paintings, and other lost forms of art. What *is* ASCII art? ASCII (pronounced "ask-ee") stands for American Standard Code for Information Interchange. It's a binary code that allows computers to display information simply.

In the early days of the Internet, computer wonks would type ASCII symbols (mainly zeroes and ones, plus some others such as @, ^, and _) to painstakingly create ASCII art. They would send miniature examples of this homespun art along with their e-mail or newsgroup messages. As the Net is taken over by a higher and higher percentage of nonprogrammers, you see less and less ASCII art. An example remains on Dan Garcia's Spam Homepage, however (see Figure 8-4).

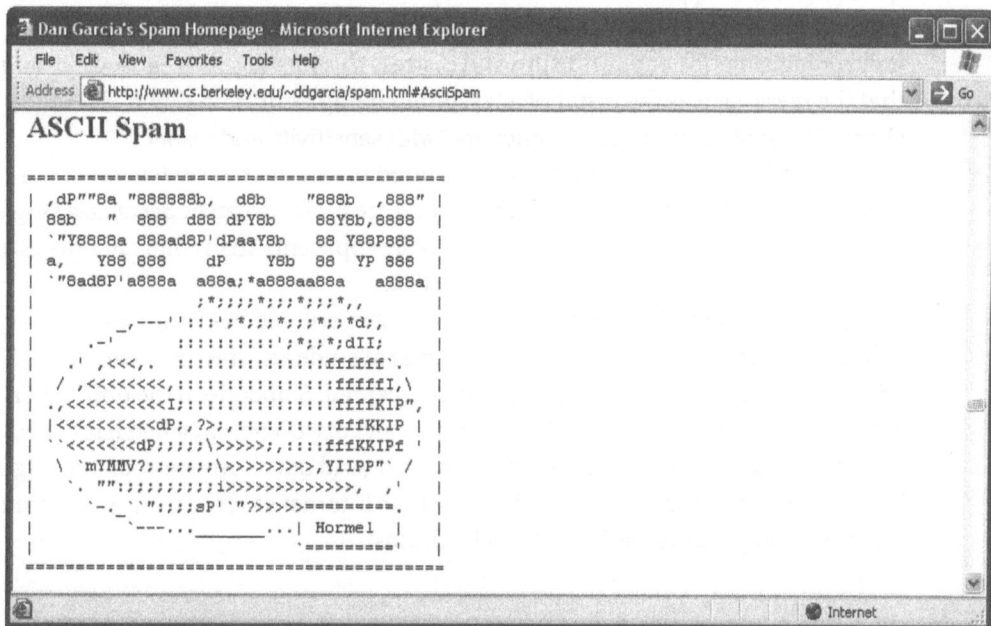

Figure 8-4. Look closely, and you'll find an image of SPAM in this ASCII art example.[4]

University Needs to Go to School on When to Click Send

One of the many wonderful things about e-mail is that you have the chance to take a deep breath, think, and read over what you're about to send before you click the Send button. One of the not-so-wonderful things about e-mail is that it is easy to send. When you're in a hurry, you're liable to forget the principle that says "read before you send" and click the Send button before you've checked over your message. Then, you're left with a sick feeling that you've sent something mistaken or embarrassing, and you can't "unsend" it.

That's what happened to an office worker in the admissions office at Cornell University in 2003. Someone mistakenly sent letters of admission to 1,700 high school students who had applied to attend Cornell. The problem was that 550 of those students had already received letters of rejection from Cornell the previous December.

Nevertheless, the letter read, "Greetings from Cornell, your future alma mater! Congratulations on your acceptance into the class of 2007!"

For high school students who take the college admissions process very seriously and wait with great eagerness for letters from colleges, this note was quite a shock.

---

4.   http://www.cs.berkeley.edu/~ddgarcia/spam.html#AsciiSpam

Their previous disappointment turned to joy and then plummeted to disappointment once again when they received a follow-up letter from Cornell admitting its mistake and apologizing "for any confusion and distress this message has caused." It said that the message was the result of a "systems coding error" and that it had fallen short of its goal of treating all applicants "with sensitivity and respect."

Such mistakes occur at universities around the world, but such letters have traditionally been sent out by "snail mail" and are easier to catch. Because a single mass e-mail was distributed instantly to Cornell's applicants, many more hundreds of mistakes were made with a single mouse click.

Cornell explained that a clerical staff member entered the wrong data to download the names and included the names of students who had been denied admission along with those who had been accepted. Someone in the office soon noticed that too many messages had been sent and discovered what had happened. Cornell officials raced to correct their error and send out another e-mail message. This was the first year that Cornell had used the Internet so extensively to communicate with applicants. Perhaps it will be the last.

Use of Multiple E-Mail "Personalities" Proliferates

Usually, if someone has multiple personalities or identities, psychologists consider this a problem to be treated. But on the Internet, when it comes to e-mail, multiple personalities can be a good thing.

Robert R. Butterworth, a psychologist who is often called upon to appear on TV talk shows as an expert in one thing or another, knows why some multiple personalities can be positive. Remember the Elian Gonzalez crisis in April 2000? A little boy floated to the United States on a raft with his mother and other Cuban refugees seeking asylum in the United States. The mother died, and Elian was embroiled in a huge controversy.

During the media frenzy over young Elian, Butterworth appeared on four networks calling for the boy's reunification with his father. This provoked the ire of many Cubans in America, who proceeded to "flame" Butterworth with angry e-mail messages.

Dr. Butterworth said it became essential to open two more e-mail accounts to isolate some of the fan and hate mail from the daily mail necessary for his work. In addition to his first e-mail address, robert@drbutterworth.net, he has another address that he is trying to turn into a more serious, and more private, work account.

NOTE   On the other hand, at least one public figure maintains an e-mail address that enables anyone to send him e-mail at any time. Jeff Bezos, the chairman of Amazon.com, the online bookseller, maintains a well-publicized e-mail address of jeff@amazon.com. He and his assistants supposedly read e-mail sent to this address—although Bezos does not respond personally to every e-mail that comes his way.

Bill Gates on Spam

The last word on e-mail in this chapter comes from no less than Bill Gates, chairman and cofounder of Microsoft Corporation, who sent out the following internal memo regarding spam e-mail:

Email is such an integral part of business and everyday life today that we tend to forget how recently it became popular.... Yet email's popularity has produced one very troubling side effect: spam. Unsolicited commercial email is a spreading plague that feeds off the unique power of the Internet to connect hundreds of millions of computer users around the world, at virtually no cost. Generally unwanted—and often pornographic or with fraudulent intent—spam is a nuisance and a distraction. Like almost everyone, I receive a lot of spam every day, much of it offering to help me get out of debt or get rich quick. It's ridiculous.

At Microsoft, as part of our drive to create a more trustworthy computing environment, we are significantly stepping up our efforts to fight spam and its pollution of the email ecosystem. ...We are building on advanced work at Microsoft Research in fields such as machine learning—the design of systems that learn from data and grow smarter over time. This kind of technology is vital to the fight against spam because every defensive action causes spammers to change their attack. Technology, to be effective, must continuously adapt, without requiring a team of people to examine messages one by one. With machine learning, a "smart" spam filter can automatically adjust to spammers' shifting tactics.

We support U.S. federal legislation that would strengthen the ability of service providers to shut down spammers by suing them on behalf of customers. And we believe that the use of automated searches to harvest addresses published on the Web and in Internet newsgroups should be banned, making it much more costly and difficult for spammers to assemble mailing lists.

At Microsoft, we're strongly committed to the goal of ending today's spam epidemic.

—Bill Gates

These are certainly admirable sentiments. However, at this writing, my own copy of Microsoft Outlook Express still receives plenty of spam, and Windows is plagued by viruses and worms, many of them distributed by e-mail.

 NOTE This memo is pretty long and has been edited. You can read the full version at http://www.internalmemos.com/memos/ memodetails.php?memo_id=1664.

Random Googling

The Internet contains countless Web sites, chat rooms, newsgroups, and other resources related to spam of all sorts. The following list contains a few I found noteworthy—a random sampling of sites that turned up after searching for the terms "spam" or "spam e-mail" on the search service Google (http://www.google.com/). Most of sites you find provide some form of anti-spam activism; I've made a point of attempting to locate some more unusual takes on spam:

- **Find the Spam (http://www.smalltime.com/findthespam.html):** This site is an exercise in existentialism. To try to analyze it further would be an injustice. Check it out for yourself, and be sure to notice the testimonials at the bottom of the page.

- **Spam Haiku (http://www.spamhaiku.com/spamhaiku/site/):** Another set of tributes to everyone's favorite spiced ham product. But this one encourages visitors to use the ancient Japanese form of poetry, the haiku, to express their love for Spam.

- **Spammimic (http://www.spammimic.com/):** You have probably heard of encryption in connection with content transmitted over the Internet: data is turned into gibberish by means of a complex mathematical formula called an *algorithm*. At the receiving end, the message is decoded using the same formula. This site operates along the same lines, but it turns messages into spam and then decodes them into the original messages again. Try it!

Low-Down, Dirty Scum in Babylon

LOTS OF PEOPLE, from impressionable youths to the morbidly curious, go online in the hope of seeing things they could never find anywhere else. They want to see faces of death and experience murder and mayhem secondhand. As long as they do so from the comfort of their computer chair, perhaps there's no harm in it.

This chapter attempts to present the darker and more sinister people and events you can encounter on the Internet. By pointing you to such places, I'm not trying to glorify them. I'm not even trying to suggest that you actually visit all of them. To paint a complete picture of all the weird and unusual events that have occurred on the Net, I couldn't avoid at least mentioning the people and places on its "dark side." It's like slowing down to gawk at an accident on the other side of the highway. There's no reason to look, but sometimes you just can't help it. The important thing is to turn away after a while and move on to more productive things.

Cold-Blooded Killers

Anyone who does anything out of the ordinary gets attention these days in the *Guinness Book of World Records* and in the media. Kill a whole bunch of people, and you generate morbid fascination among psychologists who try to figure out why you did it and among lots of people who are simply amazed at the scale of what you did. You even get admiration from a few strange folks. You'll certainly get your life story recounted—perhaps even celebrated—on the Web.

Those Mass Murders Weren't So Bad After All

Web sites that describe killers and their infamous deeds are one thing. Those that actually try to portray them as okay people who made a "contribution to society," even if such statements are supposed to be "dark humor," really disturb me. Check out the views expressed on the Art and Entropy site and see if you agree.

The site's creator explains that he wanted to design a fully functional site and needed some original content. He decided, in one part of the site, to post minibiographies of various famous killers. Each biography describes the person in question in critical terms. For instance, the page for Jeffrey Dahmer (http://www.artandentropy.com/killers/Dahmer.htm, shown in Figure 9-1) describes him as "the Cannibal Killer" and then as a "deranged introvert."

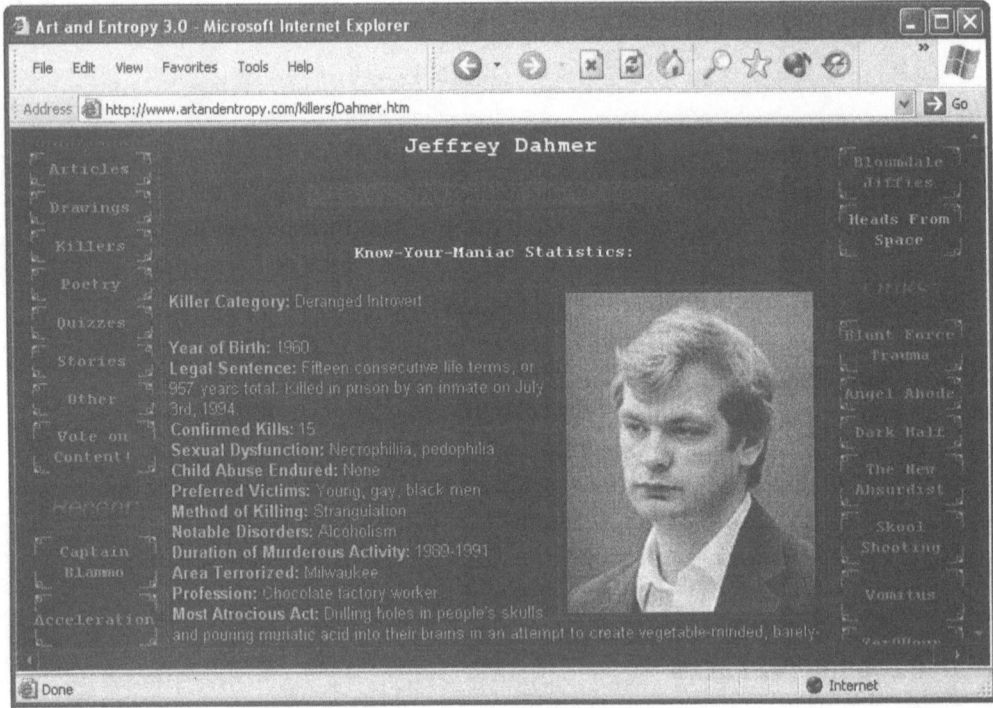

Figure 9-1. This site uses the biographies of serial killers for content and satirically praises their "contributions to society." [1]

If you read the accompanying biography, at the very end, though, you find praise for Dahmer's bizarre scientific experiments and his abilities as "an innovative artist." Statements such as the following are surely meant to be satiric: "A true renaissance man, Jeffrey Dahmer explored regions of both science and art that few authorities dare to venture." But do impressionable 15-year-olds who stumble on the page without reading about the background of the site and the disclaimers about "dark humor" actually realize that?

People routinely buy and sell objects on the auction site eBay (http://www.ebay.com/) that are associated with the most famous mass murders. For $9.99 you might be able to purchase a copy of serial killer John Wayne Gacy's death certificate on eBay. Dirt from the final resting place of serial killer Ed Gein

---

1.   http://www.artandentropy.com/killers/Dahmer.htm

has reportedly fetched $31 (but don't ask me how you know for sure whether it's Gein's grave dirt). Just search on eBay for the infamous killer of your choice, and you're bound to turn up something. I found the following recent sales:

- Gacy's autograph on a 3×5 card sold for $19.88.

- An FBI Wanted poster of Ted Bundy sold for only $3.99.

- A "true crime" book about Jeffrey Dahmer sold for $36, and his police mug shot sold for $1.75.

- A series of original articles about Jack the Ripper dating from 1888 sold for $107.50.

- A guitar pick bearing the likeness of Charles Manson went to a high bidder with the eBay user ID of kill4charlie for $6.50.

Last but certainly not least, I mention a Web page that has the harmless-sounding name: Fan Clubs and Merchandise. Sounds like a straightforward site that might sell your usual T-shirts and cups. But this one contains names and addresses of resources such as the Murder Can Be Fun desk calendar, which includes the birthdays of serial killers; Serial Killer Trading Cards; and the pleasant-sounding Catalogue of Carnage. Order your own bit of mayhem at http://members.tripod.com/ ~SerialKillr/SerialKillersExposed/fanclubs.html.

Sites Devoted to Death Row Inmates and Killers

There are Web sites devoted to murder victims, to be sure. But the number of those sites pales in comparison to the number of sites that delve deeply into the troubled childhoods, tortured adolescences, and murderous adulthoods of all too many killers. Villains who go way beyond the bounds of acceptable behavior fascinate people. The following sections show some of the indications of that fascination.

Everything You Wanted to Know About the Milwaukee Cannibal

I've already mentioned Jeffrey Dahmer in this chapter, but I have to make further note of a Web site that devotes so much attention to Dahmer's life, his family, and his crimes that it's sure to leave you shaking your head. It's called Jeffrey Dahmer's the Lair (http://www.tornadohills.com/dahmer/), and it presents everything you would want to know, and much that you probably never cared to know, about the man who killed 12 young gay men, dismembered many of them, and kept their body parts in his freezer, refrigerator, and elsewhere around his Wisconsin apartment.

The anonymous author of this site has gone through the trouble of photographing Dahmer's home from several angles; there's also a detailed section on the fate of Dahmer's brain (he was killed in prison, and his brain was cremated even though there was a request to study it). The detailed biography of Dahmer is apparently written by a minister who baptized him in prison, but this person isn't identified by name, either. Perhaps the most twisted part of this site is the area called Dahmer's Fetish, which describes necrophilia and provides detailed instructions on how to indulge in this particular pastime yourself. The text is supposedly taken from another, unidentified Web site.

NOTE   Chapter 3 describes an extensive Web site devoted to the mysterious Zodiac Killer, who has never been conclusively identified.

Friends of School Shooter Seek His Freedom

The site Friends of Andy W (http://www.friendsofandyw.org/) has drawn a good deal of criticism because it supports Charles Andrew "Andy" Williams who killed two and wounded thirteen at a school in Santana, California, on March 5, 2001. But the site also deserves credit for trying to take some positive steps as a result of a shooting: It protests school bullying as well as the handing down of adult sentences to juvenile criminals.

The site is owned by Williams's mother and run entirely by volunteers who believe the media didn't give Williams fair treatment and that he should not be confined in what the site describes as "an adult prison." Williams was sentenced to life in prison with eligibility for parole in 50 years for the shootings. His supporters contend that he was subjected to taunting and abuse at the school that led to the shootings. Williams was prosecuted under a law that requires juveniles who are charged with certain violent crimes to be tried as adults.

The odd thing is that Williams's father, Jeff Williams, runs what's described in the *San Diego Union-Tribune* as a "rival" Web site devoted to his son. The elder Williams, who was divorced from Andy Williams's mother in 1992, has sought a restraining order against the other site, seeking to keep the site from listing his (Jeff Williams's) home address, phone number, and e-mail address. Confused? Read all about it at http://www.signonsandiego.com/news/metro/santana/20030811-9999_1m11andy.html.

Meet the Texas Death Row Inmates

The site at http://www.deathrow.at/ was created to fight for the rights of the individuals who are incarcerated in Death Row in Texas—a place where they don't fool around when it comes to executing those who have been sentenced to death. View memorials to those who have been put to death; read about the Death Row novelist who won third place in a PEN American Center prison writing contest, and view photos of men with lots of tattoos.

Trenchcoat Mafia Web Sites

These are just words on a Web page, but given the authors and what they did, the words send a chill through you. It's the Web page created by the two Columbine High School students who were members of a group that called themselves the Trenchcoat Mafia. The two, Eric Harris and Dylan Klebold, killed 15 people, including themselves, and wounded 20 others on April 20, 1999. The title of the page reads "REB's words of wisdom, if you dont like it, ill kill you." The poem presented on the page includes the words "I AM YOUR APOCALYPSE" (see Figure 9-2).

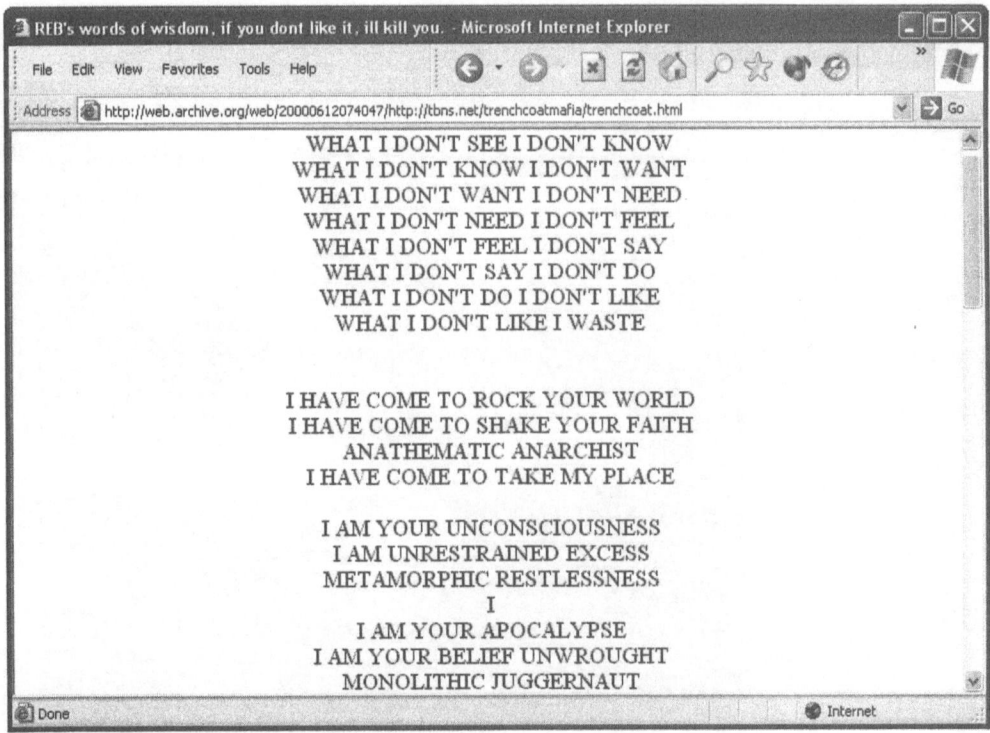

Figure 9-2. The so-called Trenchcoat Mafia left this Web page behind after the Columbine High School killings.[2]

---

2. http://web.archive.org/web/20000612074047/http://tbns.net/trenchcoatmafia/
trenchcoat.html

The page, which was established by Harris, also reportedly included instructions for making pipe bombs. A chilling message reportedly was included: "Today is my last day on Earth. Be prepared." Those words don't appear on the page shown in Figure 9-2, however.

Today, the original page is dangerous in another way. When you try to connect to its Uniform Resource Locator (URL)—which is probably not the original URL but a copy of the site—you are asked to download software that is supposed to help you view the page's contents. To me, this is a big security risk; it's safer to view the page by entering the URL (http://tbns.net/trenchcoatmafia/trenchcoat.html) in the Internet Archive's Wayback Machine (http://web.archive.org/).

One of the Web sites set up by the killers bears this polite message: "Please go to my main website: href='www.kill-society.com' Thank you!" If you go to this URL today, you view a page that has been set up to remember the students who were killed and wounded at Columbine (see Figure 9-3). They're the ones who should really be remembered.

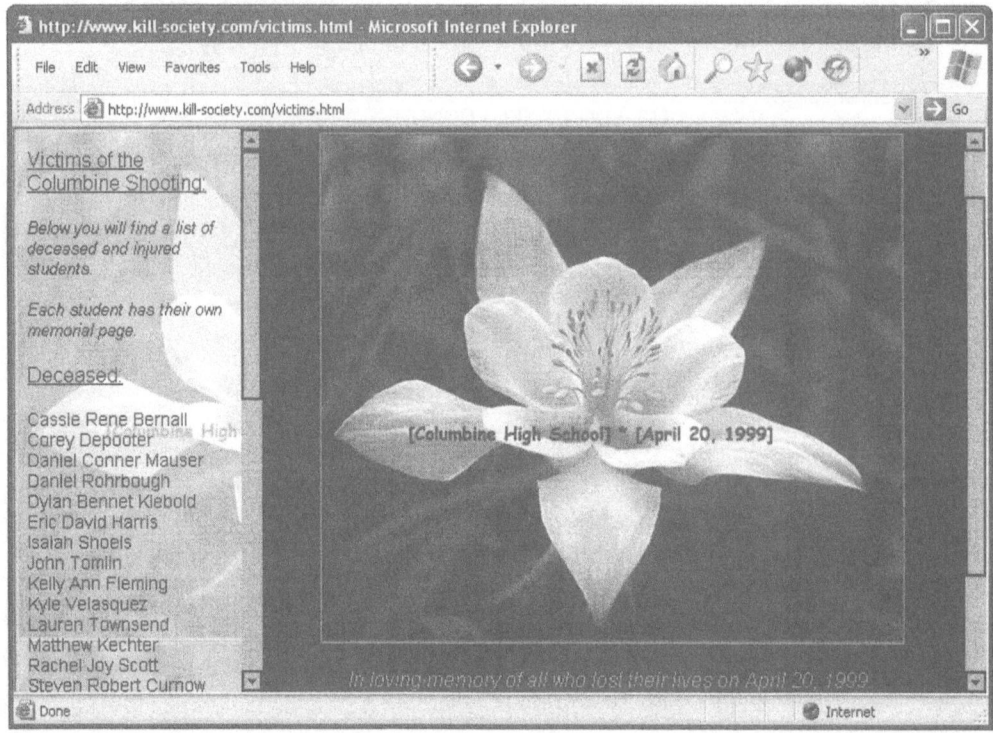

Figure 9-3. A domain once owned by the Columbine High School shooters now contains a memorial to the victims.[3]

---

3. http:// www.kill-society.com/victims.html

The Trenchcoat Mafia was apparently a small group of students at Columbine who considered themselves outcasts and boasted of owning guns. After the killings, a variety of Web pages supposedly left behind by the killers surfaced. Some were obviously hoaxes, but others contained on America Online (AOL) were not. Columnist Matt Drudge sent out a broadcast e-mail claiming to have located Web pages that contained warnings of the school massacre before the fact. Later, the page's authors admitted it was a hoax. Predictably, many of the user profiles posted on AOL were altered to include references to the Trenchcoat Mafia.

The issue of the apparently abundant warning signs that Harris and Klebold left on the Internet before the killings is one of the most important lessons to emerge from the tragedy. A teenage friend of the two reportedly saw a Web page containing detailed descriptions of the pipe bombs they were making. He told his parents, who told authorities, but apparently nothing was done. AOL's user guidelines prohibit posting instructions for making bombs online. But no one told AOL the pages existed.

TIP A service called KIDSReportline (http://www.findingstone.com/allkindsofstuff/kidscorner/kidsreportlinehome.html) gives students a place to file a report about classmates who have advocated violence or hatred and who may be embarrassed to tell others about their concerns.

Don't Trade Those Volatile Internet Stocks

Mark O. Barton (shown in Figure 9-4 in an image taken from the SpankMe's Mass Murder Web site) was a day trader: someone who buys and sells stocks quickly in the hope of making quick money. Day trading is a nerve-racking, highly risky venture in which huge amounts of money can be both made and lost in a matter of minutes. On June 9, 1999, he began a 15-day trading sequence in which he had some very big losses; in all, he was down more than $105,000. A source close to Momentum Securities, one of the places where Barton traded, said Barton had "a propensity for highly volatile Internet stocks."

On July 29, 1999, Barton bludgeoned his wife and two children to death with a hammer in an apartment in Stockbridge, Georgia. He then went to the Atlanta brokerage houses where he traded and shot and killed nine people. Before the shootings, he typed a confession on his computer in which he warned that he planned to live only long enough to kill "the people that greedily sought my destruction."

Day trading is hardly the only reason Barton may have killed his wife and children. He was suspected in the 1993 murder of his first wife and her mother. He was also estranged from his current wife. He later shot and killed himself in his van as he was about to be apprehended by police. The day trading losses weren't enough to destroy Barton financially—he reportedly was worth $750,000 and had $250,000 in liquid assets.

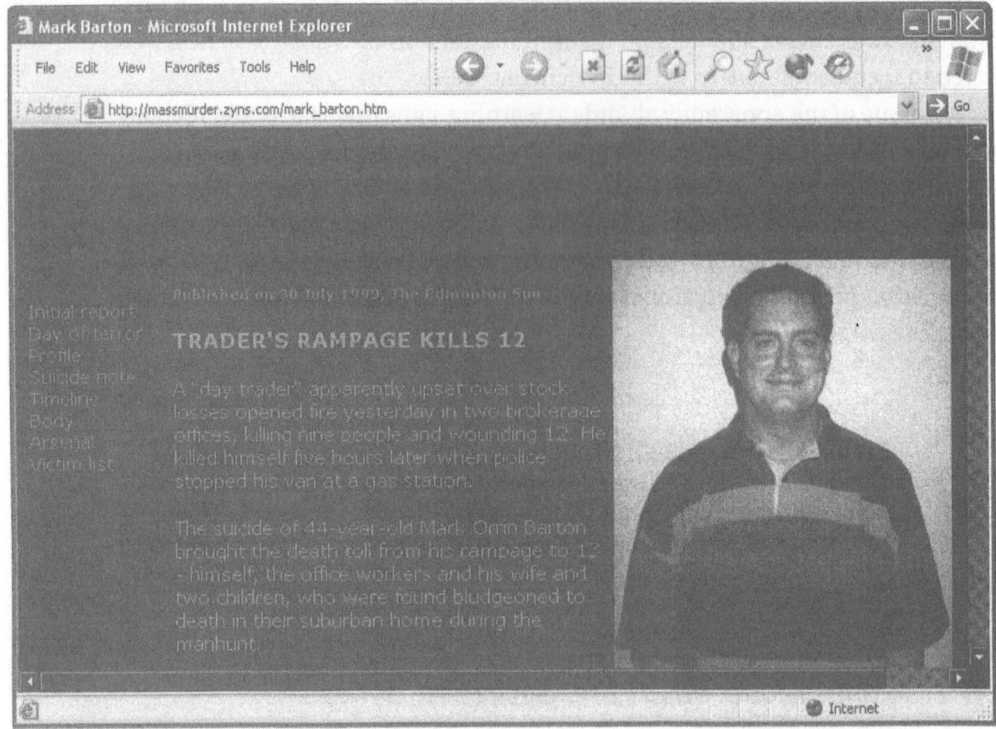

Figure 9-4. Mark Barton killed 13 people, including himself, after two weeks of trading losses.[4]

NOTE   SpankMe's Mass Murder site (http://massmurder.zyns.com/index.php) tracks murderers by the number of people they killed and by geographic region.

Hate Groups and Terrorists

Knowledge is power. The more you understand about where terrorist groups and hate groups are coming from, the less power they will have over you. Being a vigilant,

4.   http://www.massmurder.zyns.com/mark_barton.html

informed citizen isn't such a bad thing in this day and age. Almost all of the groups that are on the U.S. State Department's list of blacklisted organizations, such as hate groups and terrorist organizations, have sites on the Web. Just a few are mentioned in the sections that follow.

The Happy Aryan Nation

"If you think you have what it takes to stop being a fence sitter, and want to be a part of the solution, then you need to join Aryan Nations." I'm not making this up. If terms such as Racial Covenant Identity, the Tabernacle of the Phineas Priesthood, and lots of other racist gibberish are your cup of tea, visit the Aryan Nations Web site at http://www.aryan-nations.org/. The little icon that appears next to the site's URL—a well-known symbol used by the forces of the Third Reich during the World War II—tells you pretty much all you need to know, as does the welcoming quote from the Führer himself (see Figure 9-5).

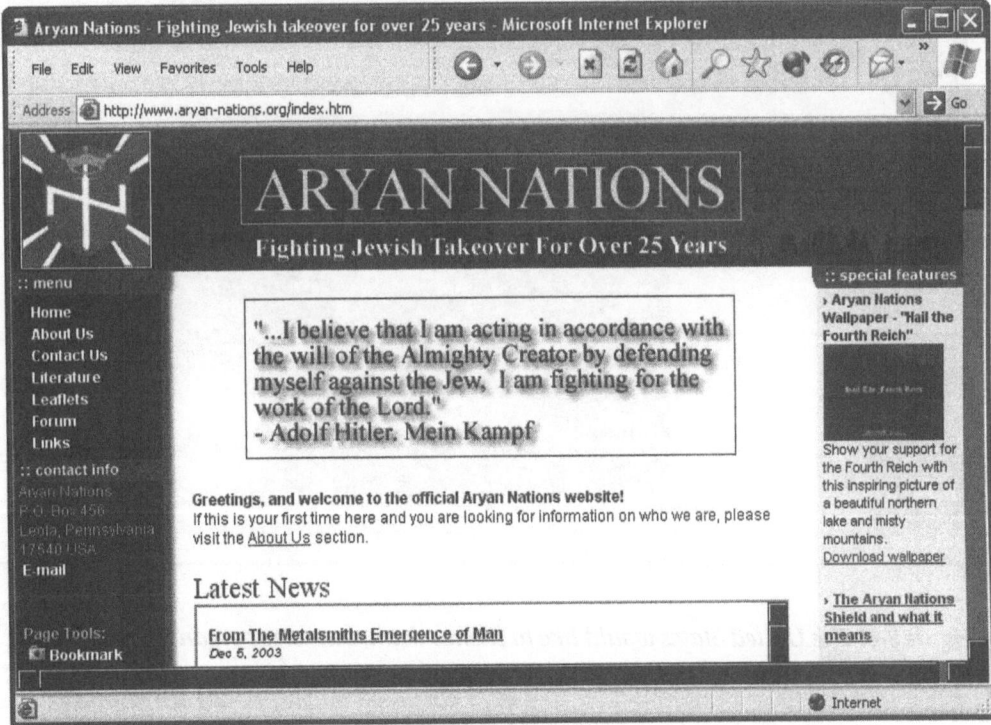

Figure 9-5. Like it or not, the neo-Nazis have their own Cyber Reich on the Internet.[5]

---

5. http://www.aryan-nations.org/index.html

You can download "desktop wallpaper" for your computer that shows a view of some mountains and the phrase "Hail the Fourth Reich."

Terror Groups Embrace the Web

The U.S. State Department tries to isolate terrorist organizations by including them on a list of blacklisted terrorist groups. But it can't keep them from creating Web sites where they issue statements, threaten their enemies, and raise funds. The Web site of the Arab terror group Hizbollah is presented in both Arabic and English. The English version (see Figure 9-6) includes statements about bombings, as well as graphic photos of masked fighters, bombs going off, and dead bodies.

Figure 9-6. *The United States would like to silence them, but terror organizations use the Internet as their mouthpiece.*[6]

---

6. http://www.hizbollah.org/english/frames/index_eg.htm

Some terror sites have reportedly tried to recruit new members through the Internet. The religious group Aleph isn't a terror group, but it was formerly known as the Aum Shinrikyo, which was responsible for a gas attack in the Tokyo subway in 1995. Some of its members did apologize in public for that incident. Aleph appeals for contributions on its Web site (http://english.aleph.to/).

 TIP The Hate Directory, a list of Web sites, mailing lists, and other online resources tied to hate groups, is the place to start if you want to research this subject. Find out more at http://www.bcpl.net/~rfrankli/hatedir.htm.

Site Raises Furor Over Der Führer

No discussion of low-down scum would be complete without mention of the head of the Nazi Party and superscum himself, Adolf Hitler. Whether you have relatives who fought in World War II or just want to find out more about the guy who inspired much of the humor in the hilarious film/musical *The Producers*, this is a good place to start. You can find examples of the Führer's artwork (he studied art in college) and see some childhood photos, such as the one in Figure 9-7.

As you might expect, this site attracts angry messages from those who suspect it is in some way pro-Hitler. I couldn't find anything that expressly sounded like Hitler idolatry, however. The sheer amount of attention paid to Hitler's words and deeds might in itself be suspect, but as they say, those who forget history are condemned to repeat it, so paying attention to the past is a good thing.

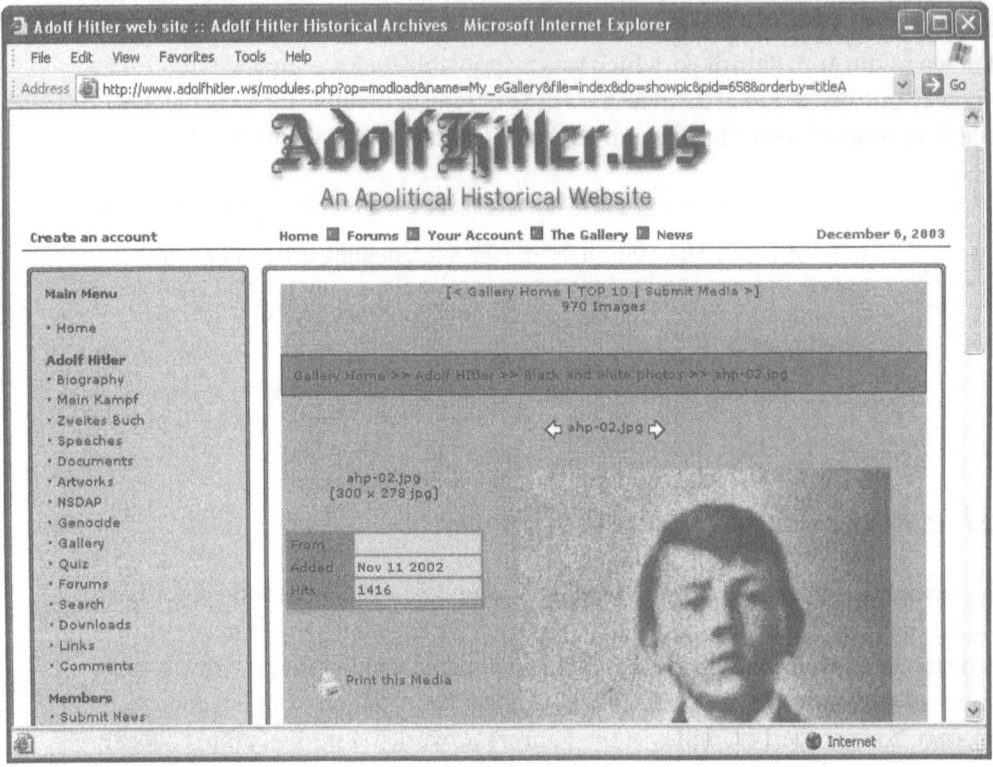

Figure 9-7. This site takes a historical, not hysterical, look at one of history's nastiest fellows.[7]

Organized Crime Influence Spreads to Internet

If you watch the television series *The Sopranos,* you have heard about the influence of organized crime spreading to high-tech arenas such as stock market trading. According to a British law enforcement firm, some real-life organized crime outfits are muscling their way into cyberspace.

Detective Chief Superintendent Len Hynds, head of the United Kingdom's National Hi-Tech Crime Unit (NHTCU) was quoted in Wired News as saying that crime syndicates in Eastern European countries, including Ukraine, Russia, and Latvia, are managing to victimize individual Internet users as well as Web sites. The NHTCU has reportedly made more than 100 arrests for blackmail and extortion as well as computer hacking in just two years of existence.

---

7. http://www.adolfhitler.ws/modules.php?op=modload&name=My_eGallery&file=index&do=showpic&pid=658&orderby=titleA

One increasingly common ploy calls for criminals to establish a fraudulent Web site that closely resembles a bank or other financial business. Unsuspecting Internet users are fooled into submitting their credit card or bank account numbers. Organized crime has also launched Denial of Service attacks against Web sites or at least the threat of such attacks—businesses are forced to pay a ransom, or the attack will be unleashed against them. Most nearly half of the NHTCU's arrests have been for offenses related to child pornography and pedophilia.

 TIP You can find out more about how to protect yourself from crime on the NHTCU's Web site at http://www.nhtcu.org/.

Forbidden Images

I remember my fascination when, as a child, I discovered a pamphlet containing photos of people who had died in automobile accidents. I hated to look at them, but I couldn't help looking, either. The pamphlet was one of those cautionary missives intended to get the reader to drive safely. Perhaps these sites will help you live a longer life.

Judge Posts Execution Photos on Web

When a convicted 344-pound murderer named Allen Lee "Tiny" Davis was sentenced to be executed in Florida in 1999, he probably never realized his death would give him a macabre sort of celebrity on the Internet. The electric chair had been rebuilt specifically to accommodate the oversize inmate. It replaced a 76-year-old electric chair. But the new chair used the same electrical system as the old one—one that had reportedly caused flames to shoot from the skull of someone who had been executed in 1997.

The controversy over Florida's death penalty law, which came up when another murderer was sentenced to death in 2000, affected Florida Supreme Court Justice Leander Shaw strongly. The court upheld the death penalty in that case. But Shaw protested by posting the gruesome photos on the Supreme Court's Web site along with his own dissenting opinion regarding the death penalty. News reports stated that eager Internet users crashed the court's Web server as they flocked to see the ugly images.

"I felt that people did not know what was really going on, how this was just inhumane," Shaw told the Naples, Florida, *Daily News*. "Blood, screaming, flames—who would have thought that in a civilized society in this day and time this would be tolerated?"

NOTE Later in 2000, the same Florida Supreme Court, including Judge Shaw, was embroiled in controversy when it overturned a lower court's decision that George W. Bush had won the state in that year's controversial presidential election. As we all know, the U.S. Supreme Court had the final say in the matter, however.

Faces of Death

Persephone, the Greek goddess, was forced to spend part of each year in the underworld and the rest of the year among the living. Harold and Maude, the unusual lovers of the classic 1960s movie, met while pursuing their obsession: attending other people's funerals. This notorious series of video/DVD collections is widely available on the Web if you, like Harold and Maude, feel connected to the underworld by the funerals of strangers.

Faces of Death has gained notoriety for its graphic depiction of dead people and other stomach-turning scenes, such as brains being removed from a monkey's head, leg amputations, and the like. In a video/DVD called *Faces of Death: Fact or Fiction*, the series director admits that some of the scenes had to be simulated. I thought the series had been banned for sale on eBay, but a search turned up plenty of copies, as well as compilations of the complete series.

Autopsy Photos

I love the television series *Six Feet Under*, but I have to admit that even the simulated autopsy scenes make me cringe. I can't imagine wanting to see the real thing, but occasionally when you're surfing through the Web investigating controversial subjects, you can't help but stumble upon some images that *really* shock you.

Anyone who looks into the assassination of President John F. Kennedy will sooner or later come across the photos of his autopsy. Both the killing of the president and the way the autopsy was conducted have been subjects of controversy for many decades. JFK Lancer, one of the better Web sites to discuss the assassination, has published some autopsy photos on its Web site (http://www.jfklancer.com/).

A case involving the death of a 36-year-old woman who died while under the care of the Church of Scientology in Florida eventually saw the release of autopsy photos of the victim. The state had originally charged that the church had abused the woman and illegally practiced medicine on her but eventually dropped the charges. The photos were released after a dispute in which the church sought to keep them sealed. The *St. Petersburg Times* declined to publish the photos in its print edition but posted two photos on its Web site. A Web site devoted to McPherson (http://www.lisamcpherson.org/) published multiple autopsy photos as well as the coroner's report, however.

Amazon.com has affiliate links with more than half a million Web sites, but it pulled its link to a Florida-based site called Website City (http://www.websitecity.com/) after the site posted autopsy photos of two race-car drivers. The site published the photos of drivers Rodney Orr and Neil Bonnett in the spring of 2001. This caused the Florida legislature to pass a law making it a felony for a medical examiner to make autopsy photos public without a court's permission. The same Web site sought access to the autopsy photos of famed racecar driver Dale Earnhardt, but the release of those photos was prohibited.

Rotten.com to the Core

If you want to see awful, disgusting photos of gunshot victims, corpses, and pretty much anything and everything, go to http://www.rotten.com/. A murder victim with a hatchet sticking out of his head, someone whose face was blown off after biting into a blasting cap, you name it—if it's disgusting, horrible, and gut-wrenching and it's been photographed, chances are it will eventually appear on Rotten.com (see Figure 9-8).

The horrible photographic content on Rotten.com might get it shut down for obscenity if the photos appeared by themselves. But the site's editorial content keeps it alive. The fellow who runs the site, who goes only by the name Soylent, publishes a regular editorial called "The Gaping Maw." A feature called "The DailyRotten" gathers news stories from around the world and includes a series of "rotten" historical events called "This Day in Rotten History."

To balance these stimulating editorial offerings, there are things such as the regular feature called F*** of the Month, which is a photo of a sexual nature that almost always manages to be repugnant in some way.

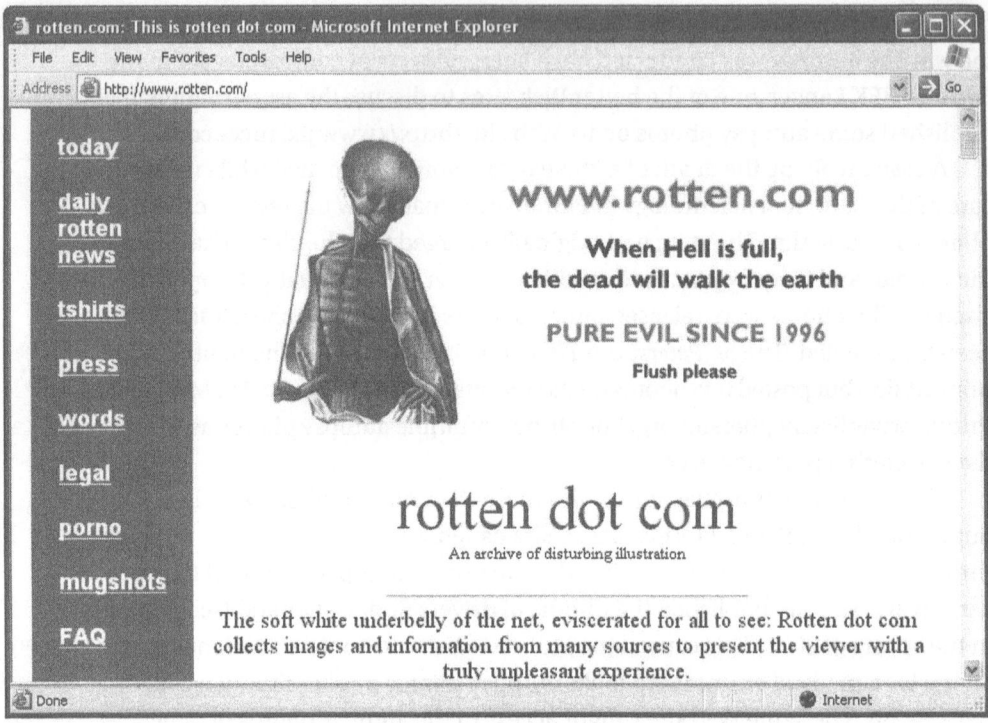

Figure 9-8. One of the few images posted on Rotten.com that this book can actually reproduce.

Soylent is described as a 30-something computer programmer with shaggy, graying hair. In the site's manifesto, he proudly points out that he posts photos that cannot be found elsewhere "Rotten dot-com serves as a beacon to demonstrate that censorship of the Internet is impractical, unethical and wrong," he states. "To censor this site, it is necessary to censor medical texts, history texts, evidence rooms, courtrooms, art museums, libraries, and other sources of information vital to functioning of free society."

In an article about Rotten.com, Salon called it "The Internet's Public Enema No. 1" and asked whether it would ever be kicked offline. That article was published in March 2001, so, for now, the answer is apparently no. Although the article berated Rotten.com in great detail for its gruesome imagery, it pointed out that an average of 200,000 visitors were attracted to the site each day. "We don't really show anything that the major television networks don't show you, it's just a matter of degree," the site's Frequently Asked Questions (FAQ) page reads.

---

8. http://www.rotten.com/

The site is, indeed, a test case for freedom of speech on the Internet. The British newspaper *The Observer* has reported that Scotland Yard and the FBI were at one time investigating Soylent for publishing an image of a man eating a baby on Rotten.com. Rotten.com was thrown out by one Internet service provider, but another that believed in anticensorship on the Internet gave it a new home.

But Rotten.com didn't start out trying to cause trouble. Soylent purchased the domain name in 1996 just because he was attracted to the name. He posted a few "joke pictures." The resulting flood of attention from visitors who kept returning to the easy-to-remember domain name convinced him to build the site into something more substantial. When radio host Howard Stern praised the site on air, it got plenty of attention, as did the publication of the alleged corpse of Princess Diana (it was widely believed to have been a fake, but it still drew more attention to the site).

Perverts and Child Molesters

When it comes to pedophiles and perverts, the Internet presents an embarrassment of "riches." I couldn't possibly list all the cases where someone has "stalked" someone else on the Internet and then arranged to meet the person with tragic consequences. I'm skipping all the many cases where young people have been kidnapped, assaulted, or murdered and have just picked a couple of incidents that got special attention in the news. Basically, you and your children *don't* want to get in the headlines the way these people did.

Pedophile Software Gets Bill Gates's Attention

The Toronto, Canada, police department, like police departments around the globe, occasionally confiscates computers from people who have been arrested or served with search warrants. Sometimes, the computers are found to hold pornographic images. Some of them hold hundreds or even thousands of images, each of a person who needs to be identified.

Detective Sergeant Paul Gillespie, a member of the Toronto Police Department's sex crimes unit, wished software could be developed that would capture the images of the young people in the photos; if the photos could be captured and compared to other photos of young people gathered worldwide, they could be identified more quickly. He told as much in an e-mail to a person of some influence in the field of software: Bill Gates, the chairman of Microsoft Corporation. Gates and his staff, who must receive countless e-mail requests asking for software to be developed, paid attention and began to get to work.

Microsoft Canada announced early in 2003 that it was working with the Toronto police to develop the software, which is designed to help track and prosecute individuals who stalk and seek to exploit children they meet online. The software is called the Child Exploitation Linkage Tracking System (CELTS). Once completed, the software will examine files on computers that have been seized by police and catalog images without forcing police to examine each photo themselves.

"Was I expecting Bill Gates to read it and actually respond, if it even made it to him? I would have considered that to be a bit of a miracle," Gillespie told the *Toronto Globe and Mail.* "Three weeks later, I got a call from Microsoft Canada, and they said, 'We'd like to come to talk to you about your e-mail.' It's like, 'You're kidding, right?'"

Pedophile Priests Go Wild

Modern Humorist, a humor Web site that creates comedy content for films and television, came up with a humorous take on the spate of Roman Catholic priests who have gotten in trouble for molesting young people (see Figure 9-9).

 TIP   Pedophile Priests, a feature of the online journal Slate, collects a series of editorial cartoons about the issue of priests who have been found guilty of this particular transgression. You can e-mail any of the cartoons to someone else. Find out more at http://cagle.slate.msn.com/news/ PedophilePriests/main.asp.

Random Googling

News, rumors, and legends surrounding criminals, spam artists, and other awful people and events are all over the Web. The following list contains a few I found noteworthy—a random sampling of sites that turned up after searching for the terms "crime," "criminal," or "evil" on the search service Google (http://www.google.com/):

- **Cruel Site of the Day (http://www.cruel.com/):** This site, a takeoff on the better-known Cool Site of Day, honors Web sites that celebrate "The World Wide Web's Bitter Aftertaste."

- **Gang Land (http://www.ganglandnews.com/):** This site examines the lives of notorious organized crime figures such as John Gotti.

- **Portal of Evil (http://www.portalofevil.com/):** Perversion, murder, and downright strangeness—this site contains links to them all.

Figure 9-9. Even the most unfunny subjects can produce a giggle when handled by the right Web site.[9]

---

9. http://www.modernhumorist.com/mh/0204/priests/

CHAPTER 10

Flakes and Fanatics in Babylon

HAVE YOU EVER CLICKED a hyperlink and immediately thought, "I can't believe I'm visiting this site?" or "I can't believe this person is doing this?" That happens to me all the time, either on the Web or when I take the plunge and visit the bizarre land of the homemade newsgroups whose names begin with the "alt" prefix.

On the Internet, you can be whoever you want. You can transform yourself into anything you want. You can change your name, your appearance, and your identity. You can turn yourself from a clumsy nerd into a chick magnet. You can also pursue any obsession or cause that's been keeping you awake at night. Just change your name to something with a "dot-com" in it, create a Web site, publish some photos of yourself, and be prepared to endure a little bit of ridicule as the price for a lot of fascination. Scores and scores of flakes and fanatics have done it.

What, exactly, is the difference between a flake and a fanatic? This can be difficult to pin down. In my mind, a flake is someone who didn't set out to do anything weird—it just happened in the course of achieving a particular goal. A fanatic is someone who is totally absorbed with a topic, event, or other object and who only wants to pursue that cause or obsession to its limit. The problem is that on the Internet there are hardly any limits at all. You'll see what I mean in this chapter.

The Flakes

Like a picture, every Web page tells a story. Many domain names have their own stories behind them, too. The problem is that the story they tell isn't one that's easy to hear. It seems crazy, off-kilter. These folks aren't really flakes. They just *act* like flakes.

Dot-Com Kid Shows What's in a Name

A young girl named Karin Robertson grew up in rural Indiana, an area covered with farms where cattle, pigs, chickens, and other animals are raised. It's one of those areas where pork and substances that go by the euphemism "pork products" are a way of life. Her mother was a kindergarten teacher, her father a biologist. She never knew anyone who was considered to be a vegetarian. Her name was normal enough, even though people always seemed to have trouble spelling it with an "i," instead using an "e" or a more exotic alternative such as Caryn.

When she was 14, Karin looked into vegetarianism for a school project. She read about testing on animals and came to a section of a book that described "factory farms" where scores of animals are raised to maximize efficiency and productivity. "This cannot be what animals go through!" she exclaimed across the house to her mother, who was cooking some pork products at the time. The book (which was probably not published by the Future Farmers of America) described chickens having their beaks pulled off when they were one day old, piglets being castrated without anesthetic, and sows being kept in cages where they can never turn around.

The moment Karin read about the supposed practices of factory farms, she stopped eating meat and eggs. Later, as a student at Bucknell University, she stopped eating dairy products as well. She became an ardent and committed animal rights activist. And in spring 2003, she legally changed her name to GoVeg.com (see Figure 10-1).

That's right: When the Person Formerly Known As Karin hands her identification card over at the library, at the airport, and whenever she signs a check, she simply writes GoVeg.com. When friends call to her, they sometimes call "Dot," but that's a name she disapproves of because it doesn't convey the vegetarian message by which she lives. She normally goes by the nickname "GoVeg."

GoVeg now works as a youth activist for People for the Ethical Treatment of Animals (PETA), which owns the Web site with the domain name goveg.com. Whenever you point your Web browser to http://www.goveg.com/, you go to a PETA Web site. The site includes a page about GoVeg.com (the person). The name, she says, reminds everyone about her antimeat message. Her mother, though, rarely uses her new name. "What are you going to do when you're married?" she asks the Daughter Formerly Known As Karin.

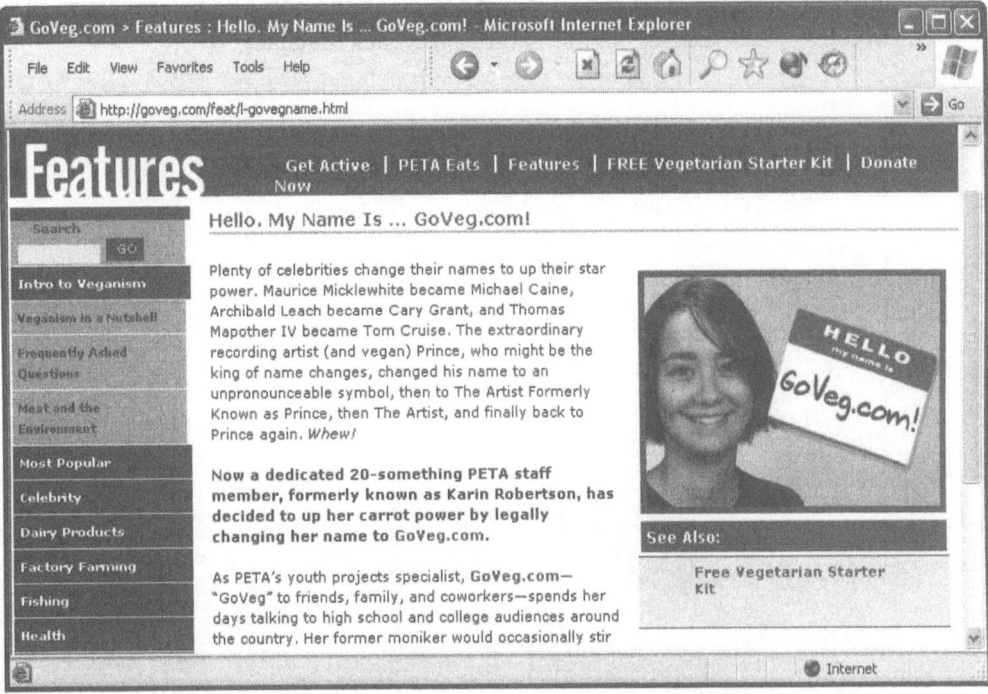

Figure 10-1. A woman who regards "dot-com" as more than a cultural term. It's now part of her name: GoVeg.com.[1]

Help Him Cut Off His Feet—Please

You've probably heard someone utter the phrase "It's like cutting off your nose to spite your face." I'm not totally sure what this phrase means, but no matter how you feel about your face, you probably wouldn't actually cut off your nose, right?

Before you answer, consider this: Suppose you lost the sense of smell and needed a new nose, but you needed $150,000 to cover the cost of the replacement. Would you cut off your nose then to raise the money, especially if it wasn't working anyway?

That's the situation Paul Morgan faced in 2001 when he created Freck's New Feet (http://www.cutoffmyfeet.com/—but don't go looking for the site now; it has been taken offline). Morgan, who goes by the nickname Freck, created one of the most controversial and universally reviled Web sites ever. He proposed selling tickets for $20 each to anyone who wanted to watch him cut his own feet off with a guillotine. Following the principle that an image is worth a thousand words, he included an

---

1. https://www.goveg.com/feat/I-govegname.html

illustrative image of what he proposed to do on the home page (see Figure 10-2, which appears courtesy of the Internet Wayback Machine).

Figure 10-2. Paul Morgan proposed to charge admission to cut off his own feet and let people watch via Webcam.[2]

Morgan, 35, who grew up and still lives in Mississippi, was hoping to raise $150,000 to cover the cost of new feet. Back in 1986, when he was returning home from a boat trip, he fell off the back of a truck and was run over by the boat trailer being pulled behind. As a result, he was paralyzed from the waist down and in constant pain. He had some ability to move his muscles above his knees but had no feeling at all below his ankles.

He was told that, if he could just obtain a new set of feet, he could train himself to walk again. But Medicare and Medicaid wouldn't cover the cost of the surgery and rehabilitation. For $20, he offered you a chance to watch him do the first part of the job—the amputation—using a homemade guillotine (see Figure 10-3). He planned a gala event, complete with director, camera crews, live band, and a video and DVD production, as well as EMT services for the immediate aftermath. He even sold a "Cut Off My Feet" souvenir T-shirt.

---

2. http://web.archive.org/web/20010922124615/http://cutoffmyfeet.com/

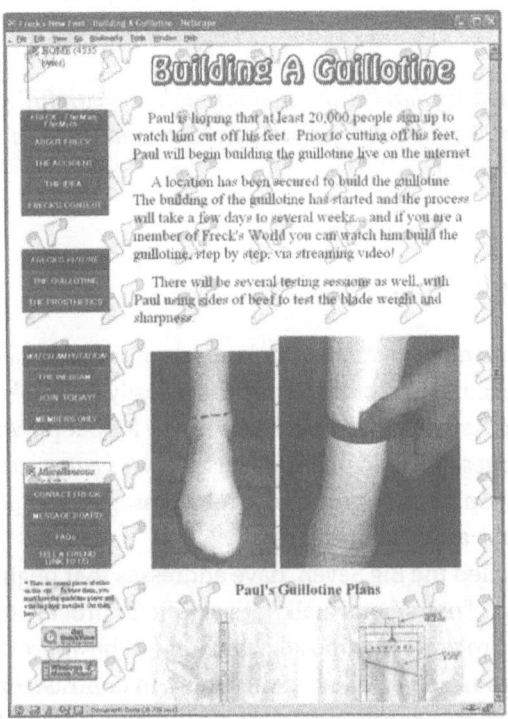

Figure 10-3. This Old Guillotine: A unique do-it-yourself project for a unique purpose [3]

A contest was held, and a man from Pompano Beach, Florida, won an all-expenses-paid trip to be present at the amputation. But the circus never took place. Morgan ran into legal troubles staging his event, and an insufficient number of investors signed up wanting to view the gruesome proceedings.

The thing that amazed me about this was not that Morgan wanted to do it—hey, if you've got to lose your feet anyway, you might as well make some money to recoup your expenses—but how little sympathy he received. Take a look at the comments on the CamChatting message board (http://www.camchatting.com/ubb/Forum1/HTML/000039.html). All participants immediately assumed he was putting them on—that it was all a "scam." So did the compassionate participants at TranceAddict.com (http://www.tranceaddict.com/forums/archive/topic/115037-1.html): "Jeez what an idiot!" exclaimed one. "What is the point?" asked another, even though the site explained that Morgan had lost a kidney as a result of his injuries and that after enduring great pain and struggling through months of rehab, he had regained some ability to walk again.

---

3. http://web.archive.org/web/20011021160100/www.cutoffmyfeet.com/build.html

The site's FAQ page included the question "Are you insane?" Morgan's answer was this:

> *No, I am not insane. This is something that I've thought through very carefully. But for all of you who still doubt, I plan to have a full psychiatric evaluation done to prove that I'm completely sane.*

Those Crazy Alt Newsgroups

The World Wide Web and e-mail are now the most popular parts of the Internet. But in many ways, the real action occurs in an older format that's easily overlooked: Usenet. Usenet (short for the User's Network) provided an early way for people with shared interests to exchange messages and hold online discussions. A *newsgroup* is simply a place on a server where people can connect, read text messages, and post responses. The resulting discussions are called *threads*.

The main set of newgroups, called the Big Seven, have addresses that begin with "comp," "misc," "soc sci," "rec," "news," and "talk." It's a difficult process to start one of these groups: You have to write a proposal, which has to be approved by the people who operate newsgroup servers around the world. In contrast, one part of Usenet has been set aside where anyone can start a newsgroup. This is the alt newsgroup area, which gets its name because all of the groups within it begin with the prefix "alt."

Whenever I venture into the alt newsgroup area, I think of that famous bar scene in the original *Star Wars* movie. The bar is populated by all kinds of bizarre creatures from around the universe, speaking a cornucopia of languages. That's what you find when you browse through the list of alt groups available on your Internet service provider's newsgroup server. The part of the group's name that follows the "alt" tells you what the group is about (more or less). The following are just a few examples:

- alt.amazon.women

- alt.antichrist

- alt.dead.porn.stars

- alt.elvis.sighting

- alt.eunuchs.questions

- alt.fetish.tongue

- alt.misanthropy

- alt.obsessive.nerd

- alt.paranormal.spells.hexes.magic

- alt.polyamory

- alt.religion.beavis-n-butthead

Simply browsing through the set of alt groups available to you is a trip. Some of them seem like mistakes in typing, such as alt.0 or alt.1d. It isn't always clear what the purpose of such groups is—attempting to decipher their meanings is amusing for a few moments, but it quickly becomes clear, in most cases, that this is a pointless activity.

The aforementioned alt.0 group, for instance, seems to be a collection of "for sale" notices. But people publish gibberish poems and nonsensical, childish sayings there as well. Some might ridicule the poems; others might attempt to analyze them in detail. Some groups are momentary jokes obviously created on a dare (for instance, alt.amanda.g.is.a.superstar) and contain only spam newsgroup postings. Others have a legitimate purpose, such as alt.ammonia.refrigeration, where refrigeration technicians discuss the merits of Freon versus ammonia or ask questions about condensers.

Some of the names of these newsgroups are all you need to know. They're likely to make you laugh out loud:

- alt.christnet.sex.fetish.fat.furry.asian.watersports

- alt.golfing-with-orson-beene

- alt.gothic.pretensions

- alt.i-like-toejam-lets-share-a-slice

Some are incredibly obscure and guaranteed to appeal to a select few:

- alt.language.urdu.poetry

- alt.lifestyle.shirtless

- alt.oj.cast-the-movie

The murky sea of alt newsgroups is constantly shifting and changing, so it's difficult to point out the "best" or "weirdest" ones. But the following are a few that have attracted attention over the years and that are likely to be around when you read this.

NOTE   You don't need to install special software to access newsgroups. Newsgroup readers are built into the major browser packages, Microsoft Internet Explorer and Netscape Communicator. You'll need to configure your e-mail to access your Internet service provider's newsgroup server, however. You can also access Usenet from the Web—it seems contradictory, but for people who are most comfortable with Web pages, go to Google (http://www.google.com/) and click Groups. Yahoo! also has a lively set of discussion groups that (at this writing, at least) is free to set up yourself.

alt.bigfoot

Bigfoot, you may or may not know, is not the basketball player Shaquille O'Neal or anyone else with impressive pedal appendages. Bigfoot is a legendary creature that is reputed to live in the woods and is related to the gorilla family. Bigfoot has plenty of people looking for him and talking about him. Alongside the inevitable junk pitches for "hot" photos and miracle products are reprints of news reports that describe Bigfoot sightings, photos of supposed footprints, and the like.

alt.treasure.hunting

As far as I can tell, this newsgroup is frequented by people who actually take their boats out and hunt for treasure, as well as those lucky enough to find valuables washed up on shore. The questions are about identifying medieval coins or comparing various machines that are designed to scour the ocean bottom and look for valuables. Even if you never intend to hunt for treasure yourself, this group gives you a glimpse into what it might be like.

alt.true-crime

This newsgroup, which gets an especially heavy number of postings, includes the same sorts of crime news you see every night on TV. If you are fascinated with crimes that involve celebrities, this is the place to go. You'll find follow-up stories on cases that have fallen out of the public eye because information is posted by those who are strongly interested in them. People who are still obsessed with mass murderers such as Charles Manson and Jeffrey Dahmer occasionally post here and find people who share their interests.

alt.tasteless.jokes

I'm not sure I agree with the name of this newsgroup. Most of the jokes, which come from one joke service, are pretty tame. If you are looking for X-rated jokes, juvenile jokes, or abusive ethnic humor, don't go here. If you are looking for a laugh at an actual joke, check it out. This is an example:

> *A tour bus loaded full of noisy tourists arrives at Runnymede, England. They gather around the guide who says, "This is the spot where the barons forced King John to sign the Magna Carta."*

> *A man pushing his way to the front of the crowd asks, "When did that happen?"*

> *"1215," answers the guide.*

> *The man looks at his watch and says, "Shoot! Just missed it by a half hour!"*

Don't Overlook talk.bizarre

Is it art? Is it just a series of drug-induced ramblings with no coherent beginning or ending? Is it one huge epic poem to which all participants add by posting messages? I can't tell, but when it comes to flaky, weird, pointless, and yet imaginative ramblings, you just have to visit talk.bizarre. The group is aptly named. Participants describe time travel incidents, news stories about 2,000 baboon noses found in airport suitcases, and the destruction of the gene pool. Frank Zappa would feel right at home here.

Devil Made You Do It? Nah, It's Just Mind Control

The truth is out there, as they said on the TV show *The X-Files*. Maybe the truth is in your own head, where the CIA and other groups are actively controlling your thought using implants they have somehow placed there.

The Mind Control Forum (http://www.mindcontrolforums.com/) was created by Edmund J. Light as a means of "resistance to the plutocracy's mind control conspiracies." In 1977, Light began experiencing intense beams of radiation that began to melt his skull. (He has X-rays of his skull on the Web, too— http://mindcontrolforums.com/v/light.htm). Since then, people "in high places" have been doing continuous experiments on him. He has been controlled remotely by satellite.

But the Web site has attracted at least 60 people who also claim to be victims of mind control and implants and whose stories are recorded on the site. What's that? You think this guy is "off the beam," so to speak? It may be mind control working on you, too. Visit the Web site for clues to unexplained scars that may indicate you are under someone else's control. You never know; you may have an excuse for the judge when you get called into court on a traffic ticket.

The Fanatics

One thing that is actually difficult to locate on the Internet is apathy. The Internet provides many points of congregation, debate, and argument for people and groups that passionately stand for something. What that something might be is likely to surprise, shock, and amaze you.

Minor Crimes Become Major Misdemeanors

Anyone who has paid attention to small-town newspapers knows where to turn to get the dirt on anyone around town. You don't go to the front page or to the letters to the editor. You go to the police blotter. The "police blotter" is the name commonly given to petty crime news taken from police reports filed in the local area over the preceding day or week.

In Annapolis, Maryland, the crime rate is (happily) so low that local residents keep track of it almost religiously. Those who appear in the blotter on a regular basis, such as a certain 29-year-old woman who was nabbed in a period of a few weeks on theft and drug possession charges, become local celebrities of a sort. In Annapolis, such incidents constitute major crimes. The police department doesn't even have a homicide unit.

The hottest ticket in town is reported to be the Daily Police Activity Report, which is prepared by the intensely laconic officer Hal Dalton, who makes officer Joe Friday look like the star of *The Music Man*. When the city of Annapolis revamped its Web site a few years ago, it turned to Dalton and his fellow officers to provide a regular source of news. Each day, Dalton arrives at the police station at 6 a.m., goes through the police reports that officers have filed overnight, and assembles a selection of the previous day's most noteworthy crimes. The list is posted each day on the city's Web site and distributed by e-mail to 400 subscribers. Some of those subscribers are local residents, and others are scattered across the country, having become addicts to the goings-on around Annapolis and environs.

Nothing is too ho-hum to make it into Dalton's report. A rock thrown through a window; 50 cents stolen from a car; pepper thrown in a restaurant employee's face, with the perpetrator still having the incriminating pepper shaker in his possession. You can even find out about upcoming appearances by McGruff the Crime Dog. You, too, can get a daily reminder of police activities in Annapolis by subscribing at http://www.ci.annapolis.md.us/citizens/myannapolis/.

Bloggers Record Day's Events, Minute by Minute

A *blog*, or Web log, is a sort of online diary in which anyone can record anything they want about any topic that's on their minds. For many people, blogging is an occasional activity, something they do once a day. Perhaps they write a paragraph or two and then move on to other things.

For devoted, committed bloggers, however, a blog can assume central importance. The blog takes on a life of its own when people begin to flock to it in droves and outsiders send e-mail suggestions for yet more content. The following are just a couple examples of the many fanatical bloggers around the world.

An Opinion on Everything and Something to Say

Glenn Reynolds is one of those people who likes to keep busy. He is a father, husband, author, law professor at the University of Tennessee, columnist for MSN, and libertarian. You would think he doesn't have enough time to contribute to a blog. But you would be very much mistaken. Reynolds makes contributions every day, sometimes many times per day, to his InstaPundit blog (http://www.instapundit.com/). He says he was one of those kids who always wanted to know everything, someone who would happily read the encyclopedia from cover to cover.

For the most part, InstaPundit consists of news stories and links to Web sites that Reynolds finds interesting. Politics is a recurring theme but by no means the only topic that attracts his attention. The following are some recent examples:

A prison rape law: "The answer is that it's not about commerce but about Congress's power to enforce rights under the 14th Amendment."

Owning multiple automobiles: "As usual, I'm surfing the wave of a trend: Ralph Kinney Bennett notes that there are now more cars than drivers in America. That includes me: The InstaPundit household has three cars and two drivers. Some people probably think that's terrible. I think it's great! I might not collect original body—style Mercury Cougars by the scores like Keith Laumer (I think he had over 50, all from the 1967–68 model year), but I like cars, and I think that it's a good thing that people can afford more of them."

VCRs: "I've got a Sony VCR that's neither the best nor the worst. (The best I ever owned was an RCA—really a Thomson, made in France, no less—that I bought in 1986 and that worked flawlessly until a few months ago.)"

You can track how often Reynolds updates his blog each day, in-between teaching, writing academic articles, and taking his daughter to or from school. In a day, he might have as many as 30 updates. He posts while brewing his morning coffee, while cooking dinner (as long as there's nothing that will burn on the stove), late at night, and when his daughter is playing computer games. His site attracts as many as 50,000 visitors each day, which is unusual for a blog that is not connected to a major media organization. And he has inspired many others to start their own blogs: You can scan the lengthy list at http://jeffwolfe.com/instapundit-inspired.html.

For All Too Many, Blogging Equals Boredom

To understand just what makes Glenn Reynolds's InstaPundit blog so exceptional (and so popular), you have to visit the many other blogs that clog up cyberspace. Most seem to be there only to entertain their owners, leaving nothing for visitors to cling to. There are so many of these that singling out any one will seem unfair; I will just take a couple at random to give you examples. But they are by no means exceptional:

Crispy Duck with Ginger (http://www.crispyduck.blogspot.com/): A series of laconic entries simply noting the author's travels to the airport, gripes about bad traffic or uncouth waiters, or fights with boyfriends: "Early flight—no problems. Hotel let us check in early. Had the rates wrong, but cleared it up later. Took the T to Fenway, looking to buy tickets for that day's game. Ended up drinking Sam Adams Oktoberfest at Cask and Flagon, a bar situated in the shadows of the Green Monster. Richie left the bar for a little bit, half drunk, and came back with scalped tickets for the next day's game. Fight started as we left the bar, continued as we traveled on the T to Harvard Square. Back to hotel for a nap that didn't materialize. Showered up and headed to Faneuil Hall area. Dinner at the Salty Dog."

The Dullest Blog in the World (http://www.wibsite.com/wiblog/dull/):
That's the name of it, and the blog lives up to its promise: "I was doing some things. After a while I decided to stop doing them and take a short break. At the end of the break I started doing the things again." All entries are pretty much like this.

World's Most Boring Blog. Promise (http://noteric.blogspot.com/ 2003_06_15_noteric_archive.html): Actually, this blog does not live up to its promise because it does discuss actual women with whom the author is obsessed, as well as albums with secret tracks and dreams the author has had. Unfortunately, it borders on nearly being classifiable as interesting.

I could go on and on with lists of boring blogs, but I leave the research up to you.

From Larva to Pupa to Obsession: Two Scientists' Love Affairs with Caterpillars

Although many providers of online content seem obsessed with themselves and their own thoughts, others use the Internet to explore a particular subject with which they are obsessed. Web sites are perfect for fanatics who seek to know everything, or who actually *do* seem to know everything, about a particular subject.

If you ever want to identify caterpillars or need to write a school report about them, visit the Web sites run by the scientists who have devoted their lives to the subject. Caterpillars come in thousands of varieties all over the world, including some that sting and some that have extra sets of fake eyes to fool predators. Entomologists who used to store their information in books, filing cabinets, or mainframe databases now store facts on the World Wide Web. In many ways, Web-based catalogs of information about species are preferable to museums: Anyone can view the data, it can be continually updated, and mistakes are corrected easily.

When Lee Dyer, an assistant professor in ecology and evolutionary biology at Tulane University, wanted to publish a book about Costa Rican caterpillars, he was persuaded to publish online by his colleague and fellow caterpillar authority, Daniel Janzen of the University of Pennsylvania.

The resulting Web site (http://www.caterpillars.org/, which also has an address of http://www.tulane.edu/~ldyer/lsacat/index.htm,), has some vivid photos and memorable descriptions of caterpillars (see Figure 10-4).

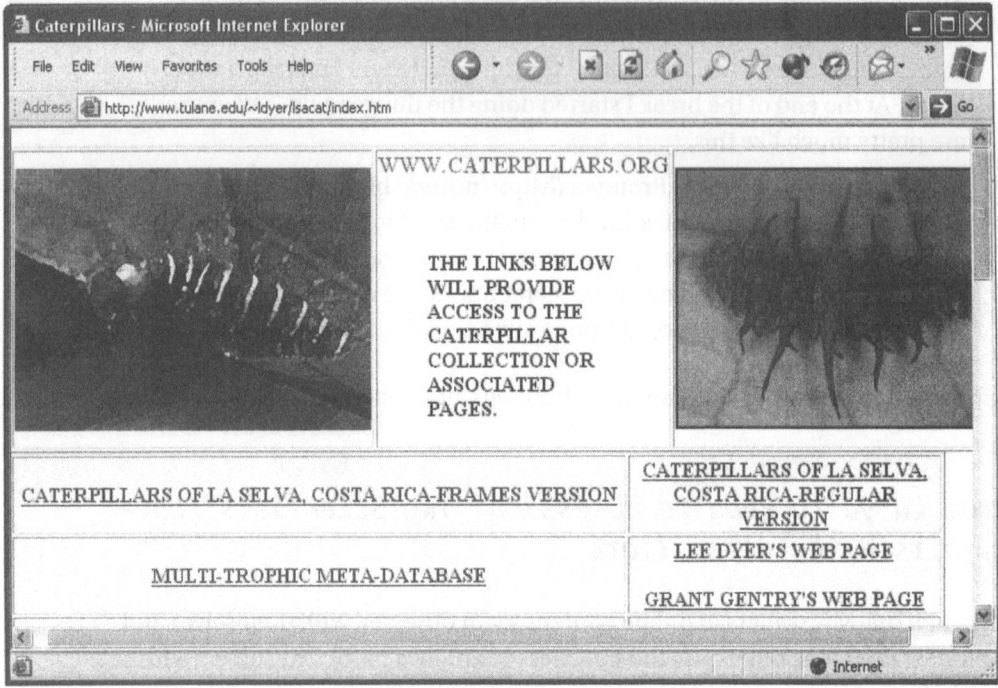

Figure 10-4. Fans, fanatics, and students of everything from cats to caterpillars can explore their subject of interest online.[4]

Dyer verges on the poetic when describing the creatures he so obviously loves. The larvae of Actinote guatemalena are described as "gregarious." The body of Nessaea aglauris is "covered with small bumps that are covered in a diaphanous pearl color (silvery blue/white)." Apatelodes erotina was observed doing a "strange forward and backward wiggle while it walked (it was agitated)." The site also lists unofficial common names of some caterpillars, including the backflip barfer, cherry-headed velvet, and fleshy crested wart butt.

Janzen's site (http://janzen.sas.upenn.edu/), which he operates with his wife Winnie Hallwachs, functions much like a virtual field guide to caterpillars, moths, and other creatures, some of which are shown in Figure 10-5.

Photos published on the Net are far easier to transmit than those reprinted and mailed or printed in a book; as a result, you can find more than 160,000 separate records and nearly 30,000 images of caterpillars on Janzen's creepy, crawly Web site.

---

4. http://janzen.sas.upenn.edu/

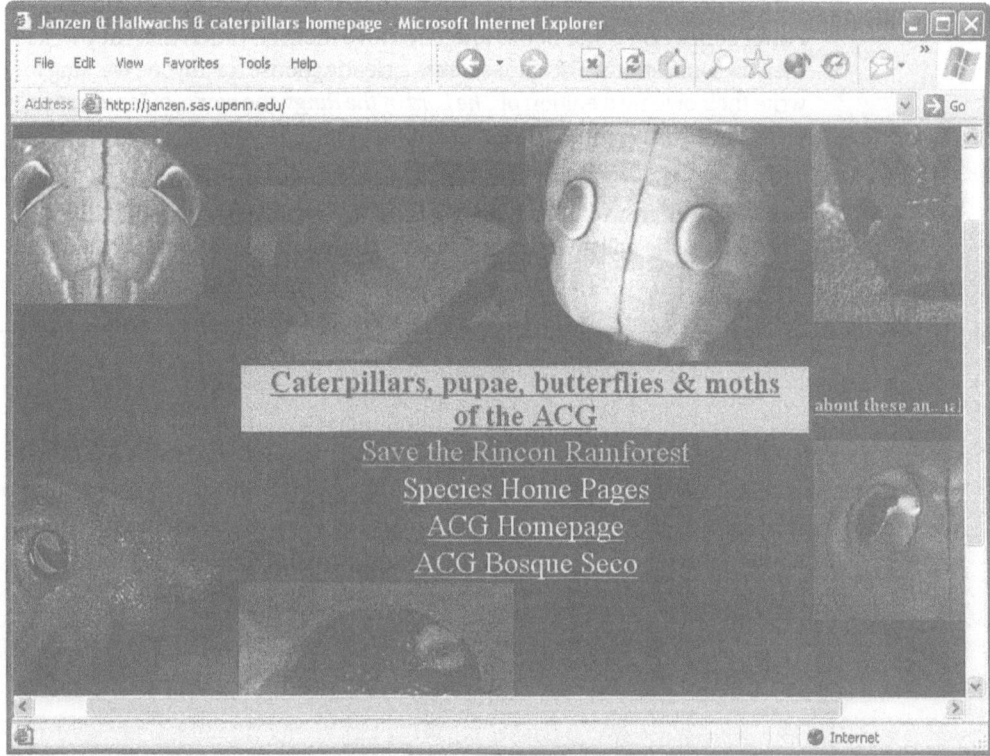

Figure 10-5. The Web is fast becoming a virtual natural history museum.[5]

Random Googling

The Internet contains plenty of Web sites devoted to the interests of fans, fanatics, and flakes. The following list contains a few I found noteworthy—a random sampling of sites that turned up after searching for the terms "fan" or "fanatic" on the search service Google (http://www.google.com/):

- **The Rat Fan Club (http://www.ratfanclub.org/):** If you already like hamsters, gerbils, and guinea pigs, it isn't such a great leap to mice and rats. This particular site launched a campaign to protest the use of rats on the TV show *Fear Factor*. Lest you think I am singling out the lowly rat for abuse, you can also visit the Little Rascals Pygmy Goat Club at http://geocities.com/littlerascalsgoats/ and the Large Black Pigbreeders Club at http://www.largeblackpig.com/club.html.

---

5. http://www.tulane.edu/~ldyer/lsacat/index.htm

- **FanFiction.net (http://www.fanfiction.net/):** Millions of fans of the Harry Potter series and other books and films love them so much that they write their own imitations. This site serves as a clearinghouse for anyone wanting to write their own next edition of *The Lord of the Rings*, the works of Jane Austen, or TV shows such as *Adam-12*.

- **Toy Fanatic (http://www.toyfanatic.com/):** Wondering what to do with that old Mork from Ork or *Welcome Back Kotter* doll laying around in a trunk? This site will give you an idea what it might be worth or buy it from you.

Part Four
Big Brother Is Watching

CHAPTER 11

Political Intrigue
in Babylon

A NEWSPAPER MAY RESTRICT itself to "all the news that's fit to print" about political figures, but the Internet knows no such boundaries. On the Net you can find out what's really going on when it's not yet ready for prime time.

Candidates for public office routinely turn to the Web to create their own Web sites. These, in turn, attract parody Web sites that often poke outrageous fun at the public office seekers. Of course, you don't have to run for office to secure a job in the government; you can apply for a job in espionage online, too.

Ordinary citizens who have access to the Internet have been able to subvert their government's authority and provide news to the outside world in times of war. The Baghdad Blogger and a cybermonk from Kosovo were both able to open a window on daily life in their countries even as they were being bombed. Finally, current office holders have found the Web to be a mixed blessing; they have run into criticism and ridicule online even as they use Web sites and e-mail for their own purposes.

Canny Candidates

The Internet's role in political campaigns is getting more important election by election. Candidates register critical domain names as soon as they decide to run for office—and, if they're smart, they also register as many variations as possible to make it more difficult for parody Web sites to be set up by those who oppose them or just want to make fun of them. Retired General Wesley Clark decided to run for president in 2003 largely because of an Internet-based campaign that was mounted to draft him.

NOTE Former Colorado senator and 1988 presidential candidate Gary Hart started what's believed to be the first Weblog by a politician at http://www.garyhartnews.com/. It's seen as a bid to build political clout.

Bob Dole's Head Explodes; Secret Service Sees Red

One of the first presidential elections to have an impact on the Net (and vice versa) was the contest between Senator Bob Dole of Kansas and the incumbent president, Bill Clinton, in 1996. Dole always seemed to be holding back some kind of dark, angry energy that threatened to burst forth at any moment. Maybe it was this aura that inspired a 22-year-old Web designer named Daniel Burford to create the Exploding Heads Web page.

The site was simple yet outrageously goofy. Visitors began by choosing a celebrity; options included Dole, Boris Yeltsin, Rush Limbaugh, Bill Gates, and Tom Hanks. They would click the celebrity's photo. Over a series of two to four images, the person would grow more and more upset, and in the final frame his head would explode, generating obviously fake blood. Hanks was included in a clip from the movie *Apollo 13* because he was "beloved by young and old alike"; Limbaugh's sequence was described as "the way things ought to explode." After looking long and hard throughout the Web, I was able to dig up the original surviving images of Bob Dole's head making like a volcano. They are preserved on Jonathan Rhoades's site (an Internet relic in its own right) called Bytes of My Mind (see Figure 11-1).

TIP Jonathan Rhoades also preserved the original images of Boris Yeltsin, Bill Gates, and the other celebrities originally featured by Daniel Burford. Visit http://www.thewebpagedepot.com/mind/expheads.htm to enjoy some further explosions.

"I didn't even expect anyone to look at it," Burford told People Online. It turns out he was wrong: The sequence of Bob Dole drew the attention of the U.S. Secret Service, which actually showed up at Burford's place of employment. Burford recounted later that the agents said they had received complaints about "pictures of a political nature." Apparently, the agents didn't understand what Web pages were.

Burford and his coworkers explained that the photos were put online only as part of a political satire; they did not intend any actual harm to Dole. (The company shot some secret video of the agents conducting their inquiry, which it eventually wanted to put online.) The Secret Service summoned Burford to its local office, where he was asked if he had ever owned a gun or spent time in a mental institution. When he answered "no" to both inquiries, he was allowed to go.

Burford took the attention in stride. He added the following disclaimer about Senator Dole to the Exploding Heads site:

I don't wish Bob Dole any harm. I hope he lives a long and fruitful life, happily exploiting the masses, oppressing the downtrodden, and taking huge "contributions" from corporate-funded PACs, until he dies a peaceful natural death WHEN HIS HEAD EXPLODES MUAHAHAHA oh god no scratch that last part.

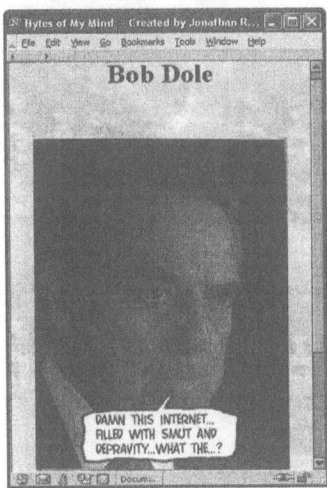  

Figure 11-1. The Exploding Heads Web page paid tribute to Bob Dole and resulted in a visit from the U.S. Secret Service.[1]

The Crazy Election of 2000: Doin' the Dubya Dance

Who can forget the presidential election of 2000? Many would like to, but its legacy lingers on whether we like it or not. Some of the few humorous moments associated with that debacle occurred online. Engineer Mike Collins created the image shown

---

1.   http://www.thewebpagedepot.com/mind/mind/expheads/dole.htm

in Figure 11-2, which summed up the confusion in Florida, where voters ran into all kinds of problems filling out the infamous "butterfly ballot" and having their votes counted accurately.

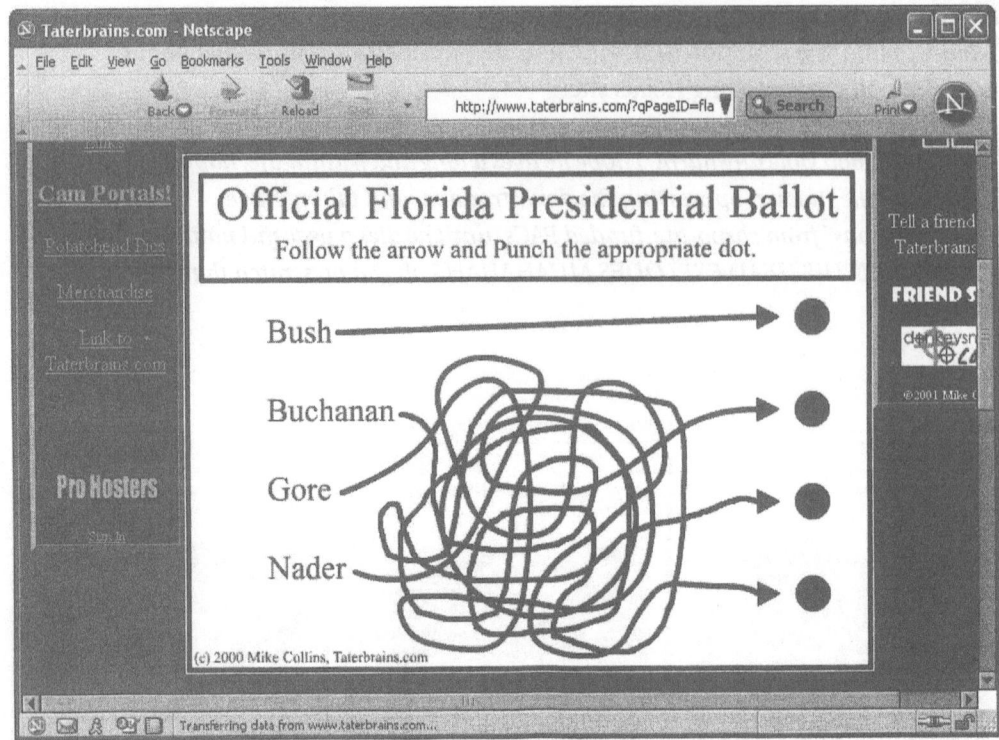

Figure 11-2. Election problems in Florida prompted one amateur cartoonist to create this classic online image.[2]

Collins, who has preserved the image for posterity on his Taterbrains.com Web site (http://www.taterbrains.com/?qPageID=fla), comments that he created the cartoon only to give some of his friends a laugh and "never in my wildest dreams expected it to become a nationwide sensation." The image was seen around the world, and Collins hired a distributor to sell T-shirts showing the ballot.

Before the election, my neighbor showed me a Web page that depicted George W. Bush dancing wildly. Many such pages circulated before, during, and after Bush became president. The original Dubya Dance page (see Figure 11-3) is still available online, too (http://www.geocities.com/dubyahump/oldsite/).

---

2. http://www.taterbrains.com/?qPageID=fla

Figure 11-3. George W. Bush danced his way into the White House through sites such as this.[3]

 NOTE Another odd aspect of the 2000 election was the promotion of an Internet Party candidate, Henry Rollins. Rollins, a heavily tattooed rock musician and poet, was boosted by an alternative-rock online magazine (or *Webzine*) called Pandomag.com.

W Tries to Silence Parody Site, Then Backs Down

During the election and all through his presidency, one of the harshest and most outrageous voices raised against George W. Bush was the Web site GWBush.com. From its earliest days in 1999, the site attracted the ire of the future president and his staff. It's not difficult to understand why. GWBush.com features video of Bush drinking and picking his nose. The site also has him "Photoshopped" into a variety

3. http://www.geocities.com/dubyahump/oldsite/

of improbable scenes and garbs, such as the Christlike outfit shown in Figure 11-4. It was posted online before Bush had chosen a running mate for the 2000 election.

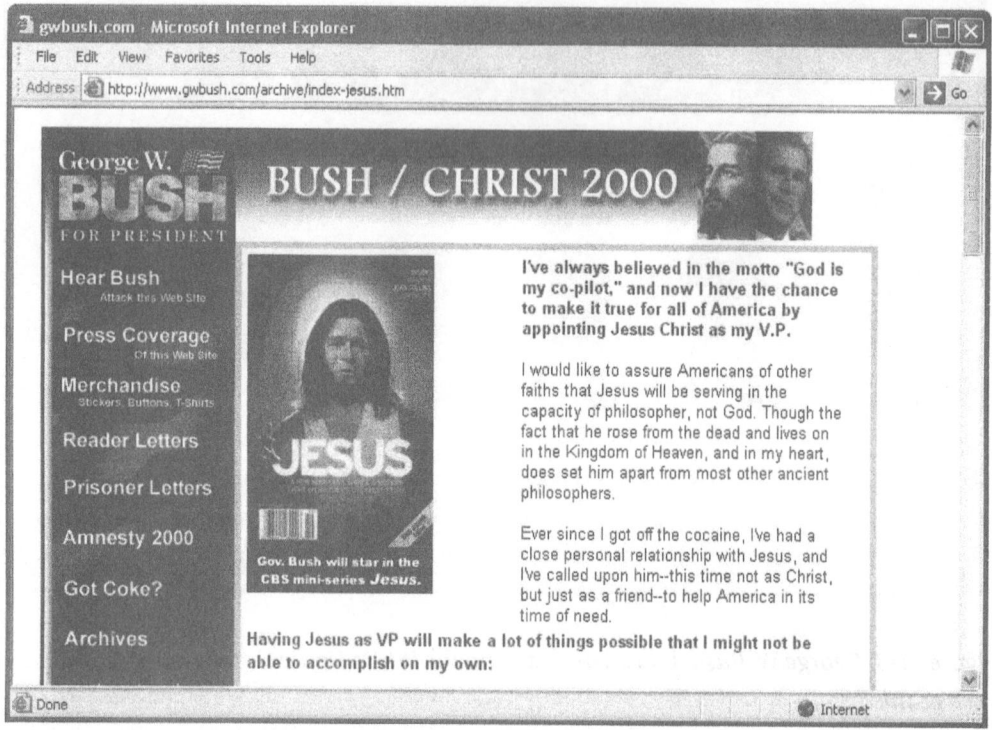

Figure 11-4. The Bush staff threatened to shut down this Web site, but it's still online and dishing dirt on W.[4]

Thirty-year-old Massachusetts-based computer programmer Zack Exley started the site. Exley is ardent in his opposition to Bush and will say or publish just about anything on his site in an attempt to disparage the Texan. He isn't alone. Volunteers have provided him with content, and donations come in to keep his site going strong. During the 2000 election, Exley first gained attention by bashing Bush's tough antidrug stance with accounts of his alleged drug use and drinking in college. As many as 10,000 visitors were viewing the anti-Bush content each day, and Exley planned to produce some anti-Bush TV ads.

---

4. https://gwbush.com/archive/index-jesus.htm

The Bush campaign responded by filing a complaint with the Federal Election Commission (FEC) regarding GWBush.com, contending that it represented a "political committee" with intent to politically ruin Bush's candidacy. When Bush was asked about the complaint at a press conference, he uttered the statement that "there ought to be limits to freedom." This comment drew criticism from advocates of free speech on the Internet and attracted nearly 50,000 new visitors to the GWBush.com site.

Exley was delighted with all the attention, which set his site apart from the other parody Web sites that are routinely established to attack candidates. The media attention about the incident caused a well-known conservative legal defense organization called the Rutherford Institute to offer legal defense to Exley. This was the same legal group that defended Paula Jones in her lawsuit against President Bill Clinton. The Bush camp quieted down, and, at this writing, GWBush.com is gearing up to sling more mud at its chosen target during the 2004 presidential election.

 NOTE Usually, presidential candidates keep their vice presidential candidate selections a secret or wait until the last minute to make a selection. Before the election of 2000, Republican candidate and millionaire publisher Steve Forbes registered the following domain names that gave a big, obvious hint as to his own preferred running mate: Florida Governor Jeb Bush. The domain names included steveandjeb.com, forbesandjebbush.net, and forbes-jebbush2000.com.

Google-Bombing Leaves President Bushwhacked

The search service Google (http://www.google.com/) has achieved a preeminent state among Internet search services because of its accuracy. The exact way in which it returns its highly accurate search results is confidential. But one thing is known: Google ranks Web pages, in part, by the number of hyperlinks that are made to those pages. If a Web page has dozens or even hundreds of other Web pages that link to it, that page is likely to appear at or near the top of a page of Google search results. The many Web blogs that countless people maintain in cyberspace can influence Google search results by word of mouth. If one blogger tells other bloggers to make links to a page, it can become popular on Google.

Bloggers have discovered their influence and taken it a step further. They have invented a bizarre activity called *Google-bombing*. They get hundreds of other blogs to link to a page and mention, in connection with that link, a word or phrase. Anyone who follows by entering that word or phrase in Google and searching for it is taken to the targeted (or, you might say, Google-bombed) Web page.

Just as this book was being prepared for press, the first known political Google-bombing took place. Bloggers decided to direct Google users to the Web page of President George W. Bush. They linked to his page on the official White House Web site. And they connected the links to a telling phrase: *miserable failure*. Before long, the word spread throughout cyberspace like wildfire: If you entered the terms "miserable failure" in Google's search box and clicked the I'm Feeling Lucky button, you were taken to President Bush's Web page.

Looking for a Few Good Spies

The Internet gives millions of college graduates a way to find employment through Web sites such as Monster.com and Jobs.com. In the United Kingdom, the increasing tendency of job hunters to post résumés and fill out applications online has not gone unnoticed. The government's security agency MI5 (the equivalent of the CIA in the U.S.) and its Atomic Weapons Establishment have taken to posting ads on job boards to recruit its newest spies and nuclear scientists.

The stereotypical image of how spies are recruited is that a professor or administrator at Oxford calls prospective spies into the office and discusses the future with them over a glass of port. Tom Hughes, managing director of the Milkround job site (http://www.milkround.com/), says that "unusual government departments need quality graduates as much as any other company, which means that more and more people can fulfill their aspirations, no matter how diverse."

MI5's employment notice on the Milkround Web site (see Figure 11-5) calls for people "of the highest integrity" who are "resilient, sensitive to others, and open to new ideas and working practices." The notice also cautions applicants: "Discretion is an important part of working for the Service, so please try to avoid telling people about your application."

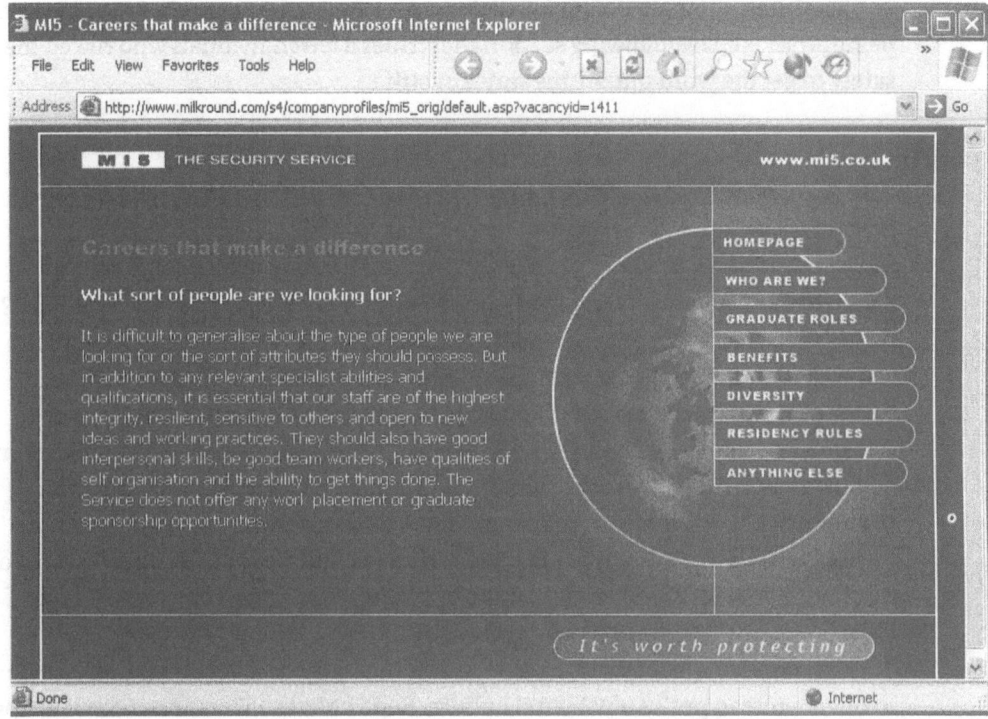

Figure 11-5. Looking for a career in the intelligence service? Now you can apply online.[5]

Wartime Observers

Past wars, such as World War II and Vietnam, were the subject of dramatic reporting by journalists who brought back news and images from the front lines. But those images were almost entirely of the forces of the United States and its allies. Once in a while, an Anne Frank provides a vivid glimpse into the horrors of war from the perspective of an ordinary citizen. All too often, those of us in the West who had been hearing about our own soldiers had no idea what war was like from the viewpoint of the people who were caught in the crossfire—the ordinary citizens of the country being attacked who had to endure bombings and all the horrors of war while simply try to survive.

---

5. http://www.milkround.com/s4/companyprofiles/mi5_orig/default.asp?vacancyid=1411

The Internet has given a voice to those who are on the "inside" of the countries being attacked. The following sections describes a few individuals who risked their safety to get the word out during times of strife.

The Baghdad Blogger, Iraq's Own Anne Frank, Finds His Voice

Salam Pax, an architect living in Baghdad began a Web log called Where is Raed? (http://dearraed.blogspot.com/, shown in Figure 11-6) a few months before the war in Iraq began in spring 2003. His pen name combines both the Arabic and Latin words for "peace." He had to choose a pen name; otherwise, he would certainly have been imprisoned by the Iraqi authorities. He provided a vivid, compelling account of the weeks and months leading up to the war including the shuttering of shops and stockpiling of food. His clandestine messages were surprisingly critical of the regime of Saddam Hussein and free in their observations of what was going on in the city—just the opposite of the image Westerners had of most Iraqis, who supposedly hated the West.

For months, speculation raged over whether Pax was a real Iraqi because he so often wrote in praise of Western culture. Reports in the West about the Web log terrified Pax, and he was afraid he would be arrested. "That's the beauty of doing things on the computer, on the Internet. Nobody has to know anything," Pax later told radio interviewer Terry Gross. "You just make sure you don't talk about it." Only one friend—Raed, the person named in the title of the blog—knew Salam was keeping a blog. His parents never knew he was sending messages to millions of people around the world from the computer in his room.

Eventually, reporters from the U.K. paper *The Guardian* tracked him down and certified his authenticity as a real Iraqi resident. Pax's blog entries were later excerpted in Guardian Unlimited, the Web site of *The Guardian*. In the fall of 2003, Pax's blog was published in book form; in the United States it's available under the title *Salam Pax: The Clandestine Diary of an Ordinary Iraqi* (Grove Press, 2003).

Pax provided the following description of what it was like to keep a blog: "It doesn't feel like you are writing a Web log and all these people are coming online to read it. It's like a conversation around a really big table where everybody is telling stories."

TIP You can find out more about Pax's book and read the first chapter at http://www.thebaghdadblog.com/book/.

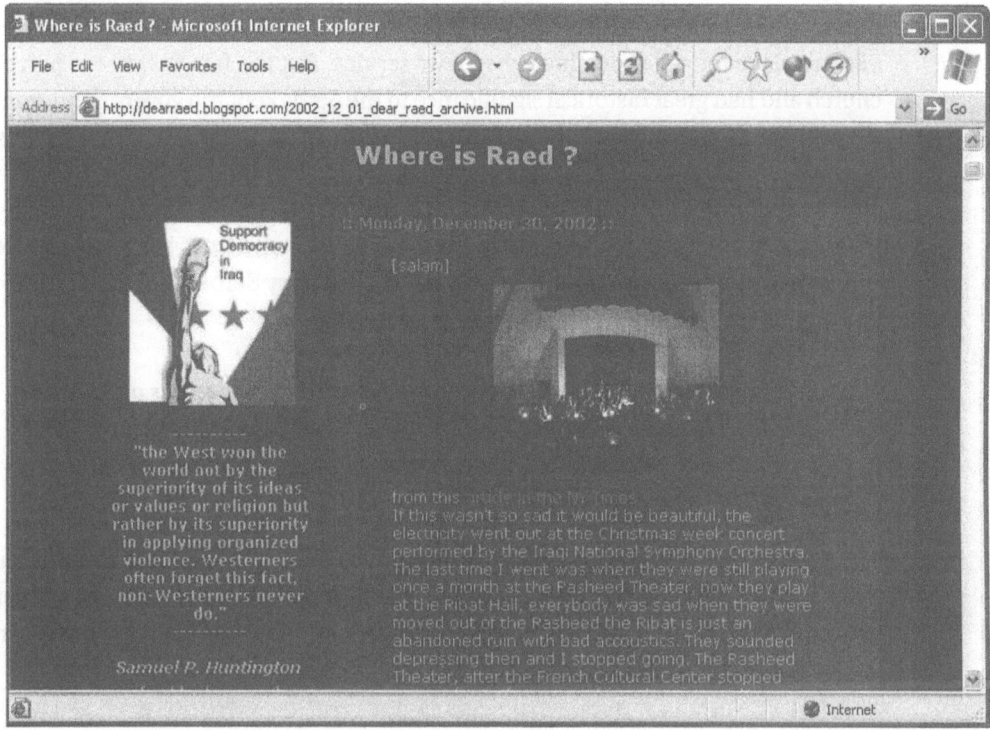

Figure 11-6. The Baghdad Blogger provided an insider's account of the War in Iraq from this Web site.[6]

Monk Starts Mailing List from Kosovo

In the late 1990s, the United States and allied nations began a bombing campaign in Serbia in an effort to stop atrocities against other residents of the former country of Yugoslavia. Serbia immediately became off-limits to foreign journalists, many of whom were expelled from its borders. Serbia's own news outlets were banned from reporting on how the country was faring under the bombing campaign.

However, one independent voice—that of a Serbian Orthodox monk who was wired to the Net and spared from persecution—was able to report by sending out e-mail messages from a monastery built in the 14th century. Sava Janjic, shown in Figure 11-7, created a mailing list of journalists and diplomats, who regularly received his news reports about the Kosovo conflict. Often, the stories he circulated were ones that had been banned for publication by the government in Belgrade but that Janjic was able to distribute to a much larger audience around the world.

---

6. http://dearraed.blogspot.com/2002_12_01_dear_raed_archive.html

The Visoki Decani Monastery, located in the western part of the Yugoslav Province of Kosovo and Metohia, was built between 1327 and 1335. It hardly seems like the place for a clandestine cybernews service. But the fact that it was part of a church and had great historical significance to the Serbs kept the government from silencing him—even though the Serbian ruler at the time, Slobodan Milosevic, was a prime target of his criticism. The monastery, which contains the bones of soldiers who fought in the battle of Kosovo in 1389, remained a tranquil refuge for many. Often, the stories Janjic broadcast to his mailing list came from refugees who fled to the monastery for sanctuary. He feared that ordinary Serbs would eventually pay a price for Milosevic's exploits. One report read:

Slobodan Milosevic is playing a wicked game with the emotions of Serbs in Kosovo. In 21st century Europe there is no place for ethnically cleansed territories, terror, or crimes. The Holy Scripture teaches us that one cannot love God without first loving one's neighbor.

A report in Salon by writer Don North reported that Janjic would rise at 1 a.m. to take advantage of better Internet connections. After saying his morning prayers, he would surf the Web and gather stories from many sources. He would then fire the stories off to his list of 300-odd reporters, diplomats, and acquaintances.

 NOTE   The Decani Monastery is depicted on a Web site at http://www.kosovo.com/edecani.html.

Today, several years after the war ended, Janjic is still speaking out about the plight of the people living around the monastery. The Web site of the Serbian Orthodox Diocese of Raska and Prizren has published a photo of Janjic and an interview with him (see Figure 11-7). In the interview, he describes the "ghettoization" of the Serb people, as well as the monks, who are separated from the neighboring Albanians for security reasons.

Figure 11-7. The cybermonk who kept the world informed on the Serbian side of the Kosovo war[7]

Web Site Puts Chinese Dissidents in Prison

Sometimes, Web sites and mailing lists can put ordinary citizens in danger even when their country is not at war. Take the case of four Chinese young people who called themselves the New Youth Study Group. They got together occasionally on university campuses to discuss political theory and occasionally posted essays on the Web.

---

7. http://www.kosovo.com/glaskim_int.html

After being held in prison for two years, they were convicted in 2003 of "subverting state power." Xu Wei, 28, and Jin Haike, 26, were sentenced to ten years in prison. Yang Zili, 32, and Zhang Honghai, 29, were sentenced to eight years. Others have been imprisoned for using the Internet and running antigovernment Web sites.

Politicians, Bores, and Hypocrites

I know what you're thinking: You're looking at the heading "Politicians, Bores, and Hypocrites" and you're asking yourself, "What's the difference?" Sometimes, these three categories do overlap. When they do, they make for entertaining online content. The following are just a few recent examples.

Boredom Has a Face, and It's Darling

Politicians don't have to be exciting. They just have to do their jobs. But Web sites such as CyberBritain.com that are looking for ways to get Web surfers to interact and visit them on a regular basis will look at anything and create a survey so people will register an opinion. They asked Brits to vote for the most boring politician in the country, and Transport Secretary Alistair Darling came up the "winner." He received nearly 3,000 of the 12,000 votes cast. Another Web site, Ananova (http://www.ananova.com/), published the scintillating photo shown in Figure 11-8.

What, exactly, goes into creating a boring politician? I decided to look around the Web. Columnist Shelagh Shepherd, writing on a site called Westminsterwatch (http://www.westminsterwatch.co.uk/diaryarchive/emag_diary020201.htm), described Darling's "boring platitudes" during the TV show *Question Time*. With admirable foresight, she called him "arguably the most boring politician on the planet."

The site of the Dull Men's Club (http://www.dullmen.com/links.htm), on the same page that gave attention to abandoned cranberry bogs, duck tape, vacuum cleaner bags, and other boring topics, also mentioned Darling. *The Scotsman*, Scotland's national newspaper, published an article online (http://www.thescotsman.co.uk/index.cfm?id=1433762002) that gave a clue as to why Darling is such a yawner: It's part of his job. He was appointed with the mission of taking the Department of Transport out of the news and overcome warring factions that previously kept anything from getting done. "Mr. Darling was chosen for his low-key, mechanistic style of government," the article explained.

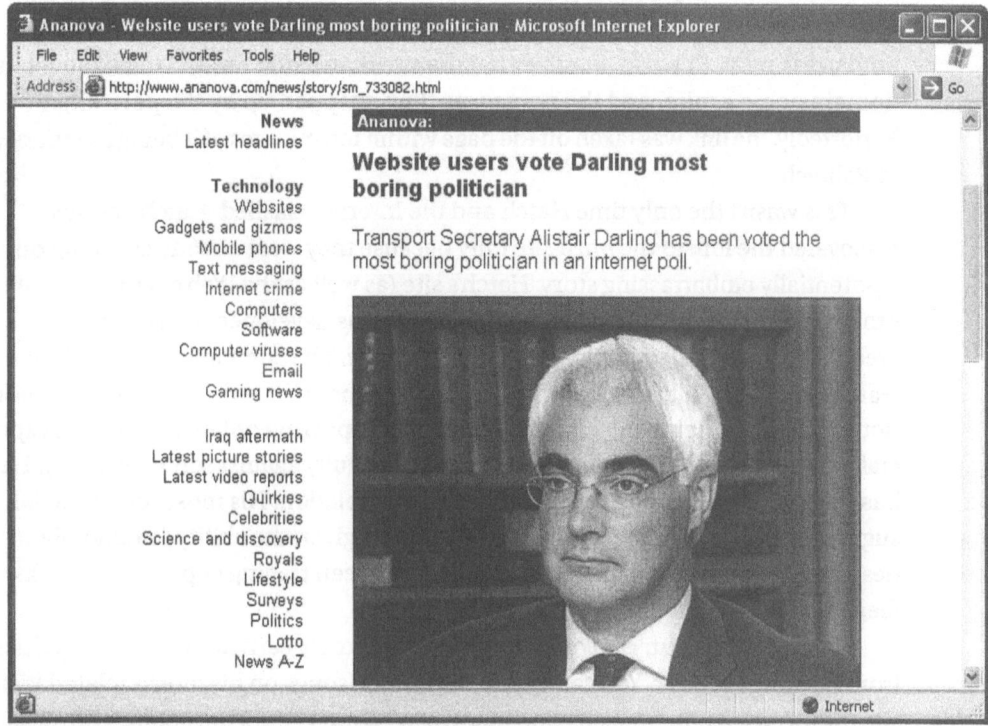

Figure 11-8. At least he gets the job done: Britian's most boring politician[8]

---

8. http://www.ananova.com/news/story/sm_733082.html

Senator Hatch and the Internet: Embarrassing Links

Orrin Hatch, the U.S. Republican senator from Utah, is one of Congress's staunchest conservatives. Senator Hatch sponsored the Child Pornography Prevention Act. The act amended federal child pornography statutes to establish a new definition of child pornography. The new definition includes any visual depiction, such as a photograph, film, videotape, or computer image, that is produced by any means, including electronically by computer.

That's why it was such a surprise when a mailing list called Politech, run by Declan McCullagh, reported that Hatch's official home page contained a link to a porn Web site. Observers speculated that Hatch was possibly the victim of an Internet Protocol (IP) hijacking, in which someone took over the original IP address associated with the link and redirected it to an extremely X-rated site to cause embarrassment. (It's also possible that the site that Hatch wanted to link to let its domain name expire, and the name was then snapped up by the porn site.) Reportedly, the link was taken off the page within ten minutes of it being mentioned in Politech.

This wasn't the only time Hatch and the Internet clashed. Hatch's critics discovered the link to the porn site only because they were already checking out a potentially embarrassing story. Hatch's site (as well as the Web sites of several other senators) uses a clickable menu bar that was developed using software created by the British company Milonic Solutions. The company that developed Hatch's site, GSL Solutions, didn't purchase a license to use the software—at least not initially. In other words, Hatch's menu was appearing online illegally. It's especially ironic because Hatch has spoken out forcefully against software piracy. He has said that there is "no excuse" for copyright violation. His most controversial suggestion was that copyright holders should be given the ability to remotely destroy the computers of individuals who have been trading copyrighted works illegally.

Hatch, it turns out, is a songwriter who reportedly earned $18,000 in royalties from his songs in 2002. You can even hear Hatch's songs on his music-related Web site (http://www.hatchmusic.com/, shown in Figure 11-9). The senator's proposal, which was made during a discussion about illegally downloaded music files, would have given offenders two warnings. After the second warning, copyright holders would have the right to destroy the user's PC. GSL Solutions avoided such trouble by quickly purchasing the required license and adding copyright information to the source code for Hatch's home page.

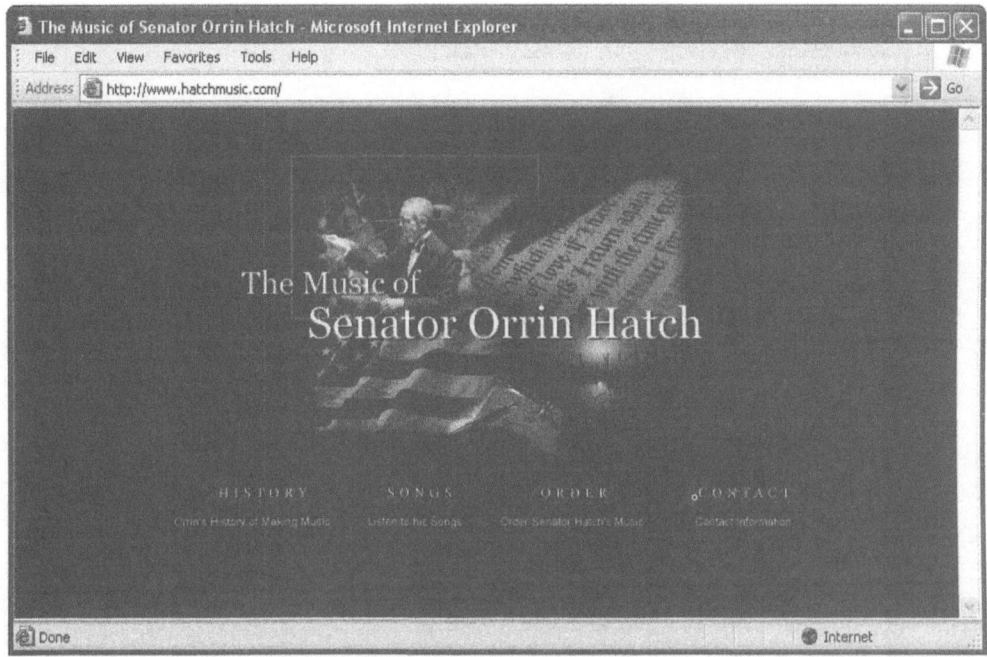

Figure 11-9. You can purchase songs such as "America Rocks!" and "The Answer's Not in Washington" on Senator Hatch's Web site.[9]

An Eerie Image of the Twin Towers and Giuliani's "Bunker"

Buck Wolf, a columnist for ABCNews.com, writes regular features about wacky news stories, some of which have to do with the Internet. The column is always entertaining. Wolf keeps archives of his old columns online, and they make for good reading. But one story and one image sent a chill through me. It originally appeared in a column Wolf wrote December 17, 2000. It was entitled "Rudy's Rampart" (http://abcnews.go.com/sections/us/DailyNews/wolffiles23.html), and it shows how dramatically things have changed since the attacks of September 11, 2001. Figure 11-10 shows the image that was depicted in the column to the right of the story .

---

9. http://www.hatchmusic.com/

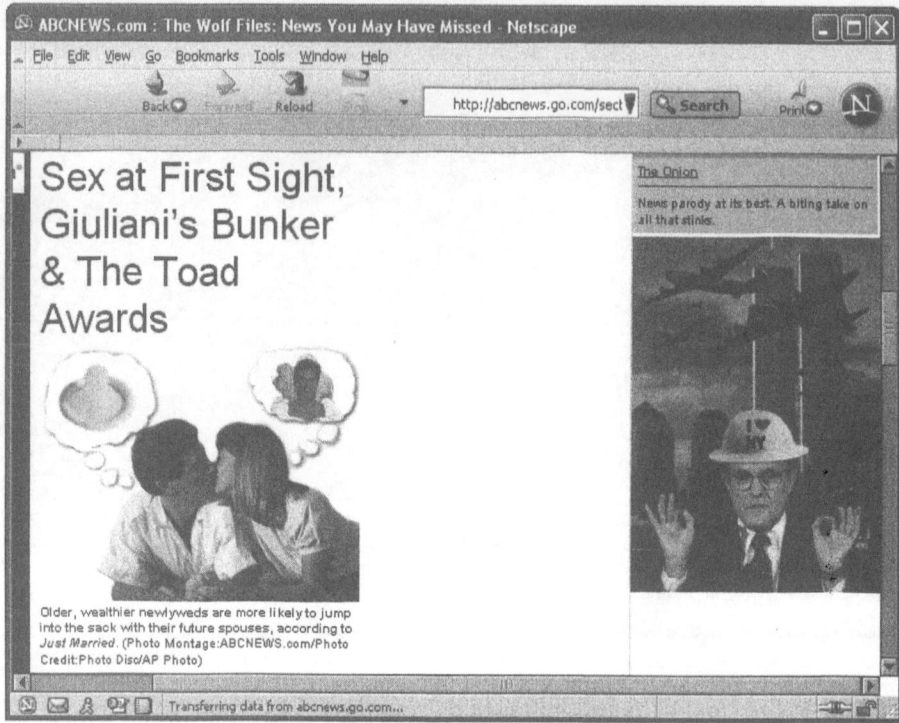

Figure 11-10. This image of New York Mayor Rudy Giuliani appeared online nine months before the twin towers were destroyed.[10]

The article and image have a harsh tone that would never be adopted today, with what we know about the attack on the World Trade Center. The article reads as follows, in part:

> *If Armageddon—or Godzilla—comes, New York Mayor Rudy Giuliani will be ready. He's building a bomb-proof, $16 million bunker in the sky....*
>
> *His 46,000-foot, state-of-the-art command center is being designed to provide refuge from biological warfare, 150-mile-an-hour hurricane winds—and all variety of terrorist attack. But can it withstand political fallout?*
>
> *"The mayor's actions are increasingly bizarre," says Council Speaker Peter Vallone, the mayor's most vocal critic. "Maybe he saw* Deep Impact, Independence Day, *or one of these other disaster movies where New York gets demolished, and it's gone to his head."*

---

10. http://abcnews.go.com/sections/us/DailyNews/wolffiles23.html

The center is to be located on the 26th floor of a building just across the street from the World Trade Center's twin towers, where a 1993 terrorist attack killed six and injured more than 100. The mayor, his family, and 30 officials would be able to live there for about a week before having to come out for air.

"We face different kinds of threats now. We should be ready for these threats," he [Giuliani] said. *"One day the city will thank me."*

He was certainly right about that last part. The city and the entire country thanked him for the leadership he displayed during the crisis. But the bunker ended up falling to the ground the evening of September 11. In fact, there has been much speculation that the fuel stored for the bunker *caused* the collapse of the 7 World Trade Center building that housed it. An article on mediastudy.com (http://mediastudy.com/articles/av10-17-02.html) reports the following:

In a culture of hawkish hyper-patriotism, all of the heroes of 9-11 became off limits for criticism. Rudolph Giuliani, for example, who in the course of one day rose from jilted husband and despotic mayor, to national hero, was actually responsible, along with the terrorists, for the collapse of the third World Trade Center building, a 47-story tower known as #7 World Trade Center. Number 7, it turns out, housed Giuliani's personal emergency command bunker, which was complete with 42,000 gallons of diesel fuel, illegally stored above ground to run the mayor's emergency generators. The fuel caught fire after the collapse of the towers and caused a structural member of the building to melt, just as the jet fuel did in the larger towers. This story, though circulating in the alternative press, was not reported by the mainstream media for nearly four months. When it finally broke, it was downplayed.

 NOTE   You can read another article about the collapse of 7 World Trade Center at http://www.wirednewyork.com/wtc/7wtc/default.htm.

Donald Rumsfeld's Online Treasury of Quotable Quotes

During my first marriage, I was distantly related to Donald Rumsfeld, at least as an in-law. But now he and I have virtually no connection except that we are both Americans. So I have no qualms about calling your attention to the Donald Rumsfeld Library of Quotations, which is provided courtesy not of an American media outline but of the British Broadcasting Corporation (BBC).

On the quotation page (shown in Figure 11-11), the BBC has captured some of the memorable sound clips from Rumsfeld's many press conferences during the war in Iraq. They are preserved as sound clips so you can enjoy their original delivery to the world. Examples include the following:

In America we have a saying: If you're in a hole, stop digging...I don't think I should have said that.

The statement I made was sound as a rock...I didn't say Iraq!

It's like stirring for troubled waters....

I would not say that the future is necessarily less predictable than the past. I think the past was not predictable when it started.

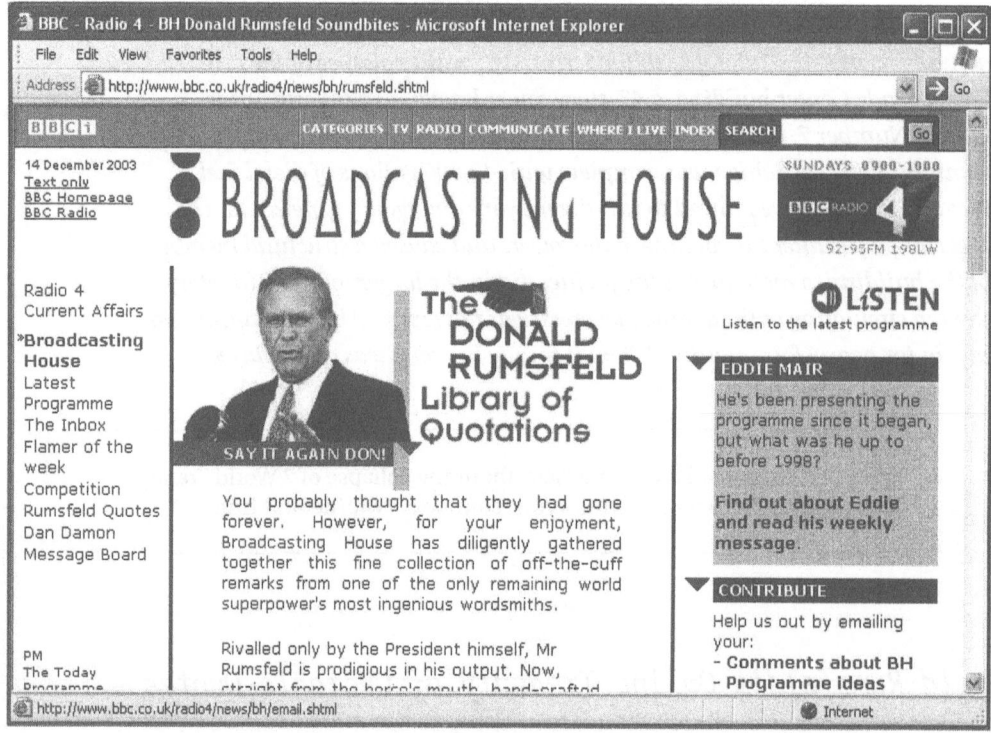

Figure 11-11. The BBC has preserved quotable quotes from the U.S. Secretary of Defense.[11]

---

11. http://www.bbc.co.uk/radio4/news/bh/rumsfeld.shtml

I wish I could convey the nasal, grating tone of voice, the sound of befuddlement, and the sense of exasperation Rumsfeld often displays when he spars with the press—but you can experience it for yourself at http://www.bbc.co.uk/radio4/news/bh/rumsfeld.shtml.

Did Al Gore "Invent the Internet?"

Former Senator and Vice President Al Gore is best remembered these days as the man who lost the closest presidential election in U.S. history in 2000. Before that, he gained notoriety for some famous (or infamous) remarks he made about the Internet on March 11, 1999, to CNN reporter Wolf Blitzer. The remarks may well have played a role in the outcome of that election. The following is the exchange that stirred up all the trouble:

> Blitzer: *Why should Democrats, looking at the Democratic nomination process, support you instead of Bill Bradley, a friend of yours, a former colleague in the Senate? What do you have to bring to this that he doesn't necessarily bring to this process?*

> Gore: *Well, I will be offering...I'll be offering my vision when my campaign begins. And it will be comprehensive and sweeping. And I hope that it will be compelling enough to draw people toward it. I feel that it will be.*

> *But it will emerge from my dialogue with the American people. I've traveled to every part of this country during the last six years. During my service in the United States Congress, I took the initiative in creating the Internet. I took the initiative in moving forward a whole range of initiatives that have proven to be important to our country's economic growth and environmental protection, improvements in our educational system.*

As you can see, Gore never actually said flat out that he "invented the Internet." Nevertheless, the remarks were grabbed eagerly by Republicans who didn't want to see Gore as president and who inflated the words and made fun of them. Senator Trent Lott claimed that he invented the paper clip, for instance. Jay Leno made endless jokes about Gore inventing the Internet. Gore tried to poke fun at himself, but the damage was done: Individual voters lost confidence in Gore and began to think that he would inflate his remarks whenever the situation warranted.

The irony is that, according to some individuals who really did play a role in inventing the Internet, Gore actually does deserve some credit. As the chairman of a congressional science subcommittee in 1986, Gore was partially responsible for creating five National Science Foundation supercomputers that played an integral role in the Internet's development. These centers created a foundation of high-speed networking from which the Internet would grow. In 1986, Gore spoke in Congress in support of funding for the National Science Foundation (NSF), which would create NSFnet, a forerunner of the Internet.

Vinton Cerf, who helped invent the Internet Protocol and is one of the real "inventors" of the Internet, participated in a forum on the Internet in June 2000. The moderator joked about Gore claiming to have invented the Internet. Cerf did not join in the laughter. He said the following:

> *I'd like to clear up one little item—about the Vice President...he really does deserve some credit for his early recognition of the importance of the Internet and the technology that makes it work.*

One of the official government Web pages for Vice President Al Gore (which is still online at http://clinton2.nara.gov/WH/EOP/OVP/) lists among his accomplishments: "While he was in Congress he sat on the relevant science and technology committees and worked to bring about what has become the Internet." Who knows where Gore—and the world—would be today if he had said as much to Wolf Blitzer back in 1999?

Random Googling

The Internet contains plenty of Web sites devoted to political rumor, ridicule, and shenanigans. The following list contains a few I found noteworthy—a random sampling of sites that turned up after searching for the terms "politics" and "political intrigue" on the search service Google (http://www.google.com/):

- **The Truth Seeker (http://www.thetruthseeker.co.uk/category.asp?ID=18):** This U.K.-based Web site explores all kinds of embarrassing political stories, and it is not limited to coverage of events in Britain. U.S. political figures as well as those in the Middle East are examined as well.

- **Politics1 (http://www.politics1.com/):** This is a clearinghouse of news about political races and current political issues in the United States. Conservative, liberal, libertarian, and other viewpoints are presented.

- **History and Politics Out Loud (http://www.hpol.org/):** This is a searchable archive of audio files that teachers and researchers can use. Excerpts from the Watergate tapes, Martin Luther King Jr.'s "I Have a Dream" speech, and other famous audio moments are available in RealAudio format.

CHAPTER 12
Scandals in Babylon

THE BILL CLINTON–MONICA LEWINSKY scandal that erupted during Clinton's second term as president was one of the first big scandals to be fueled by the Internet. Every day, it seemed, there was a new revelation about what someone said or did. It's the speed with which rumors fly; it's also the way someone's character can be tainted quickly and so severely. With JFK, everyone around the president apparently knew what he was doing in his private life, but it didn't get out of that inner circle. Now, we all are in the inner circle, thanks to the Internet.

Something happens or almost happens. A rumor starts. E-mails are sent. A chat room opens. Word gets out to one of the Internet gossip columnists. Eventually, it finds its way to the mainstream media. As new revelations occur, the cycle repeats itself.

It doesn't matter whether you look it up weeks or months after the fact. Sometimes how they got caught is just as interesting as what they were doing wrong in the first place. Find out how evildoers around the world sowed their wild oats and then were made to pay the price.

The "Zippergate" Scandal That Broke Online

The Internet increasingly plays a key role in all types of political matters. Candidates routinely create their own Web sites where they (we hope) state their positions on important matters and often launch attacks and counterattacks at their opponents. The Internet also helps both candidates and elected officials get in trouble more quickly than ever before. Scandals have been around since the Founding Fathers, but the first big political scandal of the Internet era was probably the Monica Lewinsky matter, which dogged President Bill Clinton throughout much of his second term.

The Monica Lewinsky Mess

In late 1995 and 1996, U.S. President Bill Clinton carried on a sexual relationship with intern Monica Lewinsky in the White House. Many of the details of the relationship emerged because of taped phone conversations and "wired" in-person conversations Lewinsky had with someone she met in the Pentagon and considered a friend, Linda Tripp.

Throughout the late 1990s, at a time when Web-based businesses were sprouting and Americans were connecting to the Net by leaps and bounds, the Net was abuzz with rumors, cartoons, spoofs, and ridicule about the scandal. Columnist Matt Drudge was widely credited with being the first to publicize rumors about the affair in the January 17, 1998, edition of his column the Drudge Report (http://www.drudgereport.com/), which was sent by e-mail to subscribers. The report bore the following headline:

BLOCKBUSTER REPORT: 23-YEAR-OLD FORMER WHITE HOUSE INTERN,
SEX RELATIONSHIP WITH PRESIDENT!!!

Drudge, a man with no glittering credentials who worked alone from a bedroom in Hollywood, California, scooped *Newsweek* by getting the biggest story of the decade out first. At the time, *Newsweek* was still deliberating whether to publish the story, despite the work of its reporter Michael Isikoff. They decided, using the "old-school" test for news stories, that it wasn't yet "firm" enough to go out in that week's issue. But after Drudge put it out on the Internet, *Newsweek* hurriedly published its story later that same week on America Online. Drudge preserves a copy of his plain-text scoop on his own Drudge Report archives (see Figure 12-1).

After learning about the Drudge Report's story, Clinton called his secretary Betty Currie in the middle of the night (according to Currie's later testimony to the FBI), asking her if she had a computer connected to the Internet and advising her that the Drudge Report story was out and "it was not good." He then instructed her to call Lewinsky.

This story transformed the Internet into the "go-to" place for breaking news. Webmasters, pundits, and reports alike speculated: Should Clinton finish his term, resign, or be impeached? Should Linda Tripp be applauded as a hero or reviled as a betraying friend? Each evening after returning home from work (or at work, when the boss wasn't looking), employees around the country tuned into online news sites to catch up on the latest dirt.

News organizations such as CNN, the *New York Times*, Fox News, and MSNBC saw their Web sites explode with traffic as the scandal unraveled, government bodies held hearings, and Clinton denied, denied again, and then finally admitted. Web sites set up especially for the event, such as the Monica Lewinsky Online Fan Club, dished out some welcome humor in the midst of the absurdity. The fan club included links to Lewinsky's profile on America Online and something called the Oval Office Chat Room, among other features.

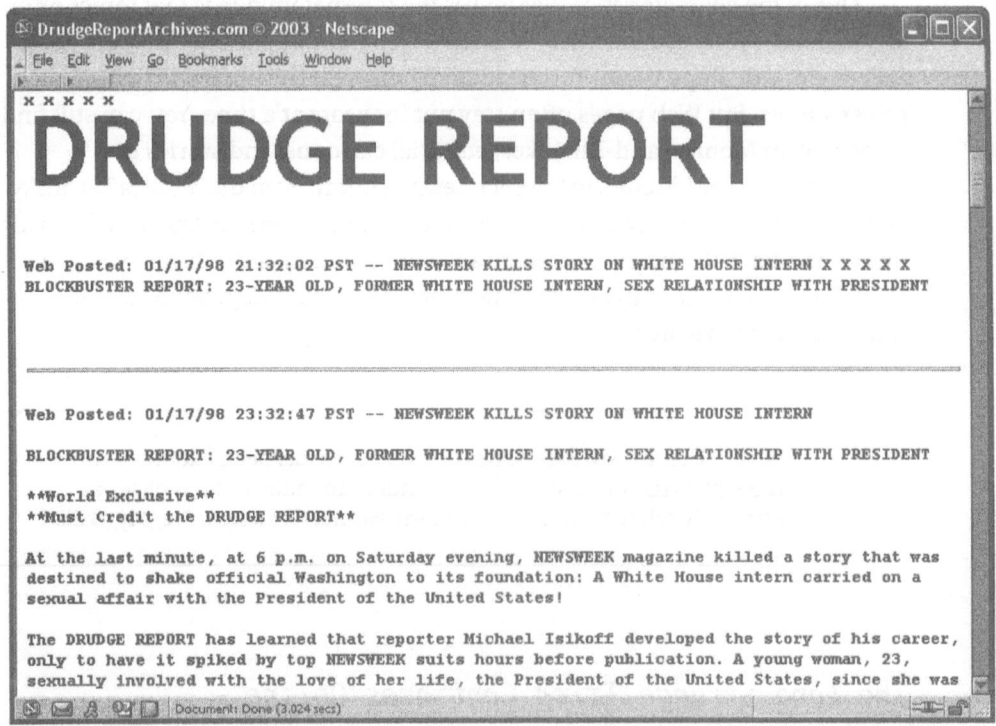

Figure 12-1. The story that beat the traditional news organizations: Matt Drudge's first report on the Lewinsky-Clinton scandal[1]

In early 1998, reporters spotted the Web page Monica's Place, billing itself as the Web site of Monica S. Lewinsky. It depicted Lewinsky as being empty-headed and trivial: "The White House, this is where I used to work.... Of course when I am not working, I am usually watching my MTV." Although the site was quickly found to be a hoax and pulled by America Online, it fooled reporters from the *Detroit News* and no less than the *Washington Post,* which declared that it "sure looked like the real home page of Ms. Lewinsky." Other sites bore names such as Zippergate and published high school photos of Lewinsky as well as her e-mail address and former work address. One of the best-known, strangest, and most tasteless Lewinsky sites was Monica Lewinsky Ate My Balls, an early entrant in the equally bizarre Ate My Balls series of Web pages. It primarily consisted of links to X-rated Web sites. A study by Harvard University reported that it was one of many Web sites blocked in Saudi Arabia.

---

1. http://www.drudgereportarchives.com/data/2003/06/04/20030604_135223_ml.htm

One of the characteristics that makes the Internet unique is that topics often stay online for years at a time. Television news reports are gone once they are aired, unless you videotape them. You need to dig through the library for old newspaper stories. But Web pages often stay put for years at a time. You can still find a page full of Monica-and-Bill jokes, editorial cartoons, and stories at http://www.keyworlds.com/m/monica_lewinsky.htm. Even the Monica Lewinsky Online Fan Club is still available, but the creator has taken it offline. If you can dig up the original URL (http://members.aol.com/monifan/index.html), you can view it (though without images) in the Internet Archive's Wayback Machine (http://web.archive.org/).

NOTE   The Ate My Balls series of Web pages has been extended to celebrities far and wide. Yahoo! contains an index to such pages at http://dir.yahoo.com/Entertainment/Humor/Tasteless/Ate_My_Balls/.

The Long Strange Tripp Continues Online

At the center of the Monica Lewinsky mess, a woman named Linda Tripp surfaced, much like green scum rising to the top of a stagnant pond. If you visit Tripp's Web site (http://www.lindatripp.com/), you discover that some aspects of the scandal—namely, the hate-filled, indignant, self-righteous, ultraconservative sentiments that kept it going for years—are still very much alive.

After Lewinsky was transferred from the White House to the Pentagon, she met Tripp and began to tell Tripp about her affair with the president. In 1997, Tripp began to tape phone conversations with Lewinsky in which she talked about the president. You can now hear excerpts and read transcripts of those 22 hours of conversations on CNN's Web site (http://www.cnn.com/ALLPOLITICS/resources/1998/lewinsky/tripp.tapes/index.html#complete).

Tripp uses her site to solicit donations to defray legal costs associated with her aborted trial for illegal wiretapping charges (the charges were later dropped) and her lawsuits against the government for allegedly revealing details about her during a job search. If you click the Support link, you go to an online store where you can donate in the interest of "helping Linda defend herself against the Clinton machine" (see Figure 12-2).

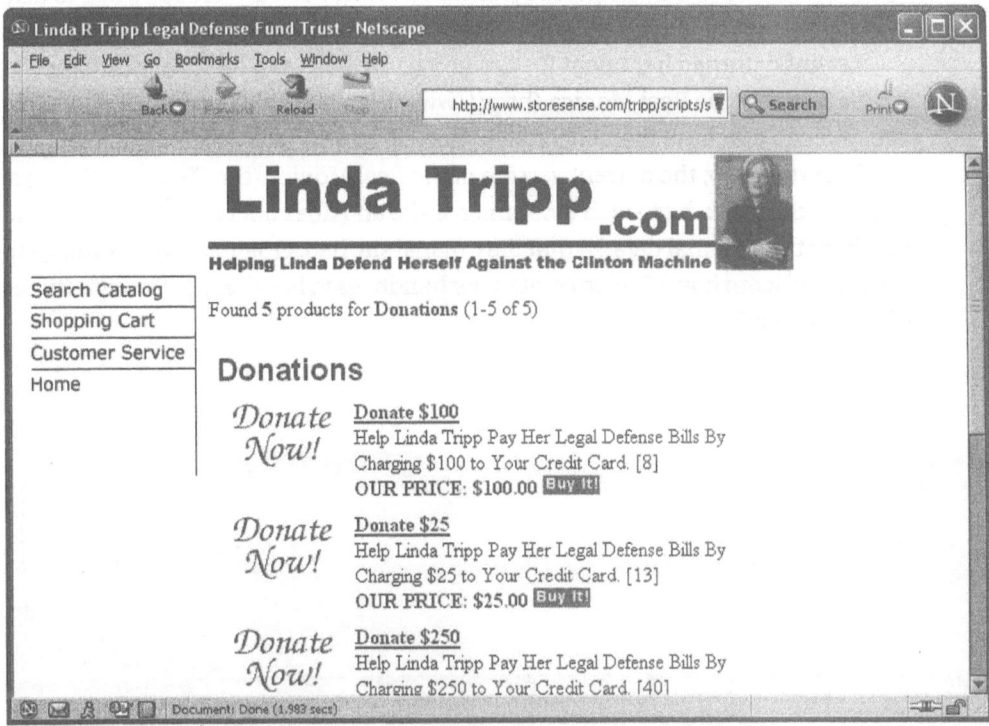

Figure 12-2. Keeping the anti-Clinton fire burning: LindaTripp.com[2]

 TIP CNN has a useful online timeline of the scandal (http://www.cnn.com/ALLPOLITICS/resources/1998/lewinsky/timeline/index.old.html) that traces the most important events and summarizes what the key figures did.

Made by Hand for You: Monica's Handbags

The Clinton-Lewinsky scandal was a time of great anxiety for many Americans, not least of all Monica Lewinsky herself. During the days when she was being pursued by reporters, called to testify before various bodies, and exposed to ridicule on the

---

2. http://www.storesense.com/tripp/scripts/store.exe/search?category=Donations

Web, she turned to a lifelong hobby: knitting. She reportedly needed a bag to take her knitting materials to court, so she designed one for herself. A new career was born.

Lewinsky turned her talent for designing tote bags and handbags into the online business the Real Monica (http://www.therealmonica.com/). On her Web site, you can purchase messenger bags, purses, and various accessories.

Unfortunately, the current version of the Real Monica (see Figure 12-3) looks like any other slick, high-tech e-commerce site and does not contain the personal touch (or the personal details) that the original site had. Originally, you could go to the site and learn how Monica created her handbags to help her get through "times of high anxiety."

Figure 12-3. Monica herself turned to the the same medium that had vilified her—the Web—to start a new business.[3]

---

3. http://www.therealmonica.com/home.php

"The long term value of Monica's totes and handbags will probably be realized when they appear on *Antiques Roadshow* in the year 2075," comments columnist Bob Brand (http://www.thebee.com/bweb/iinfo174.htm).

 NOTE Salon.com reported that a variety of domain names associated with "Monicagate" had been snapped up by X-rated Web site owners and a variety of other people. Presidentbillclinton.com was owned by a private investigator in Miami, Florida, who used it to sell spycams. Whitehouse.com and Whitehouseintern.com pointed to the same X-rated Web site. The domain name presidentclinton.com was owned by a man in Tehran, Iran, and pointed to a site called Sexflick.com.

Other Political Scandals

The Monica Lewinsky affair may have been the first Internet scandal, but others have emerged since. As cyberspace extends its reach around the world, people in other countries are introduced to the notion that their elected officials can misbehave and that the Internet is a place to go to get the latest dirt on the scandal *du jour*. The following are some examples of cyberspace connections to scandals both at home and abroad.

Taiwan Official Rides Sex Scandal to Top of Search List

On July 19, 2002, the Lycos 50 Daily Report listed the 50 most frequently used terms requested of the Web search service. At No. 1, ranking higher than Martin Luther King Jr., Britney Spears, and the NFL, was someone named Chu Mei-feng.

Most American readers are probably unfamiliar with this woman (depicted in Figure 12-4 in a BBC article about her), but she is practically a household word in her native Taiwan and in other Asian countries. It seems a clandestine video that recorded an adulterous liaison she had with a Taiwanese businessman was being sold in Southeast Asia. Before that, a Taiwanese magazine called *Scoop* gave away a CD containing the 40-minute video file.

Mei-feng had been a member of the city council of Taipei, the capital city of Taiwan. She was also a former journalist. Now, she was disgraced. What did she do? She released her autobiography, *Confessions of Chu Mei-feng*, in February 2002. She also filed a lawsuit against her ex-boyfriend, whom she accused of helping to secretly videotape her with the businessman, but she later dropped the suit.

Figure 12-4. Asian Web surfers eager for news about an infamous sex movie turned to search services such as Lycos.[4]

Journalist Loses Head; Tape Incriminates President

It sounds like the plot of a lurid B-movie. An intrepid journalist, working for a small media outlet (in this case, a Web site), criticizes the president. He disappears. His headless body is later found and then taken away by authorities before an autopsy can be conducted. A tape is released in which the president is heard ordering him to be removed. The security guard who made the tape goes into hiding.

It sounds strange, but it allegedly happened in the Ukraine, part of the former Soviet Union, in 2000. At the time, newspapers and television were considered to be under the control of the government. Gyorgy Gongadze, 31 (shown in Figure 12-5), stood out as one of the few journalists to criticize the corrupt men who ran the Ukraine. He did so from the Web site in Figure 12-5 called Ukrainian Truth (http://www.pravda.com.ua/).

---

4. http://news.bbc.co.uk/2/hi/asia-pacific/1735739.stm

Figure 12-5. Years after its editor disappeared, this crusading Web site is still active and digging up dirt about elected officials.[5]

The Ukraine, in fact, was under the control of leaders who had been bosses in the Communist Party in the former Soviet Union. One of them, former Prime Minister Pavel Lazarenko, allegedly made off with $114 million that was supposed to have been invested in energy. He eventually went on trial in San Francisco, California, charged with using the money to buy a mansion that was once the residence of actor Eddie Murphy. He eventually was able to post a mind-boggling $86 million bail and, at this writing, was holed up in a San Francisco apartment awaiting trial.

That's only a side-scandal compared to the real one, which broke after journalist Gongadze disappeared on September 16, 2003. As you can still see when you visit Ukrainian Truth, Gongadze and his coworkers published a stream of articles that were critical of the Ukraine's leaders and their alleged corruption. Many articles focused on Ukrainian President Leonid Kuchma. This sort of freedom in the press is a rare thing in Ukraine's traditional media, but on the Internet, journalists found an outlet in which they could question their officials. The problem is that most of

---

5. http://www.pravda.com.ua/en/archive/2003/september/17/1.shtml

the 50 million residents of the Ukraine, who typically earn a few thousand dollars a year, cannot afford Web connections.

But Gongadze apparently paid a price for his work. When an unidentified corpse was found in the woods about 90 miles from Kiev, the capital city of the Ukraine, Gongadze's co-editor went to investigate it. Jewelry found with the body and a scar on the wrist indicated it was Gongadze. But before she could claim the body, the Ukraine's Ministry of Internal Affairs snatched it away, announcing it would perform an autopsy.

On November 28, 2003, a politician who is a rival of Kuchma's released a tape recording. On it, a voice resembling Kuchma's is heard cursing Gongadze and other journalists and allegedly instructing someone to "drive him out, throw him out…give him to the Chechens." Although it was not immediately clear whether the voice was actually Kuchma's—and Kuchma denied he had issued any violent orders—the heat was on. The security officer who allegedly made the tapes went into hiding. He later told interviewers that he had resisted Kuchma's orders to eliminate opposition media. Members of Ukraine's parliament shouted "Murderer!" at members of Kuchma's cabinet. But at this writing, Kuchma is still the president of the Ukraine, and the investigation into Gongadze's disappearance is ongoing.

Trent Lott Gets Bloggered Into Silence

It was just a birthday party, so the major media outlets didn't give it much coverage. Although the 100th birthday party for U.S. Senator Strom Thurmond was broadcast live on C-SPAN December 5, 2002, reporters didn't notice when Trent Lott, the House majority leader and longtime senator from Mississippi, made a speech in which he stated, "We wouldn't of had all these problems" if staunch segregationist Thurmond had been elected president when he ran in 1948.

But although the major media missed the story, online journalists who keep online diaries called *Weblogs* posted scathing attacks on Lott. The journalists included conservatives such as Andrew Sullivan and David Frum. On December 6, 2002, Josh Marshall posted comments in his Talkingpointsmemo.com blog (http://talkingpointsmemo.com/) that berated Lott for his remarks (see Figure 12-6).

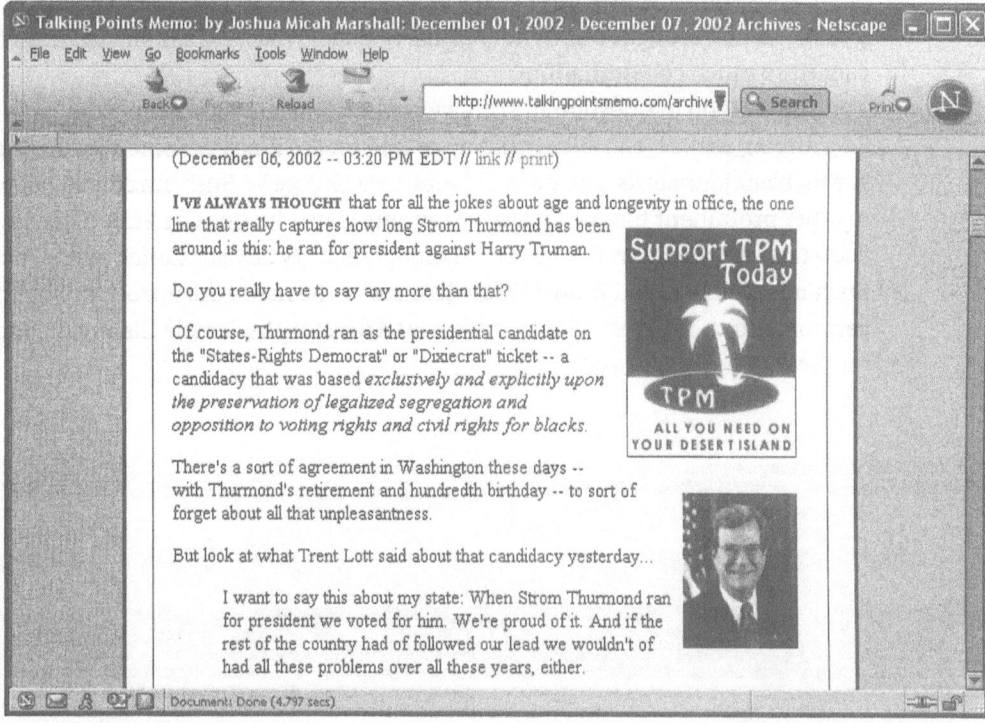

Figure 12-6. Mainstream media initially ignored Lott's remarks, but bloggers kept outrage alive.[6]

The *Washington Post* initially buried the story on page A06. But other bloggers kept the story alive, voicing their outrage. Eventually, the mainstream media figured out that there might be something worth covering here. Lott was forced to issue a lame apology, tried to backtrack in an interview on Black Entertainment Television, and eventually resigned as majority leader. A story in the *New York Post* reported that Lott was "the Internet's first scalp." I might argue that Bill Clinton preceded Lott in being skewered first on the Net, but you get the idea.

Internet Cartoon Offends Judicial Nominee

In October 2003, Janice Rogers Brown appeared before the Senate Judicial Committee, which was reviewing her nomination to the U.S. Court of Appeals for the District of Columbia. During the hearings, Republican Senator Orrin Hatch from Utah held up a cartoon that had been published on a Web site and to which

---

6. http://www.talkingpointsmemo.com/archives/week_2002_12_01.html#000451

he took exception. Brown later said she was personally offended by the cartoon and that it had brought one of her friends to tears. What was the single image that caused so much consternation?

The cartoon in question (http://www.blackcommentator.com/54/ 54_cartoon_female_clarence.html) appeared on the Black Commentator, a Web site for black journalists, and depicted President George W. Bush introducing Brown to other prominent black officials—Supreme Court Justice Clarence Thomas, Secretary of State Colin Powell, and national security adviser Condoleezza Rice. Bush mistakenly called Brown "Ms. Clarence" as he made the introduction. The cartoon, shown in Figure 12-7, accompanied the story "A Female Clarence Thomas for the D.C. Federal Court?"

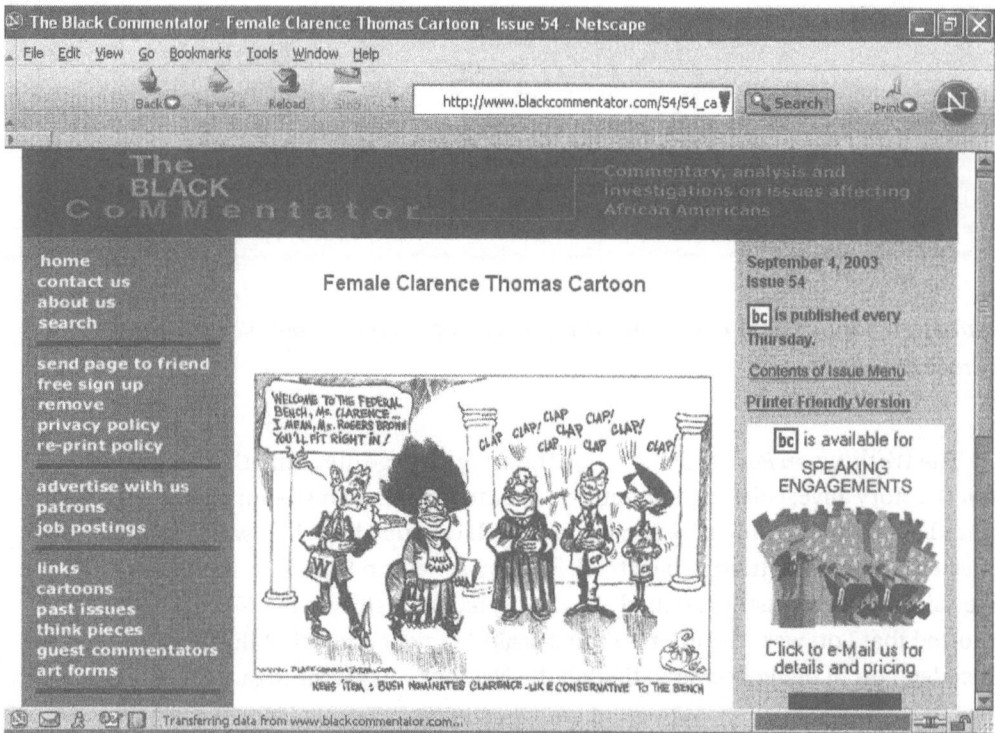

Figure 12-7. This Internet cartoon made its way offline to a Senate hearing, where it caused a new round of controversy.[7]

---

7. http://www.blackcommentator.com/54/54_cartoon_female_clarence.html

Arnold the Groper Turns Governor

As I was writing this book, one of the strangest elections in American history took place. Those of us who do not live in California looked on in amazement as citizens there voted to recall the elected governor and, in his place, voted in the movie actor Arnold Schwarzenegger.

During the campaign, desperate attempts were launched to discredit Schwarzenegger. A variety of women came forward, accusing the star of *The Terminator* and many other action films of sexually harassing them on movie sets. A Web site, We Love Arnold (http://welovearnold.com/, shown in Figure 12-8), collected many of the actor's quotable quotes—there appear to be quite a few—and reported on other humorous aspects of the campaign.

Figure 12-8. This Web site poked fun at Arnold before it actually looked like he could win.[8]

---

8. http://wwww.welovearnold.com/

Among other things, We Love Arnold repeated comments from the Drudge Report and other sources in which Schwarzenegger allegedly rebuked blacks and praised Hitler. Schwarzenegger, of course, was only one of 100 or more candidates who announced their candidacy for governor. Many of the candidates took advantage of a Web site called CafePress (http://www.cafepress.com/), which lets virtually anyone design and sell their own products online. One of the CafePress stores featured T-shirts that celebrated Schwarzenegger's macho screen image with slogans such as "The Governator" and "Conan the Republican" (see Figure 12-9).

Figure 12-9. The California recall election featured plenty of merchandise from plenty of candidates, including the "Governator."[9]

It should be noted, as an aside, that one of the CafePress stores sold a thong with a "Chickenator" graphic, apparently referring to Schwarzenegger's reluctance to engage in debates with other candidates. At this writing, it's still on sale at http://www.cafeshops.com/teasetees.7433382/.

---

9. http://www.cafeshops.com/voteahnuld/

Watergate: The Internet Scavenger Hunt

On the Internet, you don't have to sit and passively take in information, the way you do with television. Instead, you can click some links and get interactive (before you return to passively sitting and taking in more Web-based information).

The Mother of All Political Scandals, Watergate, provides an example. After you read the excellent history of Watergate at the Web site of *The Washington Post* (http://www.washingtonpost.com/wp-srv/national/longterm/watergate/front.htm, shown in Figure 12-10), you can go on an Internet scavenger hunt and try some interactive resources.

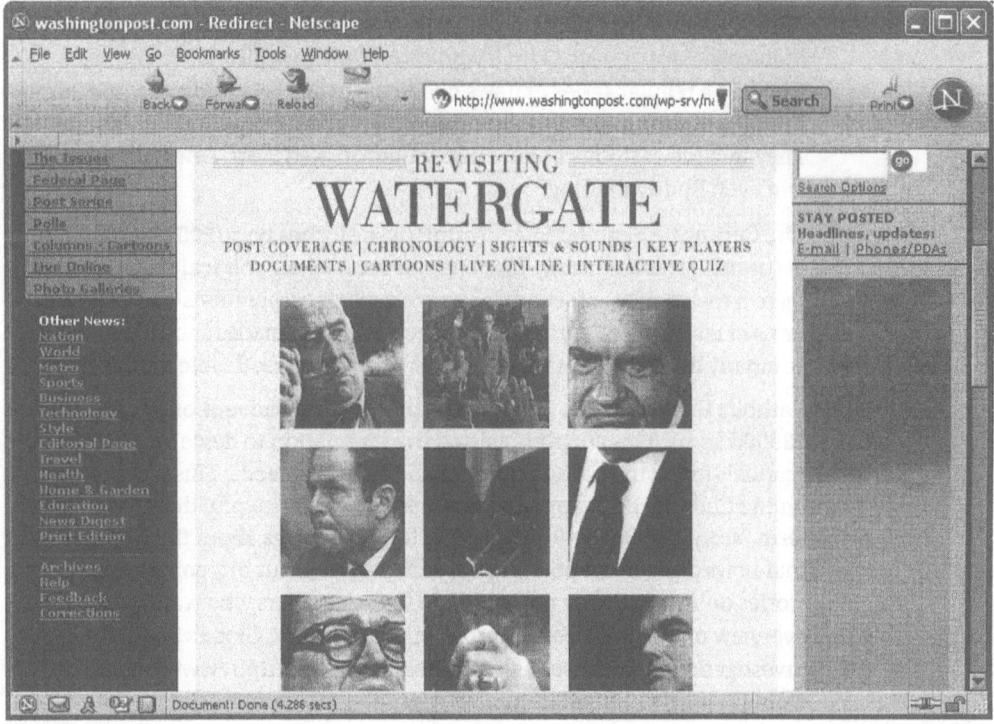

Figure 12-10. The Washington Post, *which played a key role in Watergate, provides a fascinating online look at the scandal.*[10]

You can also go to the Landmark Cases Web site (http://www.landmarkcases.org/nixon/hunt.html), click links, and try their interactive exercise. Go to various Web

---

10. http://www.washingtonpost.com/wp-srv/national/longterm/watergate/front.htm

sites, such as those for CNN and the University of California at Berkeley, and complete exercises based on what you find there. It's a terrific exercise for any student of history, whether or not you are currently in school.

Random Googling

The Internet contains plenty of Web sites devoted to scandals. But there aren't too many that discuss scandals that either originated online or in which the Internet played an important role. The following list contains a few I found noteworthy—a random sampling of sites that turned up after searching for the term "scandal" on the search service Google (http://www.google.com/):

- **White House Scandal Cartoons (http://cagle.slate.msn.com/scandal/):** Monicagate must have been a wonderful time for editorial cartoonists, who had a regular series of news headlines to lampoon. You can find some samples of professional cartoonists' work during the period on this site. They include cartoons about Hillary Clinton, Ken Starr, Lewinsky's dress, and even Buddy the Dog.

- **The Corporate Scandal Sheet (http://www.forbes.com/2002/07/25/ accountingtracker.html):** This chapter focused on political scandals, but there have been lots of scandals involving major corporations and financial firms in recent years. Forbes.com collects brief summaries about what each company did and when it occurred in an easy-to-read table on this page.

- **Catholic Encyclopedia: Scandal (http://www.newadvent.org/cathen/ 13506d.htm):** This chapter resisted the temptation to delve into the many scandals involving Catholic priests and their misdeeds. This page of the online Catholic Encyclopedia provides you with a helpful definition of the term "scandal." But seriously, one of the best things about the Internet is that news outlets can post helpful summaries about big, complex news stories online, and they remain there for researchers who want a thorough overview of the topic. For example, visit the Boston Globe's Spotlight Investigation into Abuse in the Catholic Church (http://www.boston.com/ globe/spotlight/abuse/scandal/).

- **Wikipedia: Scandal (http://en.wikipedia.org/wiki/Scandal/):** Along with a definition of the term "scandal," you get links to many Web sites that summarize scandals, as well as links to scandals in many countries.

CHAPTER 13

Government Secrets in Babylon

LIKE WATCHING SAUSAGE being made, watching government in action can be somewhat disgusting. That's why we like to find out about it from the safety of our living rooms, offices, or other places where we connect to the Internet. What the government wanted to keep secret at one point often becomes public knowledge online.

When you start looking through government secrets on the Internet, you run into all kinds of bizarre theories. You find out that the government is supposedly concealing aliens and is covering up the discovery of a 12th planet; people use the keywords "government secret" to promote themselves as private investigators. It's hard to separate what's real from what's fantasy or commercial schlock.

Hushing up isn't possible when you can find out with the click of a mouse what would before have taken years to leak out. And once word gets out, it's out there in cyberspace for years at a time. This chapter delves into different types of government secrets—both real and imagined—you can discover online.

Health and Safety, or the Lack of It

To be able to surf the Web regularly, a number of fundamental needs have to be met. Among these are health, safety, and the pursuit of information. Sometimes, the most basic needs of health and safety are called into question on the Internet, where alternative views of health crises and disasters are common.

AIDS: Not to Worry, It's All a Myth

So you thought AIDS was one of the greatest scourges of our time, a disease caused by the HIV retrovirus and one to be fought with powerful drug "cocktails?" Well, you thought wrong, according to a site called VirusMyth (http://www.virusmyth.net/aids/index.htm, shown in Figure 13-1).

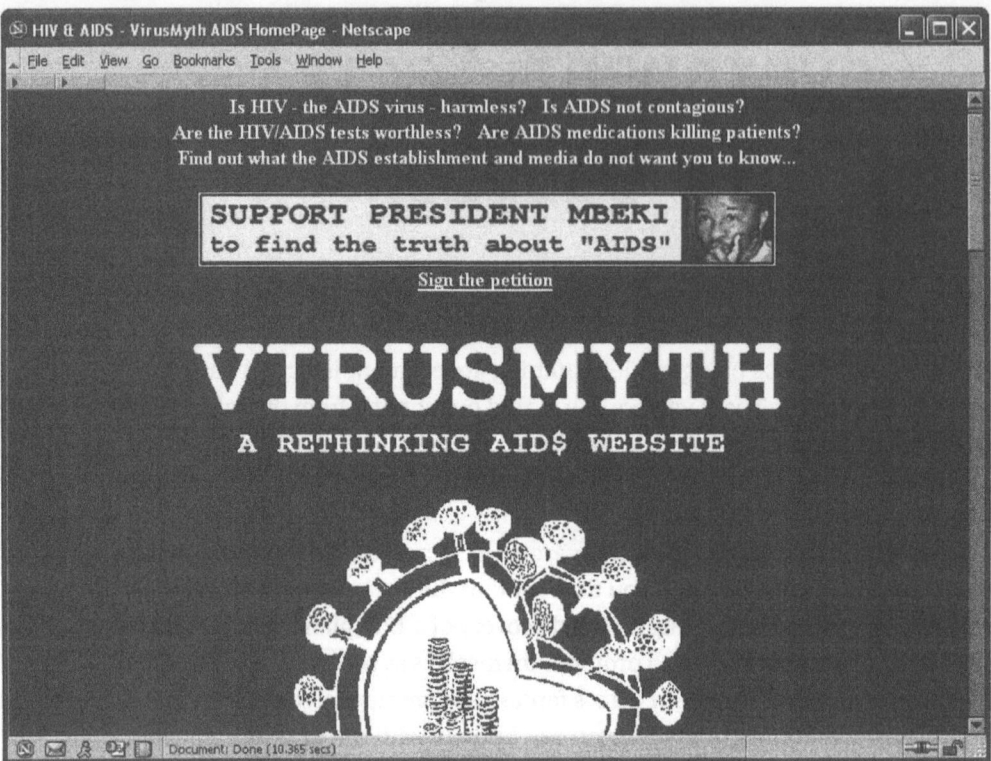

Figure 13-1. This site contends that AIDS caused by HIV is a myth perpetuated by drug companies to make money.[1]

This site cites 1993 Nobel Prize winner in chemistry Kary Mullis as stating that there should be a scientific document that demonstrates that HIV causes AIDS (and implying that there isn't one). A group of scientists called the Group for Scientific Reappraisal of the HIV-AIDS hypothesis promotes the idea that AIDS is not a sexually transmitted disease and that a single HIV may not even exist. The Web site HEAL Toronto (http://healtoronto.com/refer.html) makes the same claim. Rather, some scientists point to widespread drug use and anti-AIDS drugs themselves as breaking down the body's immune system, which, they say, is what actually causes victims to die.

---

1. http://www.virusmyth.net/aids/index.htm

The "AIDS myth" theory is a prime example of how the Web can be used to build attention for an alternative view. Each of these sites contains links to other sites that promote the idea that AIDS is a myth. All of these links have an effect: When you search for "AIDS" or "virus" on search services such as Google (http://www.google.com/), you tend to turn up these sites with fairly high frequency. They all say the billions of dollars and years of research spent on the HIV-AIDS connection hasn't come up with a better understanding of the disease. It's all a myth put forth by drug companies to make money. They also contend that the U.S. government doesn't want people to think about AIDS in ways that challenge the dominant theory.

The Mystery of TWA Flight 800

On July 17, 1996, TWA Flight 800 fell into the ocean off the coast of Long Island, New York. All 230 people on board died. Immediately, rumors were voiced to the effect that eyewitnesses had seen a missile heading toward the plane just before it crashed. A former pilot named Richard Russell wrote a memo claiming a missile mistakenly fired from a U.S. ship downed the plane. The memo went like this:[2]

> *TWA Flight 800 was SHOT DOWN by a US NAVY AEGIS MISSILE fired from a guided missile ship which was in area W-105 about 30 miles from where TWA Flight 800 exploded. W-105 is a Warning Area off the southeast coast of Long Island and is used by the military for military operations including missile firing.*

Russell further asserted that there was a Federal Aviation Administration (FAA) videotape showing images of a missile heading toward the plane. It was another conspiracy theory that raged on the Internet and that gathered support far and wide, often with amazing speed, thanks to the Internet's worldwide reach.

This particular theory might have gone nowhere if not for Pierre Salinger. Salinger, who is best known as the press secretary for President John F. Kennedy and later a correspondent for ABC News, seized on this story and ran with it. Salinger is shown in Figure 13-2 in a March 1997 *Salon* magazine article that was critical of his work.

---

2. http://www.multipull.com/twacasefile/fffax.html

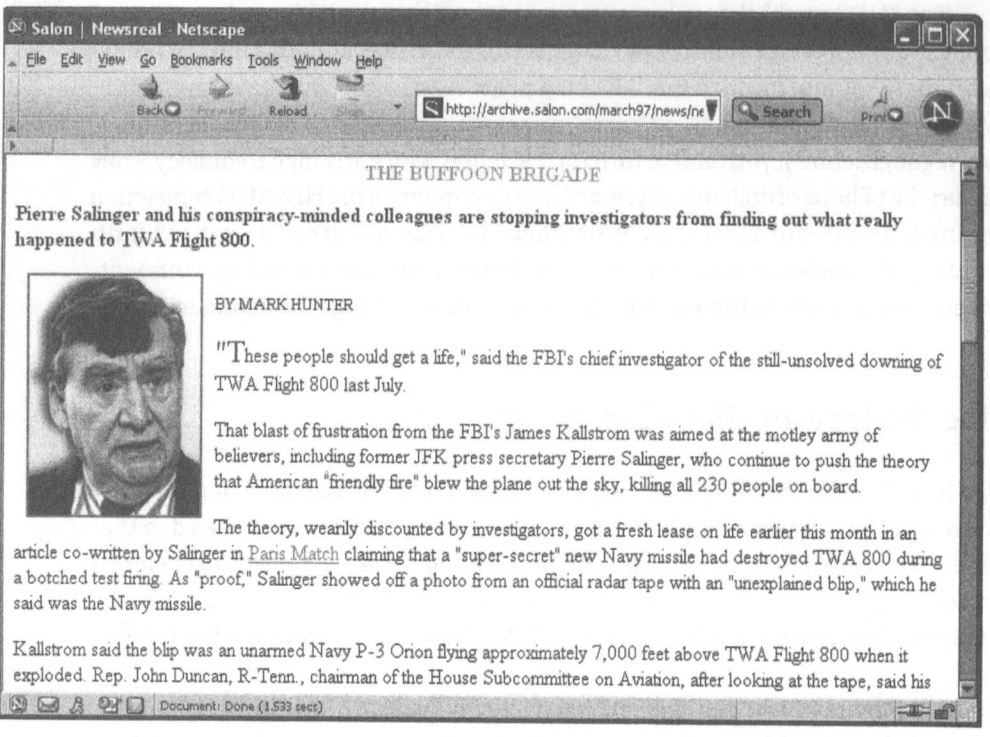

Figure 13-2. When someone famous latches on to an Internet conspiracy theory, everyone takes notice.[3]

In March 1997, Salinger produced a 69-page report and a set of radar images that he said bolstered his case. Salinger claimed the missile was fired during a "supersecret" U.S. Navy exercise off Long Island. The missile was supposed to target a Tomahawk missile but hit Flight 800 mistakenly. A Pentagon spokesman used a single word to describe Salinger's research: "bunkum." "These people should get a life," said an exasperated James Kallstrom, the lead investigator in the case.

NOTE You can read more about the suspicions surrounding the fate of TWA flight 800 on the Real History Archives Web site at http://www.webcom.com/~lpease/collections/mass/twa800.htm.

---

3. http://archive.salon.com/march97/news/news970326.html

Government Poisons Workers, Buries Information

In summer 2001, USAToday.com published an investigation of secret government programs in which civilian workers were unknowingly exposed to high levels of radiation as they processed nuclear weapons material. Any long-term attention that might have been given to the issue was diverted by the September 11 attacks that took place just a few months later. But the investigation and its supporting documents remain online, thanks to the Internet (see Figure 13-3).

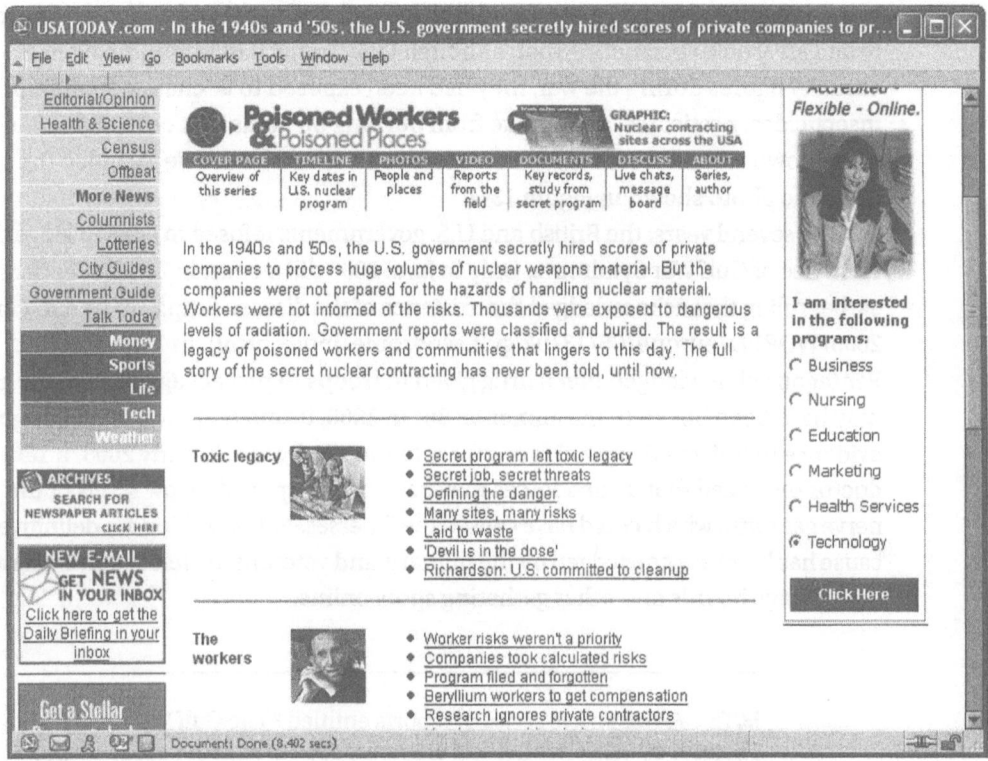

Figure 13-3. Secret government contracting programs that exposed civilians to radiation are just coming to light.[4]

Many of the original memos from government agencies such as the Atomic Energy Commission that raised concerns about levels of radiation as early as the 1940s are reproduced at http://www.usatoday.com/news/poison/docdex.htm.

---

4. http://www.usatoday.com/news/poison/docdex.htm

Gulf War Secrets Remain Online

Since the first Gulf War of 1991, veterans have made allegations about the mysterious illness called Gulf War Syndrome. The Gulf War Syndrome Message Board (http://www.healthboards.com/gulf-war-syndrome/) is now full of messages from soldiers, their spouses, and civilians who served in the Gulf complaining of a serious illness that apparently could not be diagnosed.

In 1996, an article on CNN.com (http://www.cnn.com/US/9610/07/ gulf.war.victims/) reported that a scientist had located a virus that may have infected soldiers before they were deployed to the Gulf and then was triggered by something encountered there. A publication called *Covert Action Quarterly* published an article speculating that, although U.S. troops had astoundingly low casualty figures during the war, they had been exposed to a "chemical soup" of insecticides, pesticides, and smoke from burning oil fields that caused them to come down with illnesses when they returned home. The article included the dramatic photo shown in Figure 13-4.

For several years, the British and U.S. governments refused to acknowledge the existence of Gulf War Syndrome. Only in June 2003 did a court in London back an earlier ruling that acknowledged the existence of the disease (http://www.cnn.com/ 2003/WORLD/europe/06/13/uk.gulf.syndrome/index.html). In 1999, the U.S. Pentagon acknowledged that a drug given to troops to protect against a nerve gas may have been linked to the ailments. But in 2000, it said there was not enough evidence to link the drug and four others to the syndrome. In early 2003, a Texas doctor theorized that armed forces may have been exposed to low levels of the nerve gas sarin, which could have caused the illnesses. At this writing, no definitive cause has been acknowledged by the military, and veterans are left to commiserate on message boards and other gathering spots online.

NOTE   An extensive series of reports entitled "The Gulf War: Secret History" by William M. Arkin originally appeared in *Stars and Stripes* magazine (the commercial publication, not the military newspaper of the same name). You can now read it at http://www.thememoryhole.org/war/ gulf-secret.htm.

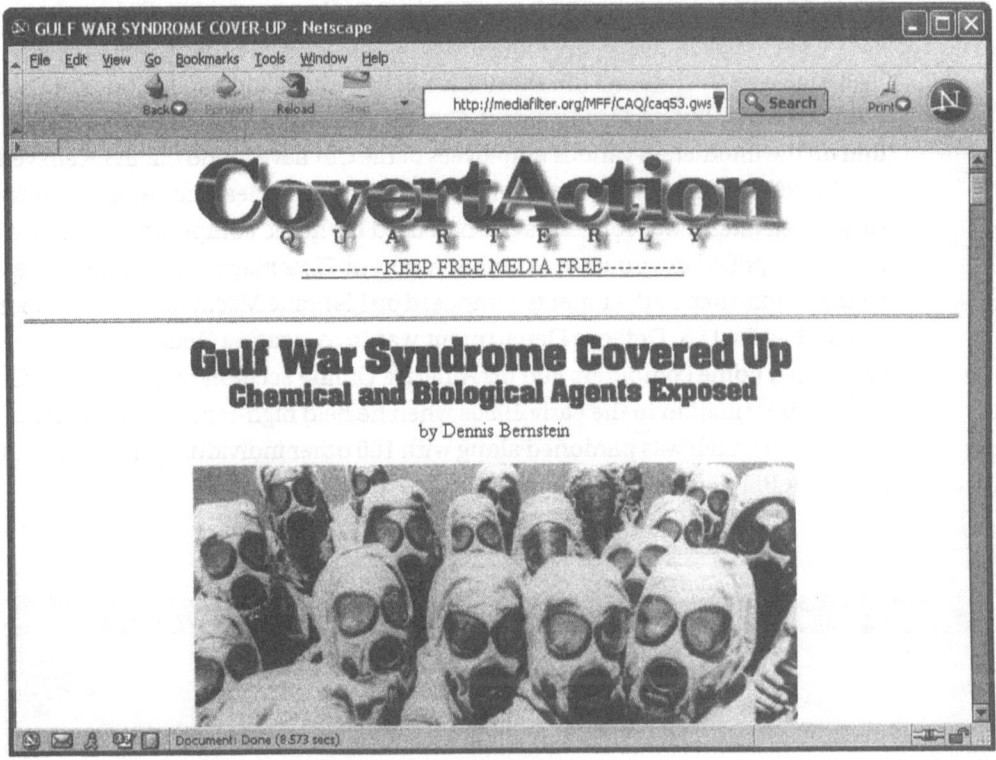

Figure 13-4. Reports, rumors, and complaints about Gulf War Syndrome continue to circulate on the Internet.[5]

CIA: Coverage on the Internet Abounds

The Central Intelligence Agency (CIA), the National Security Agency (NSA), and the "shadow government" facilities along the East Coast are supposed to be top secret. Aren't they? Not if you look around the Internet, where rumors, news stories, and speculation abound. When columnist Robert Novak identified a CIA agent in Niger, most mainstream newspapers and television outlets refused to identify her by name; on the Web, you can find her name within minutes.

---

5. http://mediafilter.org/MFF/CAQ/caq53.gws.html

CIA Agents Found in Secret Chat Room

Everyone uses the Internet to communicate these days, and that includes the ultra-secret U.S. CIA. But perfect secrecy is a concept that is difficult if not impossible to find on the Internet, as various employees of the CIA have found out in recent years.

In 1995, former CIA Director John Deutch's security clearance was indefinitely suspended after it was found that he had used his home computer to compose at least 31 classified documents. (Another report in *Time* magazine claimed it was actually more than 70 documents composed on his home Macintosh.) Other reports stated that the U.S. Defense Department was investigating Deutch's use of unsecured home computers and his America Online account to access classified defense information in the early 1990s when he held high-ranking posts in the Pentagon. Deutch was pardoned along with 100 other individuals in early 2001 by President Bill Clinton (see Figure 13-5).

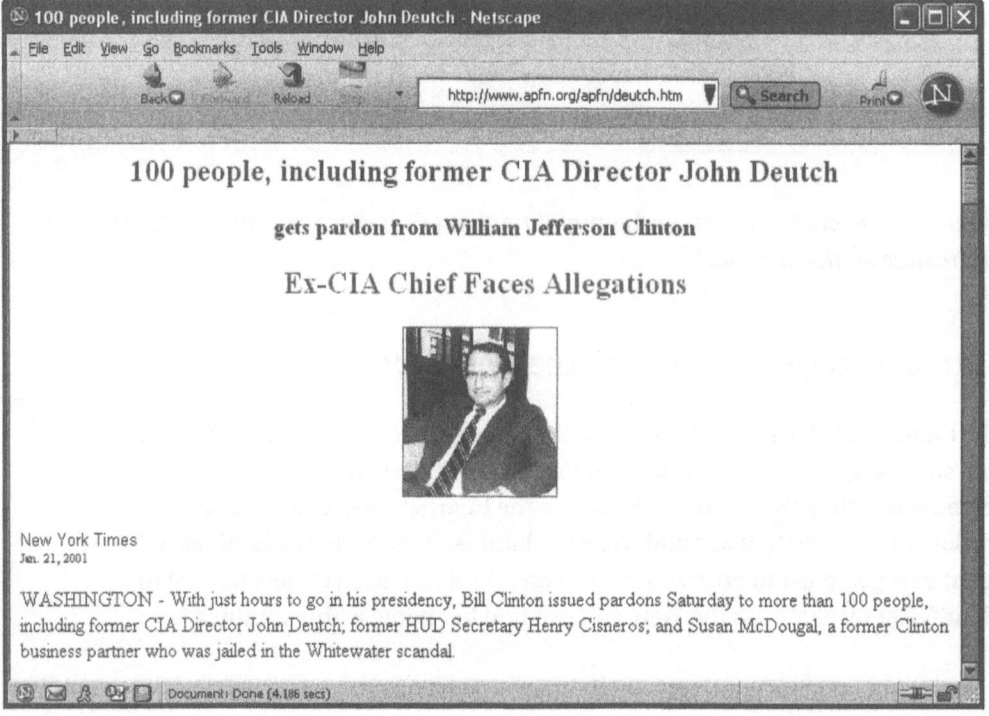

Figure 13-5. This Pentagon official, later director of the CIA, is alleged to have used his America Online account to access classified documents.[6]

---

6. http://www.apfn.org/apfn/deutch.htm

Then, in 2000, the CIA removed the security clearances of four agents, effectively firing them, and disciplined many other agents for participating in a secret chat room that had been set up on agency computers. According to a story on CNN.com (http://www.cnn.com/2000/TECH/computing/11/12/cia.chat/), the chat room was created primarily by women in the agency and was used for exchanging "sexist jokes" and other humorous material. Although no classified material was compromised, simply setting up the "secret channel" within the agency was "an abuse of the agency's internal communications system," according to one unidentified official quoted in the story. Reportedly, the chat room operated for more than five years, and participants indicated in chat room comments that they would probably have been fired if it had been discovered.

Take a Peek Inside the CIA

In October 2000, the CIA announced that it was releasing 25 million pages of declassified intelligence documents 25 years old. The files were released to the National Archives & Records Administration (NARA) and the Lyndon Baines Johnson Library and Museum.

If you go the NARA Web site (http://www.archives.gov/index.html), click Search, and enter the term "CIA," you can read some of declassified files that are now available online. Some of the files have to do with the start of the Cold War and are part of the Truman Presidential Museum and Library.

Not-So-Secret Government Activities

If it's on the Internet in the first place, it's no longer a secret, if it ever was one. It's not surprising, then, that you can find panoramic photos of the secret Air Force base in Nevada where aliens were supposedly housed at one time, and you can deduce the locations of two facilities where a "shadow government" operates in the event of a terrorist attack that disables the "public government" in Washington, D.C. Also, when the Yugoslav government briefly took over a well-respected Web site and radio station, word got out and the repression was quickly thwarted.

Hanging Out in Area 51

The words "Area 51" are well known to many denizens of the Internet. Area 51, also known as Groom Lake (and now officially called Air Force Flight Test Center, Detachment 3), is a top-secret government air force base north of Las Vegas. Those who are not conspiracy minded contend that the air force uses the base to test experimental aircraft, such as U-2 spy planes and stealth bombers. Everyone else is convinced that aliens who crashed in Roswell, New Mexico, in 1947 were taken to Area 51, along with their spacecraft. An especially imaginative subgroup within the "alien" group believes that at least one of the aliens survived and is working with the air force in Area 51.

As you might expect, Area 51 has an even more conspicuous presence on the Internet than it does in the desert of Nevada. Many Web sites purport to know what goes on in Area 51. One of the more entertaining (because it doesn't take the alien story too seriously) is the Dreamland Resort site (http://www.dreamlandresort.com/index_en.html) run by the owners of the Little A'Le'Inn, a diner and motel located near the entrance gates to Area 51 on what they call the "ET Highway." In the gift shop on the site, you can buy plastic sipper cups shaped like aliens, as well as alien Christmas tree ornaments. You can also view panoramic photos of the base taken from many miles away (see Figure 13-6).

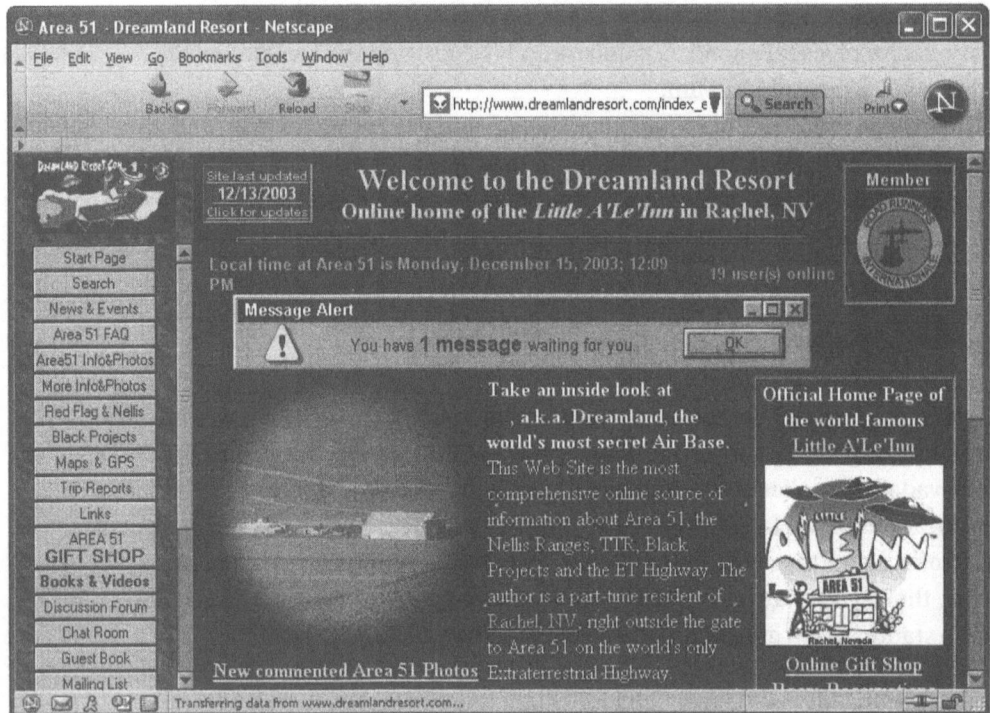

Figure 13-6. You'll be arrested if you get too near the base once called Area 51, but you can view long-range photos on this Web site.[7]

---

7. http://www.dreamlandresort.com/index_en.html

Shadow Government at Work in Secret Locations

The preceding heading is not a quotation from a tabloid newspaper. It is a paraphrase of a real headline in a story published by the *Washington Post* on March 1, 2002, which is still available online. The story states that, after the September 11 attacks, President George W. Bush sent about 100 senior managers to live and work in two secure locations outside Washington. If a catastrophic attack should hit the United States, these managers would ensure that government would continue to function.

It's called the Continuity of Government (COG) plan, and it may still be actively operating today. Those involved in the "bunker duty" reportedly live 24 hours away from their family in one of two underground facilities on the East Coast. The *Post* cooperated with the administration's request not to name anyone deployed in the program or divulge the locations of the facilities.

COG isn't exactly a secret on the Internet, however. You can read about it in the following places:

- The Research and Special Programs Administration Web site (http://www.rspa.dot.gov/oet/coop_cog.html).

- The Federation of American Scientists (FAS) Web site contains information about the origins of COG at http://www.fas.org/nuke/guide/usa/c3i/cog.htm.

- A book called *Inside the Shadow Government* by Harry Helms (Feral House, 2003) has a Web site at http://www.the-shadow-government.com/main.htm, where Helms identifies one of the supposedly secret facilities as Mount Weather and locates it in the mountains of Virginia.

- National Review Online published an article in response to the original *Washington Post* story in which the author criticized the story for revealing the existence of the "shadow government" and, in the process, repeated further details about location of the secret facilities (http://www.national-review.com/contributors/gaffney030102.shtml).

In case you can't figure out the locations of the shadow government from reading any of these articles, turn to the Temple of the Screaming Electrons Web site at http://www.totse.com/, where Amy Goodman interviews an author who places the facilities at Mount Weather and at Ravens Rock, east of Waynesboro, Pennsylvania. The fact that all these clues are online for months and years at a time should be of great comfort to terrorists of the future; before long, you can be sure to find a Yahoo! Maps listing for the shadow government facilities and a Rough Guides tour of them.

NOTE The original *Washington Post* story, "Shadow Government Is at Work in Secret," is at http://www.washingtonpost.com/ac2/wp-dyn/A20584-2002Feb28?language=printer.

The Saga of B92.net

Throughout the 1990s, a student radio station called B92 acted as a thorn in the side of Yugoslav president Slobodan Milosevic. From the beginning, the station won a faithful following thanks to its mix of music and independent news reports. Until Milosevic was finally ousted in 2000 (he is currently on trial for war crimes), B92 had to fight censorship. The station was shut down several times. But the Web site became a viable alternative for news, according to the Online Journalism Review of the University of Southern California's Annenberg School of Journalism (http://www.ojr.org/ojr/business/1017962840.php):

> *Because of government censorship and distribution problems of independent newspapers in Serbia, B92 online news has been printed, copied, and distributed throughout the country, which made it a rare case of an Internet news site being read on hardcopy on a large scale.*

When the station was closed by the Milosevic government in 1996, B92 transferred its news operations to its Web site (http://www.b92.net/, shown in Figure 13-7). The station was eventually allowed to go back on the air because of international pressure. But when NATO launched air attacks on Yugoslavia, B92 was not just shut down but virtually taken over by the regime. Eventually, Milosevic realized the power of the Web site as an alternative to radio and television, and his government took over the b92.net domain name as well. The original opposition Web site moved to freeb92.net.

Given that the B92 Web site was so popular and well respected, it's not surprising that Milosevic took it over in an to attempt to conceal the results of the election he lost. The employees who kept track of the country's Internet domain, .yu, received orders from the Ministry of Information on election night. The "Web takeover" lasted 24 hours, until the domain employees defied orders and shifted the domain name servers back to the original B92 Web servers. Other Web sites, such as FreeSerbia and Izbory2000 (Elections2000), were hijacked, thus promoting the Domain Name System to the status of target when it comes to totalitarian repression of the media.

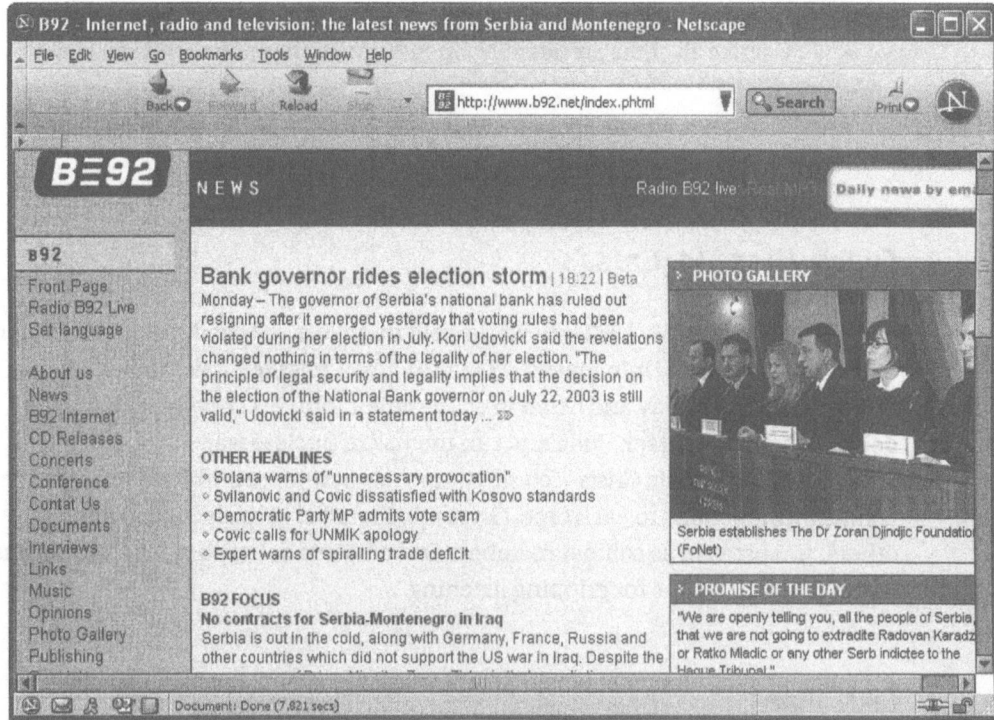

Figure 13-7. This alternative radio station's Web site was taken over by the government but eventually emerged the victor in a long battle to simply exist.[8]

Eavesdropping on the President

Everyone knows about the tapes President Richard Nixon made in the White House, which led to his downfall during Watergate. But taping actually started with President Franklin Delano Roosevelt in 1940. Harry Truman, Dwight Eisenhower, and John F. Kennedy also made tapes. Lyndon Johnson also taped; radio talk show host Howard Stern has reportedly broadcast clips of LBJ asking for trousers with "more crotch room." If you look around the Internet, you'll find places where you can be a fly on the wall of the Oval Office and listen in on some presidential conversations.

---

8. http://www.b92.net/index.phtml

TIP The Web page All the Presidents' Tapes discusses efforts to transcribe all of the presidential tapes (http://www.paulmitchinson.com/tapes.html).

Cuban Missile Crisis

From October 18 to 29, 1962, the world held its collective breath while the United States and the Soviet Union faced off in the Cuban Missile Crisis. Today, you can follow along day by day and listen in as President John F. Kennedy and his staff debate whether to attack Cuba and run the risk of nuclear war.

The Cuban Missile Crisis Web site (http://www.hpol.org/jfk/cuban/) includes textual introductions to each tape. On some, Kennedy records his thoughts. On others, you listen in as cabinet members and advisors debate how to confront the Soviet threat. It makes for gripping listening.

LBJ Tapes

The Lyndon Baines Johnson Library and Museum makes it particularly easy to listen in on LBJ's phone conversations. Some sample conversations with Jacqueline Kennedy and others are made available in RealAudio and Windows Media formats (http://www.lbjlib.utexas.edu/johnson/AV.hom/dicta_audio.asp). C-SPAN makes its own selections of LBJ taped conversations available in a searchable database (http://www.c-span.org/lbj/, shown in Figure 13-8).

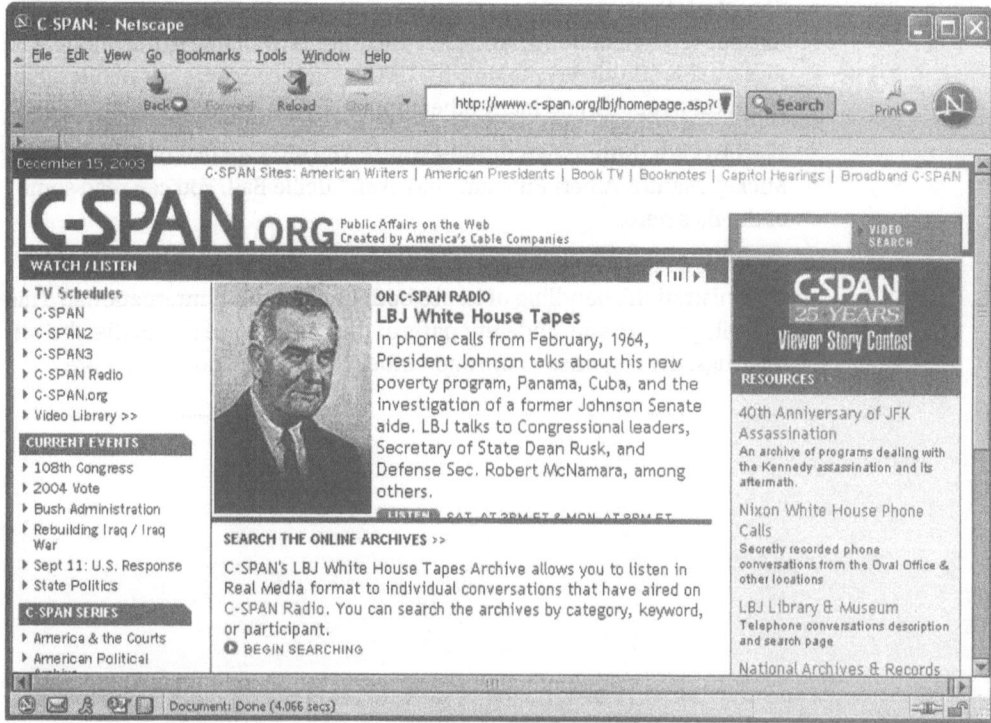

Figure 13-8. You can listen to LBJ's talks with boxer Jack Dempsey, writer John Steinbeck, and many other famous people.[9]

Random Googling

The Internet contains plenty of Web sites devoted to scandals. But there aren't too many that discuss scandals that either originated online or in which the Internet played an important role. The following list contains a few I found note-worthy—a random sampling of sites that turned up after searching for the term "government secrets" on the search service Google (http://www.google.com/):

- **Former Secrets (http://www.epic.org/open_gov/foia/secrets.html):** The Electronic Privacy Information Center (EPIC) has posted links to a variety of government documents it released under the Freedom of Information Act. These include files on the FBI's controversial Carnivore surveillance system, attempts by the government to suppress encryption systems, FBI wiretaps, the Clipper Chip, and more electronic privacy issues.

---

9. http://www.c-span.org/lbj/homepage.asp

- **The Black Vault (http://www.blackvault.com/)**: This is another site that makes Freedom of Information Act documents available to the public. The files on this site all have to do with UFOs, mind control, spy satellites, bio-chemical weapons, and many other topics.

- **The FBI Files (http://www.fbi-files.com/)**: The FBI kept files on John Wayne, Mickey Mantle, Albert Einstein, and even Lucille Ball. You can read some of the files here.

- **AlterNet (http://www.alternet.org/)**: Want to get an alternate view of the administration's handling of issues both domestic and international? This site will give it to you. Different parts of the site criticize the media, the war on drugs, the response to the September 11 attacks, and much more.

Part Five
Did You Hear the One About...?

CHAPTER 14

Tongue Lashings in Babylon

WHAT IS IT ABOUT E-MAIL, the Web, and Usenet that makes people speak so harshly to one another? To paraphrase Rodney King, "Why can't we all just get along online?"

It just doesn't work when you're sitting at a keyboard and you have access to the Internet at your fingertips. Any fight becomes quickly magnified when messages are exchanged back and forth instantly in a chat room. The fact that people can post blurbs and fire off angry comments in a matter of seconds ensures that hotter, not cooler, heads tend to prevail.

This chapter looks at flames, spams, sparks, and verbal explosions in Usenet and all types of verbal violence on the Net. One of the biggest feuds ever to take place in cyberspace—the browser war between Microsoft and Netscape—is too long to describe. Rather, I focus on individuals with an ax to grind who found their forum on the Net.

The Complaint Department: Anger and Protest

Got a complaint? For a growing number of consumers, the Web is the place to go. You can e-mail service personnel with ease and track down documentation to help you solve all kinds of problems. Of course, when commercial Web sites turn out to be unresponsive, people who are used to getting service instantly can get angrier than they ever would with a brick-and-mortar business. And people who have a gripe to make to family members can shame anyone into action.

500,000 E-Mails Helped Viewer Express His Dissatisfaction

Boston Red Sox fans are notoriously passionate about their beloved team. But at least one Boston autoracing fan can give them a run for their money. In the spring of 2001, the local Fox Entertainment TV station in Boston showed a Red Sox baseball game instead of a NASCAR auto race. Michael Melo of Boston was angry. He also knew something about computer programming. And he had access to the Internet with a broadband connection.

The result? He sent six e-mail messages to his local station, which were automatically forwarded to Fox Entertainment Group in Los Angeles. Six e-mail complaints doesn't sound like much. But Melo, who works in the computer industry, created software that sent the same six e-mails to Fox repeatedly. Eventually, 530,000 e-mails were sent. Fox was forced to shut down its Web site for several hours under the barrage of angry messages.

The Feds were hardly amused by Melo's activities, and he eventually pleaded guilty. He was sentenced to a year's probation in federal court and told by a judge to spend the first six months in home confinement. He was also ordered to pay a fine of $36,000.

Father Turns to Web to Shame Kids into Good Behavior

What would you do to keep your kids from falling into a life of crime or from misbehaving? One father in the United Kingdom turned to the Web and took some unusual steps to get his son and daughter to toe the line.

David Forward, from Malmesbury, England, got fed up when his 13-year-old son, Tom, repeatedly played truant from school and his 16-year-old daughter, Samantha, was expelled for throwing a plate of spaghetti at her school's deputy headmaster. Then, they were almost killed when they were riding in a stolen car that overturned on a country lane. He decided to quit his job at a call center to keep track of the then-unruly youngsters. Their photos are reproduced from the Ananova Web site, which reported on the incident (see Figure 14-1).

He then took the unusual step of posting a message on Malmesbury's Web site (http://www.malmesbury-memories.co.uk/menuindex1.html) in an effort to "name and shame" the kids and prevent them from falling into a life of crime.

Not only that, but he also posted the photos of others he considered to be "yobs" (troublemakers), explaining that he felt let down by police, social services, and local authorities. The police said they were concerned that such publicity would lead to disorder. But other photos on the Web site, plus the absence of any further "shaming" stories about his children, lead me to believe that his efforts were successful.

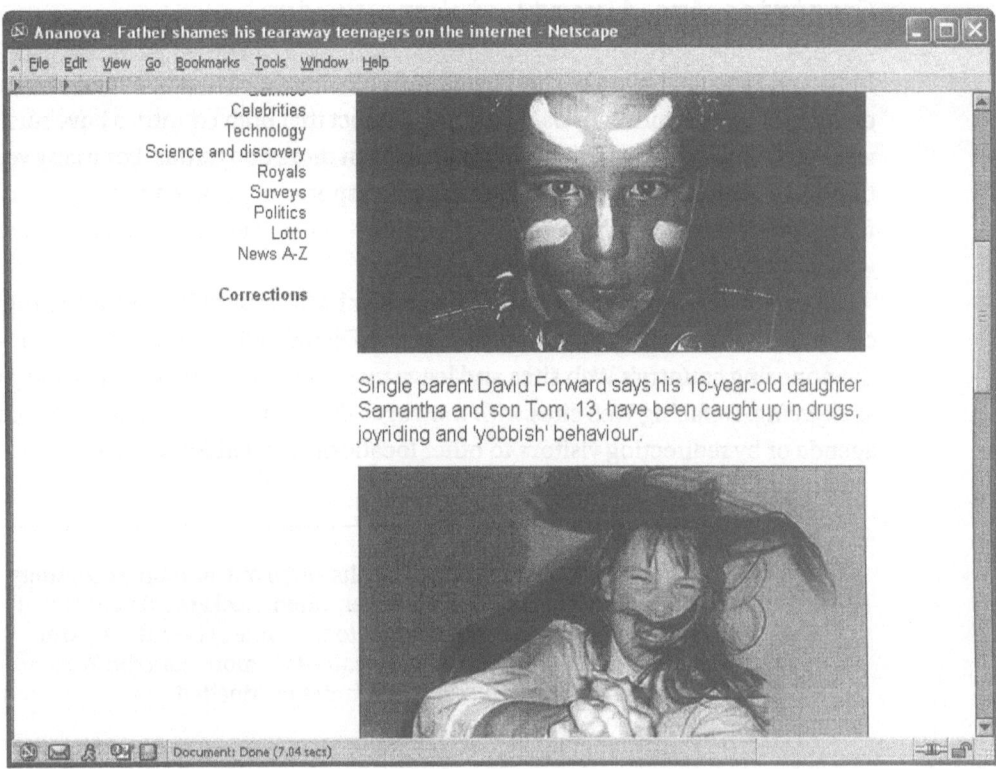

Single parent David Forward says his 16-year-old daughter Samantha and son Tom, 13, have been caught up in drugs, joyriding and 'yobbish' behaviour.

Figure 14-1. Dad published his displeasure with his children for everyone to read on the Web.[1]

NOTE People in Malmesbury who are concerned about their town's well-being voice their opinions online. When I visited the This Is Malmesbury Web site (http://www.thisiswiltshire.co.uk/wiltshire/malmesbury/news/letters.html), letters complained about "senseless vandalism," traffic congestion, and deer being killed by dogs. On the other side of the coin, some young people in Malmesbury have created their own Web site (http://www.mthreew.co.uk/) on which they complain that vandalism occurs because they simply don't have enough to do and on which they post photos of themselves drinking at various parties.

1. http://www.ananova.com/news/story/sm_737868.html

Countries Are Already at War—Online

India and Pakistan have a border that is hotly disputed and that has been the scene of many clashes against opposing troops. The fact that both countries have nuclear weapons makes any dispute between them even more dangerous. For many years, they have been having a war of words over a disputed area called Kashmir. Thankfully, they haven't actually gone to war over Kashmir—at least not in the real world where attacks can actually kill people.

Nevertheless, attacks are made on a regular basis by both Pakistani and Indian computer hackers. They plant viruses, launch Denial of Service attacks, or invade the opposing country's Web sites and leave messages on them—a process known as *defacing*. Defacing Web sites with messages that convey a particular political agenda or by redirecting visitors to other locations is called *hacktivism*.

 NOTE A Denial of Service attack results when one or more computers send multiple requests to a Web server. Often, hackers gain control of multiple computers to send requests to the same server at the same time. The resulting high number of requests is more than the Web server can handle, and the server becomes overloaded.

In 2000, Pakistani hacktivists broke into the Web site at zeetv.com. They may have been trying to attack the Indian television network Zee TV, but the two are not connected. Nevertheless, the hackers were able to place a message on the zeetv.com home page:

THE TIME IS OVER, INDIA SHOULD OBEY THE UN RESOLUTIONS AND GIVE THE RIGHTS TO THE KASHMIRI PEOPLE AND GIVE THEM FREEDOM.

This is a piece of advice to Indians to free their hands from Kashmir and stop dreaming about it.... ZeeTv's a** is kicked and we will kick the whole Indians a**.

ZDNet reported that the attack was made by the Karachi American Skool (KAS) group of hackers. Other Indian Web sites were attacked by Pakistani computer users in the same period, including at least one operated by the government of India (see Figure 14-2).

Figure 14-2. Pakistani "hacktivism" raises the question: Could cyberattacks lead to a nuclear war?[2]

The hack attacks go in both directions. The Indian newspaper the *Hindu* reported in early 2003 that the computer war has been heating up and that Pakistani hackers have allegedly launched 500 attacks against Indian servers. On the other hand, a virus launched by an Indian hacker group forced 200 Pakistani Web sites to go offline and allegedly erased the hard disks of many Pakistani government computers. Of course, it's always better than lobbing nuclear bombs across the border at one another....

Legendary Flame War Targets Software Developer

A *flame*, in Internet-speak, is an angry message sent to someone in an e-mail, in a newsgroup post, in a chat room comment, or perhaps even on a Web page. Flame messages are common in Usenet, where people who feel passionately about a subject seem to be able to fly into a rage in a moment's notice. When a series of

---

2.   http://fb.provocation.net/www.flashback.se/hack/2000/03/04/1/

flame messages is exchanged over time, a rare and wondrous event develops, one that can have the destructive force and fascinating attraction of a hurricane or tornado: a *flame war.*

Sometimes flame wars last only minutes or hours. Occasionally, they can drag on for long periods of time. The longest and best-documented flame war in Internet history concerns a software developer named Derek Smart and his nemesis Bill Huffman. The topic at hand—at least the topic that started the war—was one that many Usenet fans feel strongly about: computer games. In 1989, Smart began to create a game called Battlecruiser 3000 AD, which is typically abbreviated as BC3K. The history of the flame war recounted by Huffman (http://www.werewolves.org/~follies/archives/1History/history.htm) goes into excruciating detail on the events leading up to the war, which began in 1996 and stretched into the 21st century.

A very short bare-bones summary follows: Smart ran into problems and delays with the software, and promises were made over a period of years to actually release the software. Smart tried to implement a series of repairs called *patches*. The company that had purchased the rights to the software was determined to release it in its incomplete state. Smart allegedly undertook efforts to block the release of his own long-anticipated software. The software was released with an incomplete set of features and missing manual. All through the process, the people who were supposedly waiting for BC3K complained and ridiculed Smart. Smart fired back a series of angry messages, and the flame war escalated. Messages were exchanged not only on Usenet but on the discussion boards run by the online services America Online (AOL) and CompuServe. Inevitably, the subject of the flaming became not the game software but Smart himself.

This dry summary doesn't capture the anger and peculiar vehemence felt not only by those who opposed Smart but by Smart himself. Smart, apparently, defended himself and his game against all detractors on every message board where it was being discussed. The archive of "famous flames" exchanged in this war has short titles that give you an idea of what was going on:

- AbusedChild1.txt
- DerekWars2.txt
- DisabledInsultedAgain.txt
- EatShit.txt
- GetRaped.txt
- Kafka.txt
- RacialSlurs.txt

- SmarterThanYou.txt

- huffmanLivesInPigSty.txt

Get the idea? The flame war eventually racked up an estimated 65,000 posts on Usenet alone.

The strange realization running through the Great Flame War is that Smart was the developer of the software, and his job was ostensibly to promote the game and conduct public relations with its potential users.

It's tempting to take the side of the anti-Smart contingents, especially if your only source of information is Huffman's Flame War Follies Web site (http://follies.werewolves.org/). And Smart is by all accounts extremely combative, and he did dub himself the "Supreme Commander" of his software. But it takes at least two parties to keep a flame war going, especially for several years. In his defense, Smart says that his software was released in an incomplete state. Smart has been accused of performing rude acts with sheep, been called a liar, and received plenty of ridicule. But as he said in one message: "I will NEVER, EVER turn the other cheek." Thus, the flame war that never ends seems destined to start again at any moment—though, reassuringly, the most recent entry on the What's New at the Flame War Follies page is dated August 22, 2002.

Killed by Corporations

When the Web was young, you could say pretty much anything you wanted online without the fear of big business concerns cracking down on you. When millions of people began to go online on a regular basis, however, businesses began to take a closer look at some homemade Web sites, such as those set up to protest things their authors just didn't like. The following stories describe what happened next.

I Love You, You Love Me, But I Hate Your Web Site

Barney, for those of you who don't have young children, is a big purple dinosaur who stars in his own show on public broadcasting stations around the country. Barney is best known for an insipid song in which he tells children, "I love you, you love me, we're a happy family...."

Barney spread lots of love among kids everywhere, but he also provided a big, purple target for those who were eager to ridicule and parody him. I can't say it any better than the editors of Ghost Sites, who provide the following sage observation:

Social historians of the future may find it peculiar that so many words, and so many clicks were expended in the late 20th century attacking and defending the merits of a fictional purple dinosaur, especially when there were so many more important, real-life evils that nobody seemed to be paying much attention to.

Those same historians will also take note of how the corporate entity that owns the copyright to the Barney likeness, the Lyons Partnership, cracked down on those satiric Web sites, such as Into the Purple Abyss: The Day of the Barney Trilogy, and forced them offline. Such sites typically received a threatening letter from lawyers. Into the Purple Abyss had actually received awards for satire. The site's owner, Brian Bull, explained why he had to abandon his glorious romp: "Ideally while I'd love to put up the good fight, I've neither the time, money, or hard-fast inclination to do so."

I've no desire to run afoul of the lawyers myself, so I defer from showing any of the satirical images of Barney that originally appeared online.

Another site that took a slightly (okay, extremely) skewed look at Barney, Barney the Antichrist, didn't run afoul of the lawyers at all. Its owner shut it down because he was overwhelmed by e-mails of protest from pro-Barney supporters. He complained that his fellow anti-Barney proponents rarely contributed any of the articles he solicited, hoping to prove Barney's significance as a religious figure.

To my surprise, I discovered that the site Jihad to Destroy Barney (http://www.jihad.net/) is still online and has gone through five "editions." However, the site's home page is loaded with disclaimers explaining that the site is fictional and has nothing to do with Islamic jihad or any other terrorist organization. After the terrorist attacks of September 11, 2001, the site was flooded with angry e-mail from around the world from people who thought the site had something to do with Al Queda or terrorism. The rest of the site (shown in Figure 14-3) is quite extensive, including fiction related to Barney, a series of "scholarly works" exploring "what's wrong with Barney," and "a complete, (dys)functional Internet community."

Yet another down-with-Barney site, Top 38 Ways to Kill Barney, was also crushed by a threatening letter, which the owner reproduced on the site's home page. The opening of the letter is preserved at http://disobey.com/ghostsites/show_exhibit/top38waystokillbarney1/. The site's owner noted, as part of the reason why he was taking the site offline, "As Barney's popularity has declined, I see this as reaching for a bucket when the ship has already sunk."

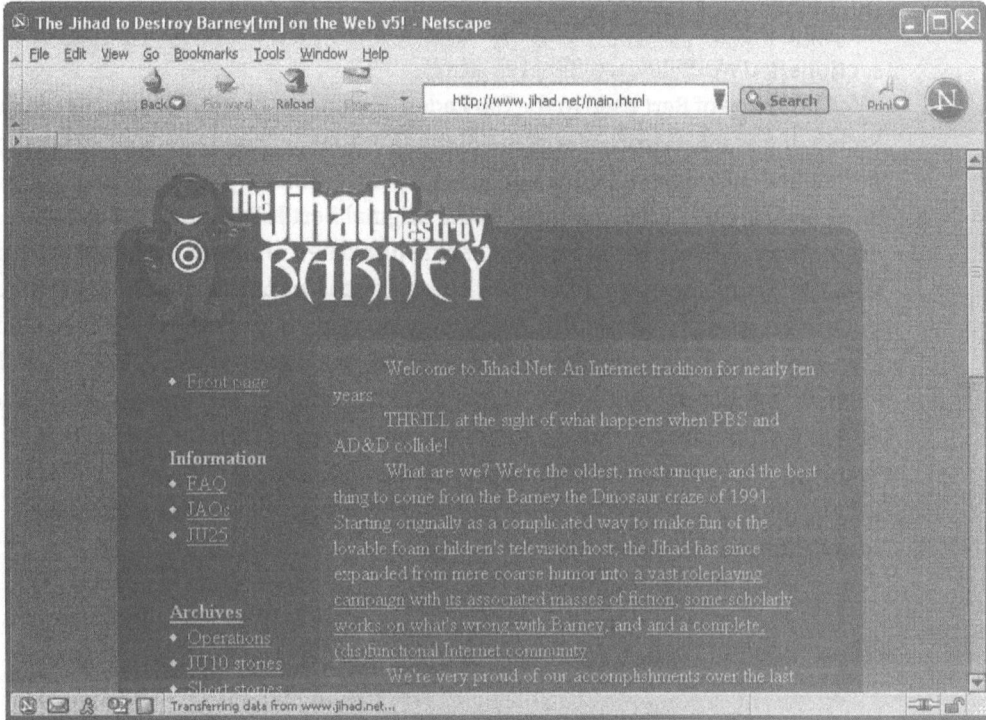

Figure 14-3. This site is a rare surviving refuge for the anti-Barney community.[3]

Bert Gets Beaten with Cyberducky

Bert and Ernie are among the most popular characters of the Muppets, the gang of hand puppets that populates Sesame Street. Dino Ignacio admits, "I myself grew up on Sesame Street, and it was an important part of my childhood." Perhaps it was out of love for the Sesame Street characters that he created a Web site called Bert Is Evil (http://www.fractalcow.com/bert/bert.htm). Perhaps, as he says in the "goodbye, Bert" message he left when he took the site down, it was a way of giving voice to the "rebellious punk" in him.

Ignacio said he killed his own satirical Web site because it was going too mainstream and was in danger of destroying "the character's credibility with children." Why did that happen? In an even more bizarre use of Bert than Bert Is Evil, some Bert Is Evil imagery was stolen and incorporated in signs used in a real (not cyber) pro–Osama Bin Laden rally in the Middle East.

---

3. http://www.jihad.net/main.html

Columnist Buck Wolf of ABC News reported on the flap, and the report included a reproduction of the scowling Bert next to Bin Laden (http://abcnews.go.com/sections/us/WolfFiles/wolffiles190.html).

The image of Bert used in the Bin Laden posters wasn't even created by Ignacio. Rather, it was taken from one of the many sites that imitated Ignacio's. The mirror Bert Is Evil site, run by Dennis Pozniak, was still online as of this writing.

The "mirror" (or online copy) of the original Bert Is Evil site is yet another example of how words and images that are published online can take on a life that goes far beyond the original creator's intent. It remains online even though Ignacio put out a request for all such mirror sites to be taken down. Bert Is Evil is certainly clever as satire. The site (which was nominated for a Webby award in 1997) includes "Photoshopped" images of Bert at the JFK assassination, Bert at Woodstock, and Bert as the Unabomber. Poor Bert, who was the subject of other speculation in years past (*Spy Magazine* originally raised the question "Is Bert gay?" which became an urban legend), still has to endure the prying eyes of inquiring Web surfers around the world.

Bleem Gets Creamed

Sony PlayStation is one of the most popular video game systems around. To play the games, you need to purchase the Sony PlayStation hardware as well as the software versions of the games themselves. A small company called Bleem.com developed a product called Bleem, which functioned as an emulator, letting PC and Dreamcast owners play Sony PlayStation games on the hardware they already owned.

However, Sony allegedly pressured retailers not to sell the Bleem software and sued Bleem.com over the Bleem emulator. The tiny company was forced out of business. The image of Sonic the Hedgehog (a trademarked symbol of Sega, one of Sony's competitors in the game field) mourning Bleem was left when the Bleem Web site (http://www.bleem.com/) folded in 2001 (see Figure 14-4).

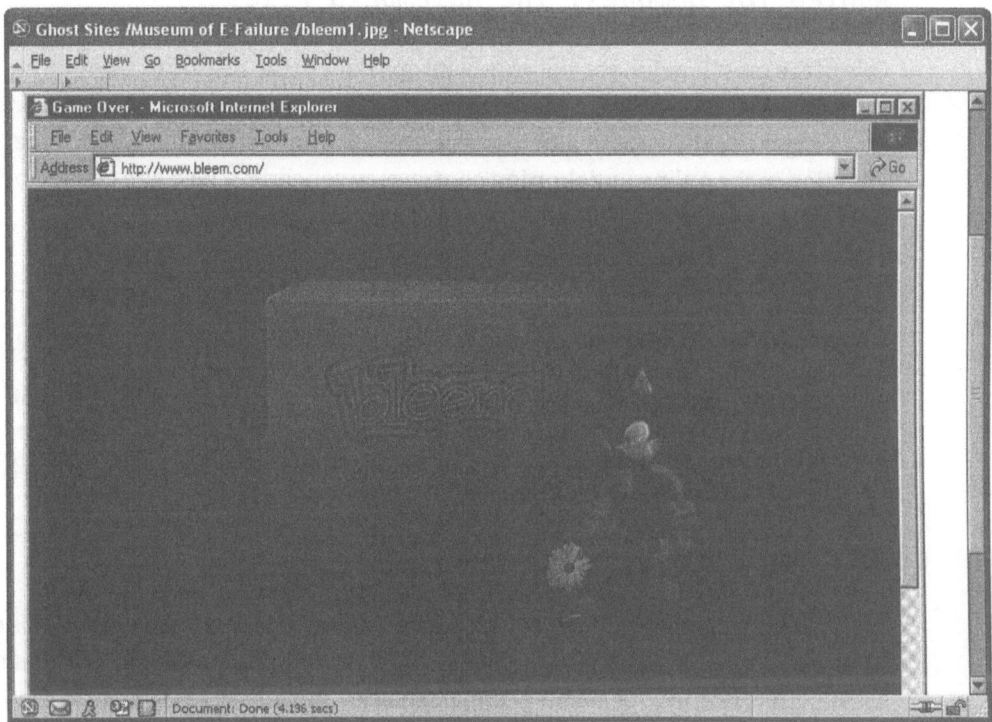

Figure 14-4. Murdered by bigger competitors: Bleem.com[4]

Just Plain Hate

By now, you know that the ability to create a Web page gives practically anyone a mouthpiece. Unfortunately, some of those mouths are best kept shut. The Web gives space to anyone with an ax to grind. The two sites mentioned in the following sections have run into problems of one sort or another. One is embroiled in a legal controversy; the other had its hero thrown into prison and has been relegated to the padded room where dysfunctional Web sites go when they die.

---

4. http://www.bleem.com/

Wanted for Damages: The Nuremberg Files

One of the most hateful, sordid, and awful episodes in the history of the Internet is still going on at this writing. It concerns the subject of abortion, which has generated more anger than just about anything I've ever encountered online. Most of the attention in the online antiabortion controversy concerns a Web site created by Neal Horsley called the Nuremberg Files (shown in Figure 14-5).

NOTE The original URL of the Nuremberg Files was not working when this book was written. The site is occasionally ordered shut down by one or another Internet service provider. You can usually find a "mirror" of the site that has been created by someone who disagrees with its statements but believes in free speech. Check http://www.xs4all.nl/~oracle/nuremberg/aborts.html.

This site rails against doctors who perform abortions and publishes photos of people going in and out of abortion clinics. The most infamous aspect of this site has been its "Wanted" posters bearing the names and addresses of doctors who performed abortions. Another disturbing part of the site is the list of doctors who were singled out as having performed abortions; the names on the list were crossed off as the doctors died.

One name in particular still remains crossed out: Dr. Barnett Slepian was killed by a sniper at his home near Buffalo, New York, in 1998. Also crossed out is the name of Dr. David Gunn, who was shot in the back and killed by an assassin as he entered a clinic in Pensacola, Florida, in 1993. Many other names are not crossed out.

A group of four doctors sued the site under racketeering laws and a 1994 law that makes it illegal to incite violence and threaten doctors who perform abortions. In 1999, a federal jury found that the Web site and its "Wanted" posters were essentially threats to kill. In 2002, an appeals court found that the site could be held liable; however, it ordered a lower-court judge to reduce the $108.5 million in punitive damages that the federal jury had awarded to the four doctors.

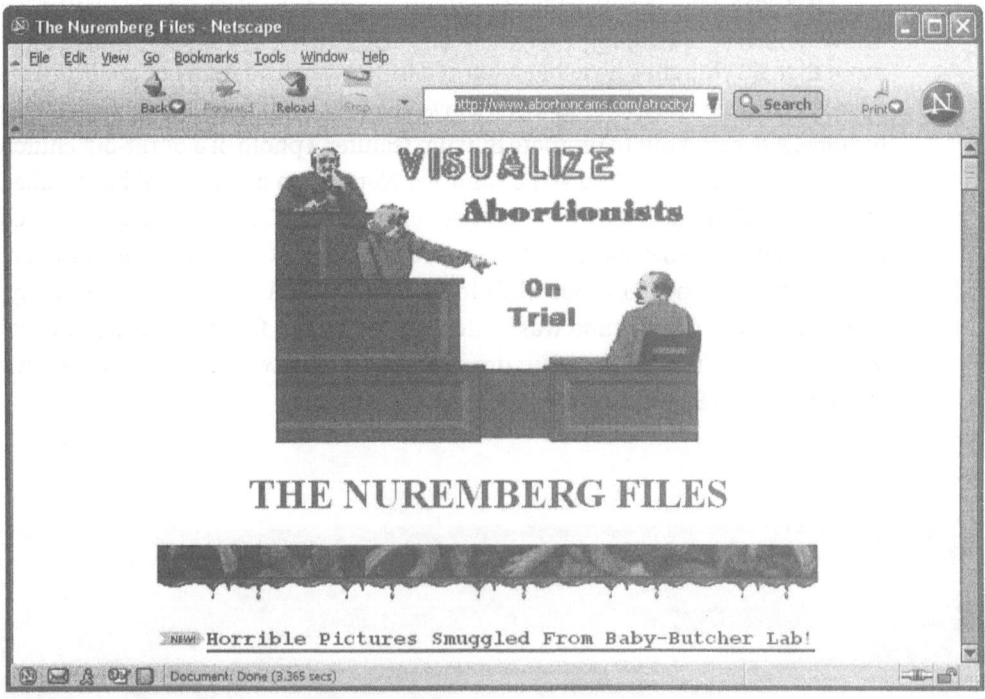

Figure 14-5. This site names doctors who perform abortions and crosses them off the list when they have been killed.[5]

Shrine to Black Metal's "Messiah" Tones Down Its Act

Christian Vikernes grew up in a small Norwegian town. He had trouble making friends because of some eccentric beliefs. First, he called himself Count Grishnackh. He also went by the nickname Varg. Second, he firmly believed that his true father was none other than Satan himself. Mercilessly picked on by his peers, he made a promise that, some day, he would exact his revenge upon the world.

Vikernes created a musical group called Burzum in 1987 when he was only 14. He was the group's only member. Burzum was devoted to a style of music called *black metal*. Black metal is a type of gut-wrenching, superfast, hard-rock music that features hissing and distorted human vocals as well as eerie, Satanic sound effects. Many of the bands that pound out black metal are considered to be neo-Fascists; some, like Burzum, have been accused of devil worship and vandalism.

---

5.   http://www.abortioncams.com/atrocity/

Vikernes's band began to release albums in the early 1990s. He began to develop a following, and his disciples created a group called the Black Circle. Since 1992, more than 50 churches have been burned in Norway, and many of the burnings have been blamed on this group. The songs Vikernes writes talk openly about church burning. A flyer put out to promote Burzum features a photo of a burnt-out church.

Burzum was overshadowed by another Norwegian black-metal band called Mayhem, which was led by the guitarist Euronymous. Count Grishnackh joined Mayhem and was their bassist for a short time. On August 10, 1993, Euronymous was stabbed to death 21 times while in his underwear. Vikernes was eventually convicted of the murder and was sentenced to 21 years for that murder and for four arson fires. The original Burzum site was pretty raw stuff; it's preserved on Ghost Sites (see Figure 14-6).

Figure 14-6. This site glorified church burning and other neo-Fascist activities.[6]

---

6. http://www.burzum.com/

Vikernes did not stop his recording career just because he was in prison. He has released several albums on Misanthropy Records that rely heavily on synthesizers. The current version of Burzum.com looks much more respectable. But click the Forums link, and you get a glimpse into the same hate-filled, unstable world. In the forums, people comment that Hitler was a messiah and that Americans require "ethnic cleansing." I don't even want to get into what they say about Jews, but their harshest treatment is reserved for Christians. At the bottom of the home page you see a tiny link leading to the United Hessian Front Web site. This group's goal is the establishment of a "naturalistic order that is less conformist and centralized than civilization." In order to go beyond civilization, it calls for the destruction of Judeo-Christianity and the separation of the races—and for the killing of "all idiots."

The Burzum site is only one place where you can get a glimpse of some scary folks. In the United States, a group called Dismembered Fetus gives the Norwegians a run for their money when it comes to advocating violence. The songs listed on their Web site (http://www.deathmetal.com/disfetus/) bear titles ranging from "Stomp on Your Face" and "Lesbian Grandma" all the way to "Beaten to Death."

 TIP   A site called DeathMetal.com (http://www.deathmetal.com/) collects links to bands that roar forth with various types of thrash metal, death metal, black metal, and other happy love songs.

The Day the KKK Got Hijacked

The Web has provided a forum for the Ku Klux Klan (KKK), which has fragmented in recent years. The many branches of the Klan, including the Knights of the White Kamellia, the North Georgia White Knights, and the National Association for the Advancement of White People, run by former KKK director David Duke, all have their own Web sites.

The site that's easiest to find on the Web, of course, is the one with the most obvious domain name. The domain name KKK.com is entered by many impressionable young people who want to venture a look at the notorious group they've read about in books and newspapers.

In September 1999, however, people who went to view the KKK.com Web site were surprised to find themselves at the Southern Poverty Law Center's Hatewatch (http://www.hatewatch.org/) site instead. Hatewatch is a site that opposes hate groups such as the KKK. It turns out that the KKK site had been hacked and hijacked to the new location—a victim of hacktivism. In this case, it occurred when someone sent a forged domain name change form to the registrar Network Solutions. However, Hatewatch's director denied that his group had anything to do with the redirect.

Having Fun with Race Relations

There are oh-so-many Web sites that take bigotry to a new level that I thought I would present a few that bring a little humor to a delicate subject. In some cases, it's difficult to tell whether satire is being attempted or whether anger is really coming through. You can tiptoe along the blurry dividing line by visiting the following sites.

Down with Whitey!

This site (http://www.downwithwhitey.com/) recalls the black exploitation movies of the '60s and '70s as well as Chris Rock's sketches on *Saturday Night Live*. The site's subtitle—Fighting Whitey with Afro-Charged Fists of Fury—sounds like it comes right out of an action movie (see Figure 14-7).

The site's creator is supposed to be an angry black man named Dwight, who is sitting on his stoop, living on welfare, and railing against the injustices "Whitey" has put upon him. Even Dwight's daughter is supposed to get in the act, drawing pictures that are reproduced on the site with captions such as "Kill Whitey."

It surprised me to learn that the creator of Down with Whitey! is, in fact, a 23-year-old white man named Justin Dagen. He lives in Massachusetts and is a systems administrator. He just graduated from college with a degree in computer science and, as he puts it, an "unrecognized minor in mischief and finding ways to exploit people's sensitivities."

Dagen created the site on a whim. He wanted to either do the site as it is currently or have the site be about a man who is "down with" Whitey in the sense that they are friends. "Whitey" is defined as "a group of social elites and business kingpins headed by the Man." There is an actual photo of "the Man" standing outside a White Castle restaurant that leads one to believe that this site is not totally serious, but the site is never clearly described as satire or not. (By the way, the man depicted as "the Man" is a researcher whose image Dagen encountered while doing a search on Google for the term "Whitey.")

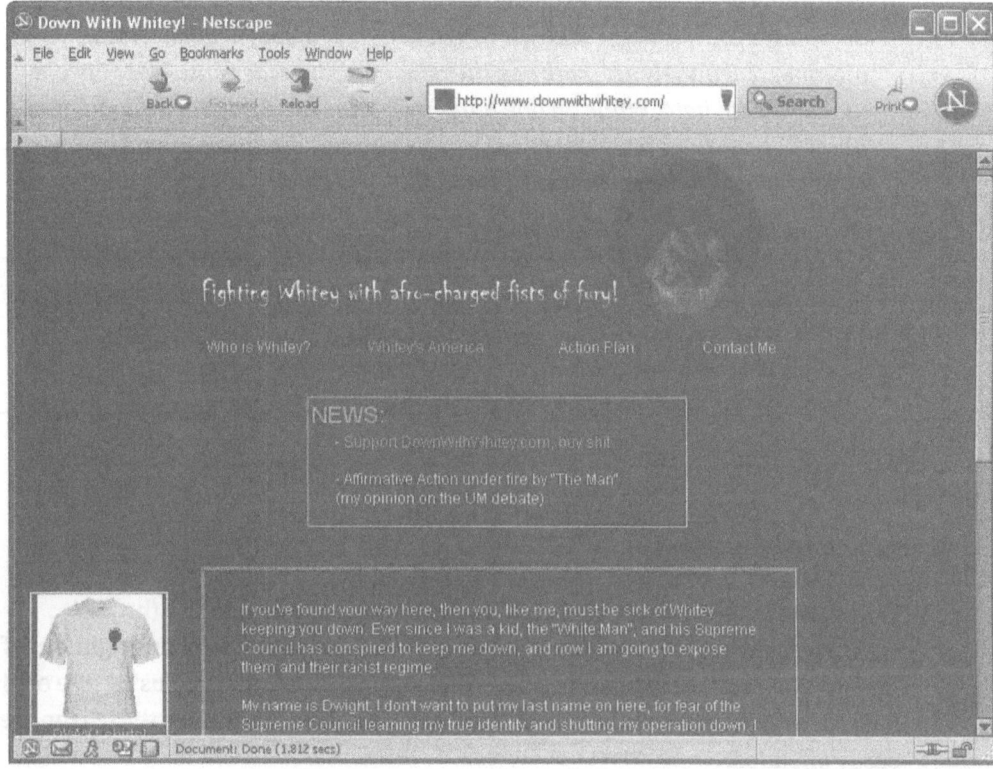

Figure 14-7. Down with Whitey! A site with an agenda and a clearly defined enemy: the Man.[7]

As you might expect, the site has attracted both positive and negative e-mail. Dagen says he wanted Down with Whitey! to "make my mark on the Internet" and elicit reactions from visitors. It was an extension of some pranks he pulled off in college—"trying to be creative, humorous, and at the same time being forced to hide who I am so as not to suffer the backlash. Quietly sitting in the shadows enjoying what I have created and watching it be appreciated by many and detested by many others." His site has received 100,000 visitors since it went online in April 2003.

Dagen intentionally left it up to the individual visitor to determine how to react to the site:

---

7. http://www.downwithwhitey.com/

Very many people do not understand the site is satire. Those who typically do are younger, often college students who will e-mail me saying the site was hilarious. I definitely get more negative than positive reactions. A lot of people are filled with hate. While on one hand it is funny to hear them rant and rave over a site that was intended as satire, it is also sad that there are still people around who feel the way these people do.

NOTE Chapter 15 describes another site that takes a funny look at race relations and that has generated quite a bit of controversy: Black People Like Us!

niggastolemy.tv

Down with Whitey! never explicitly says it's satirical, but this site (http://www.niggastolemy.tv/) is definitely not serious. The author explains right out of the box that the photos of a black person stealing a TV were staged using one of his own friends. Yet, apparently, the site still gets angry feedback from those who are easily offended.

WhiggerDressUp.com

What's a whigger? Apparently, it's someone who is white and who dresses like a black person. That, at least, is what Normal Bob Smith would have you believe. Normal Bob Smith is a Web designer and illustrator who doesn't mind creating Web sites (http://www.whiggerdressup.com/, which is also available at http://www.normalbobsmith.com/pfolio_dressup.html) that stir up trouble and generate hate mail. He's also created a Dress Up Jesus Web page that's gained him lots of negative feedback. This site purports to be a game in which you drag clothes over a bony white cartoon figure.

Pimpbuilder

A site called Dolemite Dot Com (http://www.dolemite.com/, shown in Figure 14-8) includes another dress-up interactive game but one that features a black figure— actually, it's called Pimpbuilder, so you can imagine the kinds of "threads" that are provided for you to do the dressing. *Dolemite* is a cult movie in the Blaxploitation genre.

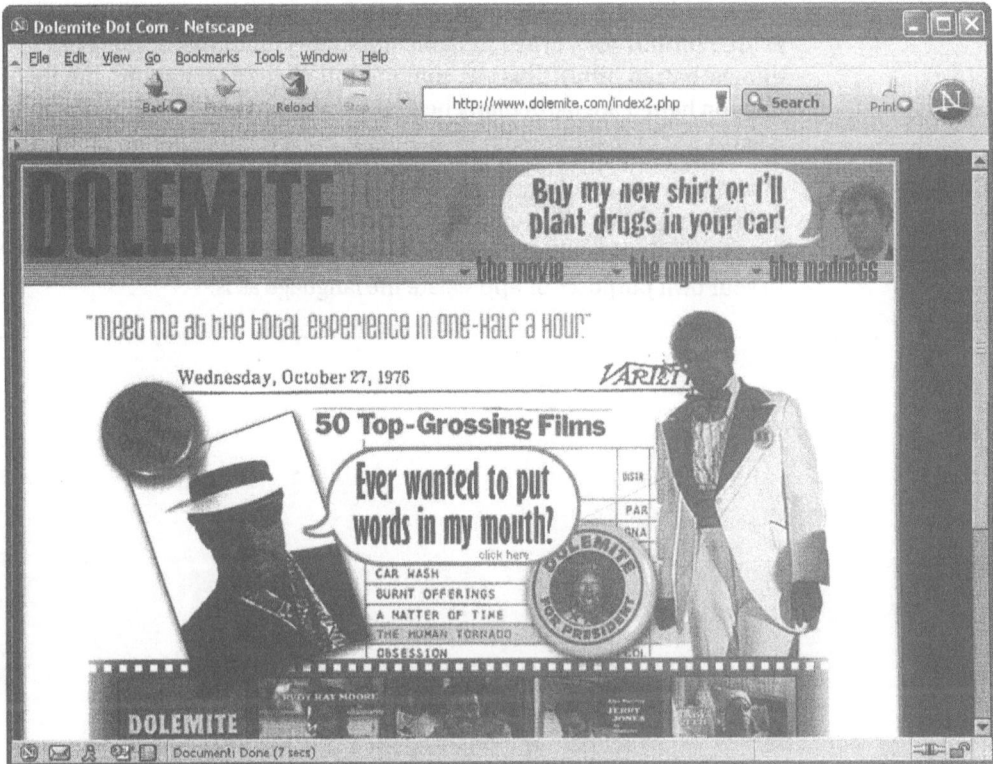

Figure 14-8. Dress up a "pimp," and view scenes from this cult movie classic.[8]

Random Googling

It doesn't take long to uncover feuds, arguments, complaints, or general tongue lashings in cyberspace. The following list contains a few I found noteworthy—a random sampling of sites that turned up after searching on the search service Google (http://www.google.com/) for the terms "insult" or "hate" or that were related to other sites described in this chapter:

- **Random Insult Generators (http://www.insultmonger.com/generators/index.htm)**: Looking for the perfect tongue-lashing to deliver to someone who rubs you the wrong way in a chat room? Visit this site, which will deliver its own insults to you or customize them to fit your description of yourself. When I visited, the following was offered: "You are in irredeemably repugnant sycophant and a feculent, nostril-offending unspeakably offensive blackguard."

---

8. http://www.dolemite.com/index2.php

- **Cyber Nation's Great Quotations to Inspire and Motivate You: Hatred (http://www.cyber-nation.com/victory/quotations/subjects/ quotes_hatred.html):** This site contains lots of good quotations, but the ones on hatred are particularly helpful to keep in mind before getting into a flame war or insulting someone online.

- **Shakespearean Insulter (http://www.pangloss.com/seidel/Shaker/ index.html):** Click a button, and you instantly receive an insult from the Bard himself, taken directly from one of his plays. You can adapt the insult to your own purposes or appreciate the language as is.

CHAPTER 15

Silliness, Fun, and Games in Babylon

LET'S FACE IT: The Internet is an increasingly serious place. We depend on it for news, for work, for homework assignments, and for finance. It wasn't always that way, though. Just a few years ago, office workers were laughing in glee and calling their compatriots to look at monitors covered with dancing hamsters or dancing babies. Anyone could make a Web site to follow up on a drunken whim, with names such as "Am I Hot or Not?"

Today, the Internet is less spontaneous and more commercial but not dramatically so. Happily, much of the Internet—the part we love to visit over and over again—is still a place where we can go to escape the anxieties of everyday life. After a grueling two-hour meeting or after a long day at work, do you flop down in front of the computer to memorize the headlines? Of course not. You head as fast as your mouse will carry you to a site that has the latest dirty jokes, to a site that describes strange things you can do with animals, or to one that devotes way too much attention to bodily functions. Thanks to some very warped imaginations, the Internet is still just plain silly. This chapter runs down some of the highs and lows of everything that the Internet has given us to laugh at in recent years.

Of Animals and Computer Keyboards

As any computer user will tell you, animals and computer keyboards just don't mix. As the owner of a lovebird who loves to perch on my computer while I'm working, I won't go into the many awful things animals can do to a keyboard. However, a number of Web sites have explored the dangers and come up with two completely different approaches to animal-computer interaction.

Keyboards Gain Nine Lives with Catproofing Tool

I freely admit that, unlike the females in my life, I'm not a feline lover. Maybe that's why I find PawSense kind of silly. After all, how often does it really happen that a cat walks across your keyboard? Don't those kitties prefer to curl up on the couch or look out the window? Do they really want to crash your computer or delete your files?

According to a company called BitBoost Systems (http://www.bitboost.com/pawsense/), this is a real danger. PawSense (see Figure 15-1) supposedly "detects and blocks cat typing." Presumably, it is able to recognize cat language and prevent cat commands from being issued via the keyboard. I'm not joking: The program's documentation states that PawSense is able to "distinguish cat typing from human typing" and can recognize a cat within just "one or two pawsteps."

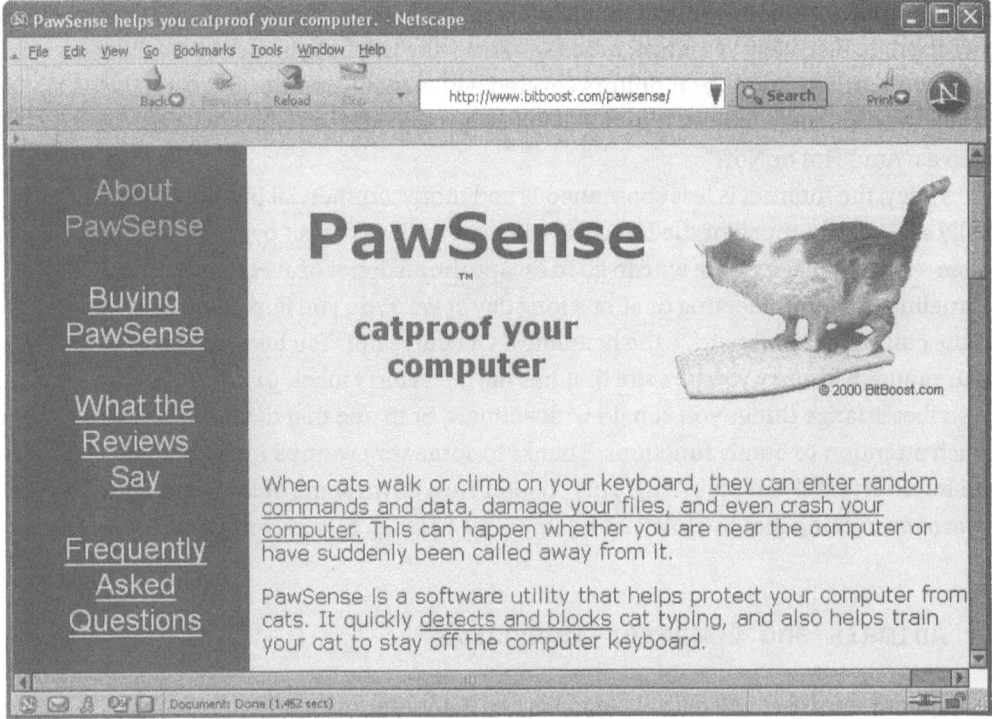

Figure 15-1. PawSense claims to be able to detect cat steps on a keyboard and emits noises that supposedly will send the animals scurrying.[1]

---

1. http://www.bitboost.com/pawsense/

The trick in developing such a program is this: How do you train the software to know when it's a cat dancing on your keyboard rather than your four-year-old learning to type or you typing gibberish after a long night out at the pubs? But PawSense goes a step further than this: It claims to be able to train your cat to stay off the computer keyboard. If it detects a cat, the program causes the computer to generate a sound that is supposed to annoy cats. You can choose between a harmonica and a hissing sound or create your own off-putting sound.

As a harmonica player, I'm offended by the notion that any member of the animal kingdom would consider this instrument offensive (though I have to admit that the birds in my house don't seem thrilled by it). However, PawSense has been around for several years as I write this, and its owner claims that more orders are coming in all the time. Would you pay $19.99 plus $3 shipping and handling for this high-tech solution? It seems much easier to shout, "Scat, cat!" You decide.

To Be or Not to Be...a Typing Monkey

You have to pity the poor monkey. Over the decades we've shot monkeys into space, turned them into television stars, and made them perform in the circus. Now, just in time for the Internet, some researchers with time and money on their hands have attempted to teach a group of monkeys to type.

Researchers at Plymouth University in England gathered together a team of six monkeys—okay, to be precise about it, they weren't your garden-variety monkeys but six Sulawesi Crested Macaques—and provided them with a computer and a keyboard. It's difficult to see in Figure 15-2, but the keyboard was covered with a plastic sheet for reasons that should be obvious. (See the "Toilet Humor" section later in this chapter if you insist on further details.) Then they were set loose with no less a goal than a duplication of the complete works of Shakespeare.

With the excruciating analysis and overly pretentious hyperbole usually indulged in by academics who need to fulfill publishing requirements to keep their jobs, the researchers provide a detailed explanation of the whys and wherefores of the test at http://www.vivaria.net/experiments/notes/documentation/. The basic idea was to see if, with the aid of technology, the creatures could leap past a few rungs on the evolutionary ladder and acquire language by pressing keys on the supplied keyboard. With an infinite amount of time, an infinite number of monkeys would eventually produce the complete works of Shakespeare in the course of pushing keys, the researchers somehow surmised.

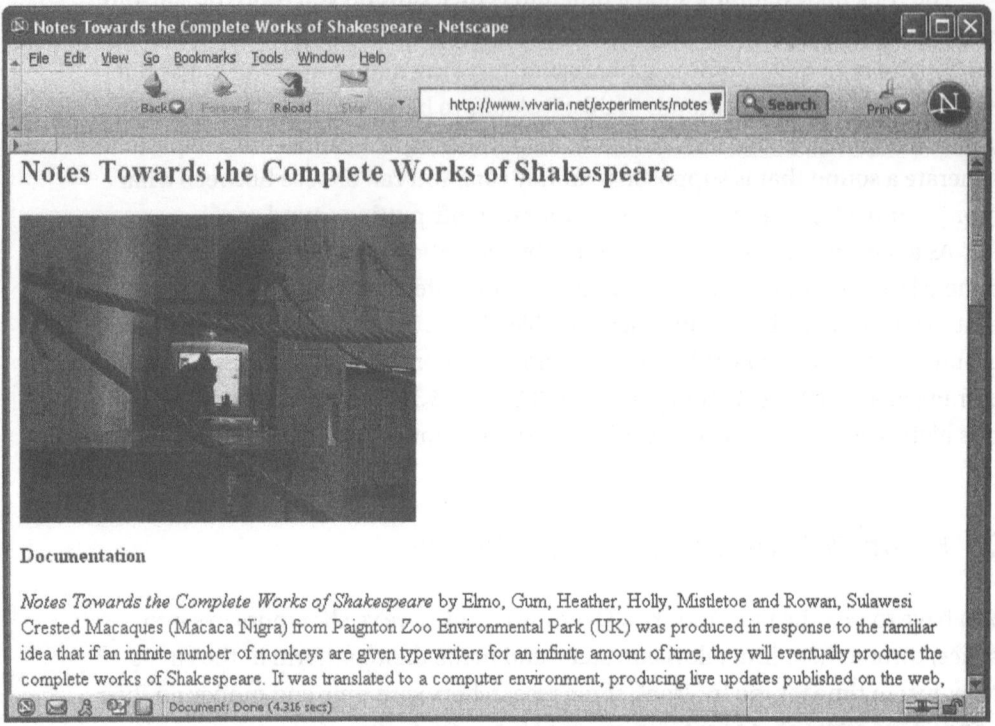

Figure 15-2. *Instant evolution: from ape to author with only the help of a keyboard* [2]

The results were pretty predictable: The monkeys typed a pile of gibberish. They didn't instantly acquire language skills just by having a set of buttons they could place under their respective butts. What's surprising is the extent of the documentation provided online. Live updates were published on the Web. Webcams tracked the activities of the monkey playwrights. You can even purchase the publication created by the six monkeys: Elmo, Gum, Heather, Holly, Mistletoe, and Rowan. It's been given the grandiose title *Notes Towards the Complete Works of Shakespeare*. For a mere 25 British pounds, you can purchase one of a limited edition of 100 16-page printed books and accompanying DVD at http://www.kahve-house.com/ society/shop/. But you can view the work for free at http://www.vivaria.net/ experiments/notes/publication/. This is an excerpt of what you can expect:

```
sssssssssssssssssssssssssssssssssssssssssssssssssssssssssssssssss-
naaaaaaaaaaaaaaaaaaaaaaaaaaaaaaaaaaaaaaaaaaaaaaaaaaaaaaaaaaaaaaaaa
aaaaaaaaaaassssssssssssssssfsssshgggggggggggssassfssssggggggggggggggggaaavlmlvvs-
```

---

2. http://www.vivaria.net/experiments/notes/documentation/

TIP Another profound study that involved research around the world, the Quack Project, seeks to determine whether ducks quack the same from country to country—whether quacks are the same in different languages in other words. The CD full of duck quacks is available for 10 British pounds. Find out more about this project, which is "designed to promote world harmony," at http://www.quack-project.com/.

Keeping Track of Monkey Business

I'm not the only one who has taken notice of monkey business online. An entire Web site is devoted to the topic: ShitThrowingMonkeys.com (http://www.shitthrowingmonkeys.com/index.html, shown in Figure 15-3) presents news stories (some fictitious, some not) having to do with the antics of everyone's second-favorite primates.

Figure 15-3. This site purports to keep track of all kinds of monkeyshines online.[3]

---

3. http://www.shitthrowingmonkeys.com/index.html

Eye Exams Done Without Seeing Patient

Eyesight is important, but the lack of firsthand eye contact doesn't hamper the activities of the Animal Eye Doctor (http://www.animaleyedoc.com/). Pet owners and veterinarians alike can fill out the handy form provided on this site and describe the eye problems being experienced by the animal in question. The eye doctor on call will respond with a diagnosis, or at least an opinion, without ever setting eyes on the pooch, kitty, or other creature. Some things, like sex, just can't be handled online; don't you think this might be one of them?

Fun with the Nine-to-Five Grind

Surfing the Web and the rest of the Internet is the guilty pleasure of many an office worker around the world. Anything to pass the time during lunch (or after lunch) or during that final hour before it's time to go home is a welcome diversion. The following are just two of the many ways to get a laugh online at the expense of bosses and annoying coworkers everywhere.

NOTE   One of the best examples of workplace humor, the comic strip Dilbert by Scott Adams, has a significant presence online. Dilbert.com, the official Web site for Dilbert, provides visitors with lots of amusement, including free comics, accessories, a newsletter, and much more.

Thanks for the Memo-rie$

Would you pay $45 to read memos issued by other companies? In some cases, it's great entertainment. You might read a hilarious notice about a toilet paper quota being established by one cash-strapped organization. Other memos, that bear headings such as "Juvenile and Repugnant Behavior" and that begin "For starters I cannot believe that it is necessary to write this email..." promise to provide many laughs around the water cooler.

That's the promise of InternalMemos.com (http://www.internalmemos.com/memos/). The site collects notices, instructions, reports, and other memos from many different organizations. The best ones usually require a subscription to read. But once in a while, you get to read something that's humorous for free. You might spy on a Web site's apology for calling the Jewish holiday Yom Kippur a "chance to party" (it's actually the Day of Atonement). Or you may stumble upon a memo purported to be issued by a well-known news service that takes employees to task for meeting other employees "with the smell of alcohol on their breath."

For a mere $45 per month, you get the privilege of reading other companies' memos as well as those produced your own employer. And that, perhaps, is the silliest thing about this Web site.

Weird Police Stories

The good old police blotter is the most fascinating source of stories in many small-town newspapers. You can find a variation on the police blotter, consisting of stories submitted by law enforcement officials themselves, on the Police Humor Web site (http://www.policehumor.com/dp/1-45.htm).

As it turns out, the police officers who submit listings to this site have a morbid sense of humor. In the Weird News section of the Web site, you're liable to encounter stories about finding body parts in unexpected places and other unpleasant things. Alongside those, you'll find some bizarre reports, including the story of the man who forced another man to fix his truck at gunpoint, the Wisconsin man who stole $100,000 worth of farm pigs to pay for breast implants for his favorite stripper, and more.

The Online Silliness Hall of Fame

Once in a while, trends and fads that originate with techie types cross over into the general population. Once in a *great* while, one of those fads takes the country by storm. Then, after a few months, the furor dies down. The sites remain and continue to grow, but they are replaced by other attractions of the moment. The following sections describe some of the most famous of the humorous, even silly, Web-based trends that have originated online.

"All Your Base Are Belong to Us"

This odd phrase doesn't seem to make any sense. But it turned out to be a huge Internet "moment" that still hasn't ended. It started out as a small-scale inside joke related to a video game. But it ended up getting attention in national publications from *USA Today* to the *Los Angeles Times*.

What *is* it, you ask? It is a phrase taken from the video game Zero Wing. The game was created in 1989 by the Japanese company Toaplan. When, in 1991, Toaplan offered a version of Zero Wing that would run on the popular Sega Genesis console, its text had to be translated into English. The English translation was remarkably awkward. One of the characters, a villian named Cats (see Figure 15-4), taunts the "good guys" in a spaceship:

How are you gentlemen. All your base are belong to us!! You are on the way to destruction. You have no chance to survive make your time.

Figure 15-4. Only on the Internet: A poorly translated phrase turns into a cult saying.[4]

Had the Japanese text been translated correctly, Zero Wing may well have been forgotten today. As it turned out, the peculiar version of "Japenglish" amused video game players considerably. They began to exchange variations of the phrase on message boards. Lively discussions erupted in which participants attempted to

---

4. http://www.classicgaming.com/rotw/zerowing/

invent scenarios using the phrase "All your base are belong to us." One Web site did a fake voice-over of the phrase in a Wayne Newton voice. Another created a video presentation of the phrase. Then, the threads died out, and the video game crowd moved on to other things. But with its usual timing, the mass media began to pick up on the craze and write about it. A whole new burst of "All your base" fever began as it was picked up by the general public—those who knew nothing about the video game. The phrase quickly became one of the top searches on the Web. The site hosting the video was flooded with more visitors than it could handle and moved to a higher-capacity server. It became the first geek catchphrase of the 21st millenium. Then, just as quickly, it faded again—until someone wrote about it in a book called *Internet Babylon*. The rest is history....

Am I Hot or Not? Site: No, It's Not

In the brick-and-mortar world, fads come and go, but they tend to last at least a few months. Beanie Babies were hot for several years. On the Internet, everything is accelerated, and that includes fads. They come and go seemingly in the blink of an eye. Some pass under the radar going completely unnoticed until someone like me takes a look back at them.

Such is the case with a Web site called Am I Hot or Not? The site (http://www.hotornot.com/) appeals to everything that makes the Internet popular. It gives ordinary people a chance to get noticed: All are invited to post photos of themselves and have visitors rate their looks on a scale of one to ten, with ten being the most attractive. It encourages instant interactivity. It doesn't require huge amounts of thought.

Am I Hot or Not? was the brainchild of two roommates: James Hong and Jim Young (see Figure 15-5). Hong found himself out of a job and with time on his hands when the air began to seep out of the dot-com bubble in 2000. Young was a graduate student at the University of California at Berkeley—just beginning his seventh year, as a matter of fact.

One afternoon in October 2000 while Hong was drinking, Young mentioned to Hong and Hong's brother Tony that a girl they had recently met was a "perfect ten." The idea percolated, fueled by the alcohol: Why not create a Web site where people could rate one another on a scale of one to ten? Young put the site together quickly, and then the pair e-mailed their friends to announce it was online. The same day, they began getting submissions from total strangers who had heard about Am I Hot or Not? by word of mouth. In just six weeks, it was getting millions of visits and rated an article in *Wired* magazine describing the site as "red hot."

The site was originally intended to let ordinary individuals submit photos of themselves so they could be "rated." Before long, porn sites were sending unclothed pictures of models. But the two developers gave visitors a way to report photos they considered offensive, and they were able to take down the X-rated photos as

well as those submitted by professional models or those that appeared to have
been retouched.

*Figure 15-5. An unemployed dot-com refugee and a perpetual grad student started one of the
Net's most popular Web sites on a whim.*[5]

Soon, the site was receiving as many as three million page views each day. Now,
Hong and Young (who had not spent a cent on advertising) were wondering if they
could turn Am I Hot or Not? into a money-making proposition. If you visit the site
today, you won't see any advertising; however, you can buy T-shirts and mugs with
the "Am I Hot" logo on them.

It's an example not only of how quickly fads come and go but of how things
become popular online. It isn't always by design. Word of mouth—otherwise known
as *viral* marketing—is what really makes things popular. One person "tells" another
about a site in a chat room or on a message board or newsgroup. Others tell a group
of others, and before long, the page is flooded with visitors. When Hong and Young
parodied their own site by creating a page called Am I Goth or Not? they told only
one person about it. Before long, the site was being viewed 200,000 times per day.

---

5. http://www.hotornot.com/

Am I Hot or Not? has inspired many parodies and imitations:

- Am I President or Not? focused on the George W. Bush–Al Gore election of 2000 (http://www.brunching.com/cgi/amipresidentornot.cgi).

- Bangable.com focused on young females (http://www.bangable.com/).

- Amihotornot.de gave German users a chance to be "in" or "out" (http://www.hotornot.de/).

- Am I Hot? works pretty much the same way as the original (http://www.amihot.com/).

Today, Young and Hong still run the site from their apartment in the center of the high-tech world: Mountain View, California. Am I Hot or Not? may not be the talk of the Web, but it still gets plenty of attention. To date, it has racked up two billion votes. Jim and James are thrilled at the coverage they received in *Salon, BusinessWeek, Playboy,* and *Entertainment Weekly.* Something else has developed as a result of the site's Meet Me feature that allows visitors to contact those depicted: Many relationships and even some marriages have resulted. The following are examples from the site's Testimonials page:

I am engaged to a very wonderful woman I met through your Web site! She lives in France and will be coming to the United States a little later in the year, and we will be getting married within three months after she gets here! Thanks to your Web site, I have finally found someone that I am compatible with, even across the Atlantic Ocean! As my fiancée says, every day is a miracle! Believe in love, it is real! Thank you very much!!!

Dear Jim and James, My husband and I recently logged onto your site together to see what was up with our favorite meeting place. Not too long ago we saw each other on HotOrNot and began chatting. A few weeks later I was leaving Minnesota to visit out in L.A. Four days later we hopped in the car, went to Vegas, and got married. Thanks for helping us find each other!!!

The following is another example:

I am quite lonely at the moment; as a recent graduate, I'm now looking for work and it can feel a little isolated. I am happy that I have a 9.3 rating, and it stays quite consistent. At this time you need all the morale boost you can get, and most people don't respond well when you say you're looking for work. Some guys have contacted me, and it makes me feel more special.

Young and Hong have received tepid ratings on their own Web site. But they are gratified by the number of relationships and marriages their site has fostered, and they've had a lot of fun.

TIP The Web site Modern Humorist helped put the "hot or not" craze to rest by creating a version related to those much-maligned members of the primate world—monkeys. Rate some monkeys for yourself at http://www.modernhumorist.com/mh/0011/monkey/.

Black People Love Them—Mostly

Chelsea Peretti and her brother Jonah are as white as can be. But they grew up in Northern California with a black stepmother. They encountered plenty of uncomfortable situations in relations between the races, which they learned to face with humor.

They decided to confront relations between blacks and whites in the same way—with humor. They created the Web site Black People Love Us! (http://www.blackpeopleloveus.com/). In the site, two characters named Sally and Johnny are shown cavorting with several of their black friends, drinking wine and boasting that they know how to communicate with black people in their own language (see Figure 15-6).

In the site's About Us page, Sally and Johnny describe something about themselves:

> *We're just regular, normal people—just like you! We grew up in your average neighborhoods doing the usual things that all people do: swimming, golf, horseback riding, arts and crafts, gardening, building tree houses, mowing the lawn, selling lemonade, etc.*

This site could easily have been trivial and blatantly offensive. But the Perettis did it up right. They never say explicitly, anywhere on the Web site, that it is meant as humorous satire. Visitors are left to react in their own way and to consider how they really feel about relations between whites and African Americans. It's never clear whether Sally and Johnny are real people. The photos are carefully staged. Subtle changes of expression from amusement to doubt to skepticism on the part of the white couple's black friends show that Sally and Johnny aren't quite as hip as they think they are. Some of the photos give a clue to the site's intent: In one, Johnny and a black friend are playing hangman. The friend shows Johnny the clue: R__ACISM. Johnny, however, looks mystified.

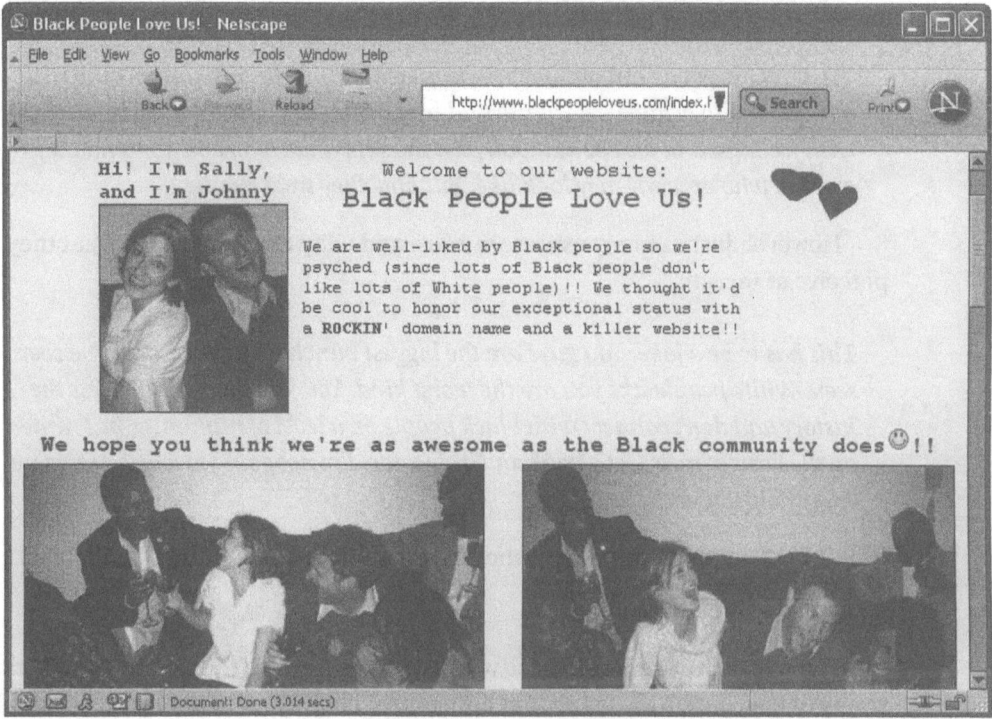

Figure 15-6. Black People Love Us! is a humorous and provocative look at race relations.[6]

"We wanted to promote dialogue, to get people talking about these issues," Jonah Peretti told the *New York Times*. The site certainly succeeds in its goal. You can tell from the page full of letters submitted by interested visitors, which is the single-most fascinating page on this site and possibly on the entire Web. "We don't really get it, but here's what people are saying," reads the introduction. The comments follow one after another in fascinating juxtaposition. Some viewers seem uncertain exactly how to respond:

That Web site is a joke, right? If not, I have to say I'm sort of appalled and EMBARRASSED by what I'm reading here.

---

6. http://www.blackpeopleloveus.com/index.html

Others praise the site and its message:

You guys are good. You really have people thinkin.' I believe that people will only get it if they have true white and black friends.... We are human beings, with feelings, and we should look past the skin and see people for who they are, not who or what they look like, but how they treat people.

However, just as many express outrage and vilify the creators for what they perceive as racism:

This has to be a joke. You guys are the biggest bunch of fuckin' idiots I've ever seen. White people like you are the worst kind. You know nothing about the history and don't connect with black people on a level of humanity, but rather on the basis of race. Get a book and a clue, too. I'm not going to waste any more energy on you pathetic losers!

—A black person who doesn't think you dumbasses "are so cool"

The interaction between those who leave messages on the site is as interesting as any of the content, as far as I am concerned. I highly recommend Black People Love Us! It's one of my all-time favorite places to visit on the Web.

TIP   Black People Love Us! has provoked discussion all over the Web. One columnist for Youth Radio says there's nothing funny about it (http://www.youthradio.org/society/kcbs2003_blackpeople.shtml). Jonah and Chelsea Peretti operate another tongue-in-cheek Web site, the Rejection Line (http://www.rejectionline.com/).

The Dancing Hamsters

As my two daughters will tell you, hamsters can grow on you (and do all kinds of other things on you). One of my kids' favorite activities for their little lovable rodents is to put them in a wooden bowl and squeal with delight as the hamsters try to get out but slip on the polished wood and end up running in place.

A hamster lover named Deirdre LaCarte loved her pet, Hampton Hampster. She, too, loved to make hamsters move in entertaining ways. She used her HamsterDance Web site (http://www.hamsterdance.com/) to make a bunch of hamsters dance in unison, as a sort of tribute to Hampton. The original Web page, shown in Figure 15-7, was simple, crude, and oddly amusing. Underneath the hamsters, a bizarre song played, which reminded one of Alvin and the Chipmunks doing hip-hop. (In reality, it was supposed to be part of a Roger Miller song from the soundtrack of the Disney movie *Robin Hood*.)

Figure 15-7. Pointless, silly, yet amusing: Hamsters danced their way into our hearts in the late 1990s.[7]

I'm not going to devote a lot of time and effort to analyzing exactly why HamsterDance became a craze that swept the Web in 1998 and 1999. I worked in an office for many years, however, and I know the importance of finding something—anything—to give you a laugh at certain times of the day. I also know how employees love to share funny things they've found online. HamsterDance seemed to embody everything that was wonderful about the Web—it was simple and homemade, it was personal, and it had no other goal than to make people smile.

This brings us to HamsterDance Mark II Mark II (http://hampsterdance2.com/, shown in Figure 15-8). You can't fault LaCarte for trying to make a few bucks off of her creation. Those hamsters, after all, do require cages, balls to run in, food, and the occasional medical attention. Accordingly, you can now purchase an album

---

7. http://hampsterdance2.com/

full of hamster songs with an accompanying music video. But the souped-up, polished, and commercialized version of HamsterDance lacks the simple charm of the original. Sometimes, office workers just want to run around in their wheels happily for a while before they are called back to the business of the day.

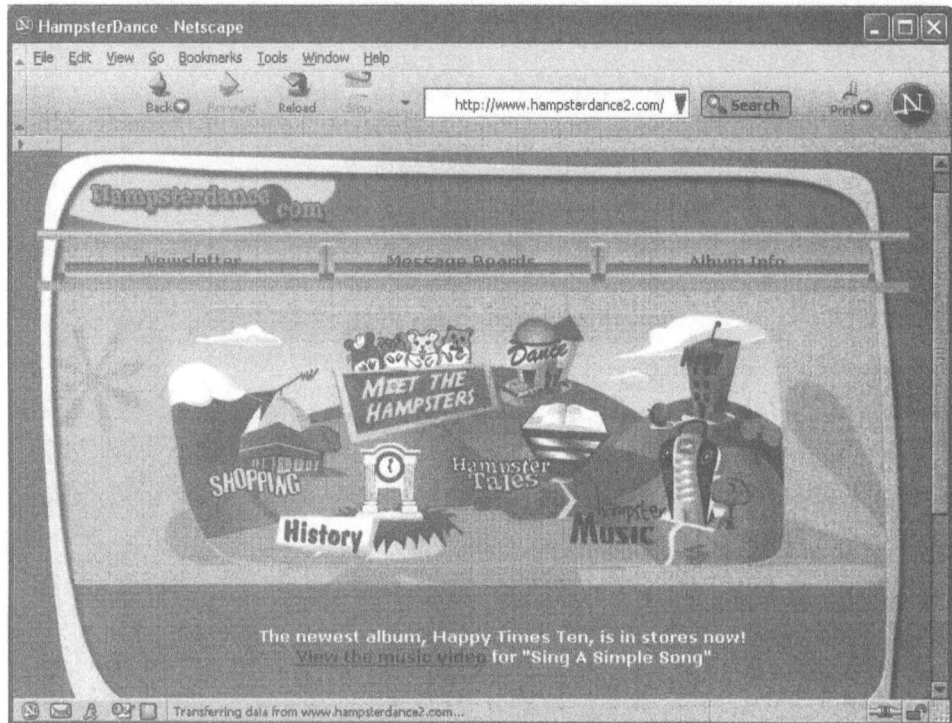

Figure 15-8. The 21st century version of HamsterDance: slick, commercial, and lacking the charm of the original [8]

...And, of Course, the Dancing Baby

If you ever watched the TV show *Ally McBeal*, you probably remember a dancing baby that kept popping up at various points, distracting the main character and usually reminding her that her "biological clock" was ticking. That show's producer, David Kelley, reportedly was inspired by the original "dancing baby," which swept across the Internet in the mid-1990s.

---

8. http://www.hampsterdance2.com/

The dancing baby, shown in Figure 15-9, was the brainchild of one of those computer graphics wizards who provides special effects for movies and television. Ron Lussier was working for LucasArts, the company that creates special effects for *Star Wars* and many other films, when he created the baby. He used the computer animation program 3D Studio Max, which is one of those applications that allow talented artists and designers to create characters that seem to move in lifelike ways.

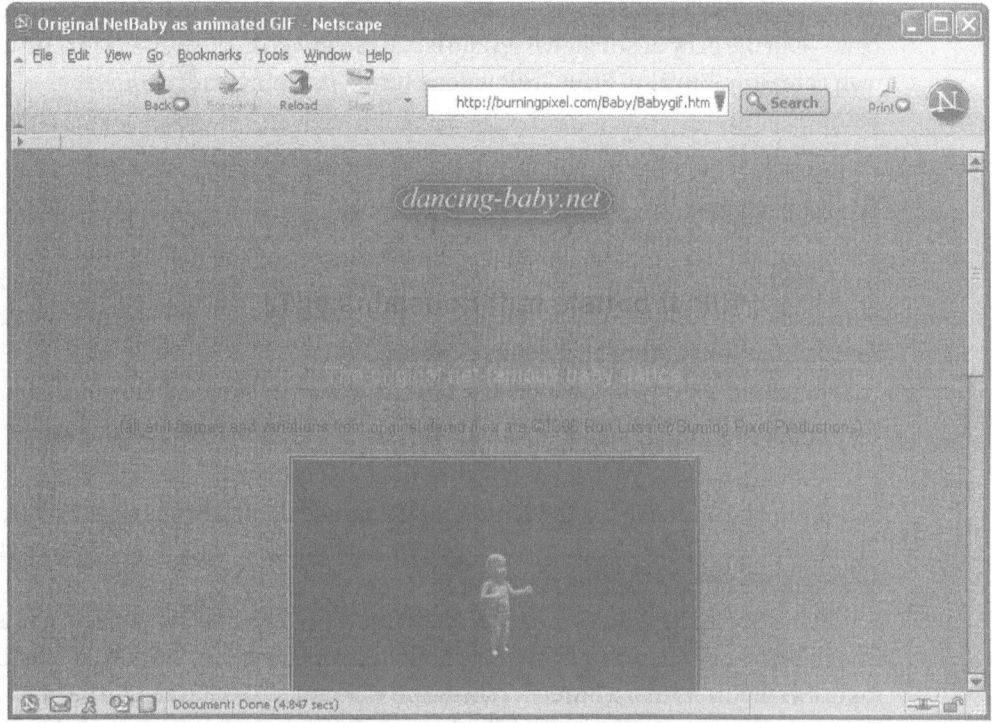

Figure 15-9. One of the earliest Web-based fads: the disturbing, fascinating dancing baby[9]

Designers love to play with new toys. One of the nice parts of Lussier's job was that he was supposed to get to know the program and explore what it could do. The demo files that came with 3D Studio Max included various characters that appeared to be in motion, including a baby. Lussier took the original baby and fixed it up: "I added some shoulder bounce, retimed the hands, retextured (colored) the surfaces, relit it, altered some skinning parameters, rendered it out...." If you get past all the techno-speak, the bottom line is that Lussier made the baby look incredibly,

---

9. http://burningpixel.com/Baby/BabyMus1.htm

disturbingly lifelike. To see a baby who looked so real doing dance moves and other things that babies just don't do naturally was morbidly fascinating.

Practically anything that appears on a computer screen and that gets viewers to go "Ah!" and smile in amazement—and keep on gazing for a period of time—is bound to become wildly popular. It was one of the first Internet fads to spread by word of mouth—first, in the company, via e-mail. Soon, coworkers began receiving copies of the animated baby from people working in another part of the country. The dancing baby fad hit its peak around 1998, when Lussier did a version for the *American Comedy Awards* show and two television commercials. Today, it's old news—but the baby hasn't grown up and is still preserved on the Web site for Lussier's own company, Burning Pixel Productions (http://burningpixel.com/Baby/BabyMus1.htm).

Toilet Humor

You just knew there would be a place somewhere in this book for some bathroom humor, didn't you? Well, this is the place. Have a seat, and I'll entertain you with some stories guaranteed to get things moving.

Surf While You Sit...the iLoo

You can surf the Internet at the airport, at the public library, in your car, in bed.... Think about it: Where else do you spend a substantial part of your day? Where else can marketers find a captive audience?

In the United Kingdom, the toilet is commonly referred to as "the loo." It was a British branch of Microsoft's Internet service provider service, MSN, that initially told news reporters that a product called iLoo was under development. The product in question was a toilet that would give its users Internet access. It seemed plausible enough: The British version of MSN was in the midst of an advertising campaign that depicted park benches in London and beach chairs in France supposedly being wired for Internet access. Why not an iLoo? It would come with a wireless keyboard, plasma screen, and toilet paper imprinted with its own Uniform Resource Locator (URL). People lining up for public toilets could use Hotmail e-mail stations so they could send and receive messages while waiting to use the iLoo.

Media outlets bought the story wholeheartedly. The Associated Press and the *Wall Street Journal* ran stories about the iLoo not being a hoax. Finally, after several weeks had passed, Microsoft issued a statement announcing that the iLoo was indeed a figment of the imagination of someone in the company's British division.

Oddly, after verifying that the story was an unsubstantiated rumor, Microsoft spokespeople stated that the iLoo was indeed under research. A Microsoft employee in—guess where?—Great Britain falsely claimed it was untrue. In fact, it had been a legitimate project being researched by MSN in Britain. However, the project was terminated quickly after the initial response: controversy, humor, ridicule, and the like. Reportedly, Microsoft ultimately decided that the iLoo was not the most effective way to extend its brand into new marketplaces.

Flush Someone's Toilet

A 23-year-old Canadian information technology professional named Kris Hanks has taken the Web to a new level of interactivity. He apparently doesn't mind having one of his toilets flush any time of the day or night. Not only has he programmed a toilet to flush remotely, but he has registered a domain name for this purpose and created a detailed Web page (http://www.ishit.ca/ishit.php).

Is this for real? I sent an e-mail to the site asking for details, but the high-tech plumber failed to respond. Perhaps he's busy hooking up pipes and wires. At the least, he has rigged his appliance with an impressive-looking set of networking equipment, some of which is shown in Figure 15-10.

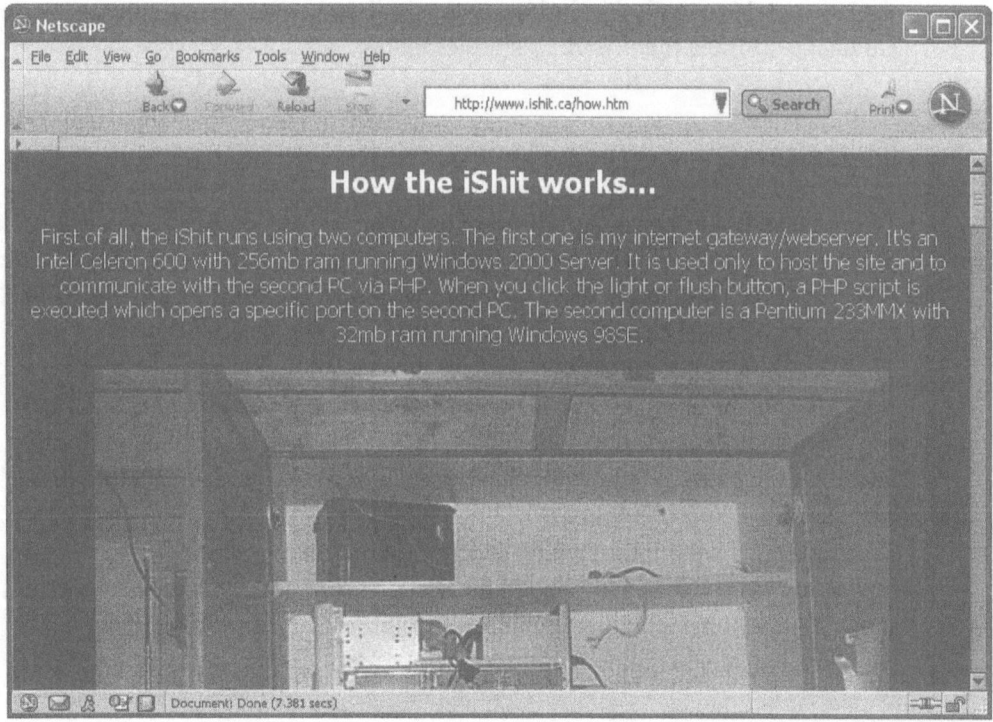

Figure 15-10. Not long ago, you could interact with a toilet in Canada in a meaningful way via this Web site.[10]

---

10. http://www.ishit.ca/how.htm

The many testimonials left on the site from amused visitors indicate that this site really worked, though it wasn't functional when I visited. Hanks admits that the site has been offline for nearly two years. But when it was up and running (so to speak), he says the following:

> *People could actually turn the light on and off and flush the toilet while watching on a live video stream. When it flushes, it is rather quiet, so you couldn't really hear it when you were in other parts of the house. The tank on the toilet is rather small, so I didn't really notice too much of an increase on the water bill.*

The statements of some visitors indicate an odd side effect of the Web's interactivity: a vicarious sense of relief.

Pick Up After Yourself, Please!

Toilet humor is pretty tame compared to much of the material you encounter on the Internet. More typical is the humor that is directly related to what goes into (or should go into) the toilet. Some examples follow.

Doodie.com

Tom Winkler not only has the chutzpah to attach his own name to this site, but he has even attracted advertising for it. This is not surprising because the site receives about seven million page views each month from people who just can't get enough feces in real life and have to supplement their daily dosage online.

The site features animations and cartoons of human beings and animals "making doodie" (see Figure 15-11 for an example). As Winkler explains on the site's Frequently Asked Questions (FAQ) page: "Wise men say, 'Follow your bliss.' Potty humor cracks me up. If you do what you love, money will follow soon. I don't love feces, just cartoons about it."

Winkler's illustrations are high quality, but the subject matter may not be so high in taste. They ought to be good; he used to be an animator on the television show *The Simpsons*. But instead of drawing Homer Simpson exclaiming "Doh!" Winkler's site now exclaims "Doo Doo!"

Figure 15-11. Following his bliss: Tom Winkler shares his doodie cartoons with millions of viewers each day.[11]

The Perfect Dump

As I writer, I have to admire anyone who can provide detailed, vivid descriptions about a subject that is often overlooked. There are many varieties of this particular bodily function. Descriptive titles include the Chili Dump, the Machine Gun Dump, the Houdini Dump...you can use your imagination. The author is believed to be Martin Riskin, who wrote *Confessions from the Bathroom* (Boston America Corporation, 1991). The text of "The Perfect Dump" has been reprinted on a variety of Web sites without citing its source or its author, however. You can read it at http://bathroomjokes.com/poop/dump.htm as well as other locations.

---

11. http://www.doodie.com/flash.php

Fart Humor

You think there's a lot of hot air on the radio airwaves, the TV airwaves, and in your local bars and cafés? Just look around the Internet at the number of Web sites devoted to flatulence in all its forms. You don't have to look far online to find sites devoted to many aspects of this particular bodily function. Fortunately, smell is not one of them—but sounds, descriptions, and stories about farts are liable to pop up just about as often as online advertisements. The following is a brief rundown of some of the many, many options for gaseous emissions on the Net.

Farts.com

First and foremost, you've got to admire anyone who was quick enough to register this rather obvious domain name. Rex Breefs also built his business from the bottom up, so to speak. As he reports on a Web page that provides the world with the history of Farts.com (http://www.farts.com/company/history.htm), he began with the Fart Line, a phone number where fart-hungry customers could purchase flatulent dolls and machines that emit appropriate noises. He expanded to Farts.com (shown in Figure 15-12), which sells products such as Blasting Bin Laden and Mr. Methane. The Weenie Dance page adds a further level of class to the site.

Breefs's history page also includes a bit of a sermon. "There are those who do not feel farts should be discussed in public, much less celebrated," he says. "These uptight people are on the other side of 'The Fart Line.' Perhaps as Rex pushes on in his fight, these folks will loosen up a bit." I'm not exactly sure what Rex's "fight" is all about—it seems to be selling fart products rather than simply celebrating them. At any rate, loosening up seems to be no problem on Farts.com.

FreeFarts.com

There may not be such a thing as a free lunch, but you'll have no problem finding free fart sounds that you can add to the backgrounds of your Web pages. The sounds have been developed by a variety of users who, thankfully, don't explain exactly how they were created. Happily, you don't have to go through the trouble of downloading, installing, and then uploading the files to your site's Web server. Just pass your mouse over the icons on http://www.freefarts.com/farts.html and enjoy.

NOTE   The developers of FreeFarts.com also provide you with more audio delights at http://www.freeburps.com/.

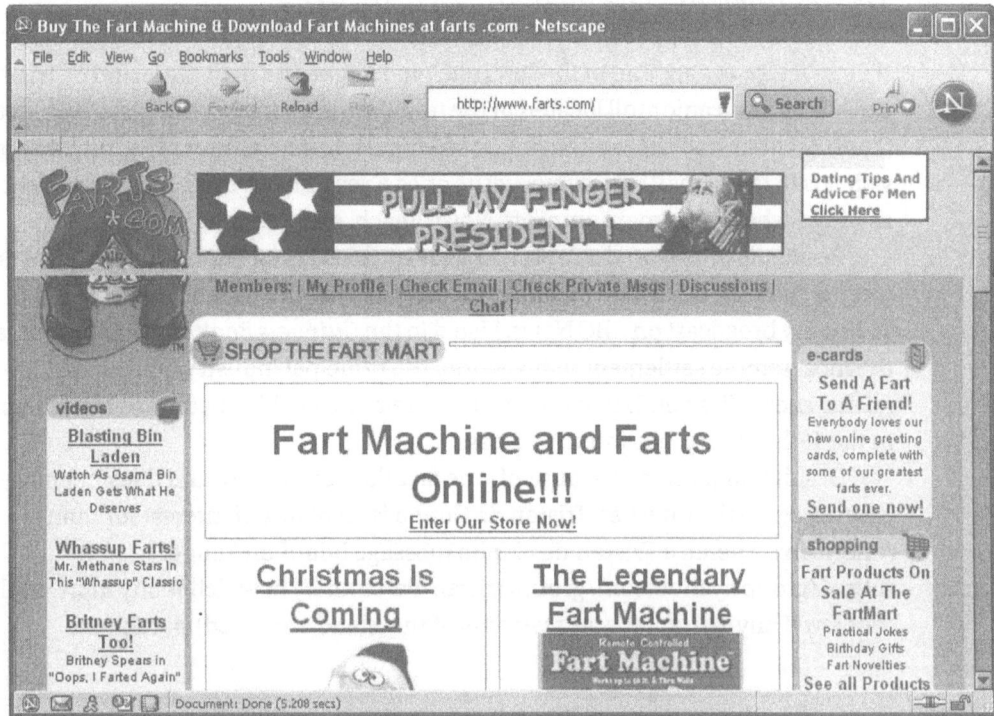

Figure 15-12. Farts.com: e-commerce or a quest for a more relaxed society?[12]

Fart.com

This site, like Farts.com, has both a desirable (in some quarters) domain name and an emphasis on fart commerce. But you'll also find jokes and riddles related to crepitation, as well as video files depicting commercials that make humorous use of this bodily function.

The Search for the End of the Internet

One of the most frequently repeated myths about the Internet is that there is an end to it. It seems we just can't get used to things that are literally limitless. But because the Internet is growing and changing all the time as people all over the world create Web pages, there really isn't a stopping point or a "last page." That doesn't stop advertisers from depicting the idea in commercials or amateurs from claiming that they're "The End," however.

---

12. http://www.farts.com/

The Island at the End of the Internet

If there really *was* an "end of the Internet," you might find it on the island of Tristan da Cunha, a volcanic atoll located in the mid-Atlantic between the eastern coast of South America and the western coast of Africa. It has no airport. The only way to visit it is to take a mail ship, which visits once a year. Places there have names such as Ridge-where-the-goat-jump-off, Noisy Beach, and Penguin Rookery.

Residents of Tristan da Cunha do have Internet connections, but the rates are steeper than the cliffs that surround the island—$10 per minute according to a 1998 story broadcast on ABC News. Listed in the *Guinness Book of World Records* as the most remote settlement in the world, the principal industry on the island is raising sheep. Even St. Helena, an island so remote that Napoleon was exiled there in the 19th century, has Internet access.

Despite (or perhaps because of) the fact that it is remote and does not have easy access to the Internet, Tristan da Cunha is an object of interest for many Americans. There's a Tristan da Cunha message board on Yahoo! (http://groups.yahoo.com/group/tristan-da-cunha/) in which many individuals (but few if any Tristanians, as residents of the island are called) participate.

 TIP   You can see photos of Tristan da Cunha and read about it on the St. Helena Web site at http://www.sthelena.se/tristan/tristan.htm.

The Page at the End of the Internet

Another "end of the Internet" site may not be hard to reach (it's at http://www.nylon.net/thateoti/thateoti.htm, shown in Figure 15-13), but it's just about as empty as Tristan da Cunha. I don't mean "empty" in terms of things to look at—there are plenty of icons, catchphrases, and links—but the anonymous author has been careful to keep everything as relentlessly silly and meaningless as possible. Even the biographical information is an exercise in futility. And the Sabrina link at the bottom of the biographical page that promises to take you to the page of the site's author actually takes you to someone completely different (though fascinating) who happens to be named Sabrina. Maybe that really is the end of the Internet—pages full of nothing supplemented by links that take you nowhere at all.

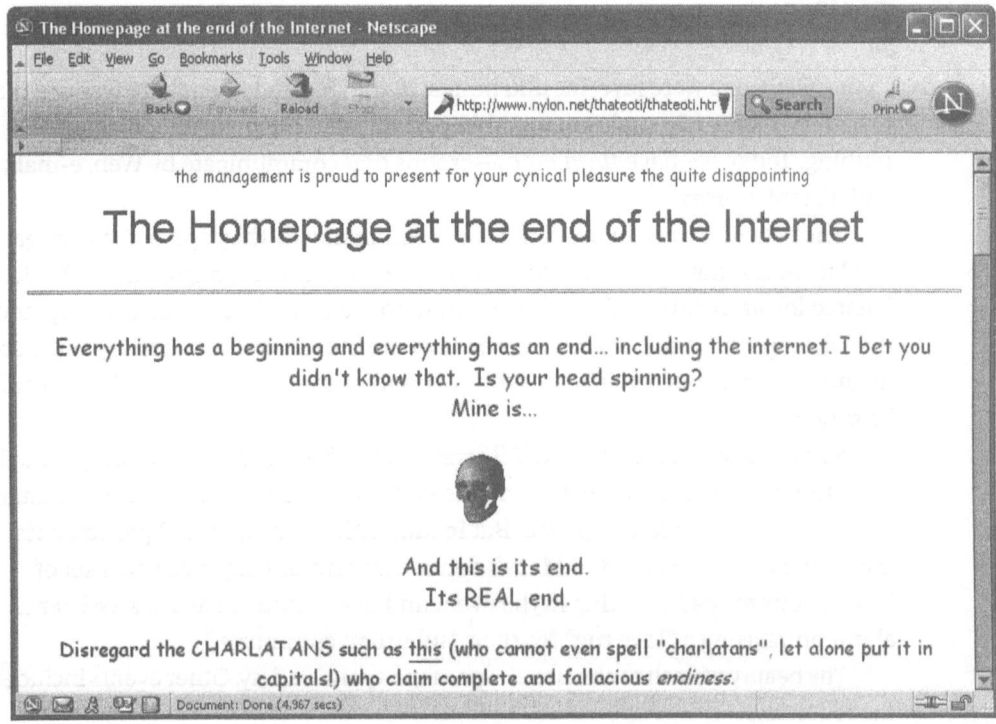

Figure 15-13. Is this really the end of the Internet? The anonymous author of this page assures us that it is.[13]

Simply Pointless Activity

Sometimes, it seems like only those of us who write about the Internet, create Web sites, or run other related services actually surf the Web with a definite goal in mind. Of course, that's not true. Plenty of people go online to check their horoscopes, download adult videos, download some music files, or perform any number of other important activities. The people I really envy are the ones who use the Net to do things that have no goal, no reason—they just are. You may never be one of them, but you can look on at their antics and hope you can one day have sufficient time on your hands to accomplish just as little as they do.

---

13. http://www.nylon.net/thateoti/thateoti.htm

Flash Mobs

In the '60s, there were love-ins and be-ins. In the '70s and later, there was the U.S. Congress. Plenty of people get together periodically to accomplish absolutely nothing. Today, we have *flash mobs*—groups that communicate by Web, e-mail, and instant messaging.

The activities of flash mobs are easily summarized. They agree to congregate at a location someone has just identified. The participants congregate at the designated location, invade the space in question, do something bizarre or silly, and then disappear. No one is hurt, and no laws are broken. Perhaps some people are inconvenienced, but it's all in the name of performance art. Jean-Paul Sartre would be proud.

Someone reportedly named Bill arranged the first flash mob, sending e-mails to 50 acquaintances and asking them to assemble as a mob in downtown Manhattan. That attempt was foiled by police. But in June 2003, a group of 100 participants met in the rug department of Macy's department store. They received a set of instructions for participating in the event and made inquires to sales assistants about purchasing a "love rug" for their "suburban commune."

The beauty of flash mobs is their spontaneity and variety. Other events included the following:

- A crowd invaded a shoe shop in Manhattan. They pretended to be tourists on a bus trip from Maryland.

- Hundreds of mob participants "perched" on a ledge in Central Park, making bird noises.

- In Rome, several hundred mob members crowded into a store selling music and books, asking for fictitious titles.

- In Berlin, 40 people took out their mobile phones in the middle of a crowded thoroughfare and shouted, "Yes, yes!"

Some Web sites purport to be "official" flash mob information centers, if only because they have obvious domain names, such as flashmob.com. However, some others are of interest, including London Flash Mob (http://www.geocities.com/londonmobs/, shown in Figure 15-14), cheesebikini.com, and smartmobs.com. The latter site is run by Howard Rheingold, author of the book *Smart Mobs: The Next Social Revolution* (Perseus Books, 2002).

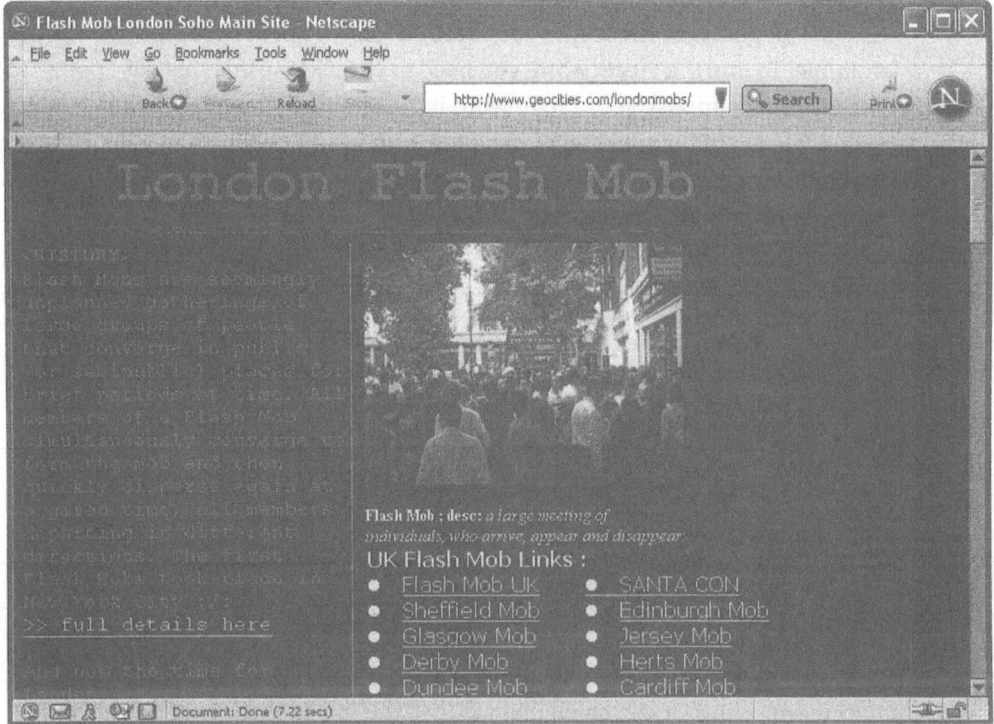

Figure 15-14. This site contains links to "mob" sites in cities around the world.[14]

Happily, these events aren't sponsored by a soda pop or candy manufacturer (not yet, at least). You cannot purchase T-shirts with the logo "Flash Mob" printed on them (not at this writing, I mean). The moment mobs get too big or too political, they are likely to fizzle and be replaced by The Next Big Thing to do online.

Google Golf

Real golf is just too difficult, as far as I am concerned. Not only do you have to endure the indignity of bogeys and sand traps, but you have to lug your clubs around and pay for the privilege. It's much easier and quicker to play a little bit of Google Golf. There are some similarities: Google Golf consists of 18 "holes." Each hole is a word that the player enters in the search box on the Google Web site (http://www.google.com/).

---

14. http://www.geocities.com/londonmobs/

To play a hole, you type one to four keywords in Google's search box and press Enter. Your goal is to encounter your desired "target word" in the fewest Web pages possible. To find the target word, you need to enter keywords that will "point" to it. For instance, suppose your target word is "allegiance." You might enter the search terms "pledge of." If your target word turns up in two pages, then your score for that hole is two. You'll find lists of Google Golf words with their accompanying par scores at http://golf.google.com/.

 NOTE   Google Golf is just one of several extremely silly games listed on the Halfbakery Web site (http://www.halfbakery.com/). Others include ICMP Pong, Internet Where's Wally, and so on.

Random Googling

The subject of silliness on the Internet is a rich and varied one. It's difficult to come up with a single search that will lead you to places that will provide you with just the sort of humor for which you're looking. The following list contains a few I found noteworthy—a random sampling of sites that turned up after searching on the search service Google (http://www.google.com/) for the term "silly" or that were related to other sites described in this chapter:

- **Black holes**: Sometimes, it seems like many locations on the Web are black holes—things that suck you in so that you are unable to escape. A couple of Web sites purport to be virtual black holes. Black Hole of the Web (http://www.ravenna.com/blackhole.html) is pretty straightforward, except that the "black hole" in this case is a black rectangle.

- **Alternatives to HamsterDance**: HamsterDance inspired many parodies and imitations. Two notable ones are the Cow Dance (http://www.cowdance.com/) and the Hamster Blast (http://www.newgrounds.com/assassin/hamster/index.html), in which you get the chance to kill the original dancing hamsters.

CHAPTER 16

Gossip in Babylon

THE PHRASE "WORD OF MOUTH" takes on new meaning in cyberspace. It used to be that gossip was spread by people who were in the same room—in the barbershop or at the hair stylist, in the lunchroom, or walking down the street together. Nowadays, the speed of communication on the Internet works to the eternal advantage of rumormongers and dirt-diggers and to the disadvantage of those caught in their spotlights. In a matter of hours, a juicy story that someone digs up can spread all over the world thanks to e-mail and the Web.

This chapter provides a selection of examples that illustrate the different ways in which gossip is used, and abused, in cyberspace. First, it contains some examples of e-mail communications that went awry when someone decided to spread them to a few acquaintances. The original senders soon realized that once you click the Send button, you lose control of whatever you communicate by e-mail: If it's considered "juicy gossip" by only one of the recipients, they will pass it on, and it can assume a life of its own.

Second, you'll learn about rumors that arise from fear and that center on the terrorist attacks of September 11, 2001. You'll get at least one example of a "vertical gossip" site that provides inside information about a particular industry (in this case, the X-rated porn industry). You'll also see how businesses have handled online gossip. In one case, gossip was initiated on purpose to build word-of-mouth "buzz" for a movie. In another, a company managed to confront false rumors and nip them in the bud before they hurt sales seriously.

Love and Sex

The Net has changed the way couples find each other, how they interact, and how they break up. Prospective mates can feel one another out, so to speak, by e-mail. They can celebrate their good times together, too, as long as one of them doesn't go blabbing to so-called friends by sending e-mail that then gets the "FWD:FWD" designation as it moves from one person to another. You'll learn about all these aspects of love-related online gossip in the following examples.

Young Man Crows, Then Is Forced to Eat Crow

Lovers used to meet over lunch, in the park, or somewhere face to face to discuss their intimate relations. They might talk on the phone, but that medium doesn't leave a record that's easy to repeat and send to others. Not so with e-mail. Once you have clicked the Send button, you have no say over what the recipient of your message is going to do with it. One of the most famous examples involved a lawyer in London, England, named Bradley Chait and a young woman named Claire Swire.

The full details of the exchange between Chait and Swire cannot be described fully—at least in polite company. Suffice it to say that the two were lovers briefly, and they had an intimate encounter of the "oral" variety. On December 7, 2000, someone sent Chait one of those staples of the e-mail medium—the dirty joke. He forwarded the joke to Swire. They exchanged a couple more e-mail messages that discussed the nature of their own intimate encounter. Then Swire issued the following comment that was to make her famous (or infamous) and that she has probably regretted ever since: "I hadn't swallowed for years, but yours was yum and very good for me, too! Apparently it's very good conditioner for your hair too…getting a funny picture in my head, giggling out loud and now having to explain to Dave what's so funny!"

Chait, feeling the need to crow a bit to his cronies about his success with Swire, forwarded the message to six of his friends accompanied by the remark: "Now *that's* a nice compliment from a lass, isn't it?"

One of those friends forwarded it to 14 others. Before long, it was all over cyberspace—by one estimate, the message reached 10 million individuals. Was it a hoax, or was it for real? A frantic media hunt ensued in Britain to find the real Claire Swire, if there was one. The Swire e-mail became a holiday season phenomenon. The Web site at Chait's stiff-upper-lip law firm, Norton Rose, crashed from overuse, and Chait was immediately dubbed "Brad the Cad" by the British newspapers. It was so big that a company in London that employs someone named Claire Swire—a different Claire Swire—received 70,000 hits on its Web site on December 15, compared with 500 on a normal day.

As it turned out, there is a real Claire Swire, and she worked for a British Internet service provider called MagicButton.net. Her photo appeared in the notorious British tabloids, and she went into hiding. You can find it now (see Figure 16-1) on the Urban Legends Reference Pages (http://www.snopes.com/), which declares this legend to be true.

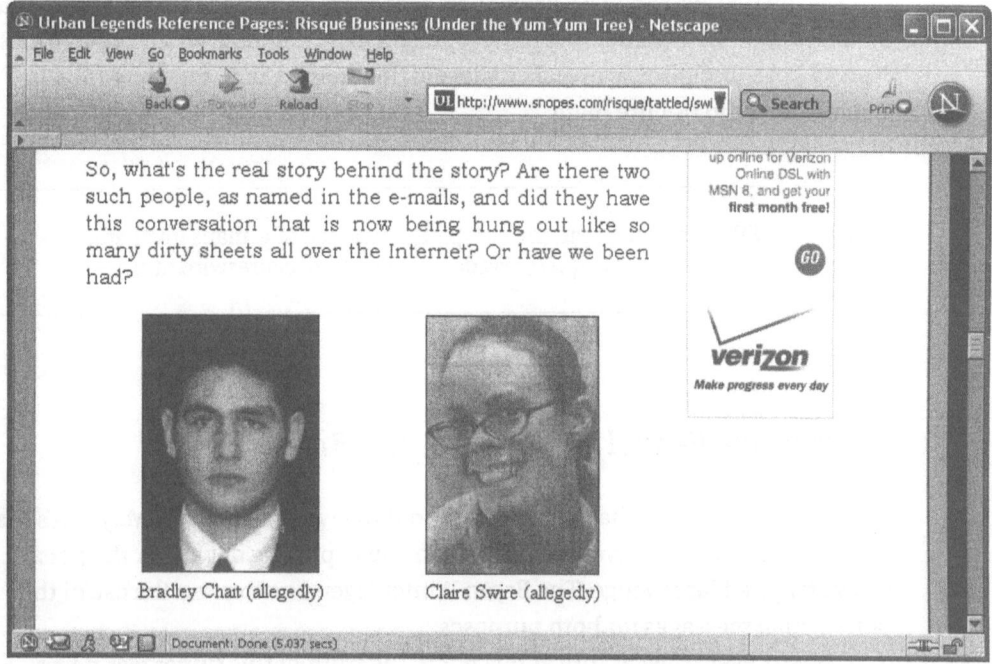

So, what's the real story behind the story? Are there two such people, as named in the e-mails, and did they have this conversation that is now being hung out like so many dirty sheets all over the Internet? Or have we been had?

Bradley Chait (allegedly)   Claire Swire (allegedly)

Figure 16-1. His was "yum": The two people at the center of the "yours was yum" controversy [1]

"I don't blame her," Swire's mother told reporters. "Would you stick around after something like this?"

All sorts of odd stories surfaced in connection with the Swire incident. One concerned an army officer in Kosovo who used all his contacts and satellite phone to try to reach Swire. Another reported that several offices have sent (presumably graphic) Christmas cards to Swire's address.

Meanwhile, Norton Rose was not amused. The same company had been the subject of a report on the BBC earlier that year, commenting about impending legislation that would enable companies to monitor private staff e-mail messages. "Naturally, we are disappointed in the behavior of certain employees," it said in a stern message on its Web site. "The employees have been disciplined."

At the Financial Services Authority, a regulatory agency in London, nine people were reportedly suspended because they passed on Swire's message to outsiders, even after the firm told them not to do so.

---

1. http://www.snopes.com/risque/tattled/swire.htm

Meanwhile, Playboy TV was searching for Swire, telling the British paper *News of the World,* "She would be the perfect person to host a show on sex topics for us." Norton Rose disciplined several employees, including Chait, for circulating the e-mail, but it did not fire them.

NOTE   You can read the complete exchange of e-mails involving Claire Swire at http://www.dazereader.com/claireswire.htm.

Revenge by E-Mail: The Hunt for Bryan Winter

What is it about e-mail that tends to bring out the worst in people? Maybe it's that e-mail is faceless. You never see the person you're putting down—or the person you've targeted for revenge. The Bryan Winter legend centers on the use of the same e-mail messages for both purposes.

The story—it's just a story at this point; the truth of this rumor was never proven despite extensive investigations by the *Washington Post* and the Urban Legends Reference Pages—is that a woman met a man while dancing and gave him her e-mail address. When he approached her by e-mail, she supposedly responded by asking a few innocent questions in an attempt to find out more about him. He then fired back the following:

> *I am at a stage in my life where I'm looking seriously and systematically for someone I can share my life with. You seem like a nice person, and I don't mean this as baldly as it might sound, but I don't have time for twenty questions by e-mail. I met five girls Saturday night, have already booked a first coffee with three of them, and meet more every time I go dancing...and I go dancing at least three times a week. I immediately rule out women who put up too many barriers. I don't do this because I think there's anything wrong with them, nor do I do it because I'm arrogant. I do this simply to economize on time.*
>
> *I know that dating in this city is difficult and scary for women. But keep in mind it's that way for the guys, too. Most of all, remember that you're competing with thousands of women who don't insist that that the man do all of the work of establishing a connection. And they live closer.*

Now, maybe you'll find someone who's so taken by a single dance with you that he's willing to negotiate by e-mail for a chance to trek to your suburban hideout to plead his case. But you might not. And if such a person does exist, and you do happen to cross paths with him—what do you imagine a guy that desperate would have to offer?

—Bryan Winter

The women then supposedly sent this e-mail message to as many other individuals as possible, with the following request:

In the hopes that this e-mail might get back to him after being seen by countless thousands of young women along the way...please send this on to a friend!

Is there a Bryan Winter? There is, but he's a hair stylist in the Georgetown neighborhood in Washington, D.C., and he didn't send the e-mail. This didn't stop people from assaulting him with hundreds of harassing phone calls at his home. Urban Legends reports that he was forced to screen his phone calls with the following message: "This is Bryan Winter," it begins. "I buy my coffee at Safeway, I only dance in my kitchen, and I don't even have an e-mail address. But if you would still like to leave a message for me—or my wife, Deborah—please do so after the tone."

Which was worse—the original e-mail (if it was genuine) or the massive e-mail distribution in an attempt to shame the sender? You decide.

Inside Information

Gossip is becoming increasingly important as a source of content on the Web. But gossip online works differently than it does in other media. The Web is perfect for people who work in a particular industry who want to get the inside scoop on it and don't mind digging through the tons of detail that Web sites typically provide. Many of these "vertical gossip" sites throw around names and jargon that only those working in the industry will recognize. Such venues give outsiders a glance into the workings of a field they'll never be involved in directly, such as the porn industry, high fashion, or the news media.

Devout Jew Dishes Stops Dishing X-Rated Gossip, Turns to Religion

Luke Ford grew up the son of a devout evangelical Christian. In his detailed biography (http://www.lukeford.net/luke_ford/bio/11.html), he describes a difficult and unstable childhood where sex was labeled the deadliest of sins. Eventually, he became a devout follower of Judaism. He also became a chronicler of the pornographic film industry. Ford (shown in Figure 16-2) became known as the most hated man in porn thanks to his Web site (http://www.lukeford.com/), which dished dirt on porn stars, film companies, directors, and anyone else "in the business."

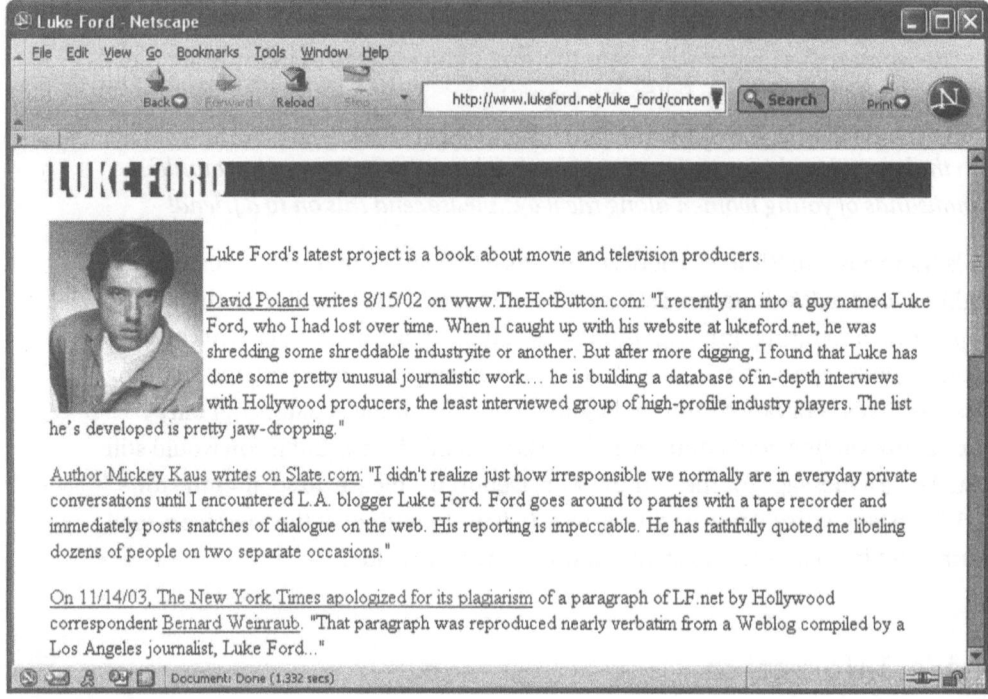

Figure 16-2. Luke Ford, onetime purveyor of porn gossip, gave up his career for his religious beliefs.[2]

Over the years, Ford dug up plenty of gossip and rumor about those who kept the X-rated film industry running. Some of it was apparently true, and some became the subject of lawsuits. He uncovered news about porn stars who were diagnosed HIV-positive and about the influence of organized crime in the porn industry. One thing that's certain: Ford's site was popular with those in the industry who wanted to find out more about their colleagues and with X-rated film enthusiasts who enjoyed getting a glimpse at those in the business. The site itself contained reports and images that were just as raunchy as any porn site, which was probably one reason for its success.

---

2. http://www.lukeford.net/luke_ford/content_luke_ford.htm

But LukeFord.com caused deep conflicts within Ford himself, who continued to participate in Los Angeles's Orthodox Jewish community and who lived in fear that his spiritual group Young Israel of Century City would find out what he did for a living and condemn him. That's just what happened to Ford when, after prayers, the group's rabbi confronted Ford about his "double life." Ford left the group, but not long after, he sold his Web site to a company called NetVideoGirls.com. According to *Wired News*, he made plans to move to Jerusalem.

Ford's current home on the Web (http://www.lukeford.net/) contains reports on various aspects of the film and television industry and stays away from the porn industry—although, when I visited, the article featured on the front page was entitled "Dildos of Shame." It was the first of a series of exposés on the mistreatment of workers in factories where those particular devices are manufactured.

Rumors About Movie Lead to Murder Mystery

Filmmaker Stanley Kubrick, the director of such classics as *2001: A Space Odyssey*, *A Clockwork Orange*, and *Dr. Strangelove*, was the subject of much discussion by the denizens of newsgroups such as alt.movies.kubrick. Throughout the 1990s, Kubrick devotees speculated about the master's project that eventually became the film *A.I.* When Kubrick died in 1999, even more speculation was aired about the project's fate. Steven Spielberg eventually made the movie. The director of such films as *E.T.* reportedly approved an innovative marketing effort that was designed to attract the same sorts of Kubrick movie enthusiasts who loved to communicate online.

The marketing campaign, which was first reported on Harry Knowles's gossip site Ain't It Cool News (http://www.aintitcool.com/), involved the creation of a series of fake Web sites. The sites themselves were real, but they depicted information about fictional characters from the movie *A.I.* Knowles reported that if you made a search on Google for one of the characters listed on the *A.I.* movie poster—specifically, the character named "Jeanine Salla, Sentient Machine Therapist"—you would find a link to a Web site that not only held fictional biographical information about the character but that held clues to a murder mystery game. The site, shown in Figure 16-3, is now only available on the Wayback Machine.

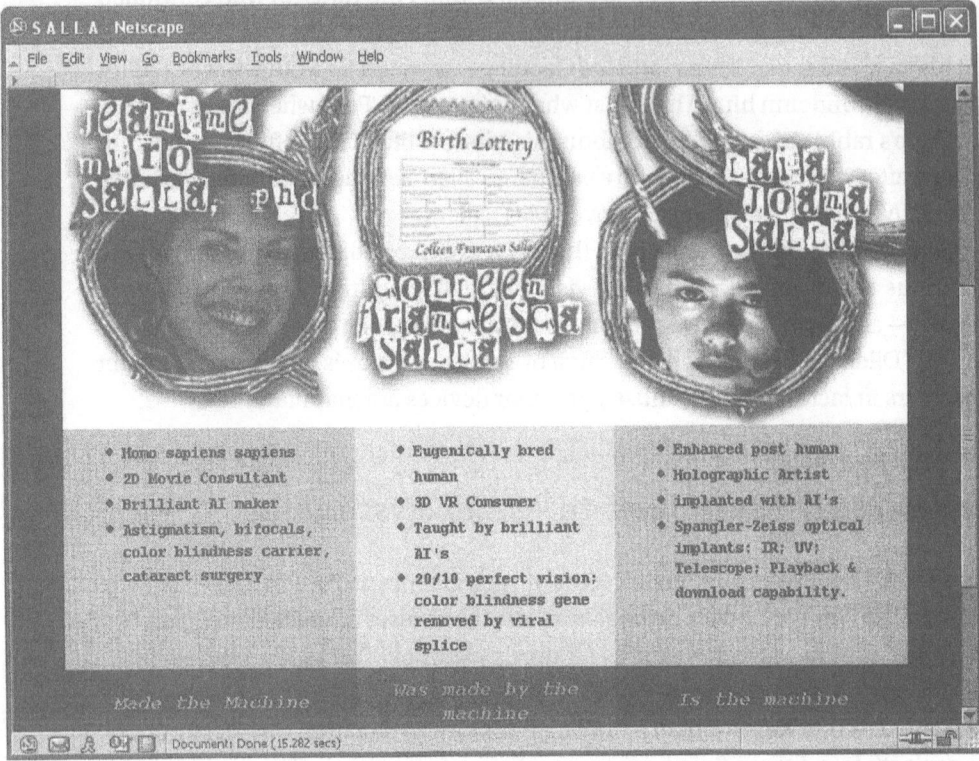

Figure 16-3. Fake Web sites such as this created a word of mouth "buzz" for the movie A.I.[3]

Other Web sites, such as cloudmakers.org (http://www.cloudmakers.org/), were set up to foster discussion about the murder mystery, which was solved in a matter of months. The site shown in Figure 16-4 purported to be set up by a group of humans who opposed robots taking over their jobs and who advocated the sort of antirobot campaign depicted in the movie itself.

---

3. http://web.archive.org/web/20011214131012/jeaninesalla.com/default2.htm

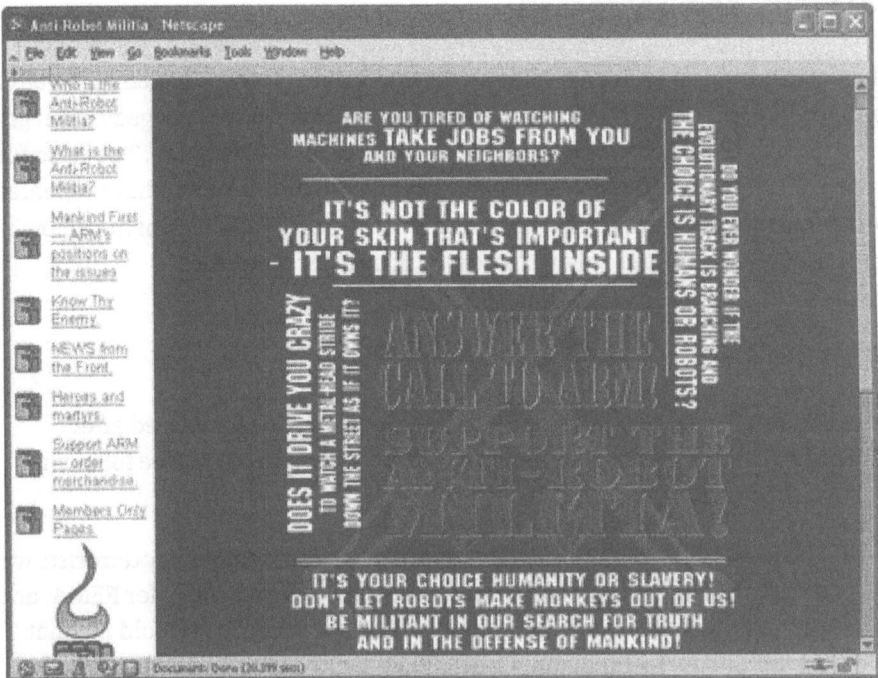

Figure 16-4. This fake antirobot site was created as part of the interactive marketing effort for the movie A.I.[4]

It's already been stated, elsewhere in this book, that the Internet is perfect for *viral marketing*—marketing that uses word of mouth passed along by enthusiasts for a product or cause. The fake Web site trail and murder mystery is an example of how online advertising can be conducted in an entertaining and unobtrusive way (in other words, one that does not involve pop-up ads).

---

4. http://unite-and-resist.cloudmakers.org/

Politics and Terrorism

Thanks to e-mail and the Web, the rumors and urban legends that emerged after the September 11 terrorist attacks spread far and wide. Fear and tragedy often give rise to stories that offer false hope to those who have lost loved ones. They also fuel hatred felt by many others. Rumors that circulate online are sometimes repeated by the mainstream media, making anything seem possible. Which of the following rumors did you hear and believe to be true, if only for a moment?

September 11: The Myths

So many fictitious e-mail messages and mythical reports circulated after September 11 that it's hard to summarize them all in one place. The following are just a few examples:

- The inevitable fictitious message about trucks being stolen by terrorists was circulated widely by e-mail. It went like this: "My dad works for FEMA, and he's really involved with the goings-on in New York City. He told me that within the last 24 hours more than 30 Ryder, U-Haul, and Verizon trucks have been reported stolen across the country, many of them rented by people of Arab descent. Be wary of these vehicles, pay attention to them, don't walk or park near them."

- ABCNews.com reported about another e-mail message concerning a woman who had been dating an Afghan man. He supposedly left a letter for her on September 10 that begged her not to take any commercial airlines on September 11 or visit any shopping malls on Halloween. He then supposedly disappeared.

- A police officer in one of the World Trade Center towers "surfed" a wave of debris down from the 82nd floor and survived.

- Another bogus e-mail message claimed that New York City's water supply had been poisoned: "We just received some off the record information from a *very* reputable source who is briefed daily, that there may be other attacks this weekend."

- One of the most persistent rumors concerned people who survived the collapse of the World Trade Center and who made phone calls from the rubble using their cell phones.

One of the strangest rumors concerned Osama Bin Laden, who was said to living in Utah, of all places. This rumor was debunked on the Snopes.com Urban Legends Reference Pages. In a story about this and other crazy rumors, *Salon* added the noteworthy image shown in Figure 16-5.

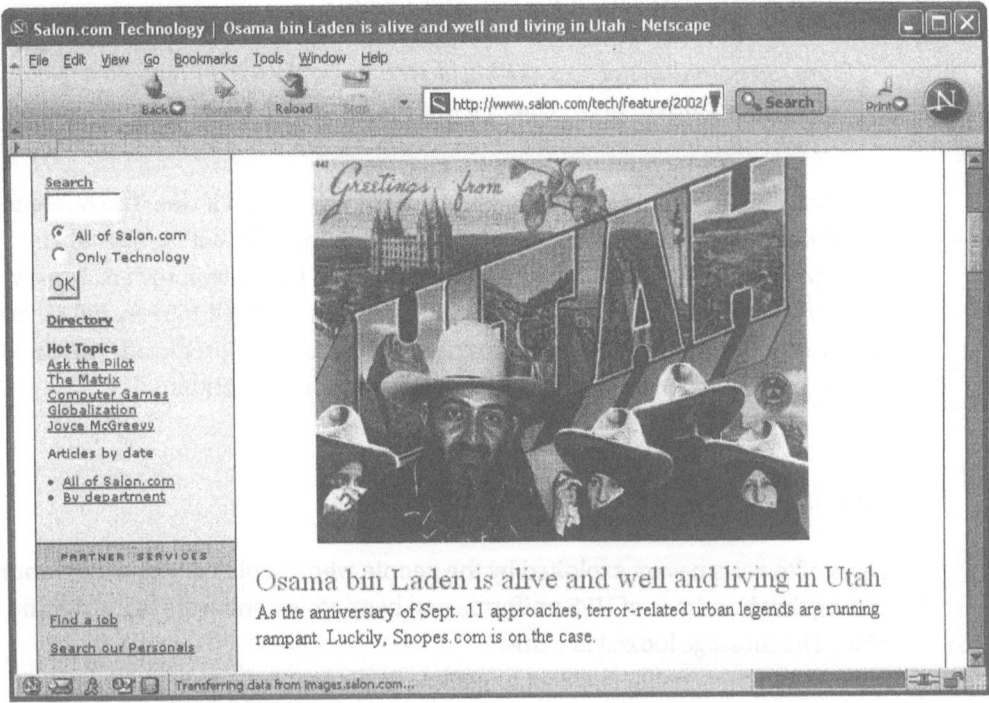

Figure 16-5. Osama in Utah? It's one of many rumors that arose after September 11.[5]

The thread that joins all the gossip and rumor surrounding the terrorist attacks is the hope that someone is alive or the suspicion that some official knew about the event beforehand. That, at least, is how the stories start. It can, of course, become more embellished and change in other ways as it moves from e-mail inbox to inbox.

No-No-Nostradamus: Prediction Was All Wrong

One of the most widely circulated stories about the terrorist attacks of 2001 was the one that involved the 17th-century figure Nostradamus. Web-based search services were flooded with requests to search for the name of the famous predictor thanks to an e-mail message that indicated he had predicted the attacks.

The message claimed that Nostradamus had nailed down the location and date of the attack on the United States. It said the following:

---

5.   http://www.salon.com/tech/feature/2002/09/03/snopes_part2/

In the year of the new century and nine months

From the sky will come a great King of Terror. The sky will burn at 45 degrees. Two brothers torn apart by chaos, while the fortress endures, the great leader will succumb.

This message could be interpreted in many ways—and it was. The reference to "45 degrees" was said to be the latitude of New York City—it is, indeed, at 45 degrees latitude. The "two brothers" were said to be the twin towers. However, astute readers would have noticed that the message was dated 1654—a full 88 years after Nostradamus died. Nostradamus is also said to have "predicted" the Great Fire of London in 1666 as well as the rise to power of Adolf Hitler.

UPS Uniforms Stolen on eBay?

Fears of terrorism were exploited by the people who circulated an e-mail rumor stating that hundreds of UPS uniforms had been stolen and were being sold on eBay. The message looked like this:

Quick security alert: $32,000 worth of UPS uniforms have been purchased over the last 30 days by person(s) unknown on eBay. Law enforcement is working the case; however, no suspect(s) have been identified. Subjects may try to gain facility access by wearing these uniforms.

URGENT N.J. OFFICE OF COUNTER-TERRORISM ADVISORY

Re: POSSIBLE IMPERSONATION OF UPS PERSONNEL SEEKING ACCESS TO BUILDINGS

The New Jersey Office of Counter-Terrorism has received a report of an attempt by an unknown individual to enter a government facility by falsely posing as an employee of the United Parcel Service....

It was all a bogus rumor. The TruthOrFiction Web site contacted UPS, which denied any uniforms had been stolen or were being sold on eBay.

Business and Workplace Rumors

The water cooler and hallway conversations that used to take up time during the average employee's day are dwindling. Some of those office workers are sitting at their computers and exchanging e-mail and chat messages. The workplace has always been a natural venue for gossip. Now, much of that gossip occurs on the Internet. The problem is, some of that gossip can come back to haunt you, as shown in the examples that follow.

Be Careful About Your Work Agenda

It's one thing to gossip about other employees. But when you gossip about yourself, be careful what you say to your coworkers. In 2001, a young Princeton graduate named Peter Chung was appointed to a lucrative job in the South Korean office of the Carlyle Group, a major international investment firm. Soon after arriving in Seoul, he e-mailed some buddies back home to report on his plans:

From: Peter Chung
Subject: LIVING LIKE A KING
Date: Tue, 15 May 2001 20:26:21 -0400
MIME-Version: 1.0
X-Mailer: Internet Mail Service (5.5.2653.19) Content-Type: text/plain

So I've been in Korea for about a week and a half now and what can I say, LIFE IS GOOD....

I've got a spanking brand new 2000 sq. foot three-bedroom apt. with a 200 sq. foot terrace running the entire length of my apartment with a view overlooking Korea's main river and nightline.... Why do I need three bedrooms? Good question...the main bedroom is for my queen size bed..where CHUNG is going to fuck every hot chick in Korea over the next two years (five down, 1,000,000,000 left to go).... The second bedroom is for my harem of chickies, and the third bedroom is for all of you fuckers when you come out to visit my ass in Korea. I go out to Korea's finest clubs, bars, and lounges pretty much every other night on the weekdays and everyday on the weekends to (I think in about two months, after I learn a little bit of the buyside business I'll probably go out every night on the weekdays). I know I was a stud in NYC, but I pretty much get about, on average, five to eight phone numbers a night, and at least three hot chicks that say that they want to go home with me every night I go out. I love the buyside.... I have bankers calling me everyday with opportunities, and they pretty much cater to my every whim—you know (golfing events, lavish dinners, a night out clubbing). The guys I work with are also all chill— I live in the same apt. building as my VP, and he drives me around in his Porsche (one of three in all of Korea) to work and when we go out. What can I say...life is good...CHUNG is KING of his domain here in Seoul....

So...all of you fuckers better keep in touch and start making plans to come out and visit my ass ASAP; I'll show you guys an unbelievable time.... My contact info is below.... Oh, by the way...someone's gotta start FedExing me boxes of domes.... I brought out about 40, but I think I'll run out of them by Saturday.....

Laters,
CHUNG

Peter Chung
The Carlyle Group
Suite 1009, CCMM Bldg.
12, Yoido-dong, Youngdeungpo-ku
Seoul 150-010, Korea
Tel: (822) 2004-8412
Fax: (822) 2004-8440
email: pchung@thecarlylegroup.co.kr

"Domes," by the way, is slang for condom, for those of you who don't run in the same circles as Chung. Poor Peter didn't learn from the example of Bradley Chait, whose boasting is described earlier in this chapter (see "Young Man Crows, Then Is Forced to Eat Crow"). Chung's friends forwarded the message to their friends, who forwarded the message to their friends.... Before long, someone forwarded the message to Chung's bosses, who quickly fired him. The Urban Legends Reference Pages account of Chung's downfall (http://www.snopes.com/risque/ tattled/chung.htm) dubs him "Chung King."

Writer Justin Pollack offered the following bit of advice to Chung: "Never send an e-mail when a bathroom wall will do." As reported in *Washington Business Forward*, Chung allegedly responded with a succinct comment: "You jealous bitch."

 NOTE   Peter Chung made No. 85 in *Business 2.0*'s list of "101 Dumbest Moments in Business."

Mrs. Fields Copes with "Crummy" Deal

After O. J. Simpson was acquitted of murder charges in October 1995, a rumor began on a tabloid television show and then spread on the Internet. The gossip stated that Mrs. Fields cookies had underwritten a party for the jurors in the case. In a matter of days, the reputation of Mrs. Fields took a nosedive.

The cookie company turned to the public-relations service eWatch (http://www.ewatch.com/) to combat the rumor as it circulated online. It's a rare case of Internet-based gossip being stopped in its tracks. eWatch began by identifying Web sites with bulletin boards where the false story was being spread. eWatch posted its own corrective messages on the boards and responded to the individuals who had placed the messages. Eventually, sales of Mrs. Fields cookies returned to normal levels, and the company's reputation was restored.

Random Googling

Gossip and rumor, especially when it concerns celebrities, is an increasingly important source of content on the Web. The following list contains a few sites I found noteworthy—a random sampling that turned up after searching for the term "gossip" on the search service Google (http://www.google.com/):

- **TruthOrFiction.com (http://www.truthorfiction.com/):** This site has a section called "Anatomy of a Rumor" that attempts to explain how some rumors spread so quickly through cyberspace.

- **Poynter Online (http:// www.poynter.org/medianews/):** Journalists try to get the scoop on newsworthy events and people. But often media figures go through the same sorts of contract disputes and personal problems that plague the people they write about. Where can you go to get the scoop on the scoopers? Try Poynter Online, which contains news about journalists and journalism for those in the media.

- **Popbitch (http://www.popbitch.com/):** This site presents observations with an edge and nastiness that you don't often find—and that I couldn't possibly quote in this book. See for yourself at this Web site, where you can subscribe to a weekly newsletter.

- **Out.com Daily Gossip (http://www.out.com/gossip.asp):** Pretty much what you'd expect—short, sweet, and bitchy daily doses of celebrity dirt dishing.

Internet Legends, Myths, and Symbols

WHEN MANY PEOPLE HEAR the term "Internet legend," they usually think of a fictitious story that took root and spread like a weed online, fooling many otherwise smart people into thinking it was true. But the Internet has been around long enough now to develop its own legendary characters, stars, heroes, and antiheroes. This chapter explores Internet legends of many sorts.

Although I describe a couple of these online hoaxes (or, as they are often called, "urban legends"), I'm more interested in presenting what I consider to be the first generation of legendary figures, images, and events that have arisen online. Every community breeds its own legends, and the Net has the advantage of being able to immediately proclaim them far and wide. You'll learn about a few unlikely legends: ordinary people who were thrust into the limelight online. You'll also learn about some of the original events that helped make the Internet such an integral part of our lives today. Finally, you'll learn about images that have become memory traces in the minds of millions of individuals and that will probably be forever associated with the Internet.

NOTE   If you want to get into some real myths, look into the life and teachings of Joseph Campbell, who wrote *The Power of Myth* (Doubleday, 1988), *The Hero with a Thousand Faces* (Princeton University Press, 1989), and many other books about myths and beliefs around the world. He's a hero of mine, and you can find out more about him at http://www.jcf.org/about_jc.php.

Unlikely Heroes

You don't have to seek out fame to get it on the Internet. In fact, it's sometimes people who are not looking to become famous and have no outstanding talents who become the most notable figures. Like the actresses who are said who have been discovered by talent scouts who wandered into a particular candy store in Hollywood, California, folks such as Mahir and the Star Wars Kid were seen by someone who had the ability, or inclination, to make them famous by spreading their images around cyberspace.

People who are actually trying to promote a particular world vision or cause, such as the Doctress Neutopia, also have their moments in the sun. They are able to stir things up on the Net for a while. But fame online is as fleeting as in the enter-tainment industry, and even those who want to gain attention sometimes disappear from the public eye faster than they would like. Some examples of both types of "Net.Fame" are examined in the sections that follow.

He Kiss You! It's the Amazing Mahir!

It often seems as though whatever is odd, quirky, and homemade will work on the Web as long as it is backed by sincerity and innocence. At least, that was true back in 1999, when a Turkish fellow named Mahir created his own Web page.

Mahir has a last name (it's Cagri), but everyone simply knows him as Mahir. In fact, if you just utter the word "Mahir" to anyone who has been online for any length of time, they'll probably say something like, "Oh yeah, that guy in the Speedo," or simply, "I kiss you!" The latter is Mahir's catchphrase, one that appeared on his original Web page, shown in Figure 17-1.

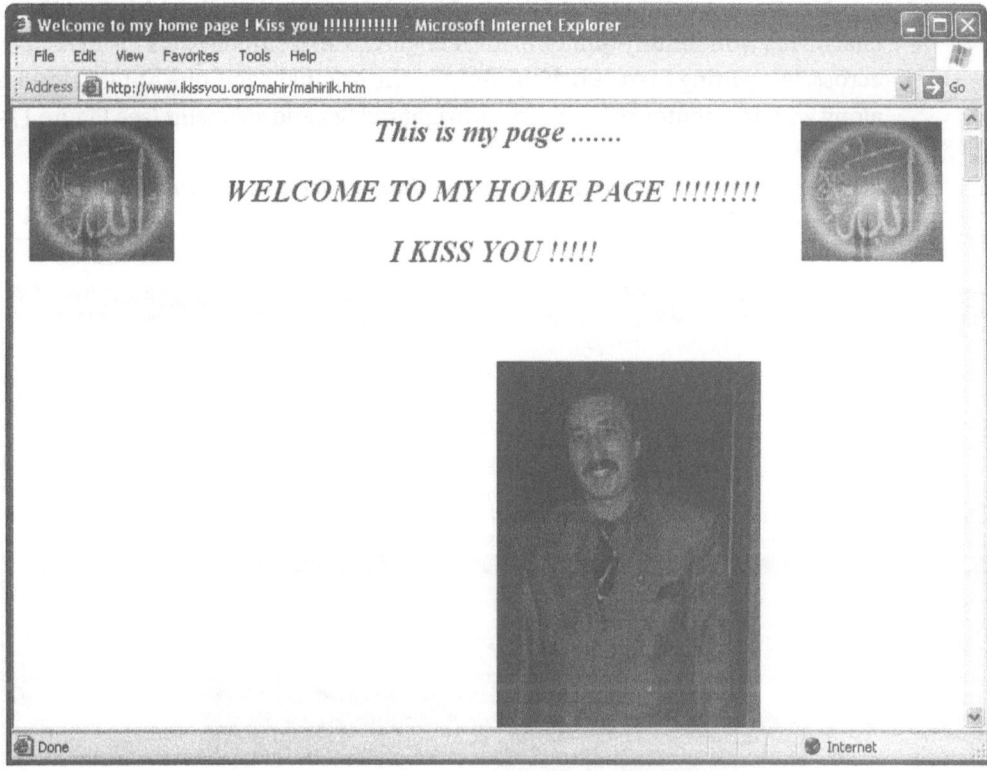

Figure 17-1. Fit as a fiddle and ready for love: Mahir's "I kiss you!" declaration became a catchphrase on the Internet.[1]

Mahir had a friend create a simple home page for him on the free Web page service Xoom. Essentially, his page was a personal ad, a plea for a worthy Muslim woman to come and be his wife (or at least his companion). He explains in the current version of his Web site (http://www.ikissyou.org/):

I decided to marry this summer soon, I want see my kids and my wife live happy life together and game together this life and other endless life too. I looking for who best wife for me from all world. I choose who have good heart and respect GOD-ALLAH, and who love kids-cooks-desserts-housework.

---

1. http://www.ikissyou.org/mahir/mahirilk.htm

A not-too-careful examination of Mahir's message reveals a big part of his charm: his wonderfully quirky, broken English. He eventually gets his message across, but getting there is half the fun. On the original page, one phrase stood out along with the photos of Mahir in his bright red Speedo swimsuit (see Figure 17-2):

Who is want to come TURKEY I can invitate.... She can stay my home.

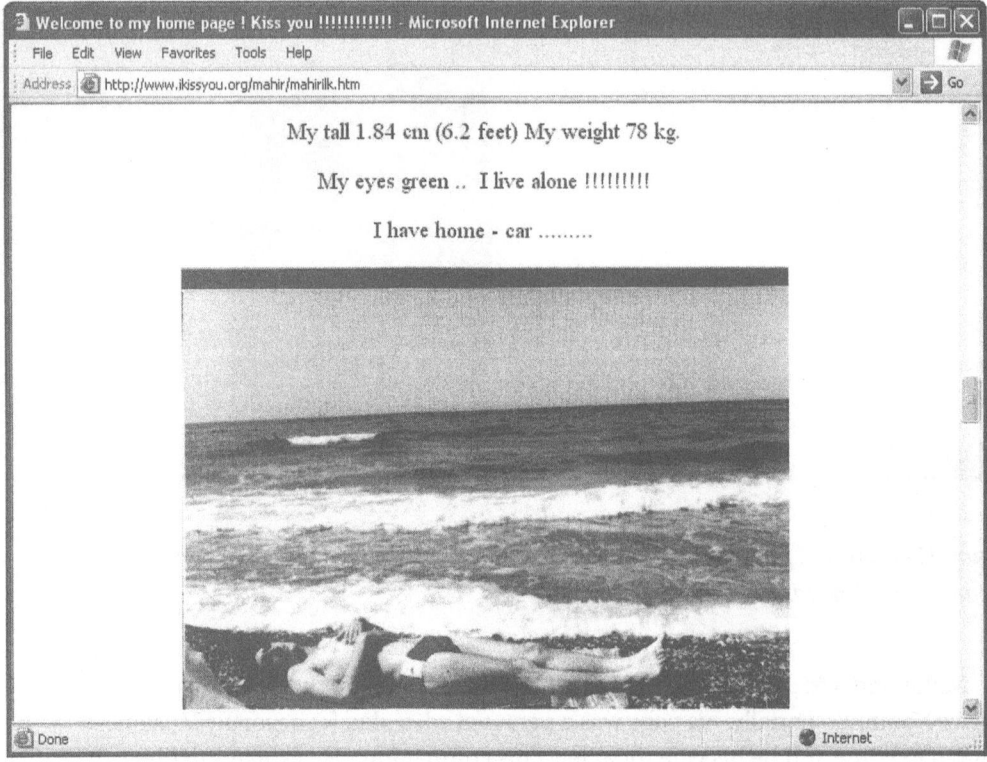

Figure 17-2. Mahir's photos illustrated what he likes to do and got his message across to the world even more clearly than his broken English.[2]

People who were amused by Mahir's search for love quickly began spreading word of his site. Mahir, who had included his address and phone number on his page, was flooded with phone calls. Early on, his page was hijacked by someone who managed to redirect it to a new location and added questionable content; the resulting furor gained more attention for Mahir. By that time the site had 700,000 visitors, and advertisers were asking to place ads.

---

2. http://www.ikissyou.org/mahir/mahirilk.htm

Mahir has charmed countless people around the world, especially because more recent versions of his site include antiwar messages of nonviolence. In the past several years, he has attracted famous fans such as Meg Ryan and David Bowie. He has been flown around the globe, he was the subject of a comedy skit on *Saturday Night Live*, and he made a record entitled (what else?) *I Kiss You*. What's more, his Web site was listed in the 2001 *Guinness Book of World Records* for the highest number of visits to a personal home page, with approximately 12 million *hits* (or page views). He also has a fan club on Yahoo! Groups (http://groups.yahoo.com/group/mahirsfanclub/). And he is the subject of one of those peculiar Web-based phenomena, the *Web ring*—a group of pages all about the same subject that link to one another in series.

Mahir was flown to New York City from Turkey by a company called eTour.com, where he met many of his fans. A contest was held with the prize of a free trip to Turkey to visit Mahir. A very embarrassed man won. Mahir was greeted by crowds who were obviously thrilled to see the real person whose image they had seen on the Web. They chanted his name, and women shouted, "I kiss you!"

On the same U.S. trip, Mahir made appearances on the *Roseanne* show and did interviews with *The New York Times*, *The Los Angeles Times*, *The Boston Globe*, *Wired*, *Forbes*, and others. What carried Mahir through it all was his honesty and sincerity and his ability to take all the attention in stride. On the latest version of his site, you can see him making fun of his famous word "invitate."

"Obviously there's an element (of ridicule) to it," an eTour.com representative casually remarked in *Wired*. "But if you've looked at his Web site, it's silly and kind of fun. What most people saw was a guy who is super nice and very genuine and taking it in stride. He's seen as an Everyman who has made good."

The Saga of the Star Wars Kid

Mahir's Web site was one thing. Mahir is an adult, and he is able to handle attention. The dark side of Internet celebrity is that it can happen to people without their knowledge and without their desire. Take, for example, the young man who didn't ask for fame but found it when his image was purloined and he was turned into the "Star Wars Kid."

Ghyslain Raza, a chubby tenth-grade student in Quebec, found himself alone in his school's recording room during theater class. He was bored. He decided to create some amusement for himself to pass the time. He put to use something that his theater class should have been exercising—his imagination—and picked up a golf ball retriever that was lying around. He turned on the class's 8-millimeter video camera and, using a videotape borrowed from a friend, began to gyrate with the retriever in the fashion of a Jedi knight in one of the *Star Wars* movies. He swooped around wildly for a few minutes, making his own light saber sound noises. Surely, Raza never intended anyone to see the brief tape except himself. But he made the mistake of leaving the tape in the camera and neglecting to erase his short episode.

The tape sat around in the video lab until some of Raza's so-called friends discovered it. Those who viewed Raza's mock Jedi fight took the liberty of digitizing the file and uploading it to the file-sharing site Kazaa (http://www.kazaa.com/), where it could be copied and viewed by millions of *Star Wars* fans and others.

Again, luck was not with Raza because his video soon attracted the attention of a Web site called Waxy.org. The bloggers who run the site are always looking for content, so they mentioned it in April 2003:

> *If you're going to videotape your* Star Wars *fighting skills on a school camera, remember to remove the cassette when you're done. Watch this embarrassingly good video.*

They posted the movie file online. The result: a predictable storm of ridicule and criticism from the site's visitors, most of whom were probably just as awkward in the tenth grade as Raza. Waxy.org, Kazaa, and various other sites quickly churned out parodies (The Chicago Kid, The Star Wars Kid Reloaded, and Star Wars Revolutions, shown in Figure 17-3). Many of the parodies had all the mean-spirited, snide humor displayed by so many Netizens. One had sounds of flatulence accompanying the boy's movements, and another was called Dork Clones. As many as two million people are believed to have downloaded and viewed the young man's moment of play in an isolated room.

Amazingly, Waxy.org's Andrew Baio managed to track down Raza, and a French-speaking reporter interviewed him (you can read the text at http://waxy.org/random/html/star_wars_kid/). When the Web site learned how embarrassed Raza was with all the attention he was getting, they began to do some unusual and noteworthy things. They removed the negative comments that visitors had posted about the video. They also wrote some thoughtful words in his defense. Then, they took up a collection to buy him a gift in compensation for the distress he had experienced. The site actually collected $4,344, and the money bought him an iPod and some other high-tech gadgets.

It sounds like a happy ending, but there's more. Unfortunately, Raza's parents were not at all amused. They filed suit against four of their son's "friends" and their parents, seeking $225,000 Canadian dollars in damages. The suit alleges that Raza was so humiliated that he had to see a psychiatrist and that he even dropped out of school because of the ribbing he was getting from his classmates.

 TIP The *Globe and Mail* in Toronto ran a story on its Web site about the lawsuit surrounding the Star Wars Kid, which was still pending as this was being written. Read more at http://www.globeandmail.com/servlet/story/RTGAM.20030723.uboyyn/BNStory/National/.

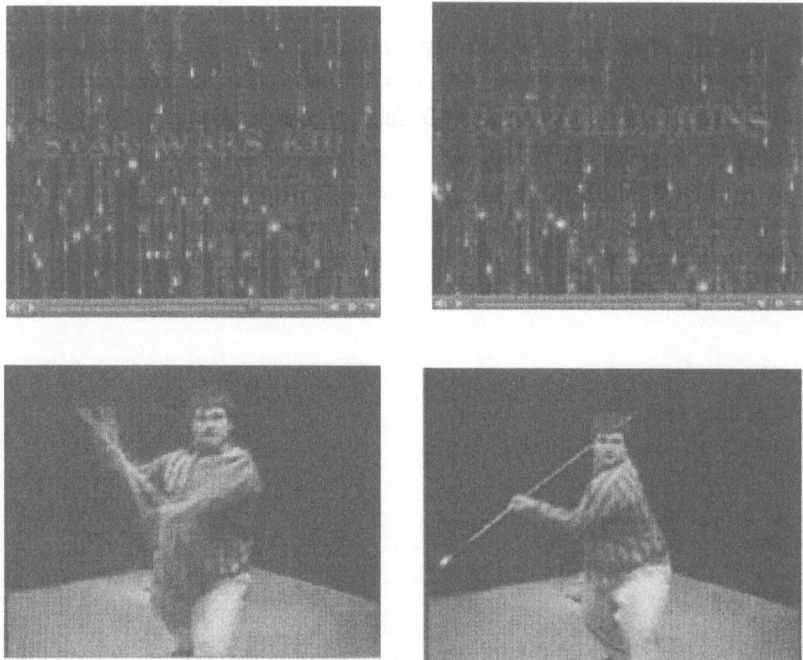

Figure 17-3. An unwilling celebrity: The Star Wars Kid in one of the videos that caused all the controversy. [3]

The Angry Drunken Dwarf

Back in the mid-to-late '90s, when the World Wide Web was but a mere babe, much of the content on it was raw, unpolished, uncommercial, and, often, downright weird. As an example, consider a brief episode involving Henry Nasiff, better known as Hank, the Angry Drunken Dwarf.

Nasiff, a diminutive "little person," was called the Angry Drunken Dwarf on the Howard Stern radio show, where he appeared regularly as one of the talk show host's sidekicks. He simply showed up one morning at 5:30 a.m. in his usual state—highly intoxicated—and the Stern show producers put him on the air. Part of Hank's shtick was getting set up by Stern to appear at various events. In 1998, listeners to the Stern show were encouraged to vote for Hank in *People Magazine's* Most Beautiful People in the World poll on People.com. Most Beautiful Person in the World poll.

Some predictable hunks, including Leonardo DiCaprio, garnered as many as 30,000 votes. But Hank outdistanced all the contestants, winning the contest with a jaw-dropping 230,169 votes. *People* magazine's statement on the debacle was as

---

3. http://www.screamingpickle.com/members/StarWarsKid/

follows: "Though we're hardly novices at handling online polls...nothing could have prepared us for the agony, the ecstasy...and, well, the angry, drunken dwarf."

Hank's statement on the event: "I think it is pathetic. Number one, I don't think I am beautiful. Number two, of course, Leo DiCaprio is beautiful, but he's a guy and I don't judge guys."

Hank passed away in 2001, but he and many advertisements for X-rated Web sites live on at his personal Web site (http://www.hankthedwarf.com/, shown in Figure 17-4).

Figure 17-4. Winner of the Most Beautiful Person in the World online poll: The angry, drunken dwarf[4]

---

4. http://www.hankthedwarf.com/

The Doctress Neutopia

Some of the people profiled in this book could fall into multiple categories. The woman who calls herself the Doctress Neutopia is difficult to classify. Should she be included in the section about flakes in Babylon in Chapter 10? How about Chapter 15, which is about silliness in Babylon?

I've put her here because, in the earliest days of the World Wide Web (1994, which is like the prehistoric era in terms of Web sites), the woman, whose real name is Elizabeth "Libby" Hubbard, gained notoriety for spreading her message of love and spirituality on the Web and Usenet. One of the first profiles of Hubbard appeared in a 1994 article in *Wired*. She frequented message boards and other sites on the Net by posting messages with the signature file shown in Figure 17-5.

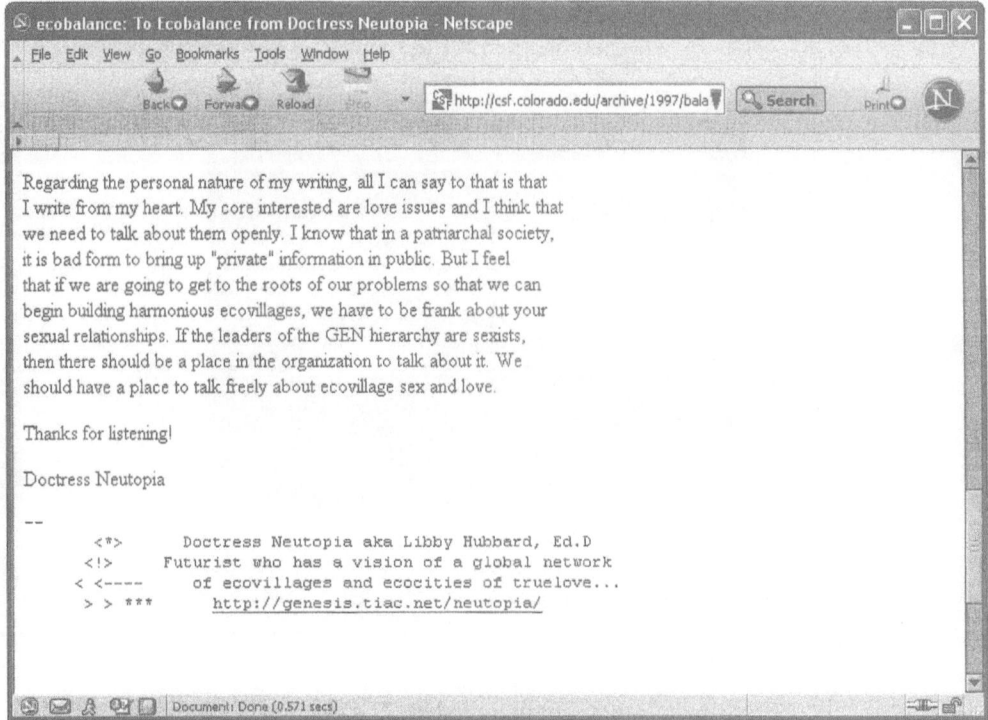

Figure 17-5. The high priestess of love and spirituality online: The Doctress Neutopia [5]

5.   http://csf.colorado.edu/archive/1997/balance3/0830.html

What, exactly, is the Doctress's message? You get an idea on her Web site (http://www.lovolution.net/resume.htm). She has published her doctoral dissertation, *Gaia: The Planetary Religion: The Sacred Marriage of Art and Science*, where she describes a utopian vision of a future in which a new society, Neutopia, turns to the goddess for inspiration and undergoes a change of consciousness fueled by love, beauty, and world peace. (The dissertation enabled her to earn a doctorate in Future Studies at the University of Massachusetts.)

The Doctress Neutopia, another figure who represents the early, flaky, fun days of the Web and Internet, lives in Prescott, Arizona, and cuts a much quieter figure online today (see Figure 17-6).

Figure 17-6. Still waiting for society to catch up to her: The Doctress Neutopia today[6]

---

6. http://www.lovolution.net/resume.htm

Foundations of the Internet

You don't think about how the water gets to your kitchen sink when you turn on the faucet. You *certainly* don't think about where the water goes when you are done with it—unless you encounter a problem with the plumbing. In the same way, even though the Internet is not a public utility, you and I take it for granted unless there's a problem with its electronic "plumbing." We assume that software will be available for our system and our computer. We assume that people will be around to answer the questions we submit to Web sites. We also take for granted that the Web, e-mail, and Usenet exist at all. The following sections examine some people and events that enable the Internet to function and that have become legendary in their own right.

Do Fish Drink Water? Ask the Webmaster

The term "Webmaster" sounds grandiose, almost like something out of a science fiction novel or a fishing show. No, he (or she) is neither a beastmaster nor a bassmaster. A *Webmaster* usually describes someone whose job is to create and maintain Web content for a corporate Web site. A small part of the job usually involves answering questions from the public and forwarding them to the appropriate staff people as needed.

At Xerox Corporation's famous Palo Alto Research Center (PARC) in the 1990s, the term "Webmaster" had a different meaning. The company was full of people who could handle the technical side of creating Web pages and programs to add functionality to Web sites. The Webmaster was supposed to assemble content, and one of the primarily responsibilities was answering e-mail from the public—every single e-mail message.

Bill McLain took his assignment seriously. With a background as a writer, he was enthusiastic about fielding every question people could send about Xerox photocopiers and other equipment. Usually, the kinds of questions Webmasters answer range from "How do I get my e-mail?" to "When will the system be back up?"

But one day someone asked:

I'm desperate; I need the Boy Scout lyrics to the song "Kumbaya." Please help!

McLain scratched his head, looked up the song lyrics, and sent the answer out of a sense of duty.

By now, you've probably read enough in this book to know how word of mouth works online. If one person gets a question answered, word spreads: "Psst…. Did you hear about the Webmaster at Xerox PARC? If you send him a question, he'll answer it—any question!"

McLain was surprised to see questions such as these begin arriving at the Xerox PARC Web site:

- "If someone has been blind from birth, do they dream?"

- "Which came first, the chicken or the egg?"

- "What do you say to God when he sneezes?"

- "What is the meaning of life?"

- "What is the correct way to eat an Oreo cookie?"

McLain saved the questions he received and turned them into the book *Do Fish Drink Water?* (William Morrow, 1999). You might think getting questions that are totally unrelated to computers or the Internet, not to mention Xerox, would annoy McLain. On the contrary—he told an interviewer for Hyperviews, the online magazine of the Society for Technical Communicators, the following:

> *I've always enjoyed helping people, and this job allows me to do that. If I can solve a customer's problem by having his machine replaced with a new one, or if I can help some grade school student understand what makes the sound when you snap your fingers, it is rewarding.*

The original Internet legend—the Xerox Webmaster will answer any question—has morphed into a more personal one. McLain, who has been called "Webmeister" and "Answer Dude," is now regarded as an Internet legend himself for assuming the role of someone who actually does "have all the answers."

The Invention and "Great Renaming" of Usenet

The World Wide Web is only one system of communication on the Internet. E-mail is another. So is chat. But the first really popular area of the Internet was called Usenet, a network of tens of thousands of newsgroups frequented by countless users each day. Usenet has been around so long that it's hard to believe any single individual "invented" it. But that's the case.

Usenet is a system of electronic bulletin boards found on servers maintained by Internet service providers around the world. It was the first way in which individuals could ask questions, share information, help one another, fight one another, fall in love, and otherwise interact online.

Jim Ellis and his fellow Duke University graduate student Tom Truscott came up with a way to connect computers so people could communicate. Their initial goal was to find a way to play chess games online. In 1979, they created software that would allow computers to collaborate using the Unix operating system's conferencing function. They used the software to connect computers at Duke and the University of North Carolina. Accordingly, one of the first newsgroups ever was Net.chess.

In 1980, Ellis did one of those things that many old-time programmers found to be a natural extension of their collaborative programming activities: Rather than sell the software and make millions, he gave it away to the world. (Contrast this with the approach followed by Microsoft around the same time, which is described in the following section.) He gave a presentation at the Academic Unix Users Group entitled "Invitation to a General Access Unix Network." The original Unix User Network could handle only a few messages at a time. Because the software was freely released, others could work on it and improve it.

In 1981, two high school students named Mark Horton and Matt Glickman released a more powerful version of the software that could handle many more posts at a time. Soon, more than 100 computers were networked, and there were about 50 newsgroups. In 1986, a group of Web site administrators referred to as the "Backbone Cabal" formalized the network's organization, came up with a naming system, and renamed the network "Usenet" in an event known as the "Great Renaming." Today, there are more than 50,000 newsgroups. Ellis, who later worked at Sun Microsystems and who always advocated access to computing systems by nontechnical individuals, died in 2001 at the age of 45.

The Stolen Microsoft Software

If you have worked with (or for) Microsoft Corporation for any length of time, you know how protective the company is about its software. Did you ever use version 1.0 of Microsoft Word back in the 1980s? Before you could type a word, you had to insert a special security disk in your floppy disk drive every time you started the program.

You can't argue that Microsoft's protective approach to its software has been successful. But it does seem more pronounced than other large hardware and software manufacturers. Where did this protectiveness come from? You might just look back to a legendary incident that occurred in 1975. That's when its first software designed for the personal computer was stolen.

On June 10, 1975, an employee of the computer maker MITS was preparing to give a presentation at a hotel in Palo Alto, California. A cardboard box was placed on a table. The box contained multiple thick rolls of the paper tape (which computers used at that time), punched with holes. On the tape was a copy of the programming language called Altair BASIC, which was written by Bill Gates and Paul G. Allen. The program was one of the first ever written for the Altair computer—the first computer aimed at home hobbyists rather than large corporations. Gates and his friend Allen had rushed to complete the program after they saw a photo of the Altair on the cover of *Popular Electronics*. It would later be named Micro-Soft BASIC, the first software product of the company that would eventually become Microsoft. The Altair came with no software provided by its manufacturer, MITS. Microsoft was thus born from the desire to put computer applications in the hands of everyday users. It marked the start of the personal computing era.

Sometime during the presentation, the MITS employee had trouble loading computer tape into the computer. At that time, the roll of paper tape had to be pulled through a mechanical reader in order to run the program. While the struggle was going on, the audience and the employee were both distracted, and the tape was stolen.

No one has ever been identified as the thief, but the software reached Dan Sokol, an engineer at a computer chip manufacturer. Sokol was a member of the now-legendary Homebrew Computer Club, which is credited with helping to start the personal computer revolution. Sokol had no qualms about having the program; his approach was that software should be shared among developers who could work collaboratively on it. Sokol brought copies of the stolen tape to a meeting full of computer programmers. When the meeting ended, the would-be hackers rushed to the podium to claim their copies.

When Bill Gates found out that his software was being shared by computer programmers, he sent a letter of protest to a variety of computer-related publications: "As the majority of hobbyists must be aware, most of you steal your software," Mr. Gates wrote ironically. "Hardware must be paid for, but software is something to share. Who cares if the people who worked on it get paid?"

The members of the Homebrew Club believed that Micro-Soft BASIC was not worth the price being charged for it. Many thought sets of programming commands should not cost money. Others began to realize that software was becoming a business and could be a lucrative one. Today, software is indeed big business. But the debate still rages about sharing intellectual property. As I was writing this chapter, lawsuits were being filed against individuals who share music, video, and software files online through peer-to-peer computing sites like Napster.

To this day, though, no one has stepped forward as the person who stole Bill Gates's software so long ago. And Sokol steadfastly refuses to reveal who gave him the software, so the theft is an enduring computer-related mystery.

Images Worth a Thousand Data Bits

When the Internet was able to combine text with images, colors, and multiple typefaces, thanks to the World Wide Web, its popularity soared, and it moved from the province of technicians to the nonprogrammers who are often referred to as "The Rest of Us." Images have become big business thanks to the Web. You can sell images, license their use, or use them to sell other services (read: X-rated services). Some images, such as the ones that accompany the listings on the auction service eBay, are online for a week or less. In contrast, the following sections look at some images that have assumed a life of their own and have become an enduring part of the landscape of cyberspace.

The Cartoon with a Life of Its Own

People just weren't writing about the Internet in the mainstream media in 1993. Not much, at least. But when a clever cartoon by Peter Steiner appeared in the *New Yorker* magazine on July 5, 1993, it did more than make people chuckle. It put the Internet in the mainstream and helped it to become a household world.

The cartoon, which regularly receives orders for reproduction on T-shirts from the Cartoon Bank Web site (see Figure 17-7), has since become the magazine's most reproduced cartoon.

In a 1996 interview, Jonathan Postel, one of the pioneers of the Internet (who is profiled in Chapter 4), said that the cartoon was pivotal because it signaled that the print media did not have to define the Internet every time it was used. It was popular and well-known enough to appear in casual conversation—or in cartoon captions.

The caption of the cartoon has become so well-known that it is sometimes simply referred to as "that old phrase" or "the adage." It was even worked into the title of a play about participants in a chat room called *Nobody Knows You're a Dog*. Steiner wasn't an especially enthusiastic booster of the Internet when he drew the cartoon, but he did have an account with an online service provider at the time.

"I feel a little like the person (whoever it is) who invented the smiley face," Steiner was quoted in a *New York Times* article. If you're wondering just who *that* person is, read on....

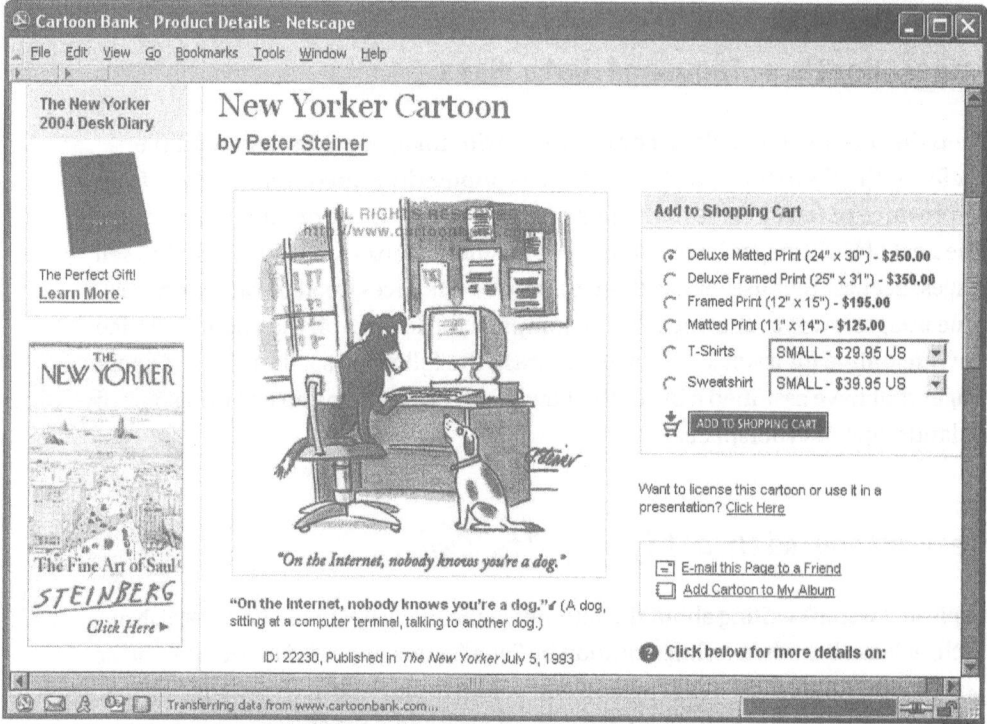

Figure 17-7. The cartoon that helped make the Internet respectable[7]

How the Smiley Was Born :-)

As Peter Steiner notes in the previous section, some symbols assume an existence that goes far beyond what their inventors originally envisioned. In 1982, Scott E. Fahlman (shown in Figure 17-8) suggested the smiley symbol during a conversation at Carnegie Mellon University, where he still teaches.

---

7. http://www.cartoonbank.com/

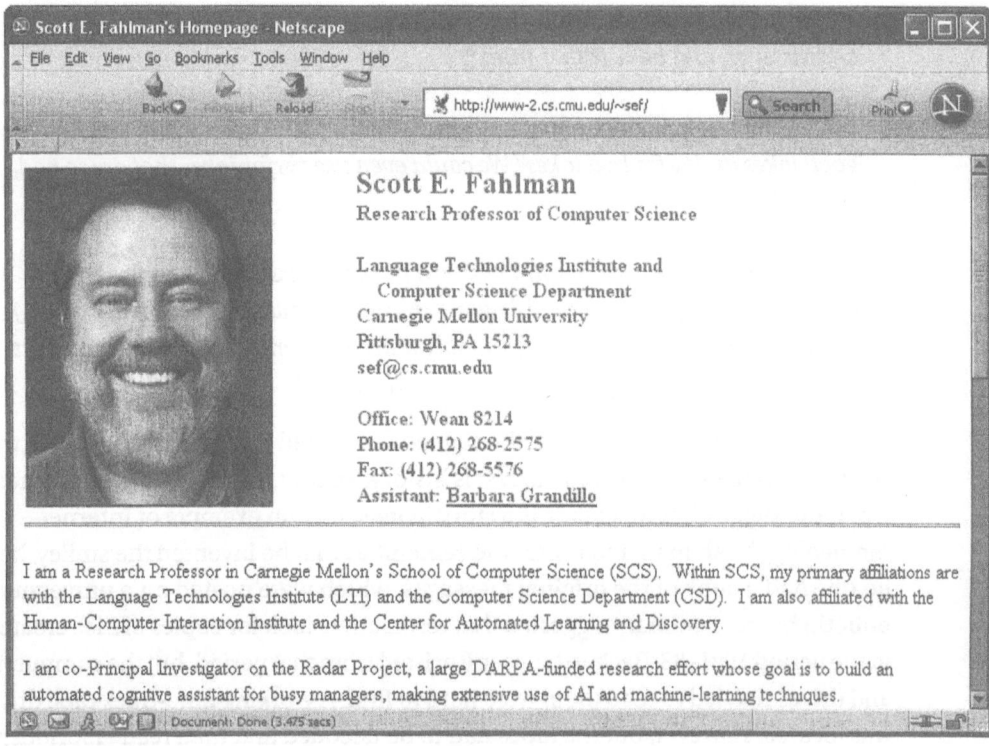

Figure 17-8. Next time you use a smiley, tip your mouse to this smiling man.[8]

It should be noted that the smiley symbol is one of a group of *emoticons*—keyboard symbols that can be used to convey emotion between people who communicate online rather than face to face. At the time the smiley was considered, someone riding in an elevator had made a joke about mercury spilling in a laboratory. Some people in the elevator didn't realize that the remark was just a joke and not a description of an actual event. This prompted staff to muse about the needs to express that a remark made on the Internet is intended to be humorous. Excerpts from that exchange follow:

> 17-Sep-82 10:58 Neil Swartz at CMU-750R Elevator posts: *Apparently there has been some confusion about elevators and such. After talking to Rudy, I have discovered that there is no mercury spill in any of the Wean hall elevators. Many people seem to have taken the notice about the physics department seriously. Maybe we should adopt a convention of putting a star (*) in the subject field of any notice which is to be taken as a joke.*

---

8. http://www-2.cs.cmu.edu/~sef/

17-Sep-82 14:59 Joseph Ginder at CMU-10A (*%): *I believe that the joke character should be % rather than *.*

17-Sep-82 15:15 Anthony Stentz at CMU-780G (*%): *How about using * for good jokes and % for bad jokes? We could even use *% for jokes that are so bad, they're funny.*

19-Sep-82 11:44 Scott E Fahlman :-) From: Scott E Fahlman <Fahlman at Cmu-20c>: *I propose that the following character sequence for joke markers: :-) Read it sideways. Actually, it is probably more economical to mark things that are NOT jokes, given current trends. For this, use :-(*

Following this conversation, the suggestion spread throughout ARPANET, the precursor of the Internet, and the rest is history. Simply rediscovering the moment when the suggestion was made is a story in itself and an example of Internet "archeology." Fahlman and others did remember that he invented the smiley, but no one had a copy of the original messages, which were posted on a university bulletin board. Fahlman suggested that researchers look for copies of files created in the period 1981–83. Backup tapes still existed from that period, but the computers and drives needed to read them were hard to find. A working nine-track tape drive was located, however, but the tapes had to be decoded and then read laboriously until the critical exchange was located.

NOTE Fahlman reports that the smiley was born on September 19, 1982. He reproduces the entire conversation that led to the invention of the smiley and provides his own views about it at http://www-2.cs.cmu.edu/%7Esef/sefSmiley.htm.

All Hail "Bob," the Head of the Church of the SubGenius

I'm not totally sure exactly what message the Church of the SubGenius is putting forth. No one except the church's scribe, the Reverend Ivan Stang, is probably sure. But chances are you've seen the church's figurehead, "Bob," before, somewhere on the Internet. He is, in fact, one of cyberspace's earliest and most enduring cult figures.

"Bob's" full name is J.R. Dobbs, and he is the founder and figurehead for the Church of the SubGenius. What, exactly, is this religion? Ah, it would take many chapters to fully explore that rich and bizarre subject, dear reader. You're better off looking up one of the worthy books, such as *Revelation X: The "Bob" Apocryphon* (Fireside, 1994), or visiting the church's Web site (http://www.subgenius.com/).

From what I have been able to piece together, "Bob's" story goes like this: A friend of Stang's named Philo Drummond discovered "Bob's" image in a piece of clip art used in the 1950s. *Clip art* is stock imagery that used to be clipped out of art books and pasted in to newspapers and other publications. Something about the comforting visage of the pipe-smoking, grinning "Bob" (see Figure 17-9) attracted Stang, who was impoverished and reduced to delivering balloons to senior citizens in the guise of a mime for $5 a delivery. Stang had already begun to write up his rants about "Bob" and Arnold Palmer, the famous golfer who was supposedly wounded by a blow by a nine iron. (The church's members worship both Bob and the Bleeding Head of Arnold Palmer, you see.)

His frustration drove him to turn his rants into *The Book of the SubGenius* (Fireside, 1987) and other volumes. He also became the host of a syndicated radio show called the *Hour of Slack*. His church, which started out as a parody of religious cults, turned out to be a huge draw for thousands of eager pilgrims hungry for its odd blend of humor and weirdness. And it has made Stang a nice living through a number of books and his ongoing radio show.

NOTE   According to the church's doctrine, "Bob" must always be enclosed in quotation marks. Apparently, the Bob that can be named is not the true "Bob."

"Bob's" image, not surprisingly, has been appropriated by lots of other off-kilter people on the Internet and transformed in many ways. For example, it was turned into an oracle that people could pray to in languages ranging from Esperanto to Pig Latin (http://www.resort.com/~banshee/Misc/8ball/index.html).

TIP   The "Ballad of J.R. 'Bob' Dobbs" sheds a little light on who Dobbs is...actually, very little light is shed. But it's an entertaining set of lyrics, and you can enjoy them at http://www.subgenius.com/bigfist/ears/soundz/10HOLE_HYMNS/X0052_BalladOBob.html.

Figure 17-9. A symbol of weirdness on the Internet: J. R. "Bob" Dobbs [9]

---

9. http://www.subgenius.com/

Did You See the Photo of the 87-Pound Cat?

I include this story mainly because it's a good example of what many people commonly call an Internet legend—a hoax or spoof that circulates online and that takes many people in. Because you don't deal with people face to face online, and because digital images can be doctored in many ways before they go online, you can never be fully certain that what you're seeing or reading is genuine.

Such was the case with the story about the 87-pound cat shown in Figure 17-10, which circulated on the Internet for several years. The story claimed that an employee with the Atomic Energy Commission Limited (AECL) in Canada found two stray cats at the AECL's facility in Chalk River, Ontario. (Specifics such as this tend to give such myths an air of credibility.) The employee and his family decided to keep the two cats, which were named Lost and Found. Snowball, the cat depicted in the photo, was supposed to be one of six kittens born to these two cats.

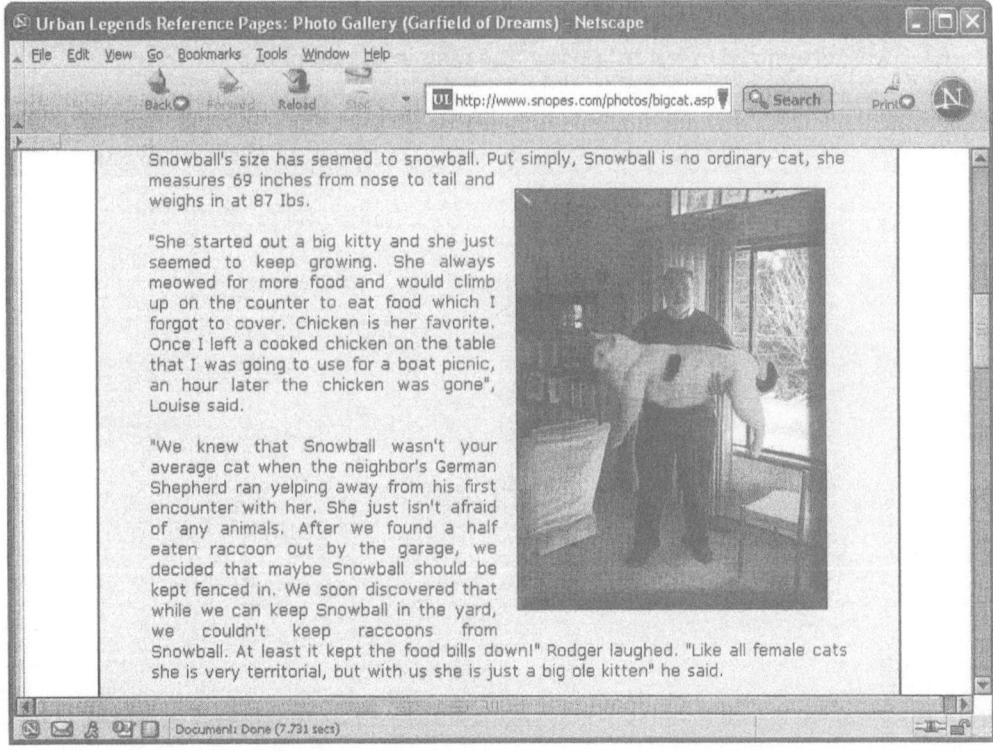

Figure 17-10. The giant cat fooled millions of viewers on the Web but was never intended to be a hoax.[10]

---

10. http://www.snopes.com/photos/bigcat.asp

Snowball's claim to fame was her enormous size: In nine years of life, she grew to 69 inches in length and 87 pounds in weight. Snowball had a healthy appetite, or so the story went—she supposedly grabbed a cooked chicken off the dinner table and ate it. The family also found a half-eaten raccoon in their garage, after which they decided to keep Snowball in the house.

In fact, the cat's name is Jumper, and he is being held by Cordell Hauglie of Edmonds, Washington. Hauglie's daughter, Jennifer, asked him to provide her with a digitized version of a photo of her cat that she could send to a friend. Like any doting father, Hauglie was eager to comply and, using the image-editing program called Adobe Photoshop, he "augmented" the cat. His son originally held the cat for one photo, and Hauglie stood in the same position in a subsequent photo. The two images were combined. "I got a little carried away," he told a reporter from the *Ottawa Citizen* newspaper.

Pleased with his electronic "joke," he e-mailed the image of the cat to a few of his friends. They mailed it to a few of their friends, and so on, and so on. Soon, he was getting e-mails from people he never met in places such as Israel and Australia, asking about the giant cat. The cat appeared on Web sites around the world. Hauglie was recognized in restaurants as "the man in the cat photo."

Random Googling

The Internet contains plenty of Web sites devoted to Internet hoaxes. There aren't too many that discuss historical legends associated with the history of the Internet itself. The following list contains a few I found noteworthy—a random sampling of sites that turned up after searching for the terms "Internet legend" on the search service Google (http://www.google.com/):

- **Kurt Vonnegut @ M.I.T? (http://www.vonnegutweb.com/vonnegutia/ commencement/mit_hoax.html):** The famous novelist and author of *Slaughterhouse Five, Cat's Cradle,* and many other books was rumored to have given a commencement address at the Massachusetts Institute of Technology in which he supposedly told students to use sunscreen. Actually, the advice was given in a column written by the *Chicago Tribune's* Mary Schmich. Somehow it was widely attributed to the novelist, who was mistakenly quoted in e-mails around the world.

- **Snopes.com (http://www.snopes.com/):** When it comes to debunking Internet hoaxes (or occasionally proving that some legends are for real), this is one of the best sources online. Urban legends are the main focus here, and they are conveniently organized by topic in a searchable database. Also check out the TruthOrFiction site (http://www.truthorfiction.com/).

- **Hoaxbusters (http://hoaxbusters.ciac.org/):** This is the place to start if you hear a rumor about some impending disaster or if you receive an e-mail that sounds suspicious in some way. Search this site's database before you forward an e-mail message or contribute to some cause.

CHAPTER 18

Dressing Up Your Home Page—and Yourself

THE INTERNET IS perhaps unique in providing a communications medium where individuals can be totally anonymous or expose themselves completely to millions of strangers. This freedom gives you the ability to shed your identity, if you're dissatisfied with it, and adopt a new one.

The freedom afforded by cyberspace also enables some extroverts to gain support and affirmation (as well as ridicule) for celebrating unusual pursuits. A grown heterosexual man can show himself wearing skirts, another can dress up as Peter Pan and Little Lord Fauntleroy, and a woman can turn herself into a professional skipper.

Finally, some gain notoriety by accident. A man discovers his wife exchanging lurid e-mail with strangers; a woman on a Webcam leaves her husband for a fan she encounters in a chat room and who lives in another country. The resulting furor creates unwilling Net celebrities. This chapter goes into the different ways in which people can bend their gender, adopt a new persona, or fall into celebrity through the Net's ability to link millions of people with astonishing ease and speed.

Making a Name—and a Life—for Yourself Online

The Internet is fast becoming a place where otherwise ordinary individuals can turn themselves into something special by adopting a new name and doing something noteworthy. The poster child for people who will do anything to become stars has got to be a Texas man named Mitch Maddox. In 1999, Maddox decided to capitalize on the growing number of Web sites that offered household commercial products and that either shipped them to your door or delivered them with their own trucks. (Remember Webvan, which would deliver groceries you ordered online directly to your door?)

It dawned on Maddox that so many products were becoming available online in 1999 that a person could order them via computer and literally never have to leave home. For most people, such realizations are passing thoughts, worth no more than a remark along the lines of, "Wow...isn't that something?" But for some reason, Maddox decided to make this thought a reality and pulled off one of the most unusual—and, as many have said, most useless—stunts in cyberspace history.

He began by legally changing his name to DotComGuy. He then announced he was going to spend an entire year indoors, never leaving his home and living off groceries and other supplies he ordered online. He lined up a group of sponsors who pledged to pay him more than $98,000 to promote the concept of making purchases online.

He found a home in Dallas, Texas, the exact location of which was carefully kept secret and which he dubbed the "DotCompound." An elaborate video setup was created in the house next door. This enabled as many as 25 cameras to keep track of DotComGuy's activities, including sleeping (the bathroom was his only privacy), and to broadcast them over the Web via the DotComGuy Web site (http://www.dotcomguy.com/, shown via the Wayback Machine in Figure 18-1). On January 1, 2000, DotComGuy entered his self-imposed exile and began to live solely off the e-commerce resources available to him in cyberspace.

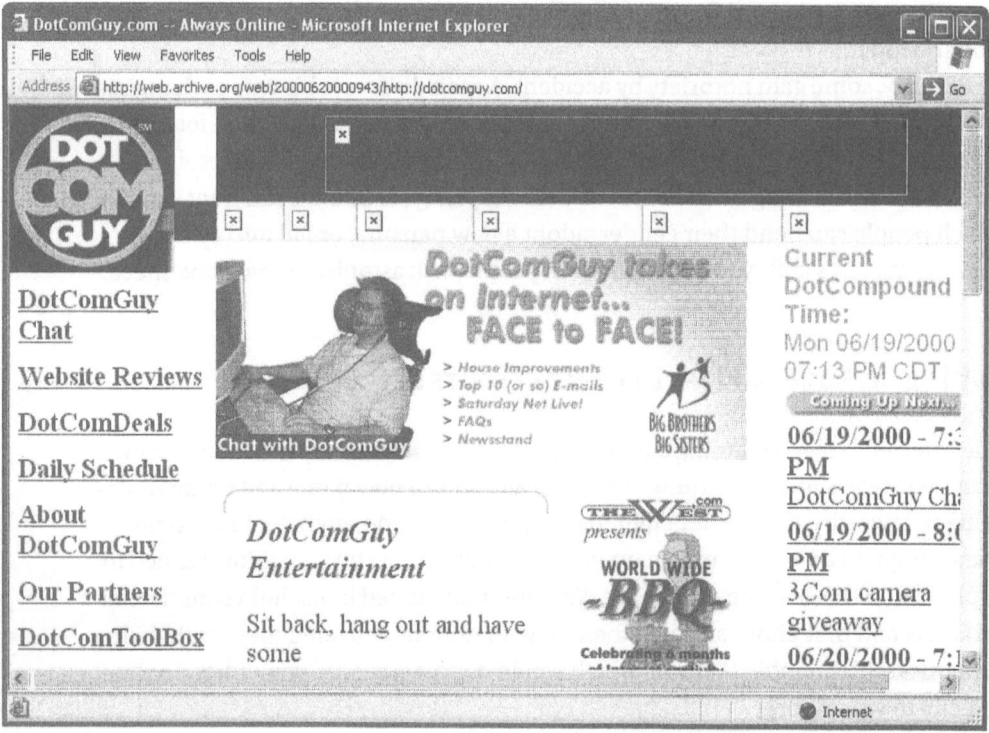

Figure 18-1. The virtual home of the Texas man who lived off the Internet's bounty for a year[1]

---

1. http://web.archive.org/web/20000620000943/http://dotcomguy.com/

Once ensconced in his cyberhome, DotComGuy proceeded to do what many of us do, only more so: He spent lots and lots of time in front of his computer. He bought furnishings for his home and stocked his refrigerator all via the Web. He exchanged e-mails, posted messages, and staged a weekly Saturday Net Live chat session. He talked to reporters. He allowed cyberviewers to watch him work out, read, or do absolutely nothing. It wasn't the most scintillating viewing, but it did get some attention in the media, at least while e-commerce was still booming. But trouble arose in cyberparadise. During DotComGuy's year at home, e-commerce became a much less popular topic of conversation as the economy sputtered. Fewer and fewer people talked about DotComGuy as the year went on, and now, he has been nearly forgotten.

One thing about DotComGuy's adventure has never been cleared up: Was he ever actually paid for his yearlong experiment in cyberspace consumerism? After spending 366 days in his home, at 12:01 a.m. on January 1, 2001, DotComGuy emerged and reportedly rode away on a small motorized scooter. Almost immediately, reports began to circulate that DotComGuy's sponsors had backed away from their original pledges and left him with no money for all his efforts. He became the object of ridicule on influential sites such as Slashdot (http://slashdot.org/), where his site was described as the most useless effort in history. But some news stories stated that DotComGuy had been paid a monthly stipend by his sponsors, which enabled him to make purchases online.

DotComGuy did not come out of his yearlong confinement totally empty-handed, however. A story on the *USA Today* Web site (http://www.usatoday.com/news/ndstue02.htm) announced he intended to marry Crystalyn Anne Holubeck, who he met in one of the chat rooms on his Web site. Her name was not destined to become DotComGal, however: DotComGuy reportedly planned to change his name back to Mitch Maddox before the wedding.

Now They Live in Private

Another experiment in Web-based virtual reality, WeLiveInPublic, followed the daily lives of Josh Harris and his girlfriend Tanya Corrin (whose biographies from the now-defunct WeLiveInPublic Web site, preserved on Ghost Sites, are shown in Figure 18-2). Harris was no stranger to high-tech projects. He founded Jupiter Communications and helped start the Webcasting company Pseudo.com. He also had a pile of money he made on those ventures. With some time on his hands, he equipped his loft in Manhattan's trendy SoHo district with 32 cameras and microphones. The expansive place included a shower cam, a toilet cam, a bed cam, a refrigerator cam, and even a cat litter cam. Harris declared the site, and his home, open to the Internet in November 2000.

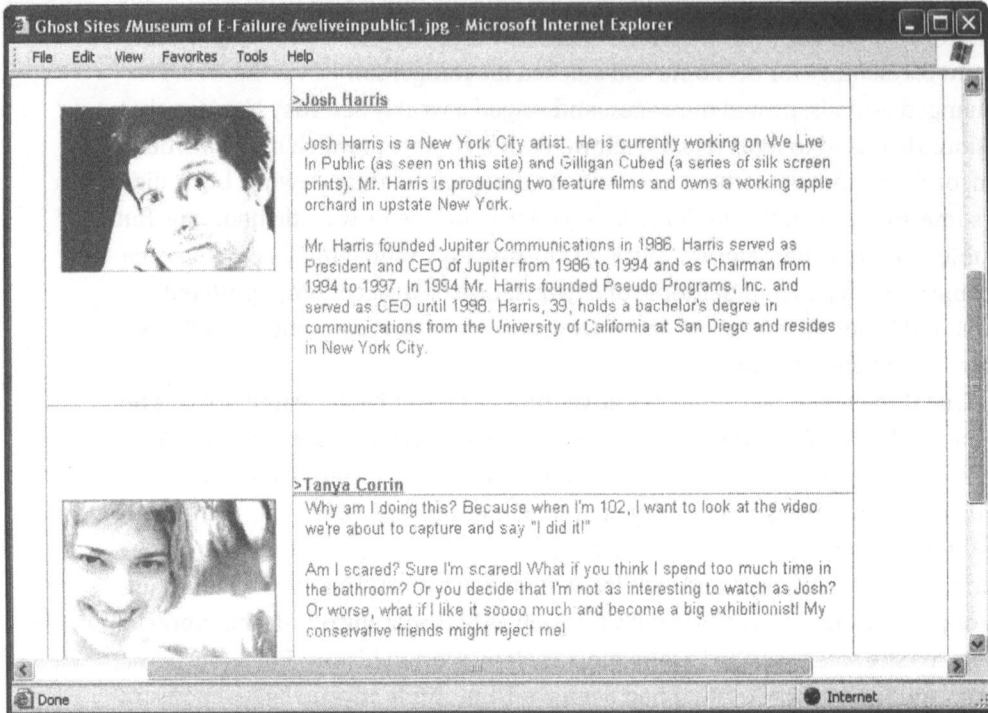

Figure 18-2. Cameras and microphones in the bedroom, bathroom, and cat litter box made them cyberstars for a few months.[2]

An article in *Wired* described Harris's vision of a high-tech utopian world in which everyone would have "intimate" contact with everyone else via Webcams: "High-speed Internet access and ubiquitous Webcams will shatter social and physical barriers, tempting us to watch one another and to enjoy this strange new form of intimacy."

A dedicated community of viewers regularly visited the site (http://www.weliveinpublic.com/), commenting on all of Harris's and Corrin's daily—and nightly—activities. In articles written after the event, Corrin said she and Harris never actually had sexual relations in front of the cameras; they would go out of town or retreat to a room where a blanket had been erected to provide a private zone. However, while they were out of town, a group of people had a "swingers' party" in the apartment, and the viewers who were hungry to watch sex online got what they wanted that weekend.

---

2. http://disobey.com/ghostsites/show_exhibit/weliveinpublic1/

Several Web sites developed fan clubs for Harris and Corrin; a regular newsletter documented their activities. About three months into the experiment, Corrin moved out. She later published a tell-all account of her nightmare (http://www.nyobserver.com/pages/story.asp?ID=3874) under the gaze of rabid chatters who commented on her every activity. She describes the moment when the cameras first started rolling and the site went online:

> *Within minutes, there were 15 people in the [chatroom]. Josh and I froze. We hadn't announced the site launch yet, so who were these guys? Before long, we got weirded out and retreated to bed, the camera whirring into focus overhead as a pack of strangers watched us cuddle.*

In a hilarious article in Salon (http://archive.salon.com/tech/feature/2001/02/26/webcam/print.html), writer Will Leitch provided an account of his own brief stay in the loft after Harris and Corrin moved out. He described how cameras all over the loft fed live video to a bank of monitors. The WeLiveInPublic chatters commented on his every activity:

> *I'm playing Radiohead's* Kid A *on the stereo, and so the chat room people debate whether or not it sucks. (They end up just making fun of my singing.) They want to know if my friend Jessica is hot. They accuse me of picking my nose.*

> *I get up to use the restroom. I rush to return. A message is waiting: "You should wash your hands."*

After they split up, Corrin and Harris (or individuals using their names) exchanged angry comments on the FuckedCompany.com Web site. WeLiveInPublic was purchased by a Web developer named Michael Auerbach, who opened the We Live in Public café in the Tribeca neighborhood of Manhattan. Auerbach was reportedly planning to develop a camera kit and software that would let anyone "live in public." Alas, that endeavor is no longer living, and at this writing WeLiveInPublic.com is dead.

 NOTE   Filmmaker Errol Morris made a story about Harris's exploits that aired on British television. Find out more on Morris's own thought-provoking Web site (http://www.errolmorris.com/).

JenniCam: Seven Years of Life Online

When it comes to Webcams, no discussion would be complete without mentioning the Doyenne of Dot-Com Display, Jennifer Ringley. Ringley is widely known as one of the first people to put Webcams in her home and broadcast day-to-day events to anyone interested. She started in 1996; seven years later, JenniCam (http://www.jennicam.com/) was still providing coverage of the home life of Ringley; her partner, Dex; and various pets. She finally decided to close the Web site on New Year's Eve in 2003.

Sometimes the cameras displayed an empty bed with piled-up covers. Sometimes they showed Ringley and Dex curled up in bed. They showed Ringley on the couch with pets, Ringley watching TV, and Ringley in the bathroom (see Figure 18-3). Whatever happened at home happened on the Web.

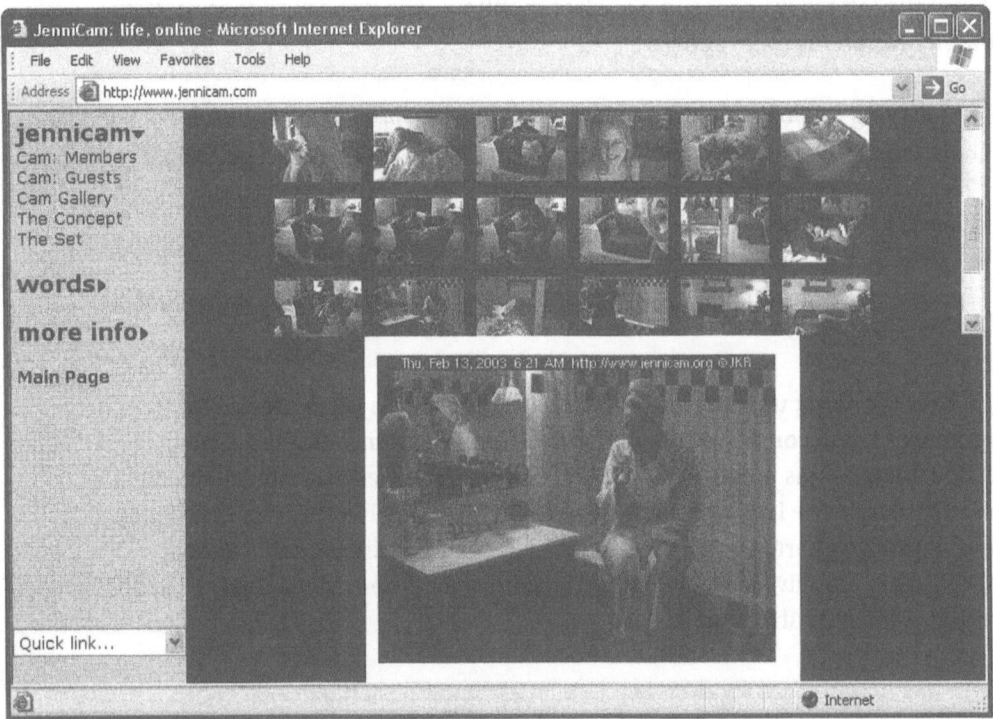

Figure 18-3. Seven years on the Web: Jennifer of JenniCam spent a good part of her life online.[3]

---

3. http://www.jennicam.com/

Because she worked full-time, Ringley just wasn't at home all that often. But then, she wasn't out to provide entertainment. She said she simply didn't mind being watched:

> *What you'll see is my life, exactly as it would be whether or not there were cameras watching. From minute to minute, it can be tough to see what it's about. The site has existed now for about seven years. As a chronicle, a long-term experiment, the concept becomes clearer.*

You wonder if, in the preceding statement, Ringley was talking about her Webcam experiment or her life. But then you have to stop and ask yourself: What's the difference?

The Couch, the Spot, and Other Cybersoap Operas

The Internet is just plain different from television, film, or other media. It's interactive, it's immediate, and it's intimate. That doesn't stop people from trying to create entertainment that was designed for one medium, such as the television soap opera, and try it online. After all, soap operas were originally created for radio, and they made the move to television pretty seamlessly. It's reasonable to assume they'll also work on the Net.

That was the thinking behind the Spot, the original Web-based soap opera (http://www.thespot.com/) and one of the first successful entertainment venues on the Web. The Spot launched in 1995, and before it ended in 1997 it developed a devoted community of a few hundred fans. The story revolved around a group of attractive young people (whose images, resurrected from the Internet Wayback Machine, are shown in Figure 18-4) living in a beach house in Santa Monica, California.

The Spot was notable for the extensive interaction it afforded its viewers. They could post messages, correspond with the writers, and even become characters in the story line from time to time. The story came to an end when the original sponsor, the American Cybercast network, went bankrupt.

Figure 18-4. The first online soap opera, which allowed fans to participate in the story[4]

Another popular online series, the Couch, featured (according to a description on Yahoo!) "eight dynamic, soul-searching, fast-living characters in group therapy with serious New York attitudes." The Couch (shown in Figure 18-5, courtesy of Ghost Sites), gave you the chance to follow these characters through their biweekly group therapy sessions. You could also explore their lives outside of therapy by reading their diaries.

---

4. http://web.archive.org/web/19970414193354/http://www1.thespot.com/

Figure 18-5. The Couch: group therapy sessions conducted online [5]

Other soap operas faded and live on only in archives. The sites include Affairs of the Net: An Internet Love Story and Dyke Street, a soap opera with a lesbian twist, which seems never to have taken off. A few ongoing series still remain online, such as As the Mouse Moves, which you can visit at http://www.readio.com/mouse/mouse1.html.

NOTE An employee at *MacUser* magazine created a Web site to celebrate an old couch he had in his office. He published photos of his coworkers actually sitting on the couch. Why did he do it? Visit http://www.romansempire.com/couch/page1.htm. If you can determine why the couch is worthy of such attention, please tell me.

5. http://disobey.com/ghostsites/show_exhibit/couch/

Web's "Oldest Woman" Documents Her Self-Transformation

There isn't anything particularly odd or bizarre about Sherry Miller's Oldest Woman on the Web site, which is part of her SherryArt site (http://www.sherryart.com/oldestwoman/, shown in Figure 18-6). I include it because it documents the transformation of a woman who apparently reinvented herself in middle age, became a Webmaster, and is thriving in the high-tech culture of California.

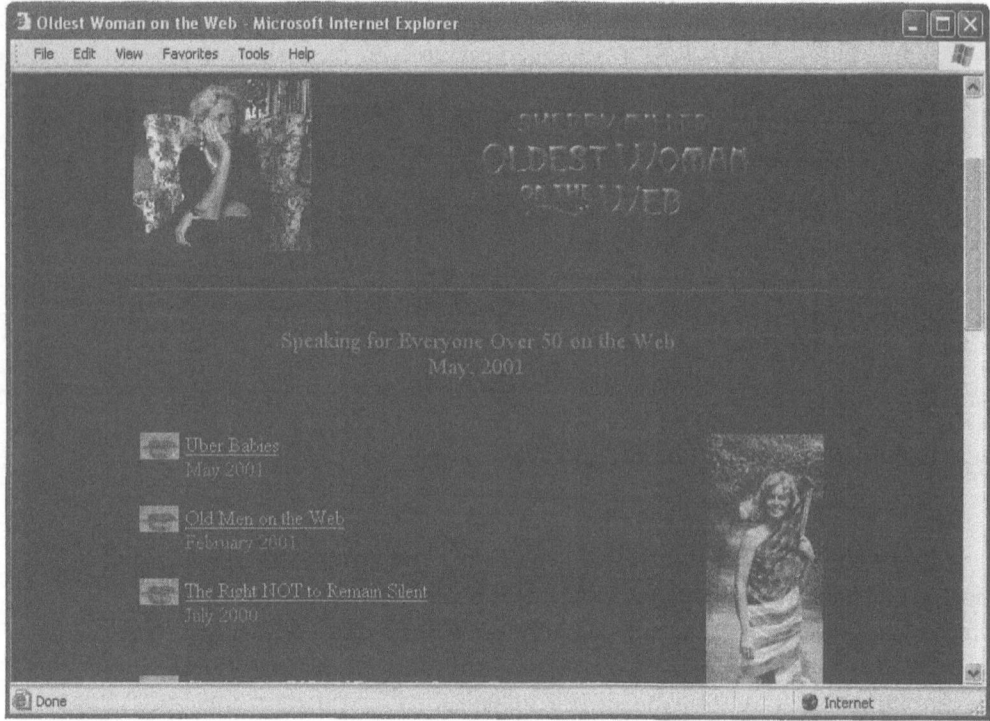

Figure 18-6. Creating an identity online in middle age: Sherry Miller[6]

That Miller managed to portray herself as the Oldest Woman on the Web shows her genius for self-promotion. She lived in Maine for many years and worked as an artist. She "fed ten children (five of them her own) every day for twenty years." She moved to California where she created several Web sites and got jobs in Web promotion, content creation, and Webmastering. Her site contains essays, examples of her artwork, and plenty of ideas for people who want to create identities for themselves on the Net.

---

6. http://www.sherryart.com/oldestwoman/

Naked on eBay: Sellers Wear Nothing to Peddle Their Wares

I stumbled across the eBay auction shown in Figure 18-7 on the very entertaining Weird Auctions Web site. It seems, at first glance, like an innocent auction of a television set, which has been put up for sale by a United Kingdom man. However, if you go to the page on which the auction is depicted (http://www.weirdauctions.com/preserves.cfm/hurl/pageid=70/preserves.cfm) and look closely at the image of the television set, you get a big surprise: The seller, in fact, has photographed himself, and his naked reflection appears in the television screen.

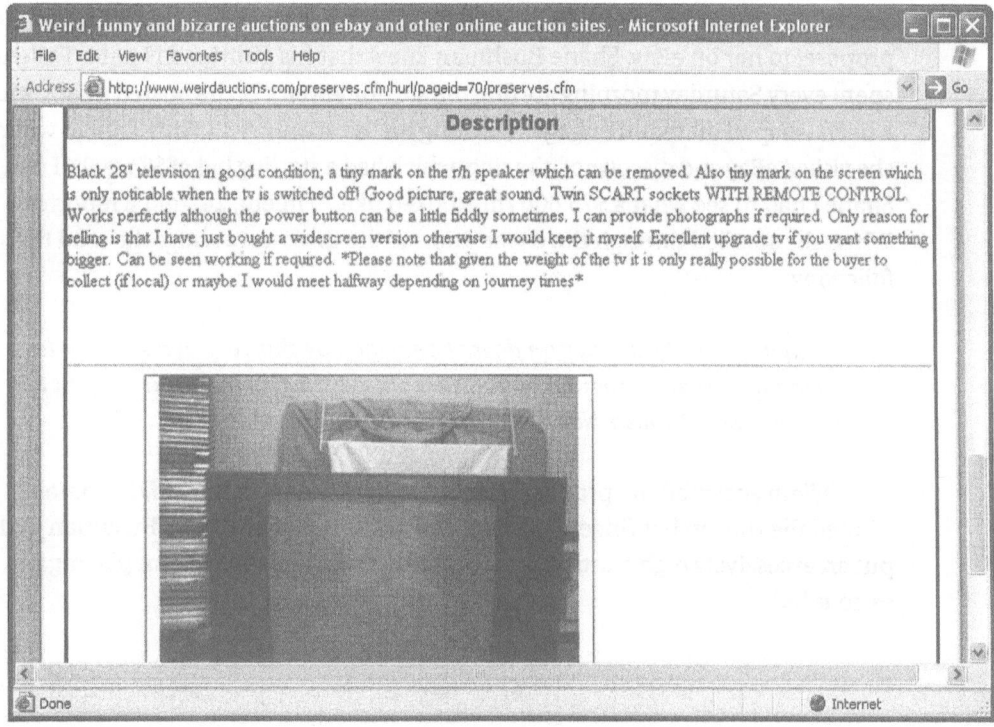

Figure 18-7. Some eBay sellers try to expose themselves as well as their possessions to a worldwide audience.[7]

---

7. http://www.weirdauctions.com/preserves.cfm/hurl/pageid=70/preserves.cfm

Little did I know, at the time, that this was a new craze on eBay and that it had been given a name: *reflectoporn*. Sellers appear unclothed in reflections on the items they are selling. Electric guitars, knives, and forks have been used to capture such reflections. An eBay spokesman was quoted in *Wired* as saying that users cannot sell erotica and are not allowed to depict genitalia in their sales, and eBay would remove any such item. This apparently has not stopped sellers from sneaking such revealing images into their sales descriptions, however.

Suitor Uses eBay to Auction Off Marriage Proposal

How much would you bid for a marriage proposal? A Florida woman turned out to be the big winner when she discovered that her boyfriend had posted a marriage proposal to her on eBay. Shane Bushman knew that his girlfriend Natalie Thilem spent every Saturday morning surfing the site for jewelry. So he posted a listing for a heart-shaped diamond engagement ring on the site. He was with Thilem when she visited eBay and discovered the ring, which had a starting bid of $75,000. "I told Shane I had to see what a $75,000 ring looked like," Thilem, 24, told a reporter. When she scrolled through the description of the three-carat ring, she read the following:

> *Bear in mind that this auction doesn't only include this ring. It also includes the eternal love and devotion of the seller...in marriage. The ring is truly fit for a princess. So...Princess Natalie...Will you marry me?*

Thilem accepted the proposal immediately. As soon as she did, Bushman slipped the ring on her finger. The ring was actually worth $7,500; Bushman had put an excessively high starting bid on it to discourage anyone from placing a serious bid.

Gender Benders and Dresser-Uppers

If you want to dress up as a member of the opposite sex, the Net is a great place to do it. You can show yourself off without attracting a face-to-face crowd; all you have to do is post some photos online and enjoy the feeling of having complete strangers ogle you in all your glory. The following are a few examples of people who are secure enough with themselves (or in the case of the would-be Peter Pan, who they *think* they are) to solicit and get plenty of attention on the Net.

Arkansas Man Skirts the Wild Side

As an example of how the Web lets people show themselves off to their best advantage, consider an Arkansas man named Dale Miller. Dale's home page looks perfectly run-of-the-mill. Of course, there's the domain name (http://www.skirtman.org/), but "skirtman" could mean a couple of different things. Chances are it means Dale likes looking at skirts, you think. That's certainly true, but that's not all. Dale also likes purchasing and wearing those skirts, as shown in Figure 18-8.

In Miller's extensive (389 items at this writing) list of reasons why women should go out with him, he includes—along with such mundane things as "I'm a good listener"—this statement: "You've probably never gone out with a man who wears skirts." After you get done talking about Miller's work as a systems administrator and the fact that he's an ordained minister in the Universal Life Church, you can compare suggestions on where to buy a floral wrap or a miniskirt.

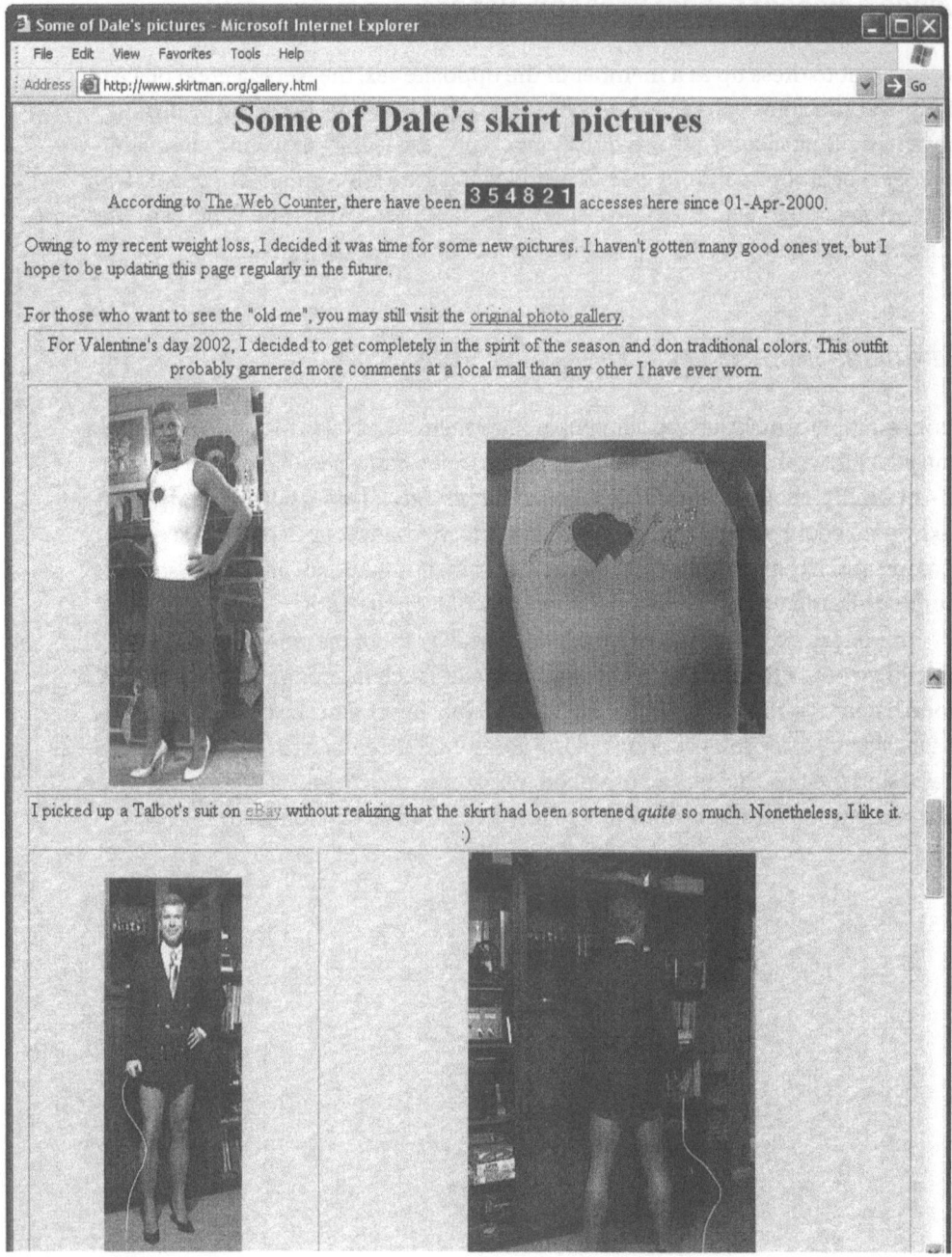

Figure 18-8. Hemming it up on the Web: Dale Miller, Skirtman[8]

---

8.   http://www.skirtman.org/gallery.html

When You Wish Upon the Web, Your Dream Comes True

Before the Web, someone like Randy Constan would only have attracted attention from his neighbors, his fellow shoppers at the local Kash n' Karry grocery stores in his hometown of Tampa, Florida, and possibly some local mental-health professionals. Thanks to cyberspace, Constan has found more than four million visitors, many of whom applaud and affirm his campaign to be a real man who happens to like dressing as Peter Pan.

The 49-year-old divorced computer programmer doesn't just want to act like Peter Pan. He wants to *be* Peter Pan. For more than two decades, he has been dressing like the famous pixie in green tights and a green top with a green elf's hat adorned by a feather. His Peter Pan Web site (http://www.pixyland.org/peterpan/) shows him dressed not only in his Peter Pan green outfit (see Figure 18-9) but in a Little Lord Fauntleroy outfit and in a frilly getup that recalls the British painter Thomas Gainsborough's famous *The Blue Boy*.

Constan's goal is to be who he wants to be, gain acceptance, and have fun. He does solicit donations on the site to cover the cost of Web site hosting and autographed photos. What's left over is given to charity. He doesn't mind when people make fun of a 6-foot-tall, deep-voiced, adult man dressed up as a pixie. When his site won a 2001 Webby award in the Weird category, he went to San Francisco and gave a five-word acceptance speech: "Weird? God loves us all."

A longer-term goal is the search for a "life partner, a soul mate"—someone he describes as his own personal Tinkerbell with whom he can share his life and presumably his love of frilly fashions.

Figure 18-9. Constan can act out Peter Pan's statement "I don't wanna grow up!" on his Web site.[9]

---

9. http://www.pixyland.org/peterpan/

Skip, Skip, Skip to Her Site

Clicking a mouse is the main activity of most Web surfers. Not so with Kim Corbin, who has dubbed herself Skipper. Corbin was walking down the street with a friend in San Francisco, where she lives, when she broke into a skip. Immediately she realized—*this is happiness*. She has been skipping ever since. At first, Corbin simply wanted to lose weight. But like so many free spirits in the City by the Bay, she had the urge to share her newfound joy with others.

The result was her Web site, Iskip.com (http://www.iskip.com/, shown in Figure 18-10). The keywords at the top of the site's pages give you an idea of what Corbin is selling: "kidagain.com," "feel like a kid," "run," "jump," and so on. She started the site in 1999 and gained a following through diary entries that conveyed the joy (not to mention the weight loss) she experienced through skipping.

Figure 18-10. Kim Corbin, whose site Iskip.com has turned her into a professional skipper[10]

---

10. http://www.iskip.com/

Corbin's life has literally skipped to a new level thanks to the attention she has received through her Web site. Within just a few months of going online, she was profiled by newspaper and TV stations in her hometown of Indianapolis, Indiana, as well as the *San Francisco Chronicle*. She also held an after-work group skip through San Francisco's Financial District.

She quit her job as a publicity director for a publishing company and is now making a living skipping and teaching the benefits of skipping and exercise. She has found disciples who have been dubbed "head skippers" and who spread the word about skipping in their own parts of the country. She gives regular group classes on skipping. She's working on a book about skipping. She mails her monthly newsletter to more than 1,000 skipping enthusiasts.

Corbin gets a wide range of reactions as she skips along the streets of San Francisco. When homeless people ask her for money, she tells them to "skip for it." When boys on bicycles make fun of her, she admonishes them to "skip off." She notices that joggers and walkers often seem to be grimacing and frowning, but anyone who is skipping seems to be smiling. She advises budding skippers not to feel silly. "It's not silly to make yourself feel incredibly young again," she says. "And it's certainly not silly to spread a little bit of joy as you go through life."

He's Forever Blowing Bubbles

Some people create Web sites so they can blow their own horn. A fellow who calls himself Bubbleman would rather make a name for himself as an online bubble blower. Garry Golightly goes by the name of Bubbleman on his Web site (http://www.bubbleman.com/, shown in Figure 18-11). Many pages consist solely of poems he has written, with titles such as "bubbleosophy" and "autobubbleography." His presence online has obviously helped him to inflate himself and his passion to new dimensions.

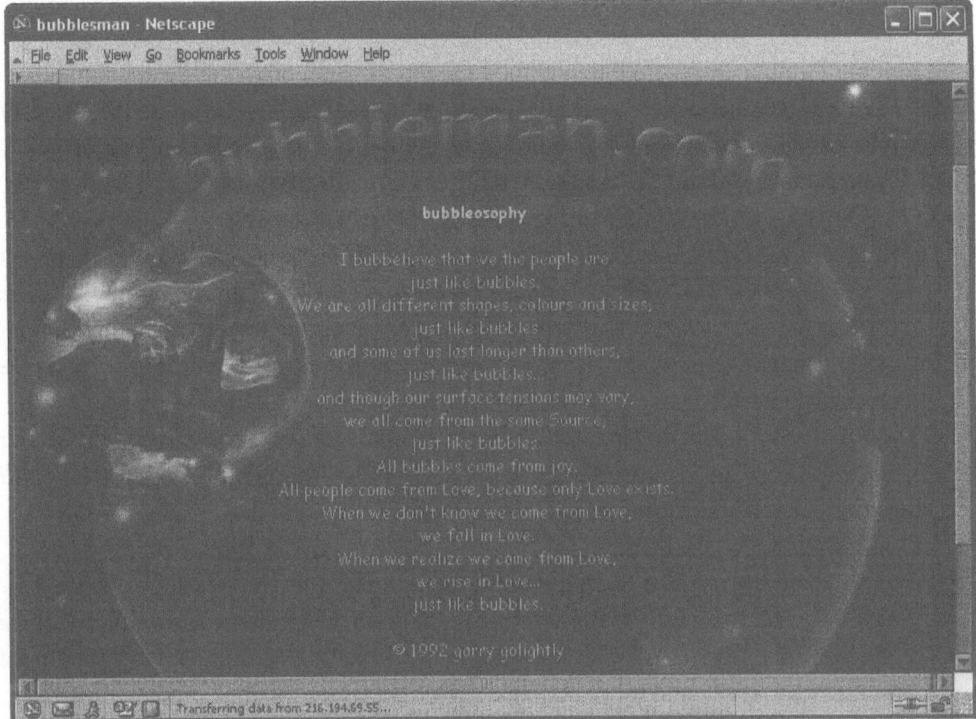

Figure 18-11. Lighter than air: Bubbleman sails through cyberspace, trailing bubbles in his wake.[11]

Kinky Communities

Some people are loners when it comes to portraying themselves on a Web site with a self-created identity or exposing intimate details of their lives (or both). But why be alone when you go online? There's not only safety in numbers, but the fun and excitement is multiplied. The following are just a few examples of online communities that allow adventurous people to try out new lifestyles, new genders, or new identities.

---

11. http://www.bubbleman.com/

One Big, Big Happy: Come Join the Baby Factory

Some families seem like baby factories. Some women probably have probably *felt* like baby factories. Only one family I know of happily bills itself as "the Baby Factory" and invites female members to live in its extended configuration of one father, several mothers, and an unspecified number of children.

It's hard to determine from the Baby Factory's Web site (http://www.babyfactory.org/) if it's for real or if it is really happening. There aren't any photos posted on it: It's a rare, all-text set of pages. The home page says the site is new; however, the date at the bottom indicates it was last updated in 1999. The two individuals who started the family, David and M. J., met one another on the Internet.

They say it's not polygamy. They say the relations between the multiple women and David are not based on sex. On the other hand, joining the Baby Factory *will* require an initiation procedure, and that procedure *does* involve sex. And there's something called the Secret Pleasure Dungeon "so that those who wish can indulge their desperate cravings by night while living in fully prim and proper denial by day." Oh, and there are the plans to make the whole formation and activities of the family into an "endless filmmaking project." If any of this sounds like your cup of tea, contact the Baby Factory at http://www.babyfactory.org/contact-us.html.

Are You a Boy, or Are You a Girl? Only the Internet Knows for Sure

One of the most mysterious and little-known areas of the Internet is the land of Multiuser Object-Oriented Systems (MOOs). MOOs are virtual environments in which people communicate with one another in creative ways. In some ways, they resemble chat rooms. But MOOs are much more: They're "playrooms" in which the rules, roles, and activities are all created by the participants. One of the largest is the oldest: LambdaMOO, which was started at the University of California at Berkeley around 1990. It has had as many as 4,000 members. A MOO was also created for fans of the television show *Babylon 5* (http://www.b5tv.com/greatmaker/news/53/).

 NOTE LambdaMOO does have a home page, and you can read about it on the Web, but you typically connect to a MOO using Telnet—which is probably why MOOs remain mysterious and an "acquired taste" on the Net. MOOs also go by the name Multi-User Dungeons (MUDs). You can find out more about MUDs at the newsgroup rec.games.mud.

MUDs and MOOs are popular venues for individuals who want to try gender switching—pretending to be someone of the opposite sex. A ponderous-sounding study called "The Social Geography of Gender-Switching in Virtual Environments on the Internet" found that relatively few participants (about 21 percent) actually do so, however. But they have provided fertile environments for cybersex: singling someone out, taking them into a private chat room, and talking them through a sexual encounter. A 1996 essay by Joab Jackson entitled "Let's Get It On Online" reported on three people who had participated in MOOs and chat rooms. A person named Rich commented the following:

> *I've actually got three different personalities on AOL. One is a bisexual male, one is a straight male, the other I play a bisexual female.... So it allows me to experiment with the other side of myself, to play around with it a little bit, and yeah, you do get aroused.... When I go online as my female screen name, I've had people ask me, "Are you really a woman?" I type back "yes" and tell them that's the end of the discussion. I have a provocative screen name. My good friend and I logged on one night and went right into the People Connection. We were not in the lobby 30 seconds, and we get three messages from three guys. They were all like "What's your measurements?" My friend and I were sitting there laughing.*

You can read the rest of the article at http://www.joabj.com/CityPaper/sex.html.

It May Be Chinese to You, but It's Greek to Me

Altering one's voice, or changing one's gender, has probably been a recurring fantasy ever since Adam met Eve. In our high-tech era, it's becoming easy to appear as the opposite sex by using a device that can change the tone of one's voice. A voice-altering machine was part of James Bond's set of gadgets in the movie *Diamonds Are Forever*. In Taiwan and China, such devices are commonly known as "gender changers." Such devices are reported to be selling well on Chinese Web sites. It's not clear exactly why. They're apparently used to play pranks on people over the phone. They may also be used by jealous husbands or wives to test whether their spouse is having an affair. There have been calls to ban the gadgets, but public security bureau officials say there is no reason to declare them illegal.

NOTE Gender bending is a popular pastime of those who play the best-selling computer game The Sims. In the game, players create virtual families and environments within which they can interact. Will Wright, the game's creator, told an audience at PC Forum in 2003 that data collected about the players indicates female players are more likely to pose as men than the other way around. However, the data collected by the game's creators also indicated that male characters were more likely to be officially ignored than females, meaning that other characters refuse to interact with them.

Home Page Wreckers

Just as people can find the love of their life (or their night) online, they can also lose their loved ones online. Because stories about love lost are almost always more juicy and interesting than those of love found, the following are some examples of relationships that have been wrecked from chat room messages or other chance online encounters.

Internet Infidelity on the Increase

"With cybersex, there is no longer any need for secret trips to obscure motels. An online liaison may even take place in the same room with one's spouse." This statement comes from Beatriz Avila Mileham, who interviewed 76 chat room participants in 2002 for her doctoral dissertation at the University of Florida. The report concludes that the Internet has made having a fling easier than ever and that "chat room cheats" are responsible for breaking up many marriages.

"All I have to do is turn on my computer, and I have thousands of women to choose from. (It) can't get any easier than that," says a 41-year-old man quoted in the report. The odd thing is that, in many cases, the cyberlovers never actually meet face to face. The participants interviewed for the report took part in two chat rooms set up on Yahoo! specifically for married people: Married but Flirting and Married and Flirting. They included construction workers, engineers, nurses, stay-at-home mothers, and corporate presidents. Some hoped for a real-world affair, some wanted only to talk about personal issues, and some wanted to engage in cybersex.

When spouses find out about the chat room "infidelities," the feelings of hurt and anger that result are just as intense as if skin-to-skin contact was involved, the report stated. Author Mileham suggests, "To prevent future problems, young couples, as well as long-term committed couples, need to talk about what role the Internet will play in their relationship."

As Home Is Rehabbed Online, Marriage Falls Apart

I can tell you from personal experience that home renovation projects are stressful on the body, the psyche, and marriages. Paul and Louise Jones seemed to have a good plan when they purchased a dilapidated house in Dorset, England. They planned to dramatically increase the value of the home through an extensive rehab project. They decided to broadcast the rehab project live over the Internet (see Figure 18-12) and persuaded more than two dozen building-supply firms to donate free supplies in return for ads. The site they established to document their efforts, http://www.internethomemakers.com/, attracted as many as 32,000 visitors each day. The project attracted as many as 400 sponsors, including Black & Decker and Laura Ashley. Everything seemed hunky-dory.

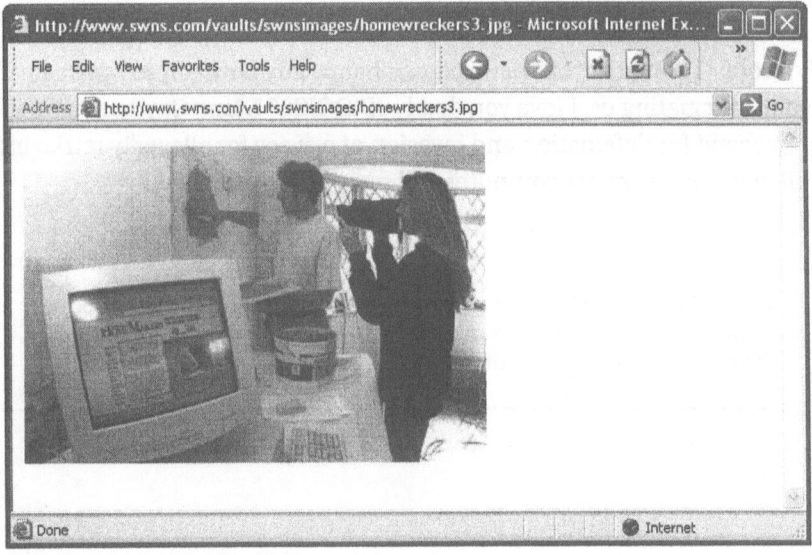

Figure 18-12. Paul and Louise Jones, the Internet homemakers, in happier times[12]

However, during the project, which took place in 1998 and 1999, Louise Jones spent hours in front of the Webcams and in the chat rooms that were set up to support the project. The chat rooms gave interested viewers a way to interact with the intrepid homemakers. It turns out that one man from Iowa contacted Louise, inquiring about more than just advice about tiling adhesive or drywall compound. They began to exchange e-mails and more e-mails, and one thing led to another.

---

12. http://www.swns.com/vaults/swnsimages/homewreckers3.jpg

Eventually, the value of the home did indeed jump from 98,000 to 320,000 British pounds as a result of the Jones's efforts. But as a result of the Iowan and Louise's efforts, none of the Jones family ended up living in the house. She reportedly told the *Times* of London, "As far as I'm concerned, the marriage is over. I have met somebody over the Internet. We met in a chat room. It was all to do with the project. He had been watching the Webcam."

E-Mail from "the Weasel" Helps Break Up Marriage

In 1996, a New Jersey man named John Goydan filed for divorce, accusing his wife of conducting a "virtual" affair on the computer with an individual she met on America Online who called himself the Weasel. He claimed that his wife, Diane Goydan, and the Weasel were planning to consummate the affair at a New Hampshire bed and breakfast.

In one of the e-mail messages quoted in court documents, the Weasel allegedly wrote: "I gotta tell you that I am one happy guy now and so much at peace again anticipating us. I love you dearly. XXOOXX." Diane Goydan, in turn, sued her husband for defamation and invasion of privacy for allegedly retrieving her e-mail messages from her computer and saving them on disk.

 NOTE The site Safer Dating (http://www.saferdating.com/) collects real-life stories and e-mail messages from couples who became involved in adultery disputes.

Random Googling

There's no shortage of Web sites that enable people to dress up and portray themselves in new and exciting ways. The following list contains a few I found noteworthy—some I found myself and some that turned up after using the search service Google (http://www.google.com/):

- **Powergen Italia (http://www.powergenitalia.com/)**: It's an Italian power company. It makes batteries. It had no idea when it chose its domain name that it might mean something else in English.

- **Webcams**: An astonishing number of people, objects, and locations around the world are being watched by Webcams. The Old Faithful Geyser Webcam is at http://www.nps.gov/yell/oldfaithfulcam.htm. The Star City Mall in Lincoln, Nebraska, is at http://www.starcitymall.com/webcam/. The Sixth Floor Museum in Dallas, Texas, points a Webcam out the window where Lee Harvey Oswald allegedly shot President John F. Kennedy in 1963 (http://www.earthcam.com/jfk/). Cloudcam Live is pointed at the sky, simply documenting cloud formations as they drift by (http://www.vmsehy.com/cloudcam/live/index.htm).

- **Gender Swapping (http://www.rider.edu/~suler/psycyber/genderswap.html)**: A search for the terms "gender switching" turned up this essay by Dr. John Suler of Rider University in which he explores the concept of gender switching in MOOs. The page is part of the intriguing Web site Psychology of Cyberspace.

Part Six
Big (and Not So Big) Business

CHAPTER 19

E-Commerce Comedies in Babylon

THE PROCESS OF BUYING or selling something online—in other words, the process known as *e-commerce*—is a totally different proposition than in the "real" world. In the real world, you can squeeze that rubber ducky to see if it squeaks or issues the sound of a "raspberry." You can see if your merchant is sporting "warning signs" of untrustworthiness such as a pound of gold chains, a Nazi helmet, or a used prison uniform. You can then act on such indicators. If you are a seller, you can see someone sign his or her charge card, and you can match the blemishes on the buyer's face with the mug on the ID card in front of you to make sure they are the same, more or less.

You can't do any of those things online. Buyers and sellers never see one another, which adds an element of danger to online commerce. So does the fact that you can buy 1,000 pounds of pink flamingoes with just a few mouse clicks. Some enterprising sellers have tried to take advantage of how perfect the Net is for impulse buyers. They've offered some strange things for sale online. Others have used yet another unique feature of e-commerce: the ability to put reams of supporting information online about products ranging from bandages and wart remover to my discontinued 1979 guitar amplifier.

Accordingly, this chapter describes some weird commercial products that have entire Web sites devoted to them. It also delves into the many strange attempts to sell online that have bombed. And, of course, no chapter about e-commerce would be complete without descriptions of the attempts to sell human beings, various parts of human bodies, or other bizarre things online.

Dot-Com Disasters

When the Web first began to get really popular, most traditional retailers (with notable exceptions such as Lands' End) were slow to embrace it as a source of sales revenue. That opened the way for some innovative entrepreneurs to try some unusual approaches to selling online. Their problem was not imagination or chutzpah. They often had good ideas but lacked the experience needed to make a business successful: quick fulfillment, good customer service, extensive inventories, and all the "back-end" processes that big catalog retailers do well.

Occasionally, though, even the "Netrepreneurs" had terrible ideas—real head-scratchers that left you muttering, "What were they thinking?" The following are some examples.

Stupid Online Pet Tricks

If you have ever had to run to the store late at night to feed your hungry pet, you know what a nuisance it is. Along those lines, John C. Dvorak nominated his own "Worst Internet Idea Ever" in his column for *PC Magazine* (http://www.pcmag.com/print_article/0,3048,a=28678,00.asp): delivering pet food by FedEx. Many dot-coms promised such service, but few could actually deliver.

For example, the online retailer Pet Express promised its customers that it would deliver all pet food orders within two days. Unfortunately, it did not always come through on this promise, and too many pooches and kitties went to bed hungry. The company ran into problems with order processing, supplier delays, and computer breakdowns. The Federal Trade Commission (FTC) launched an investigation into the company's shipping problems. Pet Express eventually reached a settlement with the FTC, but that didn't prevent the company from going paws-up.

NOTE I'm talking about the Pet Express that used to be located at http://www.petXpress.com/ and that later changed its name to ePets.net—not the Pet Express that actually seems to be delivering pet food successfully in the United Kingdom or the other businesses that use the name Pet Express.

Socking Itself Senseless: Pets.com

Here's a cyberspace version of a Rorschach test: When I say something, you type whatever pops into your head. Ready?

Dot-com failure.

That wasn't hard, was it? Did you respond with "Pets.com?" When you think about dot-com companies that went bust with a bang, many people automatically think of Pets.com. If nothing else, Pets.com deserves credit for being a trailblazer, a shining example of how retailers went public with high stock prices and then came crashing to financial ruin on the Web, a marker that many other failed dot-com ventures unfortunately tried all too hard to meet.

Pets.com was founded in 1998, at a time when it looked like practically anyone could succeed at selling online. Financial experts said Pets.com would be worth billions. It got financial backing from Amazon.com. In January 2000, the company made its most famous move, spending more than $3 million for 30 seconds of advertising during the Super Bowl. It also did something that some high-profile e-tailers thought would gain them more exposure: It started an offline print magazine that was distributed to veterinary offices.

Pets.com is best known not only for its failure but for its sock puppet mascot. The "spokesperson" for the company was a sock puppet that sang songs such as "Spinning Wheel," which had oddly prophetic lyrics that seem in retrospect to describe the company's rise and fall: "What goes up, must come down...." The sock puppet attained a cult status transcending that of the company it represented. At the height of the sock puppet craze, the Web site MBA Applicant published a story claiming that the sock puppet was planning to enroll at the Wharton School of Business (see Figure 19-1). A book even came out entitled *Me by Me: The Pets.com Sock Puppet Book* (Pocket Books, 2000).

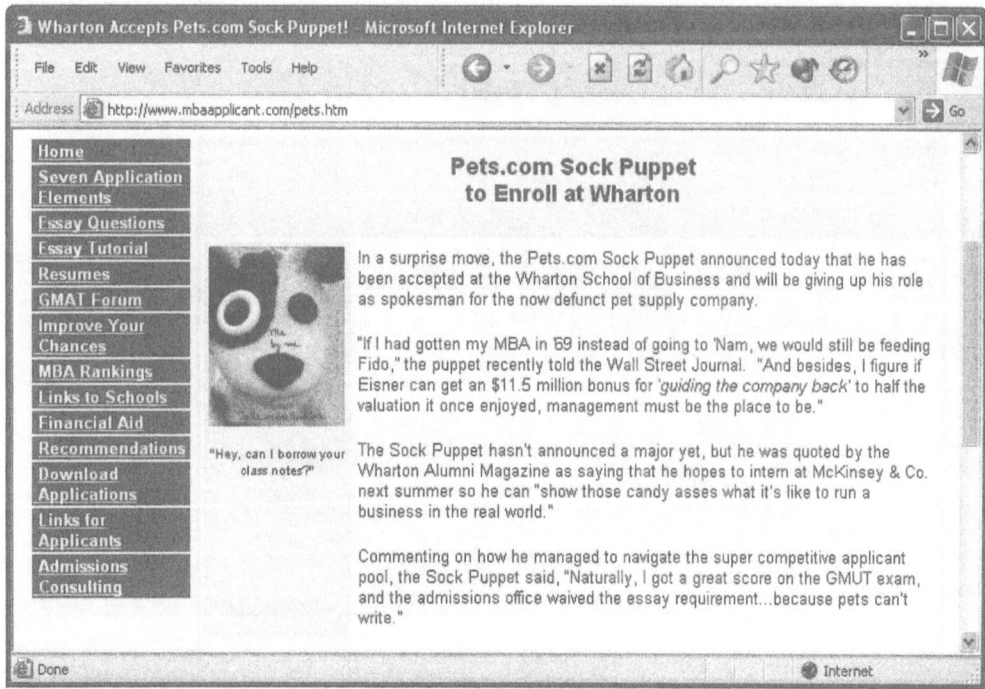

Figure 19-1. Maybe Pets.com should have followed its mascot's example and enrolled in business school.[1]

---

1. http://www.mbaaplicant.com/pets.htm

TIP The MBA Applicant page (http://www.mbaapplicant.com/ pets.htm) contains a link to a sound file of the sock puppet singing "If You Leave Me Now" by the group Chicago. *Me by Me* is still available on Amazon.com; you can relive your sock puppet days of yore for a couple of bucks—or, if you manage your money like Pets.com, you can download the e-book version of *Me by Me* for a mere $9.99.

Here, too, Pets.com stepped in the wrong direction. The company was slow to take advantage of the puppet's popularity and only began selling stuffed sock puppets in spring 2000 when it was mired in a financial tailspin. It sold 10,000 of the $20 stuffed puppets in the first week. Shortly thereafter, the actor who portrayed the sock puppet went on strike along with members of the Screen Actors Guild. The sock puppet got his own fan club, of course (http://sockpuppet.us/), which preserves clips of his TV spots for the ages (see Figure 19-2).

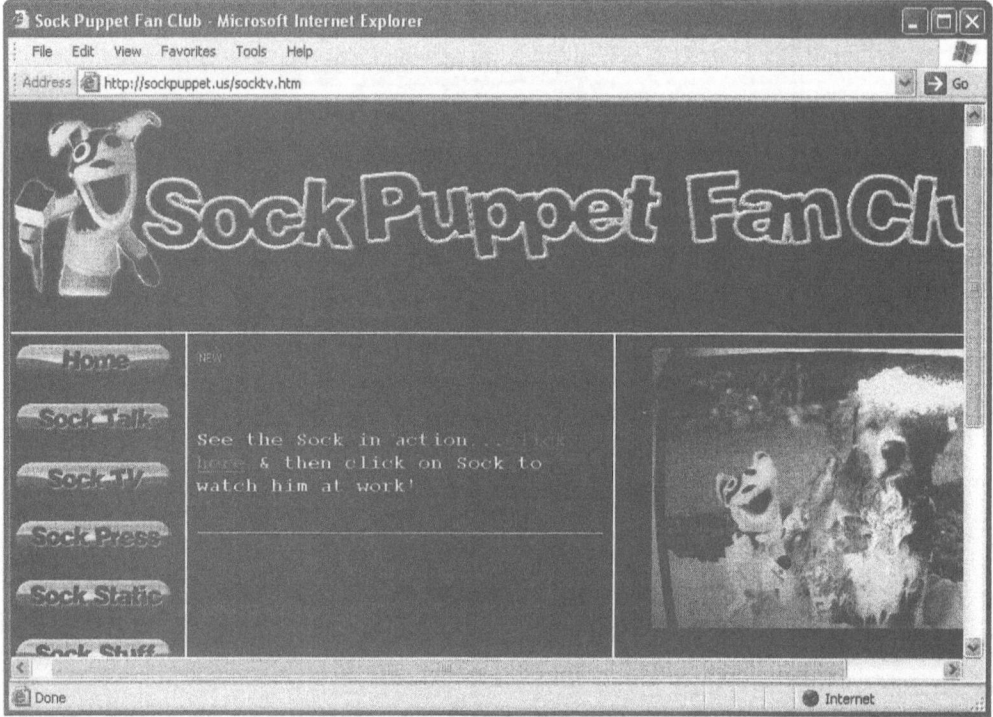

Figure 19-2. Though Pets.com is no more, its sock puppet will live forever in cyberspace.[2]

---

2. http://sockpuppet.us/socktv.htm

In February 2000, the company held its initial public stock offering and raised $82.5 million. This was despite the fact that Pets.com had lost $42.4 million during the fourth quarter of 1999. But that money didn't go far: By November of the same year, Pets.com was out of business.

Success, or the lack thereof, has not hurt the career of Pets.com's Chief Executive Officer (CEO), Julie Wainwright, however. The same executive who oversaw the sock puppet campaign and the rise and fall of the online retailer was named CEO of the photo enhancement service Bellamax in August 2003.

Dot-Com Downers Recall Days of Whine and Closures

Some studies contend that a little wine every day is good for your health. Perhaps all those dot-bombs (companies that bombed after the turn of the 21st century, when the economy took a nose dive) should have served their employees some fruit of the vine every day to keep the bankruptcy court away. Even though those companies are no more, their employees still had a chance to toast the future with a $1,500 bottle of cabernet sauvignon if they won an unusual contest.

The Dot-Com Bomb contest, held by the online wine retailer Secret Cellars, offered the pricey bottle of 1996 Screaming Eagle wine to the individual who— in 100 words or less—could tell the saddest tale of an Internet company's demise. In the bleak winter of 2000, more than 2,000 people e-mailed their stories of woe to the SecretCellars.com Web site. The prize was said to be an especially popular vintage with onetime dot-com millionaires.

One entrant told the story of an unnamed New York company that went into a "death spiral" the moment it was created: After six months, with no deals struck and $100 million down the drain, some employees—including the CEO and chief operating officer—were one day "greeted by a security guard who confiscates all their stuff and padlocks the door." Others told of ending up at the Bowl-a-Rama or working for porn Web sites.

The winner was a 31-year-old from San Francisco named Scott Bingham, who lost his job at Egreetings.com and fell on hard times:

> *Hello, SecretCellars.com. I was born in 1969, and that's when my problems began and continued until my prestigious hiring at Egreetings.com. Egreetings.com validated my entire previous existence. All those years of college; all those failed relationships; all the beatings—none of it mattered because I was an Internet professional with ownership interest in a company poised to go public. I was finally on the cutting edge, smart and getting laid. Egreetings.com's public offering failed, and they fired everyone. Now I'm broke, and I work for a free porn Web site. My mother cries when she sees me. Alcohol is, once again, my only friend.*

This runner-up's brief story is also typical of many that were submitted:

I worked at Priceline's WebHouse club. At 5:00 on Wednesday, October 4th, we received an e-mail saying we had a mandatory company-wide meeting the next day at 8:00 a.m. The strange thing was that no one was ever in the office that early! When we arrived, our founder, Jay Walker, stood on top of a desk in the middle of the office and announced that we were closing our operations! Just like that, no warning, no slow wind down, just closing our virtual doors right away. It was the most disheartening day of my life.

The misfortunes of others have turned out to be gravy for many other Web sites. The Dot-Com Bomb contest, which was suggested to Secret Cellars by a public relations firm, gained a barrel full of attention in the media. Other sites have held similar contests and made tracking dot-com failures their main source of content.

TIP   A Web site called Failurenalia (http://www.netsurf.ch/failurenalia.html) contains links to other sites that track the failures of dot-com companies. One of the best-known sites is a site called FuckedCompany.com (http://www.fuckedcompany.com/), which even produced a book full of dot-com tales of woe.

A Truly Scary Story: The Rise and Fall of Boo.com

The many stories that are being documented about the rise and fall of dot-com companies all echo one company's story. Boo.com epitomized everything that was wrong with e-commerce and with applying Web design to the buying and selling of merchandise online. Today, Boo.com and Pets.com are the poster children for what not to do with a Web-based business. But to my mind, Boo.com was distinguished not just for its lavish spending and awful business practices but for its excessive Web site design.

Don't get me wrong: Boo.com had a well-designed, professionally created site. It's just that everything was pushed to the *n*th degree in terms of technical requirements in a way that made it almost impossible for regular folks to actually use the site. It was ahead of its time in terms of producing pop-up windows and using three-dimensional animations and little bits of Web page programming called *JavaScripts* to show off products. Technology was part of the lure of Boo.com: The site promised to be able to allow shoppers to "spin" products in 360 degrees on the screen with a virtual-reality utility. In addition, a shopping utility named Miss Boo was there, popping up all over the place to help you locate products (see Figure 19-3). At the time Boo.com was created, however, most Web surfers had only dial-up connections, and simply viewing the site and waiting for pages to load was a time-consuming, laborious process.

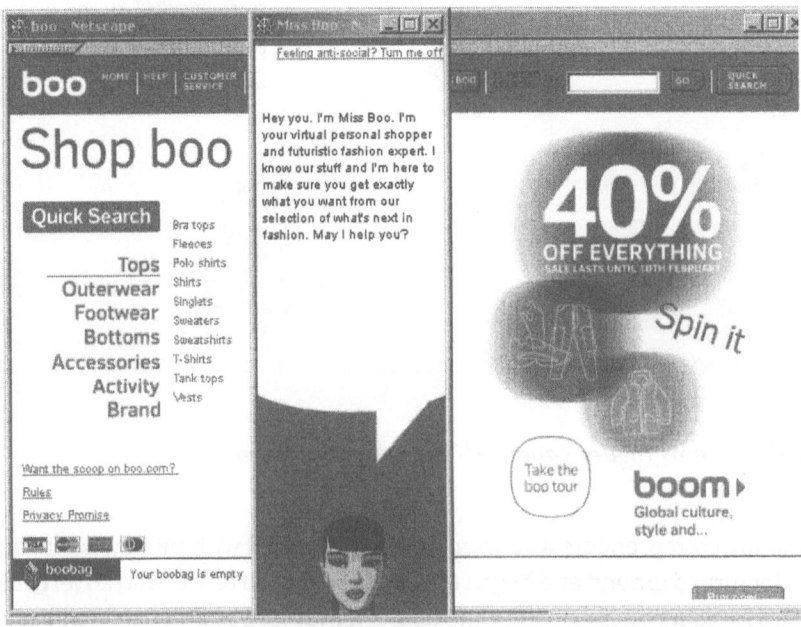

Figure 19-3. Boo-hoo: An overdesigned, difficult-to use Web site and a bad financial plan crashed Boo.com.[3]

Boo.com was started by two 29-year-old Swedish entrepreneurs, Ernst Malmsten and Kajsa Leander, both depicted in Figure 19-4 on a site created by a former employee, Patrick Gallagher. Leander knew something about fashion because she was a professional model. The site would provide service around the world in seven different languages, with the ability to handle multiple currencies. They were excellent promoters; they advertised the site in trade journals and fashion magazines before the site went online. They were able to raise $125 million from some people with deep pockets, including the Benetton family, the French luxury goods merchant Bernard Arnault, and even the investment firm Goldman Sachs.

---

3. http://www.boo.com/

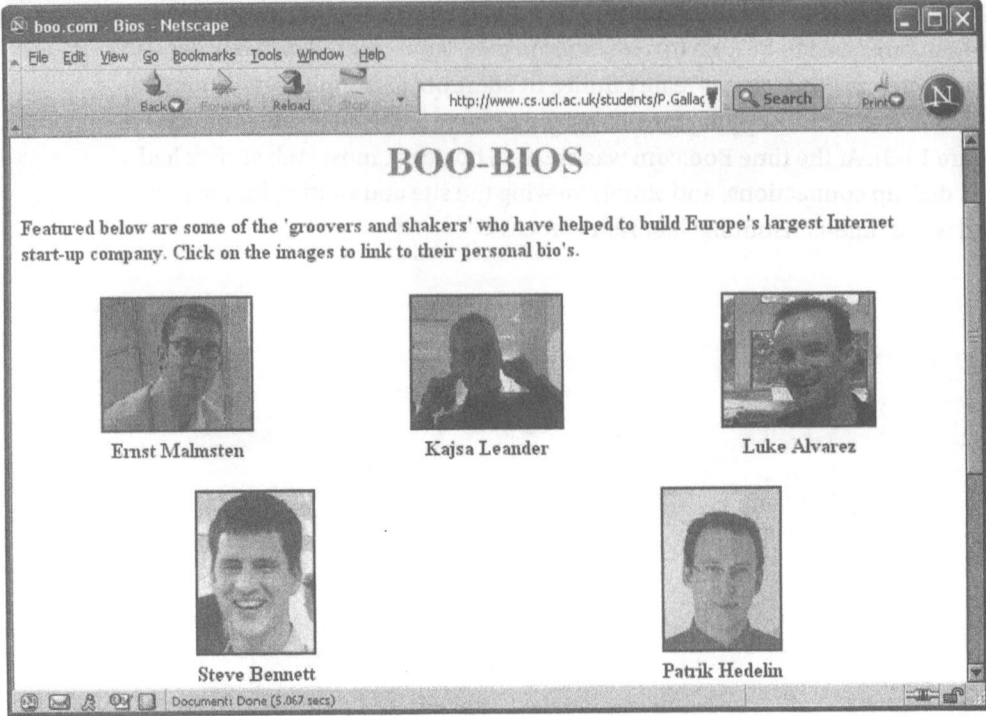

Figure 19-4. Part of Boo.com's rogues' gallery of failed dot-com executives[4]

Like many entrepreneurs who were suddenly flooded with money, Malmsten and Leander turned around and began to spend lavishly on offices and advertising. Rather than focusing on making the site user-friendly and building a distribution system, they bought an expensive office on Carnaby Street in London and then opened other offices in New York, Stockholm, and Paris. Employees were given their own laptops and Palm Pilots that they were encouraged to use both at home and at work. Rather than using the regular postal services, Boo.com used FedEx to send mail.

In just six months, Boo.com burned through all of its money and had to file for bankruptcy. Other managers attempted to resurrect the site later, but that attempt failed, too. Boo.com helped write the script that all too many would-be online retailers have followed: Raise tons of cash, overspend on advertising and daily expenses, lose money every step of the way, take the company public and raise millions, and then file for bankruptcy within a year.

The Web page at http://www.ernstmalmsten.com/ is entitled Ernst Malmsten Failed Business Man Dot Com." It contains an interesting message that apparently

---

4. http://www.cs.ucl.ac.uk/students/P.Gallagher/boo/index.htm

was created by his disgruntled Internet hosting service. The page contains Malmsten's address and phone number and a brief farewell message from Malmsten to his employees. At the bottom of the page, you find the following note: "Incidentally this domain is for sale, if Ernst or one of his *many* friends is prepared to settle my unpaid invoices this domain could be yours...." Perhaps Malmsten will be able to pay some bills from sales of his book, *Boo Hoo: $135 Million,18 Months...A Dot.Com Story from Concept to Catastrophe* (Arrow, 2001).

NOTE   Two Web sites refer to Boo.com and are apparently related to the company's 400 or so ex-employees. The site at http://www.postboo.com/ appears to be a tool used by the Boo.com designers. It contains sets of links to other online shopping sites. The Boo.com ex-employee white pages (http://www.vodkagrapefruit.com/) use the company's trial Web site name: vodkagrapefruit.com.

---

eBay Disasters

eBay has quickly become the world's garbage dump. Yes, you do find some precious objects on eBay—I have myself. Yes, it's a great place to uncover all kinds of hard-to-find objects, such as those toys you had when you were a kid. You can sell things such as rare beer cans for $19,000 or unusual fishing lures for tens of thousands of dollars, which encourages people to put anything up for sale. Sellers have tried to peddle everything from—well, the following are just a few examples.

Pieces of the Space Shuttle Wreckage

The phrase "anything to make a buck" applies to the individuals who offered pieces of the space shuttle wreckage online. Within just 12 hours after the shuttle Columbia broke up in early February 2003, killing the seven astronauts on board, an auction labeled "Columbia Space Shuttle Debris" with an initial bid price of $10,000 appeared online. A second entitled "Shuttle Columbia Debris Wreckage" was offered with an initial bid of $5,000. Both were pulled from the site, as well as a handful of similar offerings and domain names such as columbiadebris.com that someone attempted to auction off on eBay.

Buy My Family, and Become an Author, for Just $5 Million

Television writer Steve Young, who worked on well-known shows such as *A Family Affair*, put his family up for auction on eBay for a minimum bid of $5 million. He explained in a well-written auction listing:

> *If you are the highest bidder, you will receive the adoration from two congenial children with an affinity for heart-warming, homemade birthday cards and copiousness, candy-coated smiles for both family and legal benefactors. All that, plus my wife!*

(In a later comment, Young assured potential buyers that their relationship with his wife would be platonic.) Young told reporters that he was thinking of the medieval system of patronage when he created the auction. He was seeking a patron because he was having a hard time finding work. What's more, he offered to give his patron credit for any writing he did after the purchase. eBay was not amused—they removed the auction from their site, saying it did not meet their user guidelines.

Need a Body Part? A Kidney?

Over the years people have attempted to sell various items related to the human body on eBay. A lock of John F. Kennedy's hair, a set of fingernail clippings…perhaps the most outrageous came from not one but two individuals who attempted to sell their own kidneys. In 1999, a man offered one of his two kidneys for a minimum bid of $25,000 on eBay. The auction description included this statement: "You can choose either kidney. Buyer pays all transplant and medical costs. Of course, only one for sale, as I need the other one to live. Serious bids only." The bidding soared to almost $6 million before the sale was removed from the site by eBay: The buying and selling of human organs is illegal in the United States.

World's Longest French Fry

An eBay seller who goes by the User ID "reeledit" must be a master of promotion. After uncovering a six-and-three-fourths-inch long French fry at a Culver's restaurant in Wisconsin Rapids, Wisconsin, the seller resisted the urge to chomp on it and instead turned it into a gold mine. As reported on the Web site Weird Auctions (http://www.weirdauctions.com/), reeledit submitted the fry to the *Guinness Book of World Records*, offered it for sale on eBay, attracted more than 39,000 viewers, and actually sold it for $202.50. Reportedly, reeledit even marketed some "World's Longest French Fry" T-shirts, but they weren't up for sale on eBay at this writing. The original listing in Figure 19-5 is reproduced from the Weird Auctions Web site.

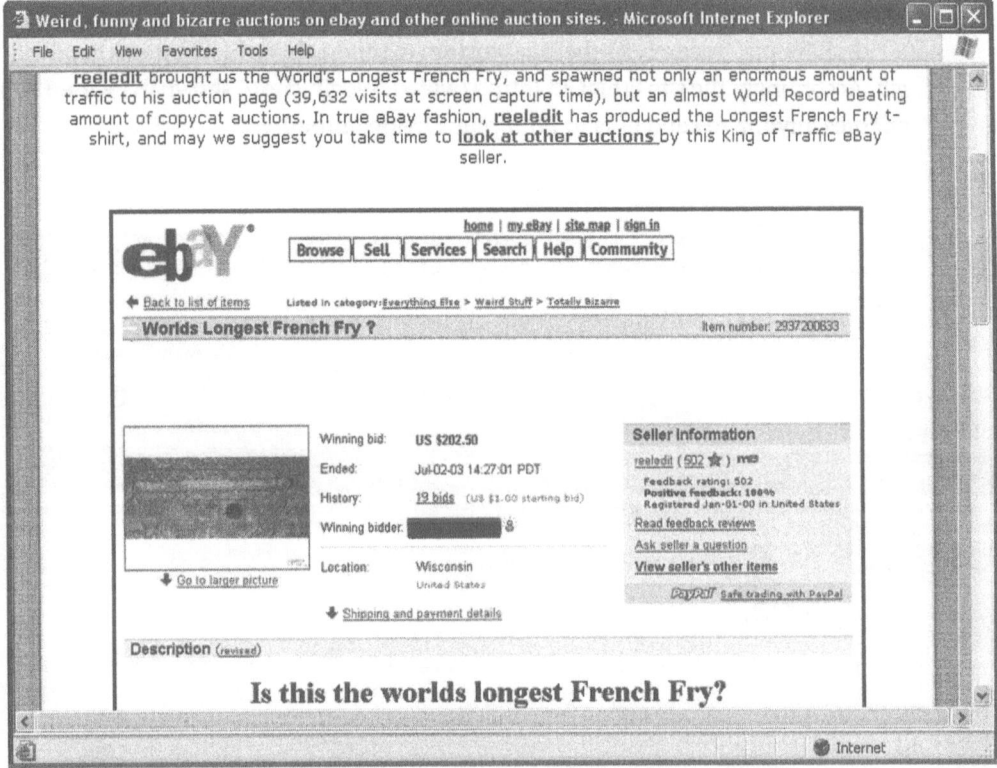

Figure 19-5. This spud's no dud: the French fry that sold for $202.50[5]

Weird and Wacky E-Commerce Hall of Fame

Usually, when people need to clean out some odd objects cluttering their closets, they hold a garage sale. In extreme cases, they simply pile everything next to the garbage. Those who are wired to the Internet have an alternative. Can you guess what it is? The following sections not only describe some oddball products that have been bought or sold online but some commercial merchandise that has been documented in excruciating detail, just for those few connoisseurs who love them.

---

5.   http://www.weirdauctions.com/preserves.cfm/hurl/pageid=53/preserves.cfm

Reach Out and Touch Someone...with a Sheep

A box of candy—really, so predictable. Flowers? Too passé. The next time you're looking for something to get that special someone—particularly if that someone happens to originate from Ethiopia—ship them a sheep via the Internet. Or perhaps a fattened ram will show them you care.

In Ethiopia, it seems, it's the local custom to send a sheep or a ram as a goodwill gift. Accordingly, the site EthioGift (http://www.ethiogift.com/, shown in Figure 19-6) enables anyone to send gifts to Ethiopians living abroad.

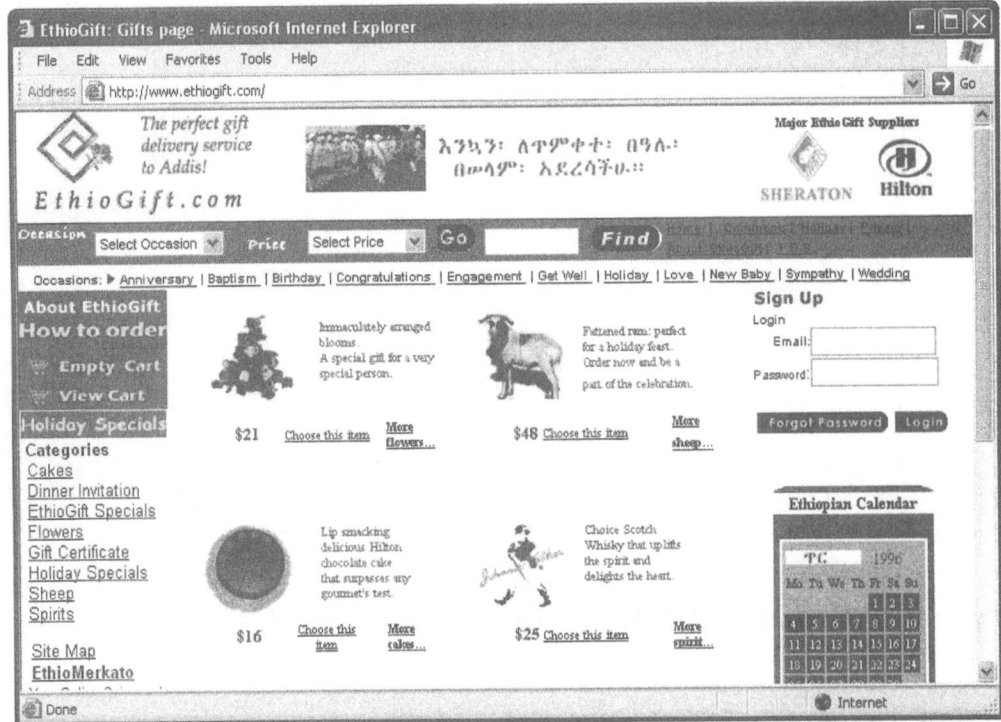

Figure 19-6. The Internet allows those living abroad to send gifts that locals will appreciate, and that includes sheep.[6]

EthioGift was started by Dawit Bekele, who was born in Ethiopia, obtained a doctorate degree in computer science, and lived in France for nine years. Bekele knew firsthand how difficult it could be to send gifts home to friends and family or vice versa. He knew that Ethiopians aren't accustomed to sending or receiving

---

6.   http://www.ethiogift.com/

flowers as gifts. But sheep are very common. So he worked with suppliers such as the Addis Ababa Hilton hotel and local livestock merchants to provide gifts that Ethiopians themselves would appreciate. In case you have a special someone who happens to be Ethiopian, you might consider sending the following gift items offered on the site:

- A medium sheep, guaranteed to be at least 25 kilograms (kg) in weight, for $48

- A big sheep of 30 kg or more

- A very big sheep of at least 35 kg

- A kilogram of Ethiopian Mokarar coffee for $16

- A holiday gift special of Mama Konjit's Mocha Cake and a medium sheep for $76

- Dinner or lunch invitations to one of several hotels or restaurants in Addis Ababa

The company's terms of service state that although the sheep will be delivered promptly, it cannot guarantee that the animal will be "of the region or type of preference of the customer."

 NOTE The gift of live animals is certain to be appreciated by poor people living in underprivileged countries. World Vision's online gift catalog (http://www.great-gifts.org/home.asp) lets you send fruit trees, drinking water, or farm animals to people around the world who really need them.

What's in a Name? Buy Yourself a Lordship and Find Out

Tired of other people "lording" it over you? You can show them who really rates by making yourself a real lord, lady, baron, or baronness. Instead of Joe Blow, you can become Sir Joe Blow, Viscount Joe Blow, and so on.

Such titles are sold on the Elite Titles Web site (http://www.elitetitles.net/, shown in Figure 19-7). The site explains how it's possible to purchase a title for yourself rather than inherit one or be granted one by royalty or the government:

"Under International and English law, 'You have the right to call yourself, and be known as anything you like' provided there is no fraudulent intention in the process of any such changes to a person's identity." The company that runs the site first checks to make sure no one else exists with the same title that has been granted by the government or royalty. "Obviously, one would not wish to cause upset or distress to that person," the site explains.

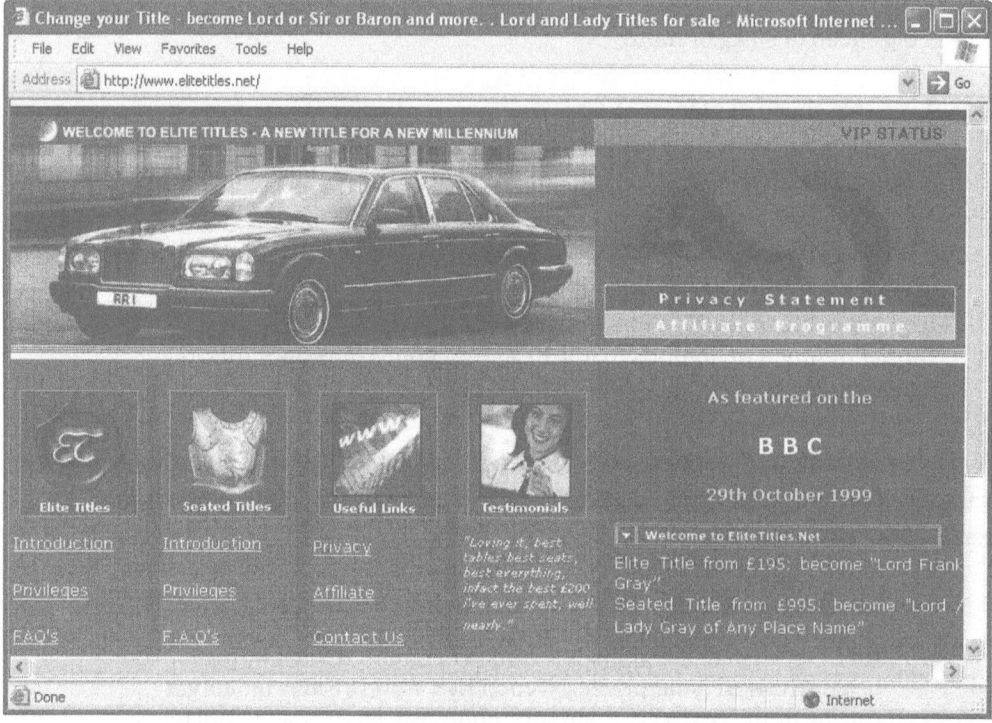

Figure 19-7. You, too, can be a lord or lady of the manor for the right price.[7]

Apparently, if a lord or lady in Great Britain has a parcel of land to be sold, the buyers can then be called Lord and Lady as well. When I visited, titles such as Lord and Lady of Hickling and Lord and Lady of Butterdale were available for 995 British pounds.

What exactly do you gain other than a sense of "coolness" from having a title such as Sir, Lady, or Lord in front of your name? Not much—but the site claims people treat you with a different attitude when you have one. Airlines might upgrade

---

7. http://www.elitetitles.net/

you; hotel staff might treat you with complementary fruit and wine or the best room in the house. The Elite Titles site states the following:

> *With a title in front of your name you will experience a difference in people's attitudes. The moment they know you are a "Sir, Lady, Lord, etc," you will be treated like some sort of royalty or famous film star.*

They cite, as an example, Richard, Seventh Earl of Bradford, who uses his title to promote his restaurant and other business interests, as well as the interest of those who sponsor him. It turns out that the Earl of Bradford has created several Web sites, including Virtual London (http://www.virtual-london.com/), which is said to receive more than 40,000 visits each week. You can read about the Seventh Earl of Bradford and get some ideas for what to do with your own title at http://www.porters.uk.com/covent/movers/default.asp?ID=8.

Psst...Do You Have Any of Those Vegan Condoms?

My first job was that of a clerk in a pharmacy. I well remember the embarrassed-looking individuals who would bypass me and go straight to the pharmacist with a request for a product of a "delicate" nature. For those who are easily embarrassed (or perhaps too young), the Internet provides blissful anonymity. Just go to the Blushingbuyer Web site (http://www.blushingbuyer.com/), and pick out one of those products you might be embarrassed to ask for in person:

- Men's and women's incontinence products

- Condomi condoms, "the only condoms approved by the vegan society," scented with banana or chocolate

- Wind-eze and other products designed to help those with stomach pain and bloating caused "by the build up of trapped wind"

- Sprays, inserts, and other products for those with smelly feet

- Snoreeze snoring relief spray and other antisnoring cures

- Waxes and other hair-removal products

- Saucy socks and slippers, with X-rated drawings on them

The site also includes reviews of many products supposedly submitted by satisfied customers. Here is one endorsement from a satisfied condom user:

"I've tried these on two women, and they both thought they'd died and gone to heaven…believe me, get them, get them now!"

Bone Up on Animal Husbandry—Order a Skeleton

They say beauty is only skin deep, but what's left after the skin and flesh is removed must be considered beautiful by the people who frequent The American HeadHunter Web site (http://www.americanheadhunters.com/). This site primarily sells skeletons of various animals. The animals, or what is left of them, are arranged in display cases. They are intended for use in classrooms.

Besides domestic animal skeletons such as dogs, cats, and rabbits, The American Headhunter also offers more exotic animals such as Macaque monkey skeletons ($1,700) or sloth skeletons ($2,000).

The most bizarre and entertaining offerings, however, are included on the Miscellaneous page. The list of oddities available includes the following:

- Preserved raccoon feet ($12 each)

- Preserved domestic cat feet ($15 each)

- Raccoon penis ($4.50; there is a photo included on the site)

- Snake fang earrings ($15 per set)

- Emu eggs ($20)

If you consider yourself an expert on bones, take the monthly contest the company holds at http://www.americanheadhunters.com/contest.html; if you identify the skull or other bones shown, you win a $5 gift certificate—more than enough to get your own raccoon penis.

The Band-Aid Museum: 75 Years of Ouchless Healing

Sometimes the most interesting and unusual commercial products found online aren't for sale at all. Rather, they are commemorated online by people who love them and never seem to tire talking about them.

Consider the humble Band-Aid, one of those products so well-known that its brand name has been given to an entire class of remedies for cuts and scratches. You'll find everything you want to know about these popular household products at the Virtual Band-Aid Museum Site (http://www.savetz.com/bandaid/, shown in

Figure 19-8). As the proprietor of the museum, Kevin Savetz, tells it, he and his wife purchased a 50-year-old house in northern California in December 1994. The previous owner didn't throw anything away and had inherited an extensive collection of Band-Aid boxes, which were used to store small nails, washers, bolts, and other hardware. Savetz decided to share his "find" with the rest of cyberspace.

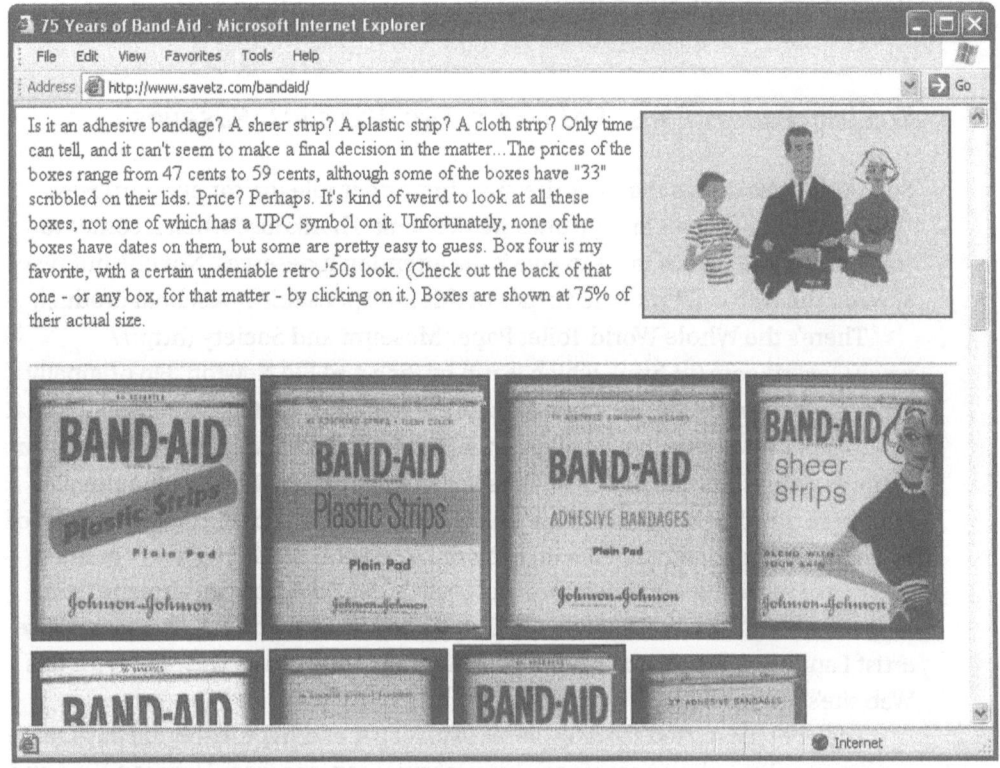

Figure 19-8. Contributors from around cyberspace have helped create this museum to Band-Aid boxes.[8]

What makes this site such a rich source of information about Band-Aids is not just Savetz's own fascination with them (which is pretty considerable) but the contributions that others have made and that have been incorporated into the museum. Back in 1996, after the museum had been online for a year, a representative of the Johnson & Johnson Company, which makes the product in question, contacted Savetz. However, it didn't complain about any sort of copyright infringement. Rather, the employee provided facts about Band-Aids, such as that they date back

---

8. http://www.savetz.com/bandaid/

to 1921. Other Band-Aid collectors have contributed many other photos. One sent a photo of himself as a child having a Band-Aid applied by his mother. The Band-Aid site, however, is just one of a Web ring of unusual museums: Others include a shrine to the musical group the Cars (http://members.fortunecity.com/cleonti/), one devoted to nails (http://home.houston.rr.com/datenails/), one devoted to sugar packets of the sort found in restaurants (http://www.the.millerfamily.name/sugar/, and did you know collectors of these things are called *sucrologists*?), one devoted to banana labels (http://www.beckymartz.com/), and on and on....

Toilet Paper Fans Roll Out Two Virtual Museums

Sometimes the things that play the most important role (or, for our purposes, "roll") in our daily lives are the ones we overlook. Thankfully, when it comes to toilet paper, the Web is there to give it the attention it deserves. Not one but two sites on the Web celebrate the virtues of this indispensable household product.

There's the Whole World Toilet Paper Museum and Society (http://www.tagyerit.com/tp.htm), which is run by Rich and Flo Newton. Flo originally envisioned the museum as a parody of all the real clubs that make everyday, trivial things great value (see the list of unusual museums previously in this chapter for some examples). In the late 1970s, she began asking friends and acquaintances who were traveling to bring back a souvenir that wouldn't cost money—a sheet of toilet paper signed and dated with a short description of where it was obtained. She began receiving donations from all over the world—from an airplane flying over the Atlantic, from artist Edward Gorey's house, from the loft of performance artist Laurie Anderson, and from Butte, Montana (pronounced as "butt" for this Web site's purposes).

Then people started sending pieces of toilet paper that probably did have some monetary value—they were signed by celebrities ranging from Harrison Ford and Penny Marshall to musician Leon Russell. Figure 19-9 shows two pieces signed by Madonna (on the left) and counterculture philosopher Ram Dass (on the right).

The donations converted the parody of a collection into exactly the thing Newton was mocking—she became a real toilet paper collector, and her museum really began to hold objects of value. The Web site that describes the museum's contents now contains a history of toilet paper, links to other toilet paper resources, and poems called "Excerpts from the Book of Toilet Paper (Excretial 10:29-38)."

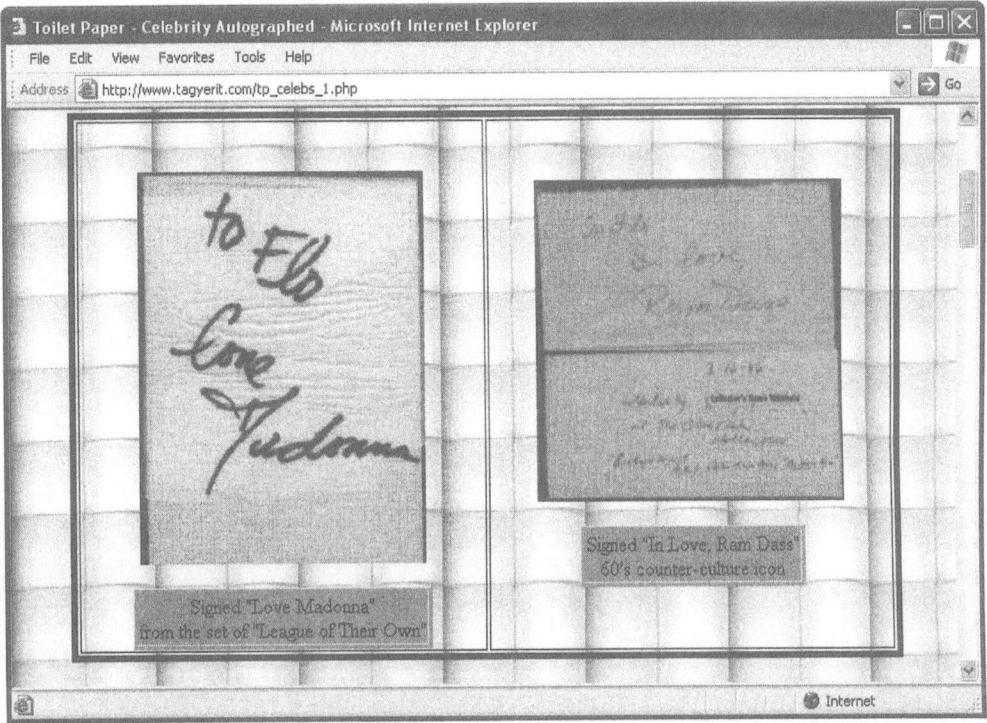

Figure 19-9. No longer the butt of jokes, this museum has managed to absorb a real toilet paper collection.[9]

There's also the Virtual Toilet Paper Museum (http://nobodys-perfect.com/vtpm/visitorsguide.html). This site also has celebrity-signed toilet paper, including a pack of Charmin signed by one of the most visible figures in toilet paperdom, television's Mr. Whipple. You'll find antique, World War II GI toilet paper and something called "electric" toilet paper. The site is set up like a "real" art museum, with exhibit halls featuring works of art that celebrate toilet paper from a wide variety of perspectives. These include the little-known work by "Michelangelo" shown in Figure 19-10. The Over or Under feature explores what the site simply calls the Great Debate: Do you roll the toilet paper so that it comes out over the top or under the bottom?

9.   http://www.tagyerit.com/tp_celebs_1.php

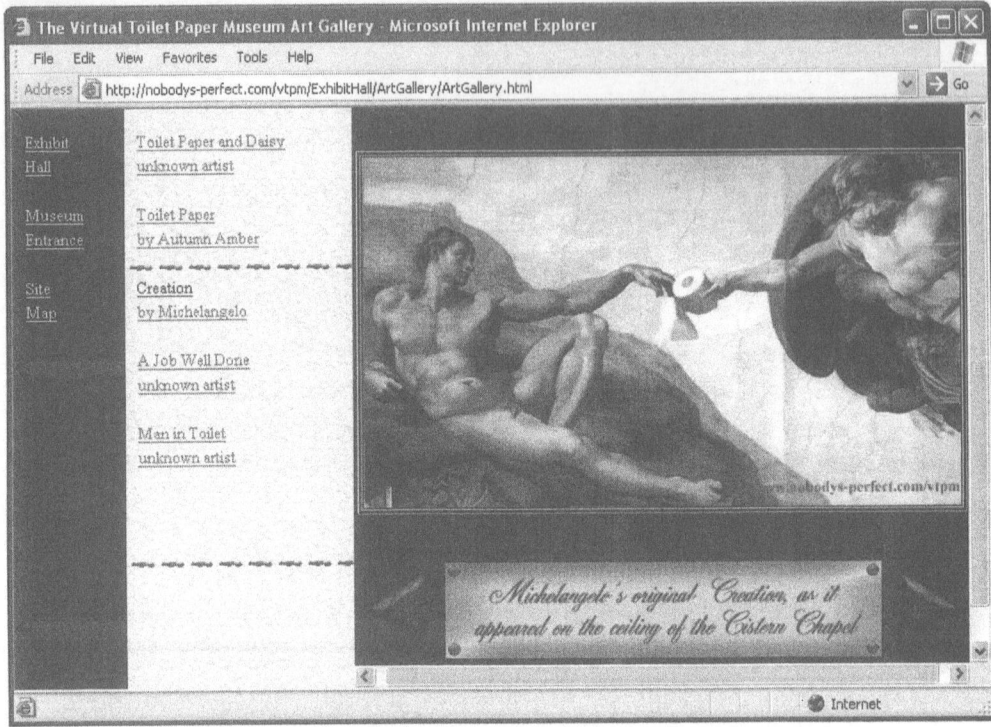

Figure 19-10. The Virtual Toilet Paper Museum takes its "roll" seriously.[10]

NOTE   The Whole World site (http://www.tagyerit.com/Madison.htm) includes information on the Madison Museum of Bathroom Tissue, a real-world toilet paper museum located in the apartment of a Madison, Wisconsin, woman.

Stinking Up the Internet: Smell-O-Vision

Entrepreneurs have a short memory. They don't always learn from the mistakes of those who came before them. Here's an example of a gimmick that was supposed to take the movie industry by storm, then bombed, was resurrected in the Internet era, and then bombed again: Smell-O-Vision.

---

10. http://nobodys-perfect.com/vtpm/visitorsguide.html

The first edition of Smell-O-Vision came in 1960. It was the brainchild of Michael Todd Jr., the son of Michael Todd Sr., who produced *Around the World in 80 Days*. After his father died in a plane crash in 1958, Todd Jr. invested all of his inheritance in the development of Smell-O-Vision. The original process called for smells, which were evocative of scenes in a movie, being pumped into a theater while the movie was playing. The smells would be sent in through pipes that led to individual theater seats. They were triggered by signals in the film itself. Only one film was ever made in Smell-O-Vision. It was called *Scent of Mystery*, and it did so poorly that Todd Jr. lost his money and left the film business for good.

Guess what? Four decades later, several separate companies were trying to help propel Smell-O-Vision back into the senses of people staring at screens. This time, however, the screens were small computer monitors. But the principle was the same: In one early example, in 1999, inventor Myron Kreuger attempted to invent a device worn on the head that dispensed scents through tubes that carried them directly to the viewer's nose.

Here's another example: In late 2001 a company called TriSenx reportedly obtained a patent for a device much like a desktop printer that would produce smells. The smells would be emitted based on data contained in a Web page. As a result, someone could download a smell from a Web site. A spokesman for another company, DigiScents, claimed that its own device, which was given the unfortunate name iSmell, would read a "digital scent file" from a Web site and re-create the smell on your desktop. The smell would then waft through your room with a small fan.

The device could produce scents to accompany digital movies; the spokesman said, "Imagine watching *The Wizard of Oz* and you smell the poppies as they're walking through the poppy field." Sound familiar? As far as I can tell, none of these inventions has hit it big yet. However, they are by no means gone. As this chapter was being written, TriSenx was launching a beta testing program for its product called the Scent Dome (http://www.trisenx.com/product.html, shown in Figure 19-11). You could purchase the dome online for $269. Will the Internet "come to its senses" and start smelling? Many would say it already smells (especially after reading this book). Just imagine what the Virtual Toilet Paper Museum (mentioned previously) and sites such as Farts.com (see Chapter 15) could do with such a device.

 NOTE Kreuger was a pioneer in the field of virtual reality and is reputed to have invented the term itself. You can read an interview with him at http://www.ctheory.net/text_file.asp?pick=328.

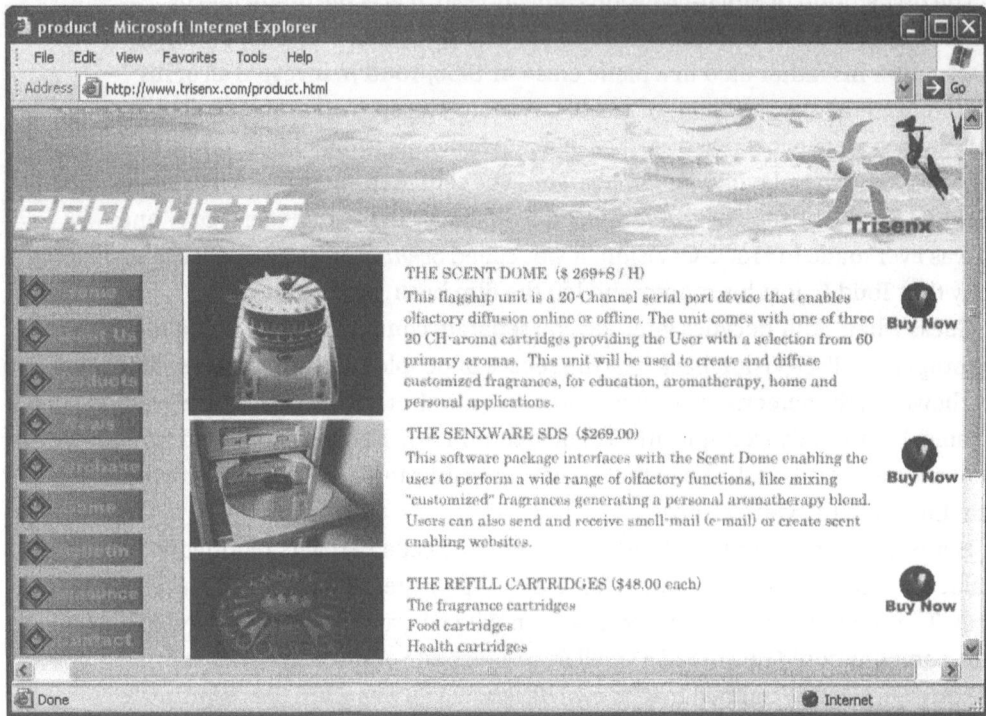

Figure 19-11. The Scent Dome, an online smell generator that could be stinking up your desktop right now[11]

Laughing All the Way to the Bank

The Web has been profitable for lots of entrepreneurs. But artists have had a tough time circumventing the normal distribution channels—record companies, publishing houses, books, music retailers, and the like.

In recent years, a number of artists bucked the trend of artists selling their works through publishers or other big media outlets by offering them online instead. Some of these episodes turned out to be funny, and others simply had a happy ending for the creators of the works.

---

11. http://www.trisenx.com/product.html

E-Book Pioneer Turns Out Online Bestseller

The publishing world has been very, very good to Stephen King. Since he sold his first book in 1973, he has written a string of bestsellers, including *Carrie, The Shining,* and *Cujo.* The problem is that in the past few decades, the number of truly independent publishing houses has dwindled. They have been purchased by one corporate conglomerate after another. Seeking to evade corporate control, King decided to experiment and offer a story on the Internet in an attempt to reach his readers directly.

It was in early 2000, when the term *e-book* was a new and mostly untried concept, when King published a 66-page story called "Riding the Bullet" online. The book would not be offered in print; it would be available only on the Internet for $2.50. He and his usual publisher, Simon & Schuster (which participated in the effort), had no idea whether anyone would download it from their respective Web sites. It also wasn't clear how an author could distribute such a work securely and induce customers to pay for it.

This first offering, however, wasn't offered for money at all—it was made available online for free. As it turned out, the sites were flooded with requests to download "Riding the Bullet." As many as 400,000 readers obtained the story. Technical glitches befell this original effort; servers were slow to respond to the heavy demand, and hackers were able to crack the code that had been used to encrypt the files.

Later that year, King made installments of a previously unpublished novel called *The Plant* on his Web site (http://www.stephenking.com/) in the popular Adobe Acrobat format, and thousands paid $1 to download each one. The successful British author Frederick Forsyth followed in King's footsteps, offering a set of stories online.

King's downloads were made available via the honor system: Readers could download for free if they wanted, but King cleverly added an inducement to cough up the nominal fee. Initially, King put only two installments of the serial novel online. He promised to write and publish the rest of the story only if at least three-quarters of the readers who downloaded the files chose to actually pay for them. King eventually published six installments online. But after the fourth installment, he reported on his Web site that only half of those who downloaded the files paid for them. He eventually suspended work on *The Plant* to pursue other projects. In the FAQ on his Web site, he says only "time will tell" whether he'll ever finish the online book.

Rock Band Says Online Distribution Is Music to Their Ears

The rock band Wilco, which hails from my hometown of Chicago, Illinois, had problems getting its album *Yankee Hotel Foxtrot* released. Their usual music publisher refused to handle it, reportedly describing it as a "career-ender." The band, while waiting for another music distributor to handle it, decided to promote the album themselves and build an audience for it by allowing downloads of individual songs online for more than a year before it was finally released.

So many people downloaded the tracks that a "buzz" was created for the album, with the result that *Yankee Hotel Foxtrot* sold well when it finally did come out under a new record label. Wilco was so pleased with the online distribution system that they made their follow-up album available for free on their Web site (http://www.wilcoworld.net/).

More Commerce Comedies

I didn't have to turn to a Web search service to suggest some hilarious and provocative sites you can visit to find more strange commercial offerings on the Internet. The following are a few sites I found noteworthy while I researching this chapter:

- **The Great Debate Series (http://www.angelfire.com/ct/tpdebate/):** You can vote on debates that have been raging for years, including the toilet paper debate (under or over?), the spaghetti sauce versus gravy debate, or the cup and glass storage debate (up or down?).

- **The Internet Tourbus (http://www.tourbus.com/bizarre.htm):** Bob Rankin and Patrick Crispen run this Web site and distribute a newsletter that tracks urban legends, virus scares, and the occasional bizarre item put up for sale on the Internet.

- **Weird Auctions (http://www.weirdauctions.com/):** This site preserves and celebrates many of the bizarre sales offered on eBay and other sites. The emphasis is on humorous rather than tasteless or illegal sales. Be sure to check out the stories of the Weird Gross Bra That Fell Out of My Ceiling that sold for $103 and the Raging Hormones Menopausal Prozac Barbie that sold for $823.46.

But Is It Art?

OPINIONS VARY as to whether art created or shown on the Web should be considered "legitimate" art. More and more art online is sold on sites such as eBay, which makes it a commodity that exchanges hands just like the schlock folks drag out of their basements.

One thing is for certain: Art on the Internet is becoming big business and is increasingly seen as a valid way for artists to display and sell their works. On the Web, art can take many forms. Celebrities and amateur artists show traditional paintings and drawings online. But some adventurous artists are using the Web itself as a medium for art. And, as you might expect from scanning this book, the Internet is full of sites that celebrate bizarre and outrageous "outsider" arts-and-crafts projects. You'll get a sampling of all of these forms of artistic endeavors in this chapter.

Celebs Can't Stop Creating

It's beginning to seem like celebrities are everywhere and like they are able to do just about anything they want. No matter what their original talent, they all seem to thrive on publicity—even if it comes from being thrown in jail or rehab or from performing dangerous stunts on television shows. Actors can give rock concerts, and rock stars can get movie parts. So it shouldn't be surprising to see people who have achieved fame for their performances cross over into art and into the Web. That's what the following famous—and, in some cases, infamous—individuals have managed to do.

Marilyn Manson, Painter

Marilyn Manson, the gothic, antichrist rock star, is best known for his well-crafted persona as a heavily made-up singer and the leader of an eponymous rock group. The two Colorado teens who shot and killed 15 classmates and themselves at Columbine High School in 1999 were reportedly big fans of Manson's, and he had to defend himself after the shootings.

But before Manson was a singer—when he was called Brian Warner and growing up in Canton, Ohio—he was a painter. Not only that, but some reviewers have touted him as a competent one. You can view his show of watercolors, "The Golden Age of Grotesque," online at http://www.marilynmansonartworkonline.com/mm.cgi (see Figure 20-1).

Figure 20-1. Marilyn Manson's artwork celebrates the grotesque.[1]

Manson's artwork is, as you would expect, grotesque in subject matter. Some images display dismembered torsos. Others focus on hands or the lack of them: Many of the figures have no hands at all or are hiding them. One work entitled *A daughter without a mother and a mother without a daughter* is described as being done in "blood/watercolor." Another is done in "pernod/watercolor."

Always careful to tend the image he has created for himself, Manson told *Newsweek* magazine that he paints in his underwear (his favorite brand: Hugo Boss). "In fact, the paint box I used for most everything is an *Alice in Wonderland* metal box made for kids," he told an interviewer for MTV.com. "I also have a 1920s mortician's paint kit used for retouching cadavers."

---

1. http://www.marilynmansonartworkonline.com/mm.cgi

TIP   Celebrity Art (http://www.artcelebs.com/) sells reproductions of paintings and other works of art by actors and other famous people. You, too, can own a painting by actress Phyllis Diller or actor James Dean.

Eraserhead's Creator Turns Webhead

Filmmaker David Lynch (best known for films such as *Eraserhead* and *Blue Velvet*) likes to keep total creative control over his work. He insists on having the "final cut" before a film is released. The Web, therefore, is a perfect medium for him. Having rejected network TV after ABC rejected his TV pilot *Mulholland Drive* (which he later made into a movie), Lynch has decided to focus solely on movies and on his innovative Web site (http://www.davidlynch.com/, shown in Figure 20-2).

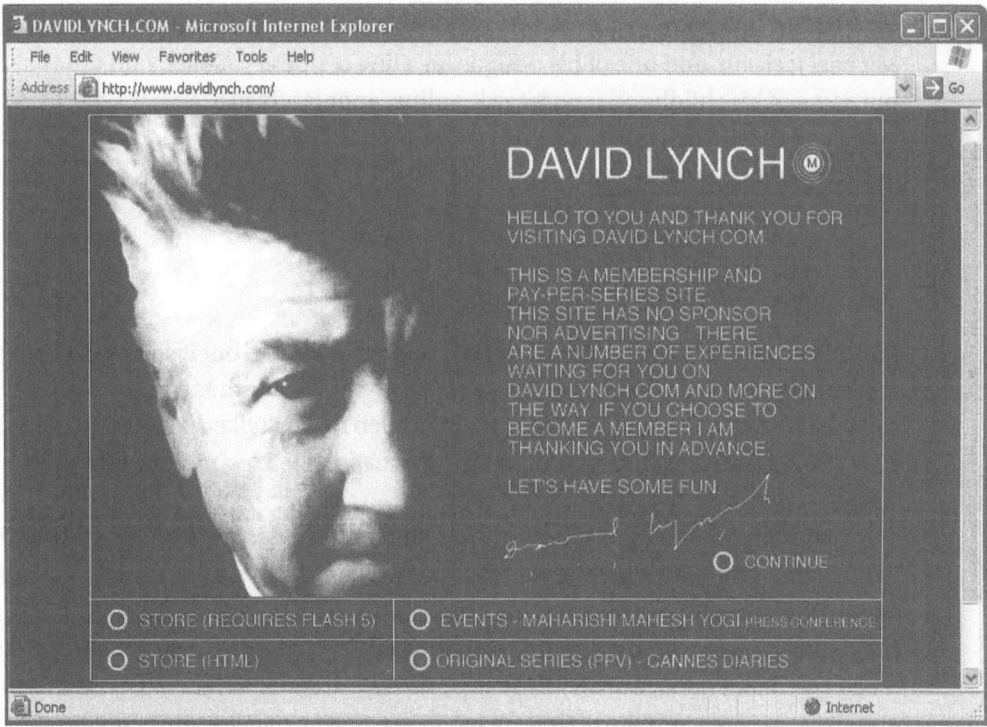

Figure 20-2. Filmmaker David Lynch has created one of the Web's unique sites.[2]

---

2.   http://www.davidlynch.com/

Lynch has made his Web site a truly creative outlet, and he is attempting to make money for his work using the site. He provides original content and has created several Web-only "series." Each series is presented in five-minute segments that are shown once a week. Lynch did all the animation for one of the series, *Dumbland*, by himself. Other series are entitled *Rabbits* and *Axxon*. Although previews are available, the full content can be viewed only by visitors who pay a monthly $9.97 membership fee. He also uses the site to sell films such as *Eraserhead* directly to the public, and reportedly this movie has sold well online.

Psychic Uri Geller Sees You Buying His Art

Uri Geller, the well-known psychic, is famous for bending spoons using only the power of his mind. He is also an artist and was once a student of Salvador Dali. You can buy his original art on eBay as well as on his Web site (http://www.uri-geller.com/). Along with the art, by the way, you can purchase Uri Geller's Parascience Pack, which includes brass dowsing rods, crystals, and other doodads for developing your own psychic abilities.

The Uri Geller's Art Work section contains photos of his drawings, a photo with Michael Jackson, and one of his designs on a line of pottery. Geller, oddly, has also put some of his childhood report cards online, apparently to assure the world that he's a real artist. They reveal that he was below par in geometry and math but did get good grades for drawing (see Figure 20-3).

It's Art to Die For

I don't know what this says about artistic talent, if anything, but it seems as though just about every serial killer was an artist of one sort or another. Even those who can't draw, such as Richard Ramirez, the so-called Night Stalker, send autographed photos of themselves to be sold on a Web site called the Lowbrow Artworld (http://www.lowbrowartworld.com/).

Lowbrow Artworld specializes in art of the sort popularized by Big Daddy Roth in the 1960s: grotesque alien creatures, cartoon characters riding in looney vehicles, aliens, and scantily clad females. The artists, with names such as Pizz and XNO, frequently appear in underground comic books. One part of the site, however, sells art by convicted mass murders. It goes by the name Serial Killers-R-Us. Paintings and drawings are sometimes sold. When those aren't available, autographs and letters are offered.

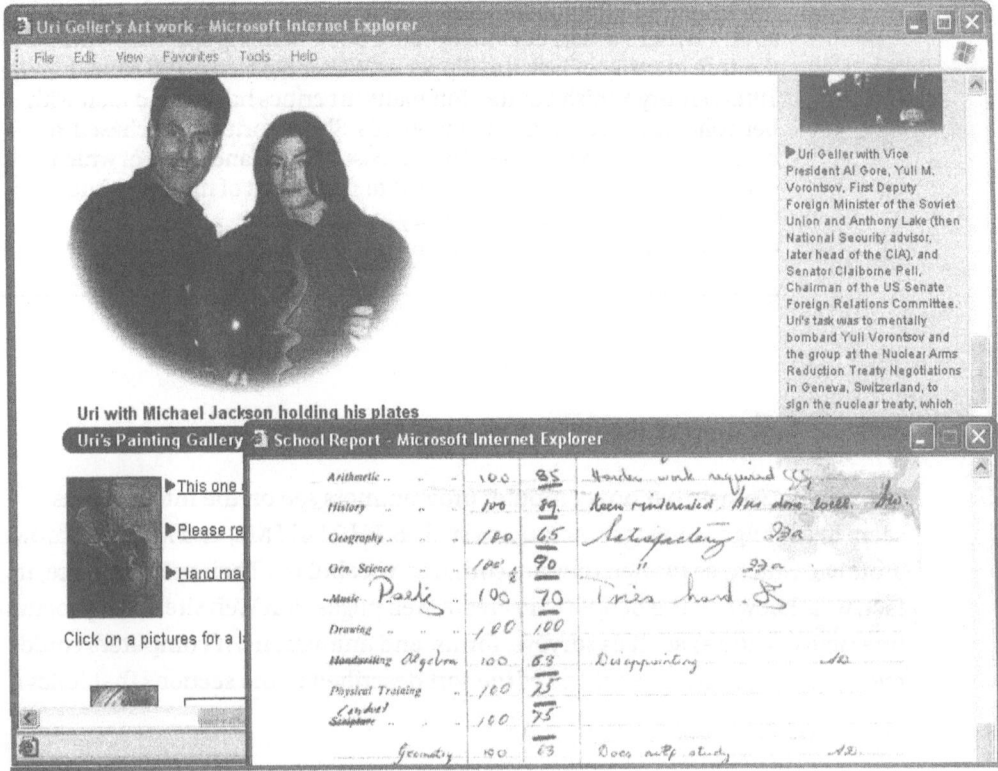

Figure 20-3. The King of Pop meets the King of Spoons.[3]

John Wayne Gacy, who killed 33 young men and boys in the 1970s, was put to death in 1994 and is no longer painting images of the Seven Dwarves or various clowns. But when I visited, Lowbrow Artworld was selling his autographed Christmas card for $90. A drawing entitled *Nightlines* by Charles Manson was available for $700. For just $125, you could own a drawing of a figure with a hatchet buried in its head, done in marker by mass murder and admitted cannibal Ottis Toole.

---

3. http://www.uri-geller.com/

NOTE   Writer Patricia Cornwell wrote a book claiming she had identified the true identity of Jack the Ripper as Walter Sickert, a well-known 19th-century British painter. But many art critics have found fault with her conclusions, as well as her methods. She reportedly purchased 30 of Sickert's paintings, some of which cost $70,000 and some of which she proceeded to tear up in an effort to find traces of his DNA. Find out more about her side of the story at her Web site (http://www.patriciacornwell.com/).

Art for Computers

Many of the things that noncomputer programmers see on the Internet must seem like foreign languages. Acronyms such as PHP, DHTML, and XML are thrown around casually, as though they are common vocabulary. Their meanings are, in fact, well-known to the people who create Web pages, run Web sites, and program interactive features such as surveys, forms, and animations. If computers could create and enjoy art, it would be of the sort described in the sections that follow.

ASCII Helps Art Get Around

One of the oldest computer acronyms around is ASCII. It stands for the American Standard Code for Information Interchange. It's a system of characters that enables a user at one computer to exchange and read data with someone at another computer who is using a different application. ASCII is most commonly used to display "text-only" word processing files. It consists of characters such as @# and numbers such as 9, 0, 1, and so on.

After tossing ASCII files back and forth for a number of years, the creative geeks who program the Internet decided to turn ASCII characters into a kind of art. Early on, ASCII was used to portray various animals and scenes. Such graphics were frequently used to accompany signature files that appear at the end of e-mail messages. More recently, ASCII and other kinds of computer-readable code have been used to create some amazing works of art. Some vivid depictions of cartoon characters are shown on the ArkWorld site (http://www.arkworld.com/ascii/). Figure 20-4 shows Cookie Monster from *Sesame Street*.

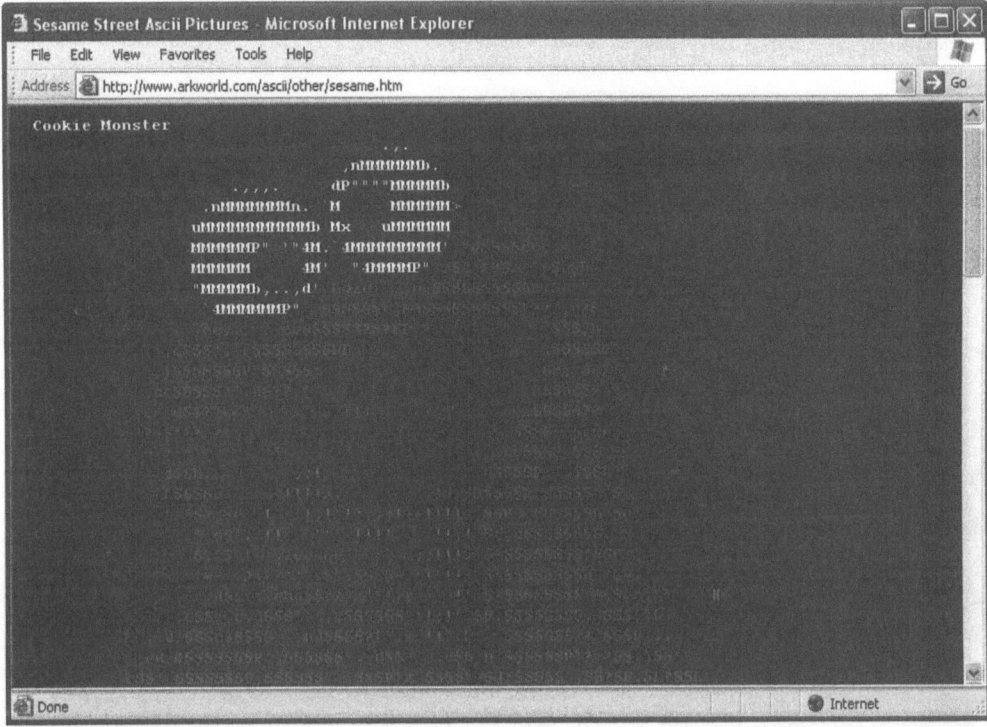

Figure 20-4. ASCII art, made up of generic keyboard characters, flourished on bulletin boards and still survives on a few Web sites.[4]

ASCII art that is used to illustrate individual still images is one thing. But some obsessive, incredibly detail-oriented individuals have attempted to reproduce entire movies in ASCII art: They draw one scene after another, put them together in sequence, and actually duplicate scenes from the movie, frame by frame. Using a computer program, they flow the frames together to create an animation.

That's what Simon Jansen, a software engineer from New Zealand, did with the task of re-creating the entire original *Star Wars* movie in ASCII characters. The project supposedly started with an e-mail joke along the lines of, "I bet you can't do the entire *Star Wars* movie...." The person who made that joke probably didn't know what he or she was starting. Jansen began his project around 1997; in 2003, when I visited the site, Jansen was still adding images to the movie (see Figure 20-5). In fact, the most recent scene added was one in which Han Solo and Luke Skywalker enter a detention cell.

---

4.   http://www.arkworld.com/ascii/ascii/other/sesame.htm

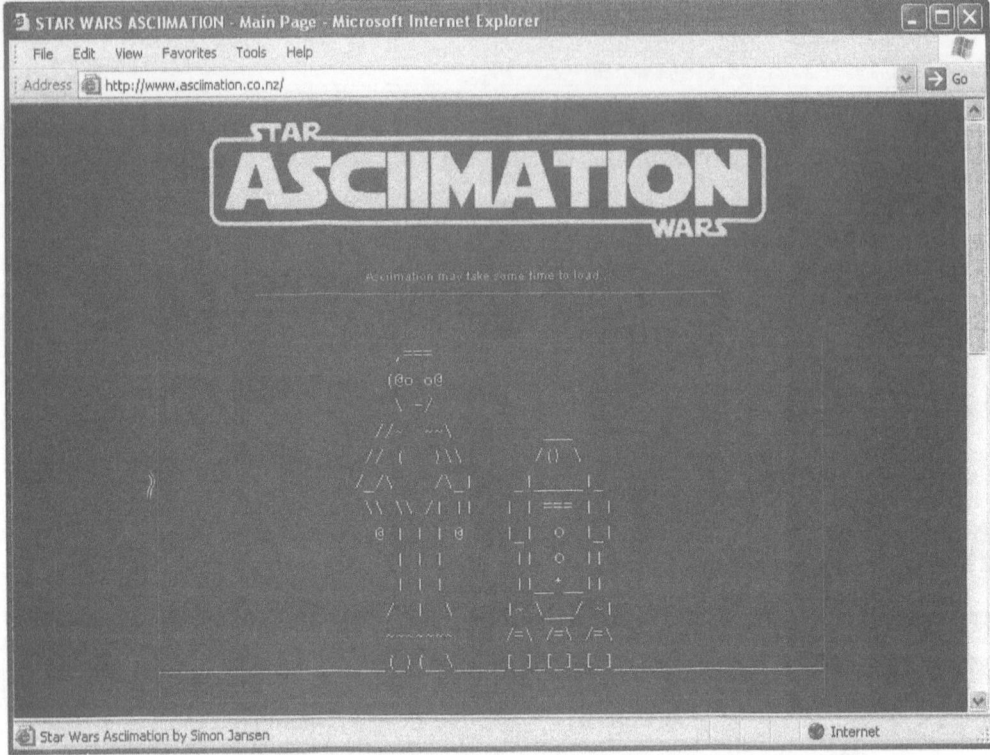

Figure 20-5. R2D2 and C3PO from the ASCII version of the original Star Wars movie[1]

Jansen has developed a cult following among fans of ASCII art. He's also admired by professional animators who praise his work while questioning his sanity. It's not always a labor of love either. Back in 1999, Jansen told *Wired* magazine that the work is quite boring: "You have to be in a kind of strange frame of mind where there's nothing else you'd rather be doing."

Jansen calls his *Star Wars* creation an *asciimation*. The Star Wars ASCIIMATION site (http://www.asciimation.co.nz/) also contains a page creating another of Jansen's creative projects: a jet-powered beer cooler.

---

5. http://www.asciimation.co.nz/

NOTE The ASCII Art Farts site (http://www.asciiartfarts.com/) has received more than 1,500 art submissions; unfortunately, almost all are offensive in some way or another. Don't go there! (See the section "If You Say 'Don't Go There,' They Will Come" for the meaning of that phrase as it pertains to the Internet.)

Web Design Mistakes Become Design for Art

I've expended a good deal of time, in one book or another, telling people how to avoid making a mess of their Web page design. One of the most obvious things is not misusing the markup language that's used to create Web pages, Hypertext Markup Language (HTML). If you use a program such as Macromedia Dreamweaver to create Web pages, you don't need to work with HTML directly. But if you do edit your own HTML, you need to make sure you use important symbols such as < and >, which enclose HTML markup, correctly. Otherwise, the commands will show on the Web page when it appears online. Most people who create Web pages don't want that to happen.

I say "most people" because a couple of artists have purposely created Web pages with jumbled, mixed-up HTML and turned it into art. Dirk Paesmans and Joan Heemskerk use the language of the Web as their medium. (Together, they call themselves Jodi.) They're part of a movement by some artists to use the technology of the Internet as a means of expression. You can see an example of Web page art in Figure 20-6.

TIP Internet art is sometimes displayed at Eyebeam (http://www.eyebeam.org/), which stages both physical and online art exhibits.

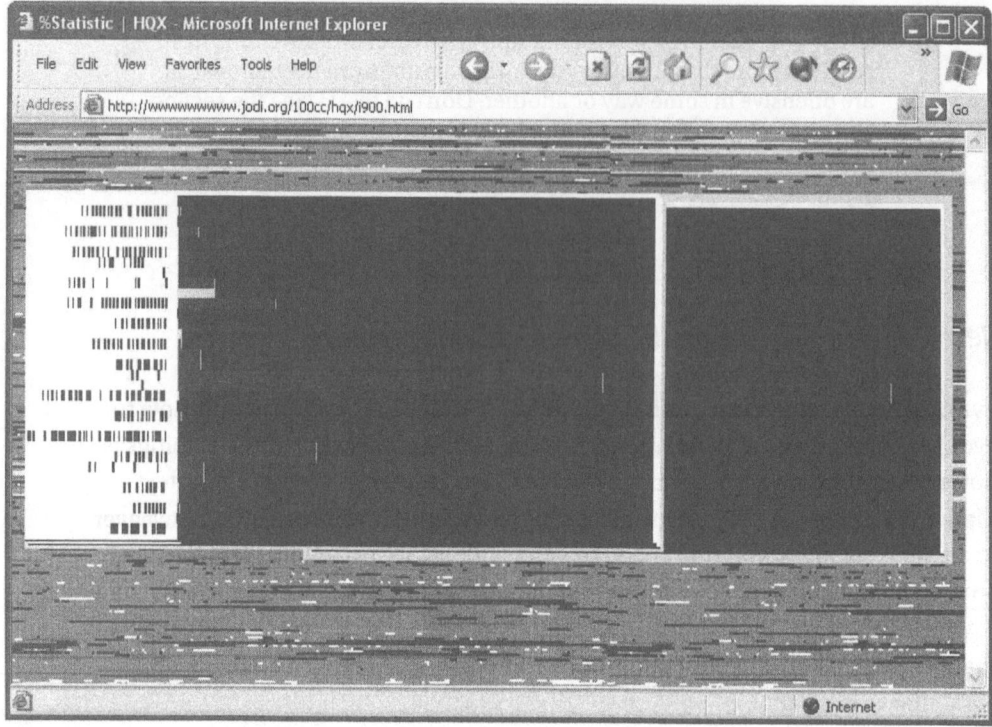

Figure 20-6. Where's the link bar? It's not a mistake; it's Web page art.[6]

Projects for Those with Time on Their Hands

Sometimes, the most fascinating arts-and-crafts projects are the ones that don't have any purpose. The ASCII art version of *Star Wars* described earlier in this chapter is just one of countless examples of the strange and useless. The projects that take on a life of their own and that involve intricate arrangement and design constitute a personal, quirky kind of Web art. See for yourself in the sections that follow.

---

6. http://wwwwwwwww.jodi.org/100cc/hqx/i900.html

Designer Lets Viewers Rummage Through His Drawers

Some people like to mold with clay. Some like to doodle. Some, like me, tend to make lists to pass the time. Matthew McClintock has carried list creation to its limit. He has created a Web site called mc.clintock.com (http://mc.clintock.com/) in which he has photographed and listed everything in his house—every desk, every drawer in the desk, and every pen, pocket knife, or roll of tape in every drawer. A Webmaster at Columbia College in Chicago, Illinois, McClintock started the site as a test of how to use the Web server software called Apache. But it's taken on a life of its own.

The site's contents are arranged according to where they are located in the house: There's an area for the first floor, the second floor, and the basement. Each drawer's contents are photographed and listed. All the books in the bookcases have been photographed. Often, stories come with the objects, such as McClintock's collection of old harmonicas or his model of the cartoon character Jimmy Corrigan. The first floor's Welcome to My Home page says the following:

I'm slowly building up a structured, visual record of everything in my house. You're welcome to browse around while I'm working—check out the kitchen cabinets, dig through my collections, or head on down to the basement and see what you can find.

Predictably, visitors quickly search out any X-rated magazines or erotica in the house. McClintock also directs visitors to a place they're sure to be curious about: his underwear drawer (see Figure 20-7). (Notice the advertisements at the top of the page, which are coordinated to match what's being displayed in the browser window.)

Why has McClintock spent so much time opening his possessions to the prying eyes of visitors around the world? "It comes down to an appreciation for documentation and lists, as well as a keen appreciation for the absurd aspect of 'revealing' the contents of my home to the entire world," he comments on the site. But he also acknowledges that "almost everyone I've spoken to sees this project as either an incredible intrusion or as an invitation to be robbed." In other words, it must be art.

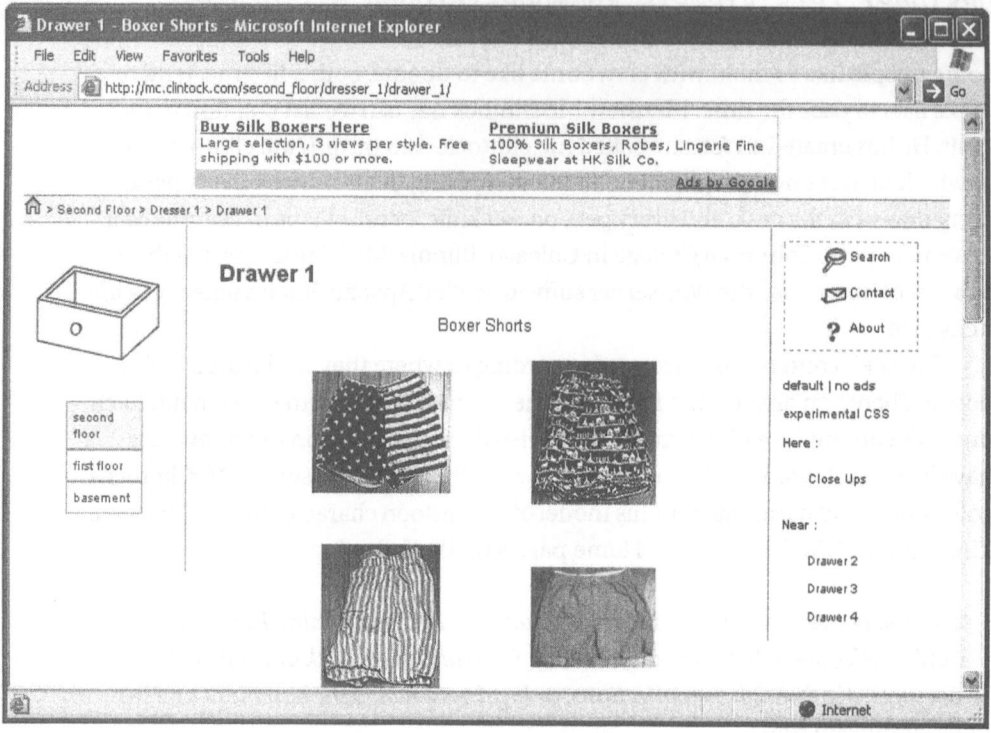

Figure 20-7. A Chicago Web designer lets visitors virtually rummage through his underwear drawer and everything else in his house.[7]

Why She's Called the "Butter Cow Lady"

Norma "Duffy" Lyon makes extensive use of the Web to promote her particular brand of artwork: She's widely known both on and offline as the Butter Cow Lady. On her Web site (http://www.thebuttercowlady.com/), the Toledo, Iowa, farm wife includes a video that shows her at work on a life-size cow made out of butter (see Figure 20-8).

---

7. http://mc.clintock.com/second_floor/dresser_1/drawer_1/

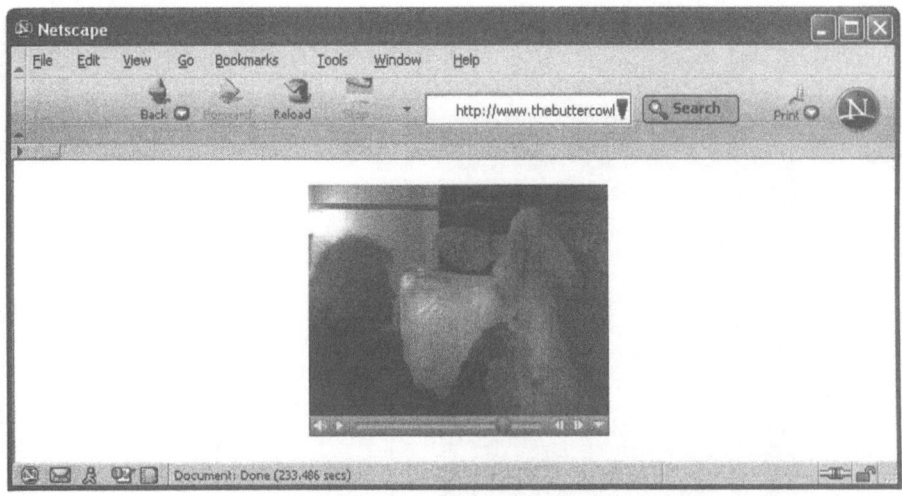

Figure 20-8. The Butter Cow Lady puts the finishing touches on one of her famous cow creations.[8]

The Butter Cow Lady site contains links to her biography, the story of a life "of adventure, achievement, friendship, dedication, and plain-spoken wisdom." Lyon, you see, studied art at Iowa State University with a colleague of Iowa painter Grant Wood, but state fair time is the only event of the year where she gets to indulge her artistic side. In 1960, she spoke out about the butter cow at the Iowa State Fair. It just didn't look right to her, and she knew she could do a better job. When the previous artist died, she was offered the job. Eventually she became the fair's official Butter Cow Lady.

You'll also see images of her other creations, such as Elvis Presley, Garth Brooks, and a version of the Last Supper (see Figure 20-9) that she did at the Iowa State Fair to commemorate her 40 years of butter sculpting. And she sculpted a Harley-Davidson motorcycle to celebrate that company's 100th anniversary.

---

8.   http://www.thebuttercowlady.com/

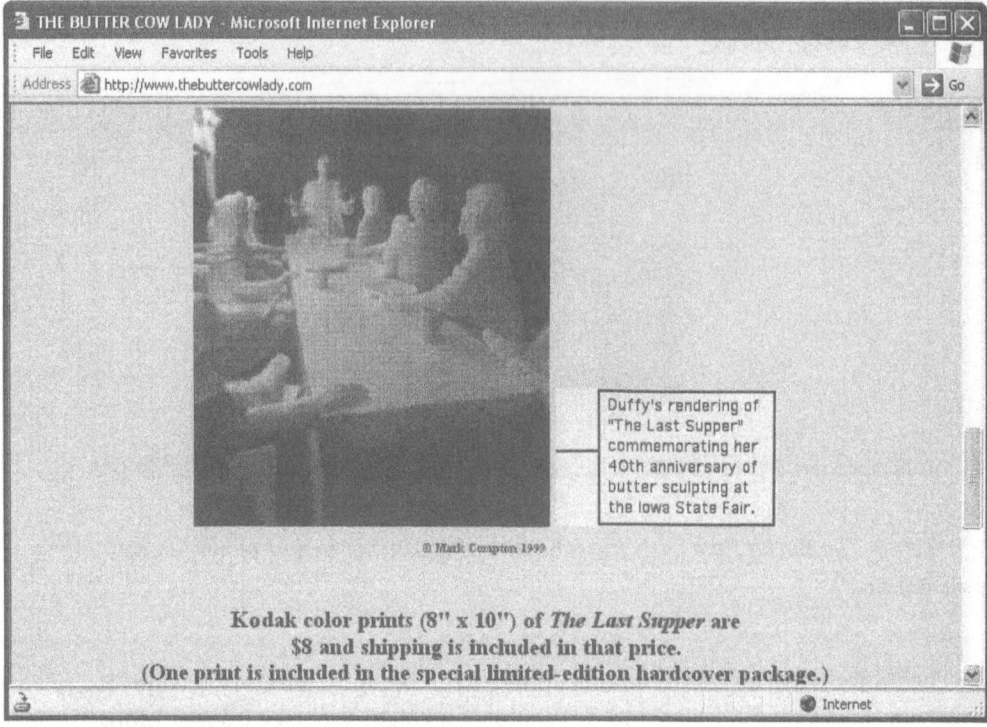

Duffy's rendering of "The Last Supper" commemorating her 40th anniversary of butter sculpting at the Iowa State Fair.

© Mark Compton 1999

Kodak color prints (8" x 10") of *The Last Supper* are $8 and shipping is included in that price. (One print is included in the special limited-edition hardcover package.)

Figure 20-9. In the Butter Cow Lady's version of the Last Supper, Christ sits at the head of the table.[9]

Lyon is apparently either retiring or slowing down her schedule; at the 2003 Illinois State Fair, another sculptor created the traditional butter cow for the first time in many years. A press release for the fair notes that after such fairs, the butter is typically removed and reused for other sculptures. Apparently, butter—unlike paint—can be recycled from one work of art to the next.

Amazing Craft Facts to Wow Your Date

Anyone who attempts to write (or read) a book about oddball exploits on the Internet has to tip their hat to sites such as the Useless Information Home Page. Since 1998, Stephen Silverman, a science teacher at Chatham High School in upstate New York, has carefully tended and written this site. The stories described on the site are ones that he has either told to his students or distributed via e-mail to his friends. You'll discover the following:

---

9. http://www.thebuttercowlady.com/

- The pink flamingo was designed in 1957 by a young man and former classical art student named Don Featherstone.

- Henry Sherwin invented ready-mix paint in the late 19th century.

- A man named Jack Hall once used 14,000 matchsticks to create a working violin, complete with a bow.

You can discover these and more bits of useless and fascinating information at http://home.nycap.rr.com/useless/.

View Digital Displays, If You Dare

There are upscale art galleries, there are small storefront art galleries, and there are informal shows you can see only in someone's home or loft. Then there are the art galleries and museums that populate the Web. Some of these contain things you'll never see in traditional locales because they're, well, a little strange. The following are just a few examples of the many extraordinary exhibits you can view online.

Yoko Usurps Museum Web Site (Not Just Beatles)

The real Web site of the Museum of Contemporary Art (MOCA) in Los Angeles, California, is at http://www.moca-la.org/index.php. In 1996, Yoko Ono created her own version of the museum Web site to publicize an art event. You can still see the home page that was created for the event and a description of what happened on the ArtCommotion Web site (http://www.artcommotion.com/Issue2/moca/).

The event, originally staged in 1971, focused on the release of a group of flies from a bottle placed in the garden of the Museum of Contemporary Art in New York City. The flies had been scented with the same perfume Ono was wearing. Eventually, the explanation on the Web states, some of the flies made their way to the MOCA in Los Angeles.

TIP Click the link One Woman Show on the fake MOCA page to read the description of the event. Then click the image of the fly at the bottom of the description to find out more about the exhibit and view photos of Ono.

Crazy Like an Artist

Dr. Silvia Helena Cardoso, a Brazilian neurobiologist, selected a group of paintings that she arranged in an online exhibit called Art & Psychosis. The exhibit (http://www.epub.org.br/cm/gallery/gall_leonardo/main.htm) contains 15 paintings, and they are all disturbing in one way or another.

This online exhibit displays art by people who were believed to have some form of psychosis, including famous artists. Some of the images were created by anonymous individuals. Others were by well-known artists such as Hieronymus Bosch (1450–1516) and lesser-known painters such as Louis Wain (1860–1939). Wain spent the last 15 years of his life in a mental institution. The page that compares his early "normal" work with his later psychotic work is especially shocking (see Figure 20-10).

Figure 20-10. You can compare normal art and psychotic art in this online exhibit.[10]

---

10. http://www.epub.org.br/cm/gallery/gall_leonardo/main.htm

Many of the images are details from some of the work of Bosch, whose visions of Hell are surreal and astonishing. But you can also study work by a 20-year-old schizophrenic with a mother fixation, a delirious Balkan peasant, and other troubled souls.

Tate Gets More Than It Bargained For

The Tate Gallery in London is one of the most respected art museums in the world. It's well-known for its extensive collections.

In 2000, when the Tate Gallery commissioned artist Graham Harwood to create an online exhibit for his Web site, it became the butt of his joke. Harwood created a parody of the Tate and the traditional art values it represents. He smeared mud from the Thames River on some of the art masterpieces that are displayed at the Tate. He combined images of his own body parts and those of his family with well-known works by Turner, Gainsborough, and Constable.

In the text for the exhibit (which lives on at the Internet Wayback Machine, shown in Figure 20-11), Harwood described the Tate as "the home of 500 years of tasty babes, luxury goods, own goals, and psychological props of the British social elite."

Although the Tate reportedly asked Harwood to modify his work, he refused to relent and happily bit the hand that was feeding him. When the site went online, it got more than 300,000 visits and plenty of media attention. The site was configured so that one in every three visitors to the official Tate site was redirected to Harwood's site. The home page of Harwood's mimicked version looked almost identical to the real home page except for the word "mongrel," which appeared throughout. (The word refers to a group of artists that includes Harwood.)

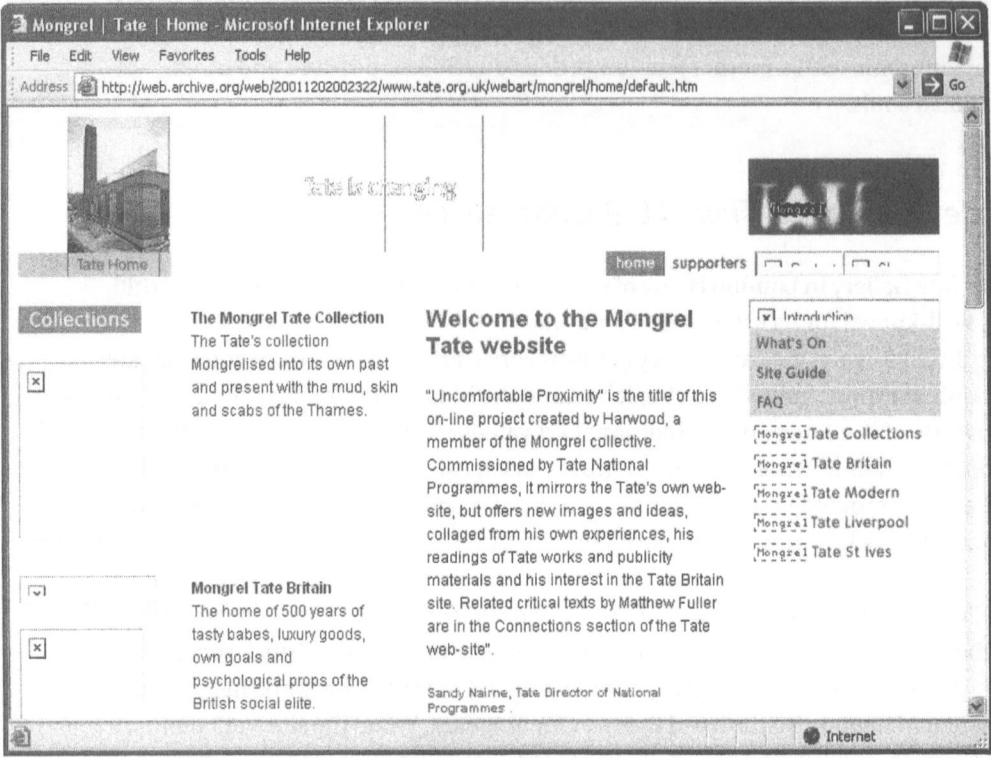

Figure 20-11. The Tate commissioned this online art project, which made fun of the Tate.[11]

It's Only One Sentence, but What a Sentence!

One of the first Web-based art exhibits to be purchased by a major art museum was a collaborative sentence first created by Douglas Davis. It began as part of an interactive performance in the Lehman College Art Gallery in New York. A live phone hookup was established with another artist in Geneva, Switzerland, who supplied the sentence's initial image and its beginning words. Visitors were then allowed to add their own words to the sentence, which quickly grew in size and complexity.

In 1995, art collectors Barbara and Eugene Schwartz purchased the interactive work. You might ask how you can purchase a work that exists on the Web and that is continually growing and changing. The Schwartz's purchased the "concept" of the work and received a signed computer disk, which contained records of the

---

11. http://web.archive.org/web/20011202002322/www.tate.org.uk/webart/mongrel/home/default.htm

earliest days of the sentence's life. Barbara Schwartz then donated the sentence to the Whitney Museum. To date, there have been more than 200,000 contributions to the sentence, which has been divided into 21 chapters.

TIP You can read about the collaborative sentence project on the Whitney Museum's Web site at http://www.whitney.org/artport/collection/index.shtml. Or, you can go directly to the project itself and add your own word or phrase at http://here.is/THESENTENCE/.

And You Thought Museums Were Boring

The following sites may not be art, exactly, but given some of the other things you've read about in this chapter, who is to say what is art and what is just crazy schlock when it comes to the Internet? Be sure to check out the following exhibits:

- **The International Banana Club Museum (http://www.bananaclub.com/Museum%201.html)**: Supposedly, there is a petrified ancient banana among the more than 17,000 banana-related objects.

- **Museum of Menstruation and Women's Health (http://www.mum.org/)**: Visitors from around the world have contributed euphemisms for menstruation. They include "little red sister has come" (China), "my steak is raw" (England), and "les Anglais ont débarqué," or, "the English navy has arrived" (France).

- **The Mütter Museum of the College of Physicians of Philadelphia (http://www.collphyphil.org/muttpg1.shtml)**: Take a virtual tour to enjoy the human horn, the giant colon, and the preserved livers (or rather, liver) of the Siamese twins Chang and Eng.

If You Say "Don't Go There," They Will Come

On the Internet, people don't like to run into barriers. They hate it when you tell them they have to pay for "premium content" or that you have to be an official member of something to view special Web pages. In an ideal cyberuniverse, they see a link and click it. If you tell them not to click it, they'll have a hard time restraining that clicker-finger.

An artist named Jack Gasoline created a simple Web page entitled Don't Go There in March 2003. As you can tell from the current content of the page (http://www.jackgasoline.com/, shown in Figure 20-12), it was originally configured so that the page would go offline after 100 clicks on a particular link.

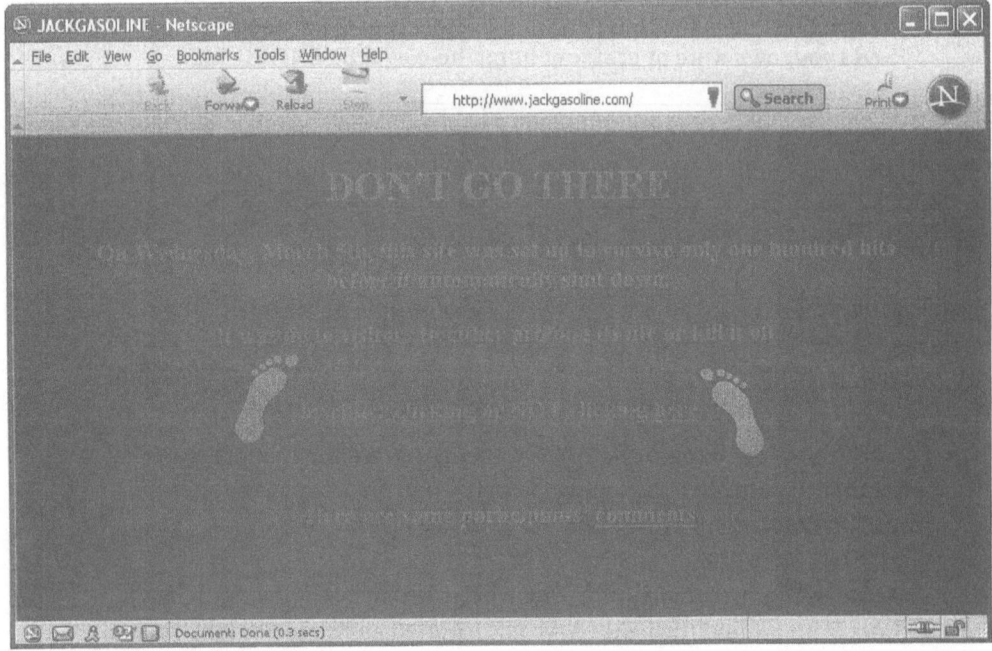

Figure 20-12. To click or not to click? That was the question surrounding this Web site.[12]

Visitors were given the choice of prolonging the site's life or sending it to its doom. Anyone who clicked the link viewed a page that told them how many more clicks were left before the site went offline. The numbers grew fainter and fainter as the number of clicks grew. Visitors were encouraged to leave messages. The following are some sample comments:

> *It is better to have loved and lost than not to have loved at all. Experiences are to be had. Resources to be used. Life to be lived. Number 32 and proud.*

> *I'm sorry; I couldn't help it. I had to go there. But to make up for it, I won't pay taxes this year.*

---

12. http://www.jackgasoline.com/

I decided not to go there. Now I am having big doubts that I might have missed out on something great, but, I believed your text and I want that imaginary site out there to keep keepin' on.

Gasoline originally hoped it would last at least 24 hours. But in only 57 minutes, it received its 100th visitor and shut itself down.

Random Googling

For artists, the Web is a dream come true. Where else can you reach a potential audience of millions, who can see your work without having to face critics or being confined within gallery walls? The following are a few art-related sites I found noteworthy—a random sampling of sites that turned up after searching for the terms "art," "artist," and "museum" on the search service Google (http://www.google.com/):

- **Art Crimes: The Writing on the Wall (http://www.graffiti.org/):** This celebrates the world of graffiti "taggers" around the country. One interactive page enables visitors to paint trains online.

- **The Gourd Artist's Guild (http://www.jkstacydesigns.com/ GourdArtistsGuild.html):** The contributors to this site do much more than simply carve pumpkins. In fact, there isn't a pumpkin in sight. They do amazing things with other kinds of gourds, however.

- **The Virtual Diego Rivera Web Museum (http://www.diegorivera.com/ index.html):** The Getty, Guggenheim, Smithsonian, and other famous museums are easy to find and have well-developed Web sites. For something completely different, visit this site, which includes collections of murals and Day of the Dead offerings made in the artist's honor and viewable as QuickTime VR panoramas.

Index

M